# EXCELSIOR

*The Story of Kappa Alpha Order*

MARTIN CLAGETT

# EXCELSIOR

*The Story of Kappa Alpha Order*

MARTIN CLAGETT

Library of Congress Control Number: 2015940557

ISBN: 978-0-9963766-0-0

Kandy Harvey, Designer
Jesse Lyons, Editor
Julie Campbell, Copy Editor
Emily Salmon, Co-Editor
John Salmon, Co-Editor

Printed with the cooperation of University of Virginia Printing & Copying Services.

*Contents*

# *Foreword*

With excellence as Kappa Alpha Order's aim, *Excelsior: The Story of Kappa Alpha Order,* has surpassed all expectations.

A hallmark of our Sesquicentennial Celebration, the book will be a treasure for the Order and all those who own a copy, have the chance to read it, or share it with a fellow brother. *Excelsior* is handsome and commanding on a coffee table, stunning as you flip through the designs and illustrations, and its prose presents a unique but natural flow of historical education.

This story takes into account more than 150 years of American and Kappa Alpha Order history. The author probably knows more about KA now than most of our members ever will. References to our birth, development, maturation, and today, are invaluable. It is a complete and definitive account, having brought together scores of facts and primary sources meticulously and academically cataloged, researched, and distilled. From the Kappa Alpha Archives to the interior of a member's daughter's attic, legend, lore, and scattered prior works are now, true to the title, subordinate to *Excelsior.*

We all share a common bond in the brotherhood of KA and I know after reading this book, you will grow in appreciation of your membership in the Order. After thirty-six years on active duty, my military associations are, of course, dominant. But over all those years, I have benefited from the continuing relationship with my brothers in Kappa Alpha.

To be clear, if you live up to the things we pledged to do, and live the way we pledged to live as members of the Order, you're going to live a good life. I'm proud to be a part of Kappa Alpha Order.

General Jack N. Merritt, U.S. Army (ret.)
Beta Eta—University of Oklahoma, 1949
Arlington, Virginia

# *Knight Commander's Introduction*

*Excelsior: The Story of Kappa Alpha Order* should make you proud to be a KA.

Today, Kappa Alpha Order boasts 127 chapters, and our members are frequently referred to as the gentlemen of the fraternity world. With well over 160,000 initiates, 7,800 undergraduate members, the most ever, and our highest GPA in history, the Order is the strongest it has been in our 150-year history.

Kappa Alpha Order provides a significant contribution to the development of college men. They come to college with their values intact; they have learned right from wrong. While in college, KA helps them keep their compass straight, enhances their values and experiences, and points them in the right direction for the future. KA is truly the moral compass for the modern gentleman.

Our founders sought to create an organization rooted in the highest ideals of the time. Those same traits of honor, chivalry, and gentility remain eternal, and are the core of the Kappa Alpha experience. KA translates these timeless ideals into the mainstream of American colleges and universities.

*Excelsior* shows us where and how all of this started. It teaches us about who helped the Order grow and spread. And, in the end, you will see how the Order's history is one of American history and that our story is continuing. It is my fervent hope that you are inspired by this story to help the Order in your own way. The next 150 years of excellence are about to begin. What will be your contribution?

May God bless the Kappa Alpha Order.

William E. Dreyer, 39th Knight Commander
Alpha Delta—William Jewell College, 1957
San Antonio, Texas

# *Author's Preface*

During the hundred and fifty years of Kappa Alpha's existence, several histories of the organization have been presented in a variety of formats—each with its own import and viewpoint. They have been written by authors with intimate connections to the organization and with personal viewpoints on the subject. The tellings of the tale have often focused on specific aspects of the fraternity's past or interpretations of the events that have either taken place or were reported to have taken place.

The purpose of this volume is twofold. The first is to look at the history as a metanarrative, which means first that major themes and events are presented in a chronological order. It is hoped that the book will present an engaging, entertaining, and informative story of Kappa Alpha's past in a way that gives the reader a comprehensive and objective version of events and people and trends that have evolved over the past century and a half. The second purpose is to attempt to set straight events, to present both sides of a case when necessary, to clarify what traditions derive from fact and which are products of imagination and invention, and to document the sources from which the information derived. In short, to create a reliable and objective history of the Order for a significant occasion—a birthday celebration.

During the history of the Kappa Alpha Order, a detached and disinterested accounting of the organization has not taken place. James Ward Wood, William Archibald Walsh, William Nelson Scott, and Stanhope McClelland Scott—the founders—gave little thought to recording the initial stirrings of the institution; for it was not an institution, not even a real organization, but rather a collection of like-minded individuals gathering together for companionship and mutual support.

Samuel Zenas Ammen, who was initiated into the lodge in the year following its inauguration, was the first to grasp the importance of tracing back to the origins of the Order's first steps. But even Ammen, at first, did not consider the history to be of special importance. He noted that in the early days "the date of our origin was of no importance, or interest; the past was not discussed. It was our future that excited concern." He confessed that he gave no serious thought to the matter until 1891, when he sat down to write the first version of events. Even the Chief Founder, James Ward Wood, was often ambiguous and vague about how the Order came into being and about what was his inspiration for its inception.

In 1918, a fraternal historian, Leroy Boyd, visited the aging Wood and asked him a series of questions concerning the origins of the organization. Wood often replied to Boyd's inquiries with feints of amnesia or confounding answers. Indeed Boyd, by the targeted nature of his interview, seems to have had a predetermined political and social agenda. But whatever he was selling, the cagey Wood was not buying.

From the 1880s to the present, internal voices have struggled to have their interpretation applied to the narrative of Kappa Alpha. And, as is often the case, facts have sometimes been fashioned to fit the theory. Major contributors to the story have vacillated from one end of the spectrum to the other; contemporary documentation has been glossed over; eye witness testimony was "smuggled & covered up"; and determinations that had been agreed on were overturned and revoked.

This history hopes to address a number of issues including the questions of when and at what place the fraternity emerged; what its basic misson was; how it expanded and developed; what was the philosophy that determined the parameters of its expansion; and who had the greatest influence on its growth and character; and, finally, how the Order came full circle and miraculously ended up on virtually the same piece of earth on which it was born.

The author Lillian Hellman prefaced her work, *Pentimento,* with the following words:

> Old paint on canvas, as it ages, sometimes becomes transparent. When that happens it is possible, in some pictures, to see the original lines: a tree will show through a woman's dress, a child makes way for a dog, a large boat is no longer on an open sea. This is called pentimento because the painter "repented," changed his mind. Perhaps it would be as well to say that the old conception, replaced by a later choice, is a way of seeing and then seeing again.[1]

Hellman's sentiment is my hope; namely, that the impact of this book will be a fresher, clearer, and more objective vision of the past of this important and beneficent institution.

Martin Clagett
Richmond, Virginia

1 Lillian Hellman, *Pentimento* (Boston: Little & Brown, 1973).

**THIS PUBLICATION WAS MADE POSSIBLE BY THE GENEROUS SUPPORT OF THESE FRIENDS AND BROTHERS OF KAPPA ALPHA ORDER.**

Barry B. Donnell (Beta Lambda-Southern Methodist '58)
William E. Dreyer (Alpha Delta-William Jewell '57)
Todd D. Reaves (Nu-Auburn '89)

Derick S. Close (Alpha Omega-North Carolina State '78)

Bensley H. L. Field (Alpha Zeta-William & Mary '54)

C. Randolph Gentz (Gamma Psi-Northwestern '68)

B. Terry Bennett (Alpha Gamma-Louisiana State '64)
Raymond B. Bottom, Jr. (Alpha Tau-Hampden-Sydney '48)
Mr. & Mrs. Clayton E. Bunting (Eta-Richmond '69)
James E. Davis (Alpha Kappa-Missouri '53)
Earnest W. Deavenport, Jr. (Beta Tau-Mississippi State '58)
James L. Ferman, Jr. (Epsilon-Emory '62)
Michael J. Garrison (Epsilon Rho-Purdue '88)
Gordon "Stumpy" Harris (Beta Zeta-Florida '57)
W. Thomas Hopkins (Psi-Tulane '72)
Eugene M. Julian (Beta Epsilon-Delaware '63)
Darren S. Kay (Alpha Eta-Westminster '88)
David T. Martineau V (Alpha Upsilon-Mississippi '88)
Charles C. Mickel (Delta Omicron-Clemson '76)
Michael V. Paulin (Beta Sigma-Southern California '60)
Vance E. Rule (Alpha Delta-William Jewel '47)
William H. Skipper, Jr. (Delta Tau-Francis Marion '80)
George A. Webster (Upsilon-North Carolina '68)

David P. Barksdale (Tau-Wake Forest '83)
Robert M. Bouse (Beta Omicron-Louisville '51)
Richard L. Burke (Zeta-Randolph-Macon '83)
M. Tim Carey (Chi-Vanderbilt '63)
LaFon C. Dees (Delta-Wofford '57)
W. Birch Douglass III (Alpha Tau-Hampden-Sydney '62)
Francis E. Gardiner, Jr. (Alpha Lambda-Johns Hopkins '59)
Norman C. George (Omicron-Texas '75)
Michael E. Gunn (Delta Epsilon-Newberry '93)
William J. Hagenah (Alpha Pi-Stanford '63)
Victor H. Hanson II (Lambda-Virginia '51)
Paul H. Kuhn, Jr. (Chi-Vanderbilt '62)
Malcolm H. Liles (Gamma-Georgia '71)
Gregory A. McCrickard (Lambda-Virginia '78)
J. Coleman McDowell, Jr. (Gamma Chi-Texas Tech '78)
SGM E. Kent McMichael (Beta Commission-VMI '95)
S. Morgan Morton, Jr. (Gamma Gamma-Memphis '60)
W. Regi Mullins (Alpha Gamma-Louisiana State '70)
David R. Murphey III (Alpha-Washington & Lee '51)
James C. Musser (Delta Mu-Eastern Kentucky '87)
James P. Myerson (Alpha Pi-Stanford '74)
James M. Ney (Iota-Furman '62)
Thomas G. Paulson II (Alpha Xi-California '49)
Hon. Robert M. Pittenger (Omicron-Texas '67)
Robert M. Pittenger, Jr. (Sigma-Davidson '99)
CPT Ronald C. Plunkett (Theta Commission-Citadel '09)
James R. Purvis (Gamma Chi-Texas Tech '85)
Robert M. Ross (Beta Kappa-Maryland '68)
Benjamin W. Satcher, Jr. (Delta Omicron-Clemson '79)
Dr. James Michael Schmuck (Alpha Eta-Westminster '69)
J. William Schulz (Alpha Kappa-Missouri '60)
Erik T. Showalter (Gamma Alpha-Louisiana Tech '02)
C. Douglas Simmons III (Beta Tau-Mississippi State '95)
Dr. Idris Rhea Traylor, Jr. (Gamma Chi-Texas Tech '70)
Joseph M. Van Name III (Beta Omega-Washington College '87)
Harvey P. White (Beta Chi-West Virginia Wesleyan '52)
Hugh P. Whitehead (Alpha Beta-Alabama '85)
Larry Stanton Wiese (Gamma Omega-Midwestern State '87)

Timothy K. Adams (Epsilon-Emory '57)
King V. Aiken, Jr. (Kappa-Mercer '83)
Dan H. Akin (Gamma Omicron-Lambuth '60)
G. Patterson Apperson III (Alpha Alpha-Univ. of the South '80)
Mr. & Mrs. Frank E. Asbury (Epsilon-Emory '44)
L. Blair Bailey (Gamma Eta-Florida State '88)
Julian B. Baker, Jr. (Delta Lambda-Middle Tennessee State '69)
William D. Balthrope (Beta Lambda-Southern Methodist '58)
L. Charles Banks, Jr. (Delta Epsilon-Newberry '02)
Richard A. Barnes (Delta Lambda-Middle Tennessee State '69)
John M. Barry (Upsilon-North Carolina '79)
Blake E. Benney (Gamma Lambda-North Texas '86)
William R. Bolen (Epsilon Iota-Texas State '05)
Dr. James L. Bowers (Beta Omega-Washington '57)
Dustin G. Brann (Alpha Omega-North Carolina State '11)
Charles S. Briggs (Delta Upsilon-Tennessee-Martin '75)
Paul R. Burns (Alpha Gamma-Louisiana State '71)

Ethan J. Bush (Delta Xi-McNeese State '97)
Scott D. Carter (Epsilon Iota-Texas State '01)
R. Craig Cass (Delta Psi-Appalachian State '81)
Jay D. Chamberlain IV (Gamma Lambda-North Texas '86)
Guy D. Colado (Gamma Pi-Florida Southern '64)
Douglas R. Coley (Delta Psi-Appalachian State '76)
Ceasar Cone III (Alpha Omega-North Carolina State '59)
C. Caleb Connor (Alpha Beta-Alabama '01)
James L. Crews II (Delta Upsilon-Tennessee-Martin '86)
Mark S. Crocker (Rho-South Carolina '74)
Dr. James W. Denham (Psi-Tulane '96)
Alfred Diaz, Jr. (Delta Iota-Texas-Arlington '84)
William K. Dillingham (Alpha Delta-William Jewell '95)
Dustin B. Donnell (Beta Lambda-Southern Methodist '01)
Jeremy D. Duke (Delta Lambda-Middle Tennessee State '09)
J. Michael Duncan (Delta Kappa-Stephen F. Austin State '69)
Garth K. Dunklin (Upsilon-North Carolina '81)
Gregory M. Eaton (Alpha Gamma-Louisiana State '67)
James R. Estes (Alpha Kappa-Missouri '60)
Douglas S. Ewalt (Beta Omega-Washington '71)
J. Kirby Ewing (Omicron-Texas '44)
Fred W. Faircloth III (Delta Omicron-Clemson '70)
COL Henry J. Foresman, Jr. (Beta Commission-VMI '76)
Stephen E. Foster (Beta Chi-West Virginia Wesleyan '68)
Michael D. Fox (Epsilon Lambda-Miami '97)
Brad B. Freeman (Beta Lambda-Southern Methodist '59)
M. Tyler Griffin (Alpha Delta-William Jewell '98)
David B. Hagan (Alpha Omega-North Carolina State '76)
Robert W. Hagan (Delta Rho-Valdosta State '74)
Loren Q. Hanson (Alpha Kappa-Missouri '50)
Otis M. Healy (Beta Sigma-Southern California '44)
R. Scott Heath (Delta-Wofford '77)
Mitchell S. Hill (Gamma Omega-Midwestern State '87)
Calvin S. Hopkins III (Gamma-Georgia '69)
Christopher S. Hoppe (Beta Eta-Oklahoma '71)
Michael E. Hopper (Gamma Gamma-Memphis '59)
Rock N. Houstoun (Xi-Southwestern '70)
CAPT Christopher A. Huff (Gamma Chi-Texas Tech '05)
Scott W. Humphrey (Gamma Epsilon-Arizona '89)
Robert P. Jordan (Rho-South Carolina '86)
James D. Kay, Jr. (Nu-Auburn '79)
Gordon L. Kinne (Gamma Beta-Missouri State '73)
Stephen H. Kouba, Jr. (Alpha Omega-North Carolina State '11)
Dr. Paul D. Kountz, Jr. (Delta-Wofford '77)
Stephen J. LaFollette (Delta Phi-Jacksonville State '84)
Sam Leake, Jr. (Beta Xi-Oklahoma State '61)
Jeffrey G. Leigh (Zeta Mu-Washington '97)
Dr. Stephen George Luckey, Jr. (Mu-Tulsa '96)
Jesse Samuel Lyons (Delta Alpha-Western Carolina '98)
George W. McCall, Jr. (Eta-Richmond '48)
George W. McCall, III (Eta-Richmond '76)
Edward D. McCrady (Lambda-Virginia '82)
David C. Merrill (Zeta Pi-Florida Gulf Coast '08)
H. Woodward Middleton, Jr. (Beta Gamma-Charleston '89)
John Michael Moore (Beta Lambda-Southern Methodist '90)
Loy B. Moore (Beta Lambda-Southern Methodist '56)
Philip P. Noftsinger (Epsilon Phi-George Mason '91)
Donald R. O'Neal, Jr. (Gamma Alpha-Louisiana Tech '09)
Matthew D. O'Neal (Gamma Alpha-Louisiana Tech '06)
Herbert Turner Odom, III (Omicron-Texas '83)
Nicholas S. Palmer (Delta Lambda-Middle Tennessee State '04)
Howard C. Pickett (Sigma Nu Fraternity)
Morris W. "Pete" Pully (Upsilon-North Carolina '45)
Gary L. Recer (Gamma Lambda-North Texas '67)
J. Derrill Rice (Beta Pi-Presbyterian '80)
Mr. & Mrs. Larry Feller Robb (Gamma Lambda-North Texas '63)
Harrison A. Robb (Alpha Omicron-Arkansas '13)
Hubel Robins, Jr. (Eta-Richmond '51)
Roy O. Rodwell, Jr. (Alpha Phi-Duke '55)
Loyd Jordan Russing (Epsilon Xi-North Carolina-Charlotte '06)
Jay F. Rutherford, Jr. (Theta-Kentucky '91)
Travis L. Sartain (Alpha Eta-Westminster '95)
C. Edward Schmidt, Jr. (Beta Alpha-Missouri S&T '62)
Brett S. Schoonover (Epsilon Delta-Texas A&M '96)
David L. Schoonover (Epsilon Delta-Texas A&M '00)
J. Carlton Showalter, Jr. (Beta Commission-VMI '82)
Gregory R. Singleton (Gamma Gamma-Memphis '82)
Robert J. Smith (Alpha Omega-North Carolina State '59)
A. Randolph Smith II (Delta-Wofford '80)
C. Michael Smith (Delta-Wofford '73)
T. Michael Stanberry (Alpha Gamma-Louisiana State '71)
Thaddeus A. Stubbs (Alpha Eta-Westminster '96)
Edward G. Sullivan (Beta Zeta-Florida '77)
E. Powell Thompson (Gamma Chi-Texas Tech '75)
Joseph N. Traigle (Gamma Psi-Northwestern '63)
John H. Turner, Jr. (Beta Rho-Roanoke '10)
Dr. Chad E. Wagoner (Delta Pi-Missouri Southern State '93)
R.M. Warren III (Kappa-Mercer '83)
Hon. David M. Warren (Tau-Wake Forest '78)
Gregory L. Waterworth (Beta Kappa-Maryland '10)
Dr. D. Wayne Whetsell (Delta Psi-Appalachian State '09)
Stuart F. Whetsell (Delta Psi-Appalachian State '06)
W. Madison Wickham (Epsilon Iota-Texas State '03)
Eddie S. Wilson (Delta Beta-Delta State '73)
Edmond H. Wilson (Delta Theta-Georgia Southern '80)
Hugh M. Wood (Gamma Alpha-Louisiana Tech '99)
William A. "Bill" Wood (Alpha-Washington & Lee '03)
LTC William Earl Wray, Jr. (Beta Commission-VMI '73)
Lewis H. Wyman III (Alpha Kappa-Missouri '63)
Ryan T. Young (Epsilon Iota-Texas State '01)
Dean S. Zang (Beta Omega-Washington '00)

Samuel Z. Ammen Court of Honor
Dallas Alumni Chapter
Mustang Alumni Chapter
Ratcliffe Foundation in honor of A.M. Ratliff, Jr.

Gamma - University of Georgia
Nu - Auburn University
Rho - University of South Carolina
Alpha Beta - University of Alabama
Alpha Delta - William Jewell College
Alpha Eta - Westminster College
Alpha Xi - University of California
Alpha Upsilon - University of Mississippi
Beta Tau - Mississippi State University
Gamma Eta - Florida State University
Gamma Omega - Midwestern State University
Delta Beta - Delta State University
Delta Theta - Georgia Southern University

This book is dedicated to the Founders, to the Former Knight Commanders, to those brothers who gave the ultimate sacrifice in defense of our country, as well as to the memories of Thomas G. Paulson II (1930-2015), Dorothy Potter Clagett (1922-2014) and Wayford Arwood Lyons (1949-2015).

KA
DIEU ET LES DAMES

# 1

## The Prelude

The history of the Kappa Alpha Order and of fraternities as student societies reaches back to the founding of the ancient Order at the University of Bologna in 1395. The organization provided proper accommodations for the students of the institutions and protected them from the extortions of the corrupt governor of the city. Bologna already had a reputation for an active student body that not only determined their courses but also their instructors and their rector.[1] The institution soon spread to universities in Florence, Oxford, and Paris and was organized for practical and spiritual purposes, with the practical aspects being drawn from local circumstances and the spiritual parts deriving, in large part, from Masonic influences.[2]

The concept of a fraternal organization in the university (and, indeed, even the name of higher institutions of learning) is likely to have found its origin in the *collegia* of ancient Rome. Collegia were, in essence, trade unions that provided certain benefits (funeral and disability), protected their members from encroachments and extortions, and socially served as an alternative system of support and friendship.[3] After the Dark Ages, as industry and trade began to reassert itself in Western Europe, craft and trade guilds came to be formed and for much the same purposes as the ancient collegia. Membership was voluntary but regularly required either an invitation or a sponsor. Craft guilds regulated the quality and quantity of goods, materials used in production, hours that their members worked, and a specified series of learning steps until the initiate produced a "master work"; trade guilds regulated the source of raw materials for production and who could sell a finished product and for what price. Both institutions, like the Roman collegia, were for mutual protection against unfair practices, against governmental intrusions, and for social interaction and political leverage. Members would gather for special holidays, guild memorials, and community service projects. Many of the social characteristics of the guilds—and later fraternities—were religious in nature and this facet was evident in their rituals and ceremonies. Thus, the medieval fraternities took on the form and function of their mercantile counterparts.

A collateral descendant of the medieval guilds and the more remote Roman collegia were the intellectual and improvement societies of eighteenth-century Britain. During the early modern period and the Enlightenment, both in England and in Scotland, intellectual societies came into prominence, often to promote discussion and plans for scientific and social improvement. In the earliest stages in Scotland, these groups were composed of aristocrats and members of the clergy and university faculties and were established to encourage utilitarian aspects of economic and spiritual improvement. They served as gathering places for scientifically minded intellectuals and professionals and increasingly included middle-class elements—especially mechanics and natural engineers. The dual realms dealt with the practical and the ethical; the practical issues embraced agriculture, science, and industry—all of which improved man's life on earth; the moral component was comprised of ethics, psychology, and jurisprudence—which governed man's relationship with his fellow citizens and God. But members joined the associations not only for altruistic reasons but also for the pragmatic purposes of fellowship, networking, and useful and mutually beneficial exchanges of information.

In the mid-eighteenth century the concept and the construct of intellectual and debating societies crossed the Atlantic to the American colonies and generated organizations such as the Virginia Society for the Encouragement of Arts and Manufactures in Williamsburg and Franklin's *Junto*, which evolved into the American Philosophical Society, in Philadelphia. The Society for the Encouragement of Arts and Manufactures was founded as a colonial sister of the London society of the same name. The organization was likely promoted by Thomas Jefferson's only professor, William Small, and supported by Governor Francis Fauquier and George Wythe. The Virginia General Assembly gave the society official recognition in 1760 and its stated purpose was to encourage the promotion in the colonies of "commodities as are either consumed in [the] kingdom or essential to it manufactures." The London group offered praemia, or cash prizes, for the best innovation or invention produced and some of the most enthusiastic participants were Small's students at the College of William and Mary. While the ostensible reason for capturing a reward was utility, very often it was the demonstration that was the loudest or most destructive that captured the prize.

Fauquier had also formed an intellectual society on his arrival in Williamsburg, which at first was restricted to the local plantocracy, clergy, and members of the college's faculty. It soon became apparent to the governor, however, that most invitees came to the meetings either to complain or to seek political favors. When two professors, who were members of the society, caused such a scandal in town, Fauquier decided to restrict attendance to a select few, who were allowed to bring visiting guests with them. In 1760, Small brought along his favorite student, Thomas Jefferson, to accompany the governor on his fiddle in his musical interlude for the evening entertainment. The group, however, immediately came to value Jefferson more for his conversation than for his fiddle playing, and the assembly became, in Jefferson's terminology, the *partie quarree*, or foursome. At these meetings he heard "more good sense, more rational & philosophical conversations than in all my life besides. They were truly Attic societies."[4] Within short order this society was augmented by Small's present and former students and, for all intents and purposes, acted like an ad hoc graduate school—Small demonstrated scientific experiments, Fauquier gave discourses on economic and political subjects, and Wythe instructed on legal theory and held mock courts.

*Governor's Palace, Williamsburg, Va.*

In the 1750s, students at the college had formed what was affectionately known as the Flat Hat Club, a boy's social club with secret codes and handshakes. Shortly after Jefferson arrived in Williamsburg he became both a member of the FHC and a permanent member of the *partie quarree;* undoubtedly other Flat Hat compatriots, who were also Small's students, attended the symposia and were beneficiaries of Small's, Fauquier's, and Wythe's wisdom and experience. Among the correspondence of St. George Tucker is a letter from Thomas Jefferson to John D. Taylor of Maryland "giving an account of the club, stating that he was a member, and that out of this club the Phi Beta Kappa, founded in 1776, may have arisen."[5] Other connections between the *partie quarree*, the Flat Hat Club and Phi Beta Kappa are overlapping memberships and many of the same faculty mentors and sponsors. George Wythe, while not being a part of the FHC, was a principal in the *partie quarree* and acted *in loco parentis* to many of its members. William Short, sometimes called Jefferson's adoptive son, was the eleventh member of Phi Beta Kappa, as were other Wythe protégées St. George Tucker, John Marshall, and Spencer Roane.

According to an early president of Phi Beta Kappa, William Short, who was also Jefferson's longtime secretary and friend, was admitted to the fraternity "by promising to invoke the Deity at the opening of meetings, not to swear or become intoxicated, to encourage new inventions in arts and sciences, and to pay his six-shilling initiation fee as soon as possible."[6] Phi Beta Kappa was primarily a debating and intellectual society whose activities "centered about a fortnightly debate between student teams of four concerning the great problems of mankind and seeking 'laws' that might govern human conduct."[7] In 1778, Elisha Parmele, who had attended Yale and Harvard, came to Virginia for his health and in Williamsburg joined Phi Beta Kappa. In 1779, Parmele decided to return home and was commissioned by the officers of the lodge to establish

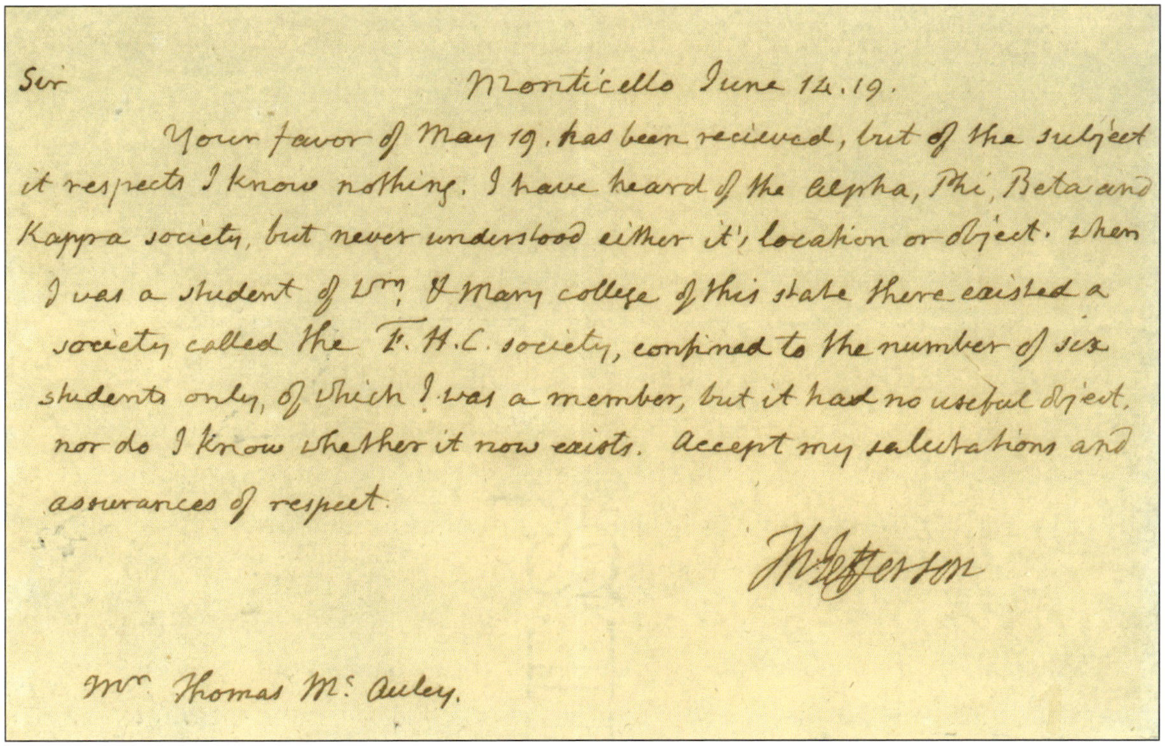

Sir Monticello June 14. 19.

Your favor of May 19. has been recieved, but of the subject it respects I know nothing. I have heard of the Alpha, Phi, Beta and Kappa society, but never understood either it's location or object. when I was a student of Wm. & Mary college of this state there existed a society called the F. H. C. society, confined to the number of six students only, of which I was a member, but it had no useful object. nor do I know whether it now exists. Accept my salutations and assurances of respect.

Th: Jefferson

Mr. Thomas Mc. Auley.

*Thomas Jefferson to Thomas McAuley, June 14, 1819*

branches of the Order at the "University of Cambridge [Harvard], in the state of Massachusetts, and the University of New Haven [Yale]."[8] Parmele established a chapter at Yale in 1780, and one at Harvard in 1781.

From the Flat Hat Club that Jefferson described as having "no useful purpose" came the genesis of the American college fraternity system—Phi Beta Kappa—which initiated a policy, later followed by Kappa Alpha and other American fraternities, of having former members establish chapters at other institutions of higher learning. During the Early Republic, the club "with no useful object" evolved into a fellowship not only for social interaction but also, in the context of the American Revolution, transformed itself into an institution with patriotic and political purposes. From that time until the present, the American fraternal orders have been comprised of both a social and frivolous side and a serious and purposeful intent, depending on the conditions of their times—a hybrid of carefree child and a deliberate man.

In pre-Revolutionary times, a student might begin collegiate classes as early as eleven or twelve years of age, although fifteen to eighteen was more common. For the most part, in the colonies, it was a worry-free time of peace, security, and plenty. Accordingly, among Jefferson's boyhood fraternity in order to thwart local busybodies, Jefferson and his friend John Page turned to using Latin names for compatriots, employed excruciating puns and puzzles in their letters, and created a secret code based on *Shelton's Tachygraphical Alphabet* in their correspondence.[9]

Nevertheless, with the discontent of the colonies and the coming of the Revolution, the same people who had participated in trivial scientific experiments and played tricks on their friends turned to more serious intent. The subject of conversation in Governor Fauquier's soirees turned, as tensions increased between the mother country and the colony, from discussions concerning scientific enquiries into political debates; parlor conversations and light musical diversions became controversies about parliamentary procedures and rights and mock trials; friendly banter devolved into heated arguments. The Flat Hat Club met at Raleigh Tavern to strategize about the impending conflict.

By the time Phi Beta Kappa came into existence, war was eminent, and its primary concern became political and patriotic rather than social and trifling.

Indeed, for the next eight decades—from the defeat of Cornwallis to the end of the Civil War—American fraternities retained an austere and resolute countenance, developed during the Revolution as a result of the fragile nature of the national condition. The uncertainty of forming a more perfect union, the fear of a British invasion, the War of 1812, disputes about slavery, and the vacillating condition of the economy, constitutional disagreements, and the secession of the South from the Union—all called for a purposeful intent in student associations. Young men at colleges formed literary societies and debating clubs in reaction to uncertain times. "For almost all of the nineteenth century, college life was centered in literary societies, [which] were organized and operated by students themselves, centers of intellectual activity in which students gained experience in public speaking, logical argumentation, formal debate and social graces."[10]

The debating and literary societies were prototypes for the later fraternal associations and existed in the 1790s at Liberty Hall Academy. Ollinger Crenshaw states that these clubs were "an invaluable educational adjunct in the nineteenth century… [which] not only trained future politicians and writers … but [also] supplemented the classical curriculum and … the social sciences."[11] Following the tradition of Scottish Enlightenment intellectual and scientific societies, subjects for discussion, or "pieces," would be preassigned and each member would present the results of his investigations. This early version of fraternal gatherings had a more somber and even clerical aura to its inception and mission. The subject of the pieces and the purposes of the gatherings, however, changed and acclimated itself to the exigencies and circumstances of its time.

In short, the form of fraternal organizations followed the function of their times. What was appropriate in times of peace and security was quite different to what was necessary in conflict and war. By the time of the founding of Kappa Alpha at the end of the Civil War, fraternities had transitioned from extensions of childhood social organizations, to bastions of patriotic zeal, coalitions of improvement, secure harbors in an uncertain world.

*The Reverend William Graham*

The histories of the Kappa Alpha Order, Washington and Lee University, and Mulberry Hill are inextricably linked. Ollinger Crenshaw, whose work *General Lee's College* is the principal source for the history of the university, wrote in his original notes, "Without a doubt the most important figure in the early history of Washington and Lee was William Graham...It was through his labors ... that the school known as Augusta Academy [1774–1776] and the Liberty Hall Academy assumed a permanent character and continuity."[12] As early as 1770 the Presbytery of Hanover had proposed the founding of a public school or academy for the western section of Virginia. Samuel Stanhope Smith, later president of Princeton College, recommended William Graham, a recent graduate of the College of New Jersey and student of John Witherspoon, as an appropriate rector of such an institution.

After the completion of his studies at Princeton, Graham was invited to preside over a rural seminary at Mount Pleasant that was located about eleven miles north of Lexington and a mile south of the town of Fairfield. The school was situated in a log cabin and characterized as "the first permanent school of its kind in the history of the valley."[13] At approximately the same time as Graham was presiding over his charges in the log cabin, the Hanover Presbytery was considering a "publick school in A[u]gusta"; in October 1773, it was agreed to "fix the publick Seminary for the liberal Education of youth in Sta[u]nton and by the following year it was concluded to "establish and patronize a publick school which shall be confined to the County of A[u]gusta."[14] Inasmuch as there was "no person to take the management of it in Staunton," the Presbytery reserved the right to fix both the place and the "person by whom it shall be conducted" for a future date. But for the present they choose William Graham.[15]

Several of the members were charged with soliciting funds in various jurisdictions for "a house, a public library, and other apparatus of learning."[16] All of these proceedings had been traditions in Scotland since the time of John Knox and the First Book of Discipline, which called for universal education so that all were able to read the Old and New Testaments without the interpretations of the Catholic Church. In the 1660s, the Scottish Parliament had passed an Heritor's Act that stated that large landowners had the responsibility of constructing a building for public instruction and a house for the master.

Ironically, by the mid-eighteenth century this practice made Scotland, although one of the poorest states in Western Europe, one of the most well educated. This, in turn, produced a highly educated society that lacked appropriate jobs. In response to the dire economic circumstances at home many young Scots immigrated to the colonies *en masse*, seeking and obtaining work as ministers, tutors, teachers, and professors.

At the College of William and Mary, William Small, educated at Marischal College Aberdeen, single-handedly taught all the collegiate classes during Jefferson's official attendance; at Princeton, John Witherspoon, a minister from Paisley, educated at Edinburgh, infused the student population with the new priorities and perspectives of the Scottish Enlightenment; at the University of Pennsylvania, James Wilson, framer of the Constitution and first professor of law at the university, had attended both the United Colleges of St. Andrews and the University of Glasgow. Even Benjamin Franklin had received his first degree from St. Andrews and Benjamin Rush his degree from Edinburgh.

Thus, much of American perspective on concepts of philosophy and politics was derived from Scotland. Both the traditions and the political and philosophical perspectives of the Scottish Enlightenment transformed American thought through the Revolution, during the evolution of the Republic, past the dangers of the War of 1812, and well into the nineteenth century.

In the spring of 1776, William Graham was appointed as pastor of the Timber Ridge congregation, and the "A[u]gusta Academy" moved southward with him.[17] Following the Scottish practice, two "heritors," Captain Alexander Stuart and

Samuel Houston, the father of Sam Houston of Texas fame, donated forty acres to establish a place for worship and edification; the community built a "Hewed Log House, 28 x 24 feet, one Storey and an half high besides their Subscriptions" and assured the presbytery that "fire Wood and Timber for the Buildings, will be furnished gratis, for at least twenty years."[18] Thus, the Augusta Academy was established and William Graham chosen as its rector. In addition, the presbytery agreed that a house would be constructed both for William Graham and for his assistant, John Montgomery.

On May 13, 1776, after transferring the property for the academy, the committee in charge of the process, also renamed the school "Liberty Hall Academy" and laid out plans for the location of the institution's several buildings. While the new school already had an adequate library and "the most essential parts of a Philosophical and Mathematical apparatus," it was still necessary to raise "a considerable sum of money" for the physical construction of the buildings.[19] Interestingly, many of the subscribers, Anglicans all, included a number of men who had been members of the Flat Hat Club, subscribers to the Society for the Encouragement of Arts and Manufactures, students of William Small, Jefferson's classmates and friends, or mentors for Phi Beta Kappa—Richard Cary, Bolling Stark, Champion Travis, Robert Carter Nicholas, Charles Carter, James Holt, Carter Braxton, Mann Page, Lewis Burwell, Benjamin Harrison, William Fleming, George Wythe, James Galt, John Page, Edmond Pendleton, Edmund Randolph, John Page of Rosewell, Fielding Lewis, and Thomas Jefferson.[20]

Graham recruited students in the fall of 1776 with notices in the *Virginia Gazette*: "An Academy to be distinguished by the name of Liberty Hall, is now established, for the liberal education of youth, on Timber Ridge, in Augusta county, where all branches of literature, necessary to prepare young men for the study of law, physick, and theology, any be taught to good advantage, upon the most approved plan." Student tuition, room and board was set at £10/s10 per annum; firewood was free, but students were to provide their own beds, washing, and candles.[21]

The progress of the war and the economic troubles accompanying it made for hard financial times for the school—subscribers were unable to pay their promises, the exigencies of the war created rapid inflation, and many young men were fighting against the redcoats rather than rebelling against the rectors. Graham made a number of visits outside of the immediate vicinity of the academy to raise contributions. Some of those appeals brought a modest response, some were totally unsuccessful.

In 1777, "Graham purchased 290 acres that included the site of the present Mulberry Hill."[22] In 1779, the situation at Timber Ridge became so dire that Graham moved to a new location near Lexington, Virginia. Without Graham's leadership, the institution at Timber Ridge ceased to exist and the library and scientific apparatus from Timber Ridge were transferred to Graham. A number of Graham's former students followed him to his new home on Mulberry Hill.

Graham as the first rector of Liberty Hall Academy, the predecessor to Washington and Lee University moved to this site and built a farm, while continuing to preach to the Lexington Presbyterian congregation and tutor students from the academy.[23] By bringing students to his own home, Graham was able to reduce expenses and, in this way, he reopened the institution in 1782. The General Assembly granted the school the status of incorporation in 1782, by which the institution was taken out of the jurisdiction of the church and thereafter maintained a nondenominational status. "Though styled only an academy, the institution was placed on the level with colleges in its ability to confer degrees."[24]

In 1781, Charles Cornwallis, Earl Cornwallis, was advancing through the Carolinas into Virginia; militias were being raised in Rockbridge and Augusta Counties, and among their ranks were a number of Liberty Hall students. Despite the opinions of some locals as to their military prowess, many students joined the army of Nathanael Greene and fought valiantly at the Battle of Guilford Courthouse on March 15, 1781.[25] At the outbreak of the war, Graham had volunteered for military service and was elected a captain in the local militia. In the summer of 1781, Lieutenant Colonel Banastre Tarleton invaded Virginia

*Liberty Hall Academy*

and caused the General Assembly to flee into the mountains, he destroyed ammunition and almost captured then governor Thomas Jefferson. Graham, "returning to Lexington from clerical business in Staunton ... fell in with some members of Virginia legislature" fleeing from Tarleton. He organized a group to warn the citizenry and urge militia officers to call up their troops to meet at Rockfish Gap to prevent Tarleton's advance, and meeting stiff resistance—the British retreated without a fight.

On October 19, 1781, Lord Cornwallis, surrounded by land and sea, surrendered to General George Washington and effectively ended the War of Independence. With the fighting over and normalcy returning to the country, the trustees of Liberty Hall renewed their efforts for revival and funding. This time the General Assembly stepped in and in December 1782 granted the first charter to an institution of learning by the Commonwealth of Virginia. State support ended the control by the presbytery and the charter itself called for "no word of creed or doctrine."[26] The charter also called for the granting of degrees—changing the status from a grammar school to one of collegiate status. In 1784, the trustees designated the second Wednesday in September as Commencement Day, and on that day twelve young men received their BA degrees.[27]

Graham continued as rector of Liberty Hall Academy until 1796. Under his leadership, the reputation and population of Liberty Hall increased and he was recognized for "his distinguished talents and that steady disinterested zeal which uniformly [increased] the prosperity of the Academy."[28]

Graham's decision to leave was based on the need to have a more lucrative financial foundation than the academy was likely to provide and he, like many others, was enthusiastic about the prospect of making money in land speculation in the Ohio Valley. There were also whispered reports that his departure was caused by the fact that he was on the cusp of being implicated in a sexual scandal.[29] The years after he left the academy, he unsuccessfully campaigned to be a delegate at the Virginia Convention of 1788, was embroiled in several political disputes, and even engaged in a litigious dispute with the Reverend Hezekiah Balch of the Abingdon Presbytery.

William Graham died in Richmond on June 8, 1799, and despite his difficult days after Lexington, he was given a glowing eulogy by former friends and students. The Reverend George Baxtor, Graham's student and successor at Liberty Academy, praised his many contributions to the community; the trustees decreed that his son William should be educated for free, and an elegant tombstone was erected in St. John's Churchyard in Richmond.[30]

*Notes* Chapter 1:


1 David Luscombe and Jonathan Riley-Smith, eds., *The New Cambridge Medieval History* (Cambridge Eng.: Cambridge University, 2004), 4:127.

2 William Raimond Baird and Jack L. Anson, *Baird's Manual of American College Fraternities* (New York: The Alcolm Co., 1905), 167.

3 Steven Epstein, *Wage and Labor Guilds in Medieval Europe* (Chapel Hill: University of North Carolina Press, 1991), 10.

4 Thomas Jefferson to Louis Hue Girardin, January15, 1815, Papers of Thomas Jefferson, Library of Congress, Washington, D.C.

5 "The Flat Hat Club," *William and Mary Quarterly* 23, No. 1 (January, 1917): 161.

6 George Green Shackelford, *Jefferson's Adoptive Son: The Life of William Short, 1759–1848* (Lexington: University Press of Kentucky, 1939), 3.

7 Ibid.

8 "A Fossil from the Tertiary," *Atlantic Monthly* 44 (Boston: Houghton, Osgood and Company, 1879), 101.

9 Martin Clagett, *Scientific Jefferson: Revealed* (Charlottesville, University Press of Virginia, 2009), 71.

10 Larry T. McGehee, *Southern Seen: Meditations on Past and Present* (Knoxville: University of Tennessee Press, 2005), 140.

11 Ollinger Crenshaw, *General Lee's College* (New York: Random House, 1969), 22.

12 Ollinger Crenshaw, Typescript Notes for General Lee's College, Archives, Leyburn Library, Washington and Lee University, Lexington, Va., 1.

13 Ibid., 43.

14 Ibid., 45, 46.

15 Ibid., 46.

16 Ibid.

17 Ibid., 51.

18 Ibid., 52–53.

19 Ibid., 53.

20 Ibid., 54.

21 Ibid.

22 Virginia Department of Historic Resources. National Register of Historic Places Nomination. Mulberry Hill. 1982. Survey File 117-10. Richmond, Va.

23 Ibid.

24 Oren F. Morton, *A History of Rockbridge County, Virginia* (Staunton, Va.: McClure Co., 1920), 190.

25 Crenshaw, *General Lee's College,* 13.

26 Crenshaw, Typescript Notes, 63.

27 Crenshaw, *General Lee's College,* 14.

28 Crenshaw, Typescript Notes, 76.

29 Ibid.

30 Ibid., 77.

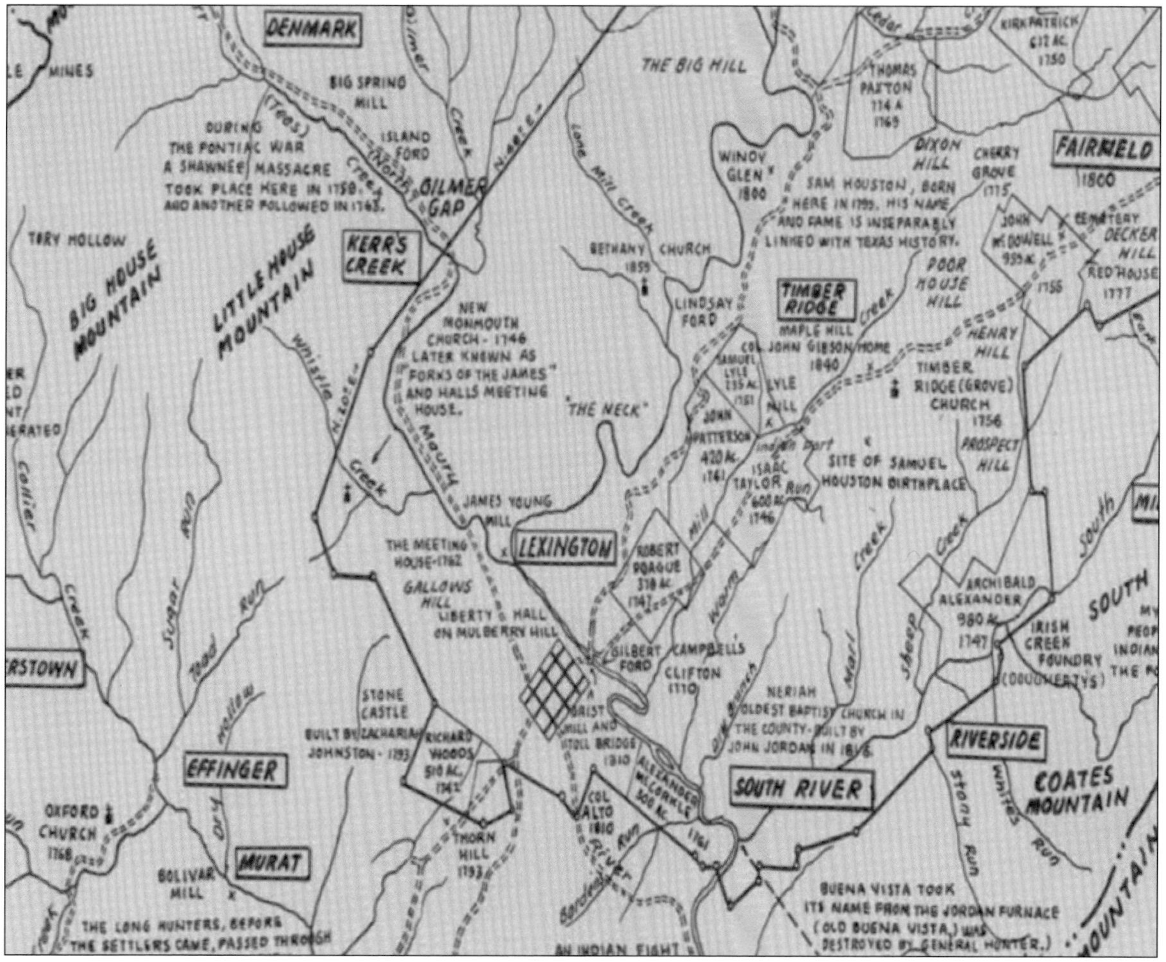


*Historic Map of Rockbridge County*

*Washington College, circa 1870*

# 2

# Washington College

The birth and development of the Kappa Alpha Order and the progression of Liberty Hall Academy into Washington and Lee University are inextricably connected. Not only did the verdant hills of the Valley provide a physical backdrop for the two institutions, but also the traditions and the missions of both formed a common heritage.

The master of Mulberry Hill, William Graham, worked diligently for the success of Liberty Hall Academy. In 1782, Graham received an act of incorporation from the General Assembly of the commonwealth. In 1785, the General Assembly of Virginia awarded one hundred shares of the James River Company stocks and fifty shares in the Potomac Company canal stocks to General George Washington in appreciation of his service and self-sacrifice during the Revolution.[1] This act of gratitude, however, put Washington in an uncomfortable position. He wrote to Thomas Jefferson for advice concerning the matter:

> Among the Laws of the last Session of our Assembly, there is an Act which particularly respects myself; and tho' very flattering, is also very embarrassing to me. This Act, after honorable, flattering, and delicate recitals, directs the treasurer of the State to Subscribe towards each of the Navigations [James River and Potomac River

> Companies' stocks] fifty Shares for my use and benefit; which it declares, is to be vested in me and my heirs forever. It has ever been my wish, and it is yet my intention, never to receive any thing from the United States, or an individual State for any Services I have hitherto rendered ... but how to decline this act of generosity without incurring the imputation of disrespect to my Country, and a slight of her favors on the one hand, or that of pride, or an ostentatious display of disinterestedness on the other, is the difficulty. [2]

Jefferson replied that "the world would be pleased with seeing them [honors] heaped on you and would consider your receiving them as no derogation from your reputation. But I must own that the declining them will add to that reputation."[3] In the end Washington decided to accept the stock, but only with the understanding that the funds "would be applied to some public purpose."[4]

Washington first considered using the funds to support two charity schools; his next thought was the prospect of establishing a national university in the Federal City. In addition to a national institution, Washington wanted to provide for his home state, "his country," as well. Once again he sought the counsel of Thomas Jefferson and influential members of Virginia's General Assembly in this matter. They recommended that an institution should be placed in the upper country at a place that would be convenient to the inhabitants west of Tidewater.

In 1794, with the facilities of Liberty Hall expanding, the trustees again appealed to the Virginia legislature for financial relief. At that very time, several alumni were making a case for Liberty Hall to receive the coveted stocks. One of these men dined with Washington in New York in 1790 and presumably mentioned his alma mater in this connection.

On January 28, 1795, Washington informed the commissioners of the Federal City that he had "vested in perpetuity fifty shares of the Potomac stock" toward the establishment of a national university to be built in the capital. Thomas

Jefferson nurtured the concept of a scientifically oriented institution to be centered in Richmond and staffed with the transported faculty of the University of Geneva. He applied to Washington for the remaining shares of the James River stock. Washington demurred.

In March, Washington wrote that he wished to give his stock to "a seminary of learning with an enlarged plan, but not yet coming up to the full idea of a university."[5] He sought the advice of Governor Robert Brooke and some old friends in the Virginia legislature. Two of the influential members that Washington consulted were also trustees of Liberty Hall Academy—Francis Preston and Andrew Moore: "Moore was sent for by the Father of his Country to be consulted about appropriating the shares to some literary institution above the falls of the river. Gen. Moore presented the claims of Liberty Hall, and after a consultation with his colleague … Gen. Francis Preston, who united with him in urging upon Washington the claims of the Academy, he wrote to the trustees, who presented their case in an able argument."[6] The trustees took Preston's advice and sent an appeal to the already-inclined president that, in part, read:

> In the year ninety three it became necessary to fix upon a spot where permanent building should be erected—the Academy enjoys an extensive prospect of the circumjacent country and a full view of the Town it possesses, Agreeably to the great design of its institution, a calm and undisturbed retirement for study: The situation of the neighborhood for health and fertility as well as for pleasantness yields to no high lands in the upper parts of the State…. By voluntary contributions and some sacrifice [*sic*] of private property we were enabled to erect plain but neat buildings sufficiently capacious to accommodate between 40 & 50 students. The business of education is now in full train.[7]

Persuaded in part by the arguments of Preston and Moore, Washington decided on the struggling school in the shadows of Lexington, for he wrote

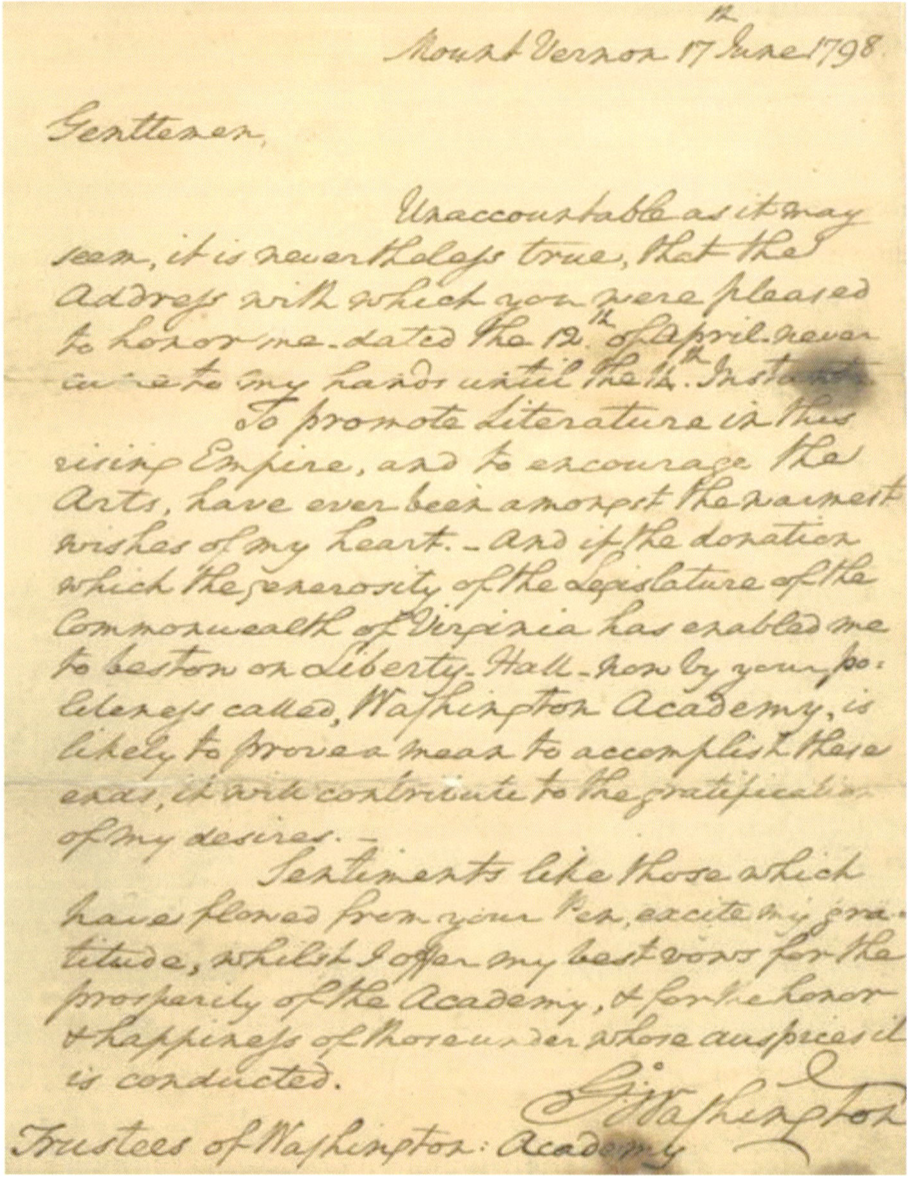

Mount Vernon 17th June 1798.

Gentlemen,

Unaccountable as it may seem, it is nevertheless true, that the address with which you were pleased to honor me, dated the 12th of April, never came to my hands until the 14th Instant.

To promote Literature in this rising Empire, and to encourage the Arts, have ever been amongst the warmest wishes of my heart. — and if the donation which the generosity of the Legislature of the Commonwealth of Virginia has enabled me to bestow on Liberty-Hall — now by your politeness called, Washington Academy, is likely to prove a mean to accomplish these ends, it will contribute to the gratification of my desires. —

Sentiments like those which have flowed from your Pen, excite my gratitude, whilst I offer my best vows for the prosperity of the Academy, & for the honor & happiness of those under whose auspices it is conducted.

Go: Washington

Trustees of Washington Academy

*George Washington to the Trustees of Washington Academy*

to his friend Robert Brooke several months before the eloquent appeal arrived from the trustees, "After careful enquiries, … I have, upon the fullest consideration of all circumstances, destined those Shares to the use of Liberty-Hall Academy, in Rockbridge County."[8] The officials of the school, however, wrote to the president, "It was not earlier than September 1797 that we were officially informed of your liberal donation to Liberty Hall Academy."[9] Washington graciously replied that "unaccountable as it may seem" he had not received their letter of April until the middle of June. "To promote Literature in this rising Empire," Washington wrote, "and to encourage the arts have ever been amongst the warmest wishes of my heart. And if the donation which the generosity of the Legislature of the Commonwealth of Virginia has enabled me to bestow on Liberty Hall, now by your politeness called Washington Academy, is likely to provide means to accomplish these ends, it will contribute to the gratification of my desires."[10]

Three months after Washington's announcement of his choice, the General Assembly passed "an act for erecting Liberty Hall Academy into a college."[11] The act had the unintended consequences of aborting Liberty Hall's charter of 1782 and named a board of visitors that included no clergy and only a few of the gentlemen who had birthed and nurtured the nascent institution. The trustees instantaneously and vociferously protested the changes. Zachariah Johnston, a trustee and a member of the House of Delegates, brought the matter to the attention of the legislature "and early in 1798 the act was repealed. The status quo under the charter of 1782 was explicitly restored, with the unexceptional change in the name to Washington Academy."[12]

The Reverend William Graham tendered his resignation in 1796 and for almost three years after his departure Washington Academy "was committed to the care of tutors."[13] One of those tutors, George Baxter, was appointed rector of the institution and served in that capacity until 1829. The canal stocks did not immediately produce the anticipated revenues and for several years the school languished on the brink of insolvency. In 1802, however, the canal stocks began to provide returns, and the school was able to pay its most pressing debts, purchase some books, and buy fire insurance. In early 1803, Liberty Hall Academy was consumed by flames with only some of the books, scientific apparatus, and bedding being rescued.

With the school's having been destroyed, the faculty and students were suddenly homeless. The collected group found refuge in town at the brick

*Ruins of Liberty Hall Academy, circa 1890*

house of Edward Graham, brother of the former rector, tutor at the academy, and future professor at Washington College. The school resumed its normal functions after a fashion and the fire brought Washington Academy into the bounds of Lexington.

The townsmen were anxious to have the school located in Lexington "whereby they might most conveniently educate their own sons, and most copiously extract money from the sons of others."[14] The trustees were offered several sites around town and finally settled on the property of Andrew Alexander, which consisted of thirty acres of land including an old frame house that served as the president's residence until 1844. Between the money paid out by the insurance company and the dividends of the James River stock, the trustees were able to erect new buildings on the purchased property.[15]

In addition, a local gentleman, John Robinson, also took an interest in the institution and began to make donations to fund the construction of the new buildings.

The original plan was to raise three buildings, two wings, and a large central hall. "It was determined to erect the wings first, and to postpone the main building till a more convenient season. These wings were about 60 yards apart; each was 75 feet long by 20 wide, and two stories high, with two cross passages, and four rooms in each story. In the east wing two of the upper rooms were thrown into one for a chapel and recitation room. There were fourteen rooms therefore for the accommodations of students and tutors."[16]

Graham Hall and Union Hall were the first two buildings raised up on a ridge in the town in 1804, and at such a distance as to permit a central hall to be built between them at a later time. In 1813, the General Assembly passed an act changing the name and status from Washington Academy to Washington College. In 1822, architect John Jordan, whose first professional job had been at Mulberry Hill, designed the center building, or Washington Hall, as a three-story classical temple with a Tuscan portico. In 1831, monies from the Robinson mortification were used to construct a new building, which was then called the Lyceum and now is known as Payne Hall; it was three stories in height with a hipped roof and a balustrade to be used as an observatory. Combining form and

*Graham Hall (1804–1835)*

function the architect used brick made from clay on the site and in the process the unintended consequence of developing a series of terraces occurred, giving the whole area a pleasant and balanced perspective.

In 1835, the administration decided to tear down the former Graham and Union Halls and to replace them with a twin to the Lyceum to be constructed on the opposite side of the Center Building in order to give the whole classical dimensions and uniformity. Center Hall was crowned with a statue of George Washington, or "Old George," in 1844. A second building was christened Robinson Hall after its benefactor "Jockey" Robinson. All future improvements were, by necessity of the Civil War, deferred.[17]

George Washington's donation not only increased the physical dimensions of the College, but also provided an elevated status by the reflected glory of its benefactor's name and amplified its worthiness by his choice—it encouraged students to attend, caused alumni to be supportive, and increased the giving of others to a small school that had been chosen by the Father of the Country—a man of unassailable character, charisma, and fine judgment. "To be sure, the Washington donation did not bring affluence, or even provide immediate solution to the most pressing difficulties; but it created a unique identification, and was the first great step in the second transformation of this institution—from a provincial academy to one of the countries distinctive smaller universities."[18]

The patronage of Washington had other and more immediate financial ramifications as well. The Society of the Cincinnati was initiated at the home of General Friedrich von Steuben in Fishkill, New York, in May 1783, while the British were still occupying New York City. The attendees of the dinner at the general's house were American and French military officers zealous to expel the British. During the meal, General Henry Knox, supported by Alexander Hamilton, proposed a fraternity to be composed of patriots of a certain officer rank to keep alive the dedication to freedom and maintain the friendships forged in battle. The Virginia contingent of the Society of the Cincinnati was founded on October 6, 1783; its members pledged their "sacred honor" to one another until death. The first president of the Society of the Cincinnati was George Washington, who like the eponymous founder of the society, Lucius Cincinnatus, had left off plowing the fields of his farm to save the Republic and returned to his humble occupation after the successes of the battlefield and the glories of a conquering general. Unlike the Orders of the society in many other states, the Virginia Cincinnati did not include a provision for a hereditary membership, likely in deference to the sentiments of Washington. Thus, the society was chartered to expire with its last member, setting the stage for its own demise. Because of the prominence of its members and the respect of its missions, donations, and mortification to the society were substantial.

By the beginning of the nineteenth century many of the society's members were dying off and, pragmatically, the membership planned for the funds and investments that it had amassed. On December 16, 1807, the Virginia branch resolved "that the whole of the funds be presented to the seminary of learning denominated Washington Academy, near the town of Lexington, in the county of Rockbridge."[19] The resolution also included the provision that "there shall be established and continued in the said seminary *a military school in which shall be taught (at least) the sciences of fortification and gunnery*."[20]

In 1814, the General Assembly passed a provision that incorporated the wishes of the Virginia Society of the Cincinnati to "receive the funds into the treasury of the commonwealth, upon the terms and for the objects specified in the above resolutions of the society, and subject to their Order… [and] that the treasurer should pay the pensions charged on the funds, and other demands of the society."[21] In 1824, with only a few members remaining, the secretary of the society, Major James Gibbon, ordered the funds to be delivered to the treasurer of the Commonwealth. It was at this time that it was discovered that the treasurer of the society had taken a substantial portion of the funds and, being insolvent, he committed suicide. His estate was sued and the matter remained in litigation until 1848, when the Commonwealth finally received the endowment, $25,000, and transferred it to Washington College.[22]

It was during this period of fits and starts that the precursors of fraternal organizations began to spring up in the town and at the college. Although sessions of this sort had taken place at Liberty Hall Academy under William Graham's supervision, the first official meetings of "literary" or "debating" societies appeared in Lexington about 1800. The first recorded group styled itself "Belles Lettres" and the members met weekly to discuss topics of interest.[23] The subjects were preselected, speakers were invited, and fees were established to maintain the premises and build a library. Membership and attendance were by invitation only. The name of the group was changed first to the Union Society and then to the Franklin Society. In 1816, the General Assembly granted a charter to the group under the name of the Franklin Society and Library Company of Lexington.[24]

Two such societies competed at Washington College, the Graham Philanthropic Society and the Washington Literary Society, and they "did much to fill the gaps in the curriculum in the areas of literature and the social sciences.... They maintained libraries and sponsored prominent speakers ... but their most significant activity was the weekly debate session ... [in which they] thrashed out ... the foremost national, state and local issues."[25]

Moreover, the literary and debating societies resembled fraternities in some respects and their public functions drew attendance from the elite of the community. In 1816, a member of the Washington Society, David Moore, wrote to his friend from home, Calohill Mennis, concerning the activities and rivalries of the two improvement clubs. He made clear that "the two societies "competed for members and prestige ... and that a student could only belong to one."[26] The groups also had the hallmarks of the social fraternities—secrecy, exclusivity, and complete loyalty.

Moore remarked that the number of members projected for the next year (1817) was about equal and that "young men who came to Washington College from a distance were seldom predisposed to one or the other of the Societies ... but believed that the Society with the larger membership would be of the greater advantage."[27] He added that whichever group had the greatest number of members for the following term would gain the "ascendancy ... and retain it for many years." Moore urged his neighbor to look up local students planning to attend Washington College "in order to prevail upon them" to join the Washington instead of the Graham Society.[28] Historian Ollinger Crenshaw pointed out that "this type of action suggests the "rushing" proclivities of modern college social fraternities.[29] A later society member, John Coles Rutherford, a Washington College student in the 1840s, wrote to his father that after initiation "you take an oath, never to divulge … any of the proceedings of the Society to which you belong."[30]

*Henry Ruffner (1790–1861)*

One of the great ironies was that literary and debating societies were looked on with great favor for they created a forum for a free exchange of information and ideas, nurtured intellectual curiosity, and encouraged practical application of abstract philosophical and political concepts. By contrast, secret social societies were looked on with great suspicion and distrust and were often considered by college officials as the genesis of social discord and political unrest. Nevertheless, in a very real sense the social fraternities were offshoots of the debating and literary societies and likely were composed of many of the same members. Fraternities at Washington College did not come in existence until the mid-1850s and were a bane to President Henry Ruffner's replacement, George Junkin.

*George Junkin (1790–1868)*

In Lexington, in 1849 the trustees of Washington College found a suitable replacement for President Ruffner, who had been outspoken in his opposition to slavery. George Junkin, the trustees' choice, held views diametrically opposed to those of Ruffner. Junkin began his academic career as rector of an academy in Germantown, Pennsylvania. From that institution he progressed to Lafayette College in Easton, Pennsylvania. After a short stint in Easton, he was elected as president of Miami University in Ohio "where he was thrown into the whirl of the abolition storm."[31] John C. Calhoun declared that the speech that Junkin delivered before the Synod of Cincinnati was the finest proslavery argument that he had ever heard.

The speech both made Junkin the focal point of criticism at the northern college and at the same time brought him to the attention of Dr. Archibald Alexander, a trustee of Washington College, who urged him to apply for the vacant position in Lexington. In 1848, George Junkin took his place as the college's new president and, at first, was viewed very favorably. Throughout the 1850s, President Junkin, the trustees, the students, and the townspeople were on the same page concerning slavery but were becoming more and more divided on political issues. As the decade ended, Southerners were feeling increasingly threatened by Northern demands and actions. South Carolina was toying with the idea of secession and was supported in its view by many of the residents of Lexington and students at the college.

In a public letter in the *Lexington Gazette* on January 8, 1861, Junkin wrote that secession or disunion by armed force was treason. He became increasingly insistent on the point and wrote a series of letters to the paper echoing President Andrew Jackson's proclamation that nullification was a "practical absurdity" and condemning "the heresy of great Southern confederacy."[32] Trustees, citizens of the town, and students became increasingly angered by the president's opinions and taunts. When Junkin lectured the students about their secessionist tendencies "in the face of jeers, catcalls and hisses [which rose to a fever pitch when he ... defiantly shouted] in his shrill squeaking voice the hated word Union."[33] Soon acts of defiance and rebellion at the college broke out.

One of the most frequent and favored acts of protest among students at Washington College was the practice of flag-raising. During the winter of 1861, the sentiments for succession were becoming more vocal and aggressive; the advice and angry admonitions of President Junkin more visibly challenged. A son of one of the trustees, H. Rutherford Morrison, and six classmates made a flag "blue with one blood red star in the middle and DISUNION painted in large letters above it and hoisted it on the roof of the college."[34]

When Junkin discovered the banner the following morning, he was "pale with rage [and] threatened to cane the traitorous fellow [who had instigated the outrage] if he could find him."[35] The incandescent president ordered the servants to pull down the flag, but the students, in anticipation of the action, had removed all the ladders. Eventually the servants retrieved ladders from the town but were unable to put them up because of the high winds blowing at the time. The next day it was finally removed, Junkin sentenced the flag to be burned, he invited local dignitaries to witness the execution—but was foiled by the resourceful agitators who "filched" the flag from the president's room and concealed it. Junkin, having been thwarted, raged from student room to student room "squealing" for the despised banner which was never uncovered.[36]

Dr. Junkin endured more tribulations; the students referred to him as the Pennsylvania Abolitionist, the column opposite of his lecture room was adorned with "Lincoln Junkin," and flag-raising incidents took place with increasing frequency. In March, a Palmetto flag was wrapped around the statue of Washington on the top of Center Hall in support of the calls for succession. Junkin commanded it to come down and was determined not to allow the rebels to trick him again. He had the servants hold the offending standard in the sight of all and put a match to it, while shouting out, "So perish all efforts to dissolve this glorious Union."[37] Nevertheless, the recalcitrant students tore "ribbands" from the burnt flag "which they wore in defiance of their president" and draped the statue of Washington in mourning.[38]

Junkin suspected that the social fraternities, which had first appeared on campus in 1855, were at the bottom of the flag-raising ceremonies. On May 28,

1857, the Beta Theta Pi fraternity held an anniversary dinner, and it was also recorded in the *Lexington Gazette* that a "Symposium" of "unusual elegance" was held by Phi Kappa Psi at the Lexington House.[39] The existence of secret societies on campus was longer hidden.

Shortly after the account in the newspaper, President Junkin took exception to the report and alerted the trustees that although they (the fraternities) had "not done much damage so far… they would undermine the authority of college government" and that he was of the opinion that is was appropriate "to exclude these excrescences altogether."[40] President Junkin concluded that fraternities were contrary to Section 8, Chapter 9, of the Laws of Washington College—in that they were both secret societies and promoted the consumption of alcoholic beverages. He drew attention to the fact that in other institutions fraternities had "produced the most disastrous consequences… that their secret ties overrode all others, those to the college, those to the [Literary and Debating] societies, and even to classmate fellowships."[41] He warned the trustees that this cancer must be eliminated immediately or it would become "uneradicable."[42]

The trustees took Junkin's recommendation to heart and ordered that "no student of this College shall be permitted to hold a connexion with any Society whose character is not approved by the faculty."[43] Junkin threatened, even from this early date and even before the disunion banners appeared, to expel any student with fraternity ties.

The first recorded fraternity at Washington College, Phi Kappa Psi, was established there on March 2, 1855, by Charles C. Wertenbaker, and by the end of that year had sixteen of the college's leading men in its fold including the scion of Mulberry Hill, Samuel McDowell Reid, and John B. Brockenbrough, the son of Judge J. W. Brockenbrough, then a trustee of the college and founder of the Lexington Law School, which evolved into Washington and Lee School of Law. "The newness of the fraternity idea, the dense veil of secrecy drawn about their every action, and the prominence of the members excited the greatest curiosity among the faculty and students, as to what were the aims and rites of the new organization…. Beta Theta Pi appeared at Washington and Lee at the next session, and a strong rivalry immediately arose between it and Phi Kappa Psi. The older organization maintained a sure supremacy until the time of the opening of the Civil War."[44] In October 1859, a new organization, Delta Delta, was organized at Washington College by John C. Van Fossen.

After Fort Sumter fell on April 14, 1861, and Virginia seceded on April 17, the students of Washington College again raised a disunion flag over Washington's statue. This time, however, they sent President Junkin a note informing him that anyone attempting to take the flag down would be considered an enemy to the State of Virginia. Junkin's response that he would "never give another lecture or hear another recitation ... until the flag was taken down, and, if the Faculty did not have it removed at once, he would ... hand in his resignation."[45] The faculty ignored Junkin's ultimatum and ordered that the offending flag be permitted to remain. Within twenty hours of the faculty resolution, Junkin submitted his resignation and soon departed for Pennsylvania, leaving behind his possessions, his two sons (who were Presbyterian ministers), a daughter Margaret (who was married to the commandant of VMI, Colonel J. T. L. Preston), and the grave of his daughter Elinor (who had been married to Stonewall Jackson).

It was not the exhortations of Junkin, however, but the exigencies of the

*Fort Sumter, April 15, 1861, after Anderson's surrender*

Civil War that put an end to fraternal activities. The few students remaining at the College were either too preoccupied with worry or too burdened by the unrelenting assignments of the remaining professors to indulge in the luxury of pleasant company or frivolous amusements. All official activities of the antebellum societies were in abeyance during the conflict but "with the influx of students after the Civil War the ante-bellum Phi Kappa Psi and Beta Theta Pi were reactivated and a number of other fraternities were introduced."[46] And indeed, the nature of these organizations and the hearts and minds of their aggregate members may well have gone in a different direction had it not been for the college's next and most important president.

*Notes* Chapter 2:

1 Herbert Baxter Adams, *Thomas Jefferson and the University of Virginia* (Washington, D.C.: Government Printing Office, 1888), 33.

2 George Washington to Thomas Jefferson, February 25, 1785, George Washington Papers, Library of Congress, Washington, D.C.

3 Thomas Jefferson to George Washington, July 10, 1785, George Washington Papers, Library of Congress, Washington, D.C.

4 Ollinger Crenshaw, *General Lee's College* (New York: Random House, 1969), 27.

5 Adams, *Thomas Jefferson and the University of Virginia*, 42.

6 Hugh Grigsby, "The Founders of Washington College," in *Historical Papers: 1890,* No. 2 (Baltimore: John Murphy & Co., 1890), 61.

7 The Trustees of Liberty Hall Academy to George Washington, December 7, 1796, George Washington Papers, Library of Congress, Washington, D.C.

8 George Washington to Robert Brooke, September 15, 1796, George Washington Papers, Library of Congress, Washington, D.C.

9 The Trustees of Washington Academy to George Washington, April 12, 1798, George Washington Papers, Library of Congress, Washington, D.C.

10 George Washington to Washington Academy Trustees, June 17, 1798, George Washington Papers, Library of Congress, Washington, D.C.

11 Crenshaw, *General Lee's College,* 29.

12 Ibid., 31.

13 Ibid., 71.

14 Henry Ruffner, "Early History of Washington College," in *Historical Papers (1890)* No.1 (Baltimore: John Murray, 1890), 88.

15 Ibid., 89.

16 Ibid., 90.

17 *Preservation Master Plan for Washington and Lee University* (Charlottesville: John Milner Associates, Inc., 2005), Chap. 2, p. 6.

18 Crenshaw, *General Lee's College,* 26.

19 Henry Ruffner, "Early History of Washington College," 102.

20 Ibid.

21 Ibid., 103.

22 Ibid.

23 Charles W. Turner, "The Franklin Society, 1800–1891," *Virginia Magazine of History and Biography* 66, No. 4 (October 1958): 432.

24 Ibid., 434.

25 Crenshaw, *General Lee's College*, 106.

26 Ibid.

27 David E. Moore to Calohill Mennis, December 18, 1816, MS, Calohill Mennis Papers, University of Virginia Archives, Charlottesville, Va.

28 Ollinger Crenshaw, Typescript Notes for General Lee's College, Archives, Leyburn Library, Washington and Lee University, Lexington, Va., 433.

29 Ibid.

30 Crenshaw, *General Lee's College,* 106.

31 Ibid., 112.

32 Ibid., 118.

33 Ibid.

34 Ibid., 119.

35 Ibid.

36 Ibid., 120.

37 Ibid., 122.

38 Ibid.

39 Crenshaw, Typescript Notes for General Lee's College, 429.

40 Ibid., 423.

41 Ibid., 429.

42 Ibid., 425.

43 Ibid.

44 Charles Liggett Van Cleve, *The History of Phi Kappa Psi from Its Foundation in 1852 to Its Fiftieth Anniversary* (Philadelphia: Franklin Printing Co., 1902), 172.

45 Crenshaw, *General Lee's College,* 124.

46 Ibid., 211.

*Jo Lane Stern in a Confederate uniform of his own making*

# 3

## The Civil War and Washington College

The situation at Washington College was unique before, during, and in the immediate aftermath of the Civil War. Ollinger Crenshaw put it succinctly in *General Lee's College*: "Although many Southern institutions of higher learning closed their doors during the Civil War, Washington College struggled on with its work of education. It operated, however, with altered and restricted dimensions, as military service called away most of its students and many youths who otherwise would have become students."[1]

With the departure of the Liberty Hall Volunteers in June 1861, the administration and faculty of Washington College faced the sober and somber obligation of maintaining academic standards, to the best of their ability, for the duration of the struggle.[2] Faculty members played dual roles as educators and patriots. With a reduced staff, a meager student body, and funds rapidly being depleted by inflation, extraordinary measures were taken—the literary societies were suspended, students were expected to attend drill when thought expedient, those over the age of eighteen were compelled to leave, new and returning students were urged to bring their own books and supplies, and provisions of every sort were in a diminished state.

The Union troops, under General David Hunter's command, burned Virginia Military Institute and Governor John Letcher's family home, and inflicted heavy damage on Mulberry Hill. The houses of local citizens were vandalized and looted, livestock was appropriated and carried off, and fences and crops were destroyed.

Hunter's men seemed to have taken special delight in damaging Washington College itself—the libraries of the literary societies were either mutilated or carried off; carpets, pictures, and furniture were broken or ripped up; laboratories and specimen cabinets torn apart and pulled down. The Federal soldiers pelted Washington's statue atop Center Hall with stone, thinking the figure to be that of Jefferson Davis. The Federal troops were on the verge of setting fire to the college when an officer on Hunter's staff, and a Virginian, implored him to spare the institution.

After Hunter departed, the College was used as a makeshift hospital. The trustees of Washington College offered both the use of classrooms, and the chapel and quarters to the faculty of its sister institution, Virginia Military Institute, which now lay in ruins. The college reopened for the fall-winter session of 1865–1866.

From 1861 to 1865, those students who conceivably would have been meeting for classes were busy attending to the business of war. For those who were of an age to matriculate, the delay of the intervening years gave them a sense of purpose and sobriety; for those who were still children, the war provided a catalyst for accountability, discipline, and maturity, but, at the same time, it took away the transitional joys and the triflings of adolescence.

Thus, the new students returning from the rigors of war were not of uniform backgrounds or similar ages. Three such individuals were Jo Lane Stern, who was a mere twelve years old when he first became involved in the Confederate cause; James Ward Wood was almost sixteen and would likely have been preparing for college at the time of his enlistment; and, Samuel Z. Ammen, who arrived in the fall of 1866 and at the ripe old age of twenty-two. Their combined experiences and backgrounds provide an interesting and unusual sociological study of the first years of Washington College under General Robert E. Lee's administration.

The last to enroll and the first to be born was Samuel Zenas Ammen, the son of Benjamin Ammen, of Swiss-German heritage, and Naomi Cross Ammen from a Scots-Irish background. He was the youngest of nine children and was born on October 22, 1843, on the family farm at Mill Creek about three miles from the town of Fincastle, Virginia.[3] Samuel Ammen's father, Benjamin, was born circa 1800 and his mother in 1810. Naomi was the daughter of Thomas Cross, who owned a mill in Rockbridge County. Benjamin was mechanical by nature and early in life installed machinery in local mills.[4] In 1826, he purchased Cross Mill from his father-in-law. "The mill consisted of a flour and grist mill, sawmill of the old type, a hatter's shop in the basement, and a carding mill to make rolls of wool. This, the women of the country spun into yarn from which hosiery, cloth and other apparel were made....The Ammen Mill became famous for its Fincastle patterns, woven into woolen blankets... and furnished vital supplies to the Civil War Commissary Department."[5]

The Ammen homestead was described as "a Substantial two-story dwelling erected close to the factory. The thick brick walls rested on a heavy stone foundation. The basement rooms are large and have high ceilings where they cooked and ate. The interior decorating is finely carved and the door locks bear English crests... the main door is particularly beautiful decorated with a fan and side lights" and there is fine rope molding throughout.[6]

According to the article in the *Baltimore Sun*, Ammen "was given the best educational advantages possible at the time. At 8 years of age he was sent to a school kept by a Presbyterian clergyman." After his tutelage with the minister, Ammen attended McCue's and Wilson's Latin School on Academy Hill in good times, and, in less prosperous circumstances went to "Robinson's [school] over the fire engine with its poor white trash ruffians."[7] According to his biographer, Ammen showed his abilities and enthusiasm in academics by maintaining top marks in all of his studies—Latin, Latin Composition, Algebra, Spelling, Reading, English and Declamation.[8]

During the winter session that began in January 1861, the students "of the academy formed a military organization known as the Home Guard, and when the interruption of the Civil War closed the doors of the academy at Fincastle, students old enough to bear arms hastened to the defense of their native state," Ammen remembered, "We boys 'on the hill' organized the Junior Guards. . . . We wore white trousers, red shirts and black caps, drilled with music, in great style, halting for display usually where an ice cream treat was most likely. Our popularity was immense."[9]

Ammen enlisted at Centreville, Virginia, on August 7, 1861, in the Fincastle Rifles, Company D, 11th Virginia Infantry, as a private and was discharged on May 19, 1862. This regiment was in the brigade initially commanded by General James Longstreet and afterward by Generals Richard S. Ewell, A. P. Hill, and George E. Pickett. The Fincastle Rifles were composed of regular citizens of the county and formed in the fall of 1859, during a period of increasing sectional tension. In its early days, the company's uniform consisted of civilian pants and a linsey hunting shirt. The re-formation of the cohort was precipitated by John Brown's insurrection at Harper's Ferry. The first meetings were held in the jury room of the Fincastle Courthouse and drill was practiced in the nearby fields.[10]

A few days after he enlisted in the Confederate States Army, Ammen found himself at Fairfax Court House, where his unit skirmished with Northern troops in sight of Washington. "At Upton's Hill I acquired a piece of Gutta-percha, copper covered [telegraph] cable used, I was told, to connect McDowell's Army to the White House."[11]

Ammen's first major encounter was at Dranesville, Virginia, in December 1861, when his detail foraging for food for their horses ran into a much-larger contingent of Federal troops. Ammen later recalled, "I took part, December 19, 1861, in a bloody little fight at Dranesville, near the Potomac, between a Confederate force of about 2,000 led by General J. E. B. Stuart, who took wagons to get stacks of hay for his cavalry, and a force of 4,000 Yankees, who by chance went the same day to get the same hay. Jeb this time was badly beaten, and the Yankees got all the hay."[12]

Both sides were deployed on opposite sides of the road with the artillery in the middle of each line. After several hours of fighting the superior Northern force threatened to overwhelm Stuart's men and he ordered them to withdraw.

In the end the Southerners lost "all but one horse, which Sergeant Theodore Hammond aided by Private Sam Ammen, guided through the mud."[13]

Ammen's next, and most dangerous experience of the campaign, occurred in April 1862, near Fort Magruder, which was located between Yorktown and Williamsburg. Under attack, young Ammen had left his foxhole to answer nature's call, when, all of a sudden, "a direct hit was scored on [his] knapsack—tearing it up and blowing the bottom out of a canteen."[14] The following days were equally as fierce, the 11th Infantry was harassed by rain, artillery fire, and snipers. A comrade of Ammens' noted that there was "no, fire, no comfort, no hope" and if he were lucky the best he could wish for was "three soggy crackers downed by dirty water for breakfast."[15]

The Confederate forces then receded toward Williamsburg with "horses and mules ... pulled under the mud by sinking artillery and left for dead."[16] General George McClellan's army, too anxious for victory, followed the army retreating to Richmond in disarray, and, Ammen wrote, "We were victorious driving the enemy through the woods and across a clearing, inflicting and suffering heavy losses. I slept the night before the battle on the campus of the College of William and Mary with my mess-mate Ed James. I never saw him again. He, being taller than I, was to my right in the line of battle, and fell with a bullet through his temples. Two others, close to me in line, were killed, and several more were wounded. Toward night, rain fell; and about 10 p.m. we withdrew to a plowed field near town, to sleep in the mud on a floor made of fence rails. As we were leaving the battlefield through the clearing of fallen trees, a pitiable moaning of the wounded, left behind in the rain and darkness, attended us."[17]

Suffering from many close calls, Company D drew back from the area, and "after a long and starved march through the Chickahominy Swamp we reached 'Camp Stumpy' a few miles out of Richmond," Ammen continued. "I was in rags and tags; at Warwick River a long shell had struck my pillow—my knapsack—and destroyed my clothes."[18]

By now, Ammen's father had arrived in Richmond, determined to have his son moved out of harm's way. His father, Benjamin Ammen, arranged for a

*Battle of Williamsburg, May 5, 1862*

change of post, and the son was "detailed as chemist to make dyestuffs needed in the manufacture of cloth for the Confederate army."[19] The Ammen family had such a factory in Fincastle, which made uniforms and blankets for the Southern forces, and Ammen soon returned home to help in his father's factory.[20]

On February 22, 1864, however, the young man "perversely and successfully volunteered again," he recalled, "this time for the Navy." He was assigned to the *Drury [Drewry],* a dispatch boat with a crew of "rascals, thieves and cut throats." He soon "suffered greatly from malarial fever," wrote William Doty."[21] As the ship's doctor was administering quinine to Ammen, the *Drury,* was attacked. Ammen recalled that they were hit in several places but managed to limp "into 'the basin' at Richmond [where] extensive repairs were found necessary."[22]

He recalled that, not wanting to wait, "[I] bestirred myself to some purpose" and obtained the assistance of a local congressman to be transferred to a mounted guerrilla unit operating near the borders of West Virginia, "west of Lewisburg, where the region was rough and I had some adventures, not without danger." At the end of the war, he surrendered, received a pardon at Lewisburg, and returned home.[23]

Ammen wrote that "on June 1, 1865, I went to McCue and Wilson's Classical School [until] June 1, 1866." During this enchanted year, he fell in love with the daughter of a professor, Mollie Sealey, who introduced him to the art of love, while her father instructed him in French and English literature. Half nostalgic, half ashamed, Ammen recalled, "Mollie took me by storm and kept me captive for months in 1865 and 1866.... We caressed merely for the delight of semi-carnal passion.... After we parted, my successor were Marcus, John, James, Kent, and others less fastidious. The net effect on me was bad; my heart, I felt, was burnt to a cinder."[24] It was then that Ammen decided to become a surgeon and determined that Washington College would be the best choice for his future education.[25]

Our second student, Jo Lane Stern, the youngest, was born in Caroline County on December 23, 1848, and attended a local school until the outbreak of the war.[26] While the coming hostilities were still on the horizon, Stern "beat the drum for a Military Company, afterwards known as Company E 30th Infantry" which was organized in his district and "acted as a sort of a messenger between the soldiers of his neighborhood ... carrying provisions, etc." [27]

In 1861, the Confederate government established the "Military and Railroads Stations at Chesterfield Station" near Ruther Glen in Hanover County. [28] The telegraph operators in charge of the operation "found board and lodging in the home of the Stern family"; at the time Jo Lane Stern was "12 years of age." These operators took a fancy to young Jo and, in turn, he was obsessed with the telegraph instruments and in an incredibly short time became a good operator.[29] Stern made quite an impression in the spring of 1862, when substituting for one of the resident operators who was away, he alerted the authorities in Richmond about an imminent Union attack. As a result of this action, he was commissioned by the Confederate government to assist the operators of the telegraph that stretched from Ashland to Hamilton's Corner near Fredericksburg on the Richmond, Fredericksburg and Potomac Railroad.[30]

The following year, at the age of thirteen, "Stern was taken into the service of the Confederate States as military telegraph operator."[31] In 1863, Stern joined the Confederate army, he was thirteen. In this capacity, he came under fire at Fredericksburg. He wrote, "I was sworn into the secret service of the Confederacy early in 1863, and [was] assigned to duty with General P.M.B. Young," who "commanded Stuart's Cavalry Brigade." He was shuffled back and forth between different generals until he was assigned to Robert E. Lee's Army of Northern Virginia, from the Battle of the Wilderness until Cold Harbor. "It was Stern who intercepted a message from Sheridan and sent Lee's order to Stuart," wrote Governor Garland Pollard in 1932, "which brought about the defeat of the former [General Philip Sheridan] at Yellow Tavern, and saved Richmond from the invader."[32]

Stern met the general in May 1864, when Lee had positioned his army "at a halt on the North Anna River" near Hanover Junction. "I was on duty there as military telegraph operator, and as such received a message over the line from the Secretary of War for General Lee. His tent was on the opposite side of Central Railroad from the telegraph office, a short distance, and being anxious to get as close as possible to this great man and see how he looked after fighting almost every day for a month, I took the message to him myself instead of sending it by one of the couriers."[33] Mustering up the courage, the young Stern folded the telegraph, made himself as presentable as possible, and crossed the pontoon bridge.

He approached the commander's tent and found Lee "alone, sitting on a box, writing on a board on his knees. The sides of the tent were rolled up, and it occurred to me that I might get a chance to put my hand upon him, which seemed to me to be as great an honor as would in all probability ever come to me. So I flanked out to one side and came up behind him and touched him on the shoulder. Not knowing what sort of reception this kind of familiarity was going to receive, I had my cap off in a second, and with the other hand was holding the message in an unmistakable envelope, so he could see it as he turned. He spoke in the gentlest, kindest manner, as if it were an everyday occurrence for boys to punch him on the shoulder, thanked me for bringing the message and asked me to wait till he could see if it required an immediate answer. When he finished I told him that I was the operator and not a courier, and he said, 'Then I will not keep you waiting. You had better go back to your office and I will send the answer.' I could but be struck with the quiet dignity and gentleness which characterized the man, and the fact that the surrounding exciting circumstances and the approach of a hostile army of a hundred thousand men seemed to have no terrors for him."[34]

The young telegraph operator again encountered General Lee on the following day as General Ulysses S. Grant's troops were nearing Jericho Mills and battle was imminent. Stern recalled, "The next day I saw him and Colonel Taylor and another officer down near the river, where one of Grant's corps was crossing to the south side. My business that day was with Colonel Taylor, and he told me to get out of the range of the firing. It struck me that what was good for him and General Lee ought to be good enough for any one else."[35]

General Lee may have thought that the situation was too perilous for his young friend and immediately transferred him to the relative safety of Richmond. On May 23, 1864, Stern became the night operator at "the main office of Confederate States Military Telegraph, 11th Street, Richmond."[36] In September 1864, Stern was ordered to return to Hamilton's Crossing and served for some time on the line of the Richmond, Fredericksburg and Potomac Railroad with several commanding officers until the fall of Richmond, April 3, 1865. With the city having been taken, he was ordered to go to Lynchburg but the army surrendered before he could make it there. Stern "surrendered at Richmond, May 2, 1865, and was paroled."[37] For a short while he attended school in Richmond, and then enrolled at Washington College.[38]

A photograph of young Stern in a Confederate uniform of his own making

*Jericho Mills, North Anna River, May 23, 1864*

was donated many years ago to Kappa Alpha. This representation of Stern the soldier, telegraph operator, some say spy, was given as a reward to a former comrade only identified as Jack in regard for doing his "duty so perfectly" at the reunion of United Confederate Veterans in 1929. On the reverse he described the story of the portrait, "In December 1864, Operator Stern decided to have his photograph taken and had to devise an uniform for the occasion, as shown in the illustration. The coat was made from a captured blue-gray blanket, with Union buttons, and the vest and trousers from a Confederate blanket. A calico collar—and he was all dressed up!"[39]

The portrait demurely hangs in the former carriage house that has been converted into a stylish and efficient office for the present archivist of the Kappa Alpha Order, Sergeant Major E. Kent McMichael. General Stern, known for setting styles and breaking hearts all his life, began his sartorial career at an early age and in an efficient and utilitarian fashion.

Midway in age among the three subjects of our narrative was James Ward

*Major General Thomas Lafayette Rosser*

Wood. He was born on December 26, 1845, in Lost River, Hardy County, now West Virginia. The Wood homestead had originally been surveyed by George Washington and Wood descended from some of the earliest settlers in the region. Wood's mother, Susan Inskeep Branson, was related to the Inskeeps and the Bransons. As a boy Wood received a proper English education in local schools and his father maintained a substantial library at home. As the Civil War approached he had plans to go to college and study law.[40] Instead, he became a soldier.

A story has been related that young Wood accidently wounded himself and spent a part of the war convalescing at home. His diary for 1864, however, gives a robust account of his time with Company C, 7th Virginia Cavalry. It begins "Sat. Jan 9th 1864: I leave home to-day for the C.S.A. Crossed the North mountain to Furman's Furnace. Captain Keyhendall, John Inskeep & myself in company. Picked up an old magazine containing the following lines which seem very prophetic of a soldier's life.

Our life is but a tale, a dance, a dream  
A little wave that frets and nibbles by  
Our hopes the bubbles that it bears  
Born with a breath & broken with a sigh[41]

He spent much of the next month and a half in camp beset by foul weather, cold, and excruciating boredom. By February, the Seventh Cavalry was playing cat and mouse with the Union army: "Thurs 4 Feb Yankees advance on [Generals] Early & Rosser at Moorefield. Their Com. By Mulligan, Averill, & Shoburne. Rosser wanted to fight but Early would not let him." On February

27, Wood wrote to his father: "The men are in fine spirits & most of them think the spring campaigns will end the war but I cannot see why. It is also the general opinion that the confederate army will masse & go into Maryland & Pennsylvania in the spring but of course no one knows."[42]

The winter made for terrible traveling conditions, maintaining supply lines, and foraging for food. Soldiers, both North and South, usually spent this time in intermittent training and reconnaissance but most often in total tedium sitting in cold and wet tents with little to eat and less to amuse themselves with, except unreliable opinions. With summer approaching and spring in full bloom, however, military activities commenced apace. On May 5, 1864, he began to describe the horrific events that transpired during a time of intense conflict:

> Thurs 5: Our pickets are driven in by the enemy we are then formed and charge them down . . . their force consisting of Kilpatrick's Division & another Brig. Numbering . . . 9000 men . . . I now could attend to nothing but those events transpiring immediately around me. Lt. Com waved his old shotgun over his head & shouted come on my boys follow me, come on Co. F follow me & with a tremendous yell we followed him. We charged down the road about 300 yds when we came in view of about 800 men. Sharpshooters deployed for action in the edge of the woods. The Regt charged them in the face of a hailstorm of solid shot shell & grape just here. J. Johnson of our Co was wounded in the neck by a pistol ball & carried to the rear & just then Lt V's horse was killed under him.... About 3 o'clock the fight was going on to the very greatest degree of heat possible & shot & shell flew like hail stones.[43]

From this point on there were few lulls in the fighting which, raged in a continual and unforgiving manner; on the 15th of the month Wood reported that his unit found "many of the enemys dead behind their lines some of whom have been dead so long that they are almost entirely decomposed and worms may be seen preying upon their carcasses to the number of millions of millions—Great God our Heavenly father shall harvest of death never cease? The stench is almost intollerable—They also left many caissons the mud being so deep that they could not convey them to the right where they were massing their forces. The only wonder is that they did not burn them."[44]

Wood and the 7th next deployed to the North Anna River and at the very same time that Jo Lane Stern was there with General Lee. Wood's diary recorded a series of eventful days at the North Anna River. On May 22, he wrote: Go out to sharp shoot at N. Anna bridge. Enemy do not come, then move down to-wards Hanover Junction and go into camp near Caroline and Hanover line. Mon 23rd: Go out to sharpshoot at another N. Anna brige. Enemy come this time, have a very spirited fight—balls fly by the handful."[45]

As the summer progressed the injuries became more serious, the privations more extreme, the loss of life greater on both sides. Wood's entries describe frantic movements, changes in campsites, and the direction of the fight, his account ended on August 1, 1864.

Although the narratives of all three soon-to-be students at Washington College followed varied paths to the end of the war, a common thread ran through all three. Those who endured the trials of battle came out men, not boys. They were more sober, more serious, more resourceful, more confident, and more determined than they would have been without the experience. Many who entered Washington College after the war were of a different and more-tempered metal than those who came before. The college that General Lee would command became distinguished not only by dint of his leadership but also on account of the character of those who made up the student body of the time. That the college became an institution dedicated to unification and betterment, instead of one devoted to factions and revenge is a testament both to the providential leadership of the college and to the temperament of the students.

The stories reflected in the history of these three men were not at variance

*Chesterfield Bridge, North Anna River, May 23, 1864, by Timothy O'Sullivan*

with the background of many coming to Washington College at the end of the war. They are especially interesting as they are the narratives of the three individual most important to the story of Kappa Alpha. Their character, and those of many of their comrades, classmates and instructors, along with the tempered direction of the new president of Washington College, affected the nature of that institution and reflected a set of principals that healed the nation and shaped its history.

## *Notes* Chapter 3:

1 Ollinger Crenshaw, *General Lee's College* (New York: Random House, 1969), 127.

2 The Liberty Hall Volunteers was composed of students from Washington College under the leadership of Professor of Latin, James J. White. The name of the organization had originated with a group of patriotic students who had attended Washington College's precursor, Liberty Hall Academy, during the Revolutionary War. See John Apperson, *Repairing the March of Mars* (Macon: Mercer University Press, 2001), 109 n. 13.

3 "Dr. S. Z. Ammen Hailed as Father of Kappa Alpha," *Baltimore Sun,* March 18, 1923, p. 3.

4 J. W. Austin, *Related Families of Botetourt County Virginia* (Baltimore: Clearfield Press, 2000), 3.

5 Ibid.,10.

6 Ibid.

7 Samuel Ammen, My History, Typescript Copy, Kappa Alpha Archives, Lexington, Va., 56.

8 William Kavenaugh Doty, *Samuel Zenas Ammen and the Kappa Alpha Order* (Charlottesville: Surber-Arundale Co., 1922), 10.

9 "Dr. S. Z. Ammen Hailed as Father of Kappa Alpha," 3; Ammen, My History, 58.

10 William O. Doherty, *Snowballs and Skirmish Lines: A History of the Fincastle Rifles* (West Haverstraw, N.Y., N.D.), 2.

11 Ammen, My History, 61.

12 Doty, *Ammen and the Kappa Alpha Order*, 16.

13 Doherty, *Snowballs and Skirmish Lines*, 7.

14 Ibid., 8.

15 Ibid.

16 Ibid.

17 Doty, *Ammen and the Kappa Alpha Order*, 16.

18 Ammen, My History, 61.

19 Doty, *Ammen and the Kappa Alpha Order* ,17. Benjamin Ammen, Samuel's father, established "in 1826… a flouring mill, next a tannery and shoe-making business, and finally, in 1842, a flourishing manufacturing business for the production of woolen cloth, blankets, yarns, etc., for the surrounding countryside and more distant counties." Doty, *Ammen and the Kappa Alpha Order*, 9.

20 Doty, *Ammen and the Kappa Alpha Order*, 9

21 Ibid., 17.

22 Ammen, My History, 60.

23 Ibid.

24 Ibid., 62, 64.

25 Doty, *Ammen and the Kappa Alpha Order*, 21.

26 Samuel Z. Ammen, "Founders of Kappa Alpha: General Jo Lane Stern," *Kappa Alpha Journal* 38, No. 1 (November 1921): 19.

27 Ibid., 1921, 19: The school was Fountaine Hill Academy, conducted by Professor Squires. Greenlee Letcher, "Stern Biography," March 4, 1935, Kappa Alpha Archives, Lexington, Va., 2.

28 "The New President of the Old-Time Telegraphers," in *Telegraph and Telephone Age,* April 16, 1921, p. 186.

29 "Old-Time Telegraph Operators to Meet in Richmond Virginia," *Miami Daily Metropolis Newspaper,* October 18, 1921, p. 6.

30 "The New President of the Old-Time Telegraphers," 186; "Old-Time Telegraph Operators to Meet in Richmond Virginia," 6.

31 "The New President of the Old-Time Telegraphers," 186.

32 Ibid. Governor Garland Pollard to Gardner Waller.

33 Jo Lane Stern, "General Lee, Pretty Girls and Traveller" *Richmond Times-Dispatch*, January 20, 1907, p. 3.

34 Ibid.

35 Ibid.

36 Ammen, "Founders of Kappa Alpha," 21; see also "The New President of the Old-Time Telegraphers," 186.

37 "The New President of the Old-Time Telegraphers," 186.

38 Whether Stern attended Richmond College or nearby Randolph-Macon is not known at this time, but, it is interesting to consider in that he planted branches of the Kappa Alpha Order at both institutions.

39 Archivist's Office, Kappa Alpha National Headquarters, Lexington, Va.

40 Samuel Ammen, "The Founders of Kappa Alpha: James Ward Wood," *Kappa Alpha Journal* 37, No. 3 (May 1921): 218.

41 James Ward Wood Diary, January 9 through July 21 1864, Accession number 25506, Archives, Library of Virginia, Richmond, Va., 1.

42 Ibid., 12; James Ward Wood to Angus Wood, February 27, 1864. ibid., 3.

43 Ibid., 40.

44 Ibid., 70.

45 Ibid., 74.

*View of Confederate Gunboat Drury (Drewry)*

*Lexington and environs, circa 1865*

# 4

# General Lee to the Rescue

The *Evening Star,* a Washington, D.C., newspaper, reported on Monday, April 10, 1865:

> SURRENDER OF LEE AND HIS WHOLE ARMY! GRANT'S TERMS ACCEPTED!
>
> All the Arms, Artillery, and Public Property turned over to our Government. Officers and Men Paroled. The Officers allowed their Side Arms and Horses. Lee's Army Allowed to Return Home. Grant Wishes to Spare Life. Lee Desires the Restoration of Peace. Congratulatory Order of Secretary Stanton. A Grand Salute to be Fired in Every Part of the Union. Official War Bulletin—War Department. Washington, D.C. April 9, 1865, 9 p.m—The Department has just received official report of the surrender, this day, of General Lee and his army to Lieutenant General Grant, on terms proposed by General Grant. Details will be given as speedily as possible. Edwin M. Stanton.[1]

With these words, the war ended for the most part. The hopes of the South were dashed, but the prayers of many were answered—an end to the fighting and killing and destruction. Thoughts turned to a new reality and the prospects for a better future both in the North and in the South. In its own way, each side exhibited remarkable restraint, an almost immediate desire for reconciliation,

*Union Troops in a victory parade, May 1865*

and, for the most part, a preternatural lack of ill will and the desire for revenge against their recent foes. Much of this level-headed approach was brought on by a weariness of war and the feeling of pure waste but it also was encouraged by the actions and words from the leaders on both sides.

The prospect of rebuilding society and the economy seemed unattainable and the prospect of a restoration of a system of higher education impossible. Following a time of destruction and desolation, when jobs are rare, the only source of hope for a future for soldiers is in education. Without hope and without employment, men accustomed to fighting often turn to desperate and dangerous measures. In the South, the expectations for a quick revitalization of institutions seemed especially grim. Thus, a dispirited congregation of trustees for Washington College met in the middle of June 1865 to determine the future of the institution. It was decided that the college would reopen in the fall and that a new president would be elected.

On August 1, 1865, the trustees reconvened and Bolivar Christian nominated Robert E. Lee for the office of president. Although the recommendation was met with unanimous and enthusiastic approval, nobody was quite sure of

*Governor John Letcher*

the genesis of the proposal or any reason why a person so venerated as General Lee might accept. Years later, Greenlee Letcher, son of the wartime governor of Virginia and future leader of the Kappa Alpha Order, reported that his own father had written to Lee on the subject two days before the meeting, urging him to accept the offer should it be made. Implicit in this reminiscence is that Governor John Letcher proposed the same to Bolivar Christian.[2]

After the meeting the trustees sent forth Judge John White Brockenbrough, the new rector, to approach General Lee on the matter. "He left on borrowed funds and … in a borrowed suit."[3] In the election of Lee the trustees hoped to bring to the college not only a man of the highest reputation and character but also a magnet to attract students from all over the state, all over the South, and even from the North. And after all, alone among the other institutions in the state, Washington College was in possession of the Cincinnati endowment and the Father of the Country had conferred his favor on the school more than a half a century earlier. News of the election quickly spread. William Thom, who was a freshman at the time, wrote to his father, "The Board elected Genl. R.E. Lee President and Judge Brockenbrough, one of the Committee, has gone to see if the Genl. will accept the position, if he does so, it will be a great thing for College, about the best thing which could be done."[4]

Brockenbrough returned with the general's promise to consider the matter. Lee's biographer, Douglas S. Freeman, wrote, "As he canvassed the idea, however, it seemed to Lee that the summons was providential, in that it both offered him a livelihood and a opportunity of service to his people."[5] Lee spent several weeks after Judge Brokenbrough's visit consulting friends and advisors. Chief among his concerns was the potential for bringing "animadversion" to the college because of his exclusion from the Amnesty

Proclamation and the ill will toward the South from certain members of Congress.

On August 24, 1865, he wrote to the trustees from Powhatan, Virginia, that he had delayed "from a desire to give the matter due consideration." He continued by mentioning several reasons why the board might want to consider its decision further, but should it continue in that determination that he would "yield to your judgment & accept."[6] On August 31, 1865, the Board of Trustees joyfully welcomed Lee's decision to become its next president.[7]

The sentiment expressed by William Taylor Thom was fully endorsed by a great majority of the community at Washington College and the citizens of Lexington. It was even reported in a number of northern newspapers with approval. On September 7, 1865, the *New York Times* reprinted the announcement, unchanged, from the *Lexington Gazette*. The article proclaimed, "The accession of this distinguished gentleman to the faculty of this venerable college, and as its honored chief, is destined, we trust, to mark the commencement of a new era in its history, and most cordially do we congratulate its numerous friends on this most auspicious event. The high, noble and patriotic motives which impelled our beloved chief, in accepting the honorable, but comparatively humble, position tendered to him by the authorities of the college, must win for him a new title to the admiration and love of his countrymen. The college, under the administration and supervision of Gen. Lee, will resume its exercises on the 14th inst."[8]

In his letter of acceptance, General Lee wrote, "It is the duty of every citizen, in the present condition of the Country, to do all in his power to aid in the restoration of peace and harmony, and in no way to oppose the policy of the State or General Government directed to that object"; and that "it is particularly incumbent on those charged with the instruction of the young to set an example of submission to authority."[9] Brockenbrough noted that these were "sentiments that cannot fail to commend themselves to the approval of the President of the United States, and to the unqualified assent of all sensible and virtuous citizens."[10]

Lee reiterated these sentiments in more specific terms to former governor Letcher:

> The questions which for years were in dispute between the State and General Government, and which unhappily were not decided by the dictates of reason, but referred to the decision of war, having been decided against us, it is a part of wisdom to acquiesce in the result, and the candor to recognize the fact. The interests of the State are therefore the same as those of the United States. Its prosperity will rise or fall with the welfare of the country. The duty of its citizens then, appears to me too plain to admit of doubt. All should unite in honest efforts to obliterate the effects of war, and to restore the blessings of peace.[11]

In the very first words of connection with the institution that would become the focus of his last years, Robert E. Lee expressed his hopes, his plans, his duty in order to establish a clear vision for the college and future generations. Douglas S. Freeman wrote that Lee's advice was the law to men of moderate passions and noted that "necessity forced Southern men to set their jaws and to strengthen their hearts for the black vigil of reconstruction; General Lee's example made it easier to do so."[12]

On September 15, Lee mounted Traveller and started out from Powhatan on a four-day journey to Lexington, he wore a gray suit without its former buttons and ribbons, many of which he had given to the children of family friends as gifts. He arrived in the small college town in the afternoon of the 18th ahead of schedule and prepared to secure a room at the Lexington Hotel, when he was greeted by his old friend Captain James White, who was now a professor at the college. White insisted that the general come to stay at Mulberry Hill, home of his father-in-law, Samuel Reid.[13]

Lee's son later recalled that "when he first arrived, the family, very naturally, stood a little in awe of him. This feeling, however, was soon dispelled, for his simple and unaffected manners in a short while put them at ease.... With these kind and hospitable friends he stayed several days."[14] On the morning after his arrival, Lee sat down to write a short letter to his wife:

> Lexington September 19, 1865
> My Dear Mary: I reached here yesterday about one p.m., and riding up to the hotel was met by Professor White, of Washington College, who brought me up to his father-in-law's, Colonel Reid, the oldest member of the trustees of the college, where I am comfortably quartered. To-day I will look for accommodations elsewhere, as the Colonel has a large family and I fear I am intruding on his hospitality. I have not yet visited the college grounds. They seem to be beautifully located, and the buildings are undergoing repairs. The house assigned to the president, I am told, has been rented to Dr. Madison (I believe), who has not been able to procure another residence, and I do not know when it will be vacated, nor can I tell you more about it.... I shall go after breakfast to inquire after my trunks. I had a very pleasant journey here.... The scenery was beautiful all the way. I am writing before breakfast and must be short. Last night I found a blanket and a coverlid rather light covering, and this morning I see a fire in the dining-room.
> Most affectionately yours, R.E. Lee.[15]

Lee visited that day the campus of Washington College where he met with the trustees of the college to discuss plans for his administration and he expressed a desire for the ceremonies to be as plain as possible. It was reported in the *Staunton Spectator* the following week, "Inauguration of General Lee: At the opening session of Monday (2d instant) the Board of Trustees, Faculty and Students of Washington College assembled to witness the inauguration of Gen. Robert E. Lee. Nothing could surpass the simplicity of the ceremonies on the occasion."[16]

*C. A. White's Lexington Hotel, circa 1865*

The first of our former soldiers to arrive at Washington College was James Ward Wood. Wood's grandmother wrote to James's brother Branson, exactly one week later, on October 9, 1865, and recorded James's departure from his home, "Your father started early today to Harrisonburg with James on his way to Lexington to school, he does not expect to be home for ten months, One, by one, you leave me.[17]

In a letter to his brother Branson, James Wood wrote that from Harrisonburg he took a stage to Staunton and spent the night in a hotel; the next morning he caught the train to Goshen and from that place took the stage coach for the thirty-odd mile trip to Lexington, where he promptly had dinner at Bath's Restaurant, got a shave, and checked into the Lexington House Hotel, where General Lee was then residing. He next secured temporary lodging at a boarding house and soon obtained a room at the college.[18]

At the end of the month he wrote to his brother, "I lodge in the College. It is situated on a hill N.W. of the town (Lexington) and on the same chain of hills with the VMI it consists of two main buildings called Paradise & Cattails and two dormitories—N & South. My room is No. 4 (on the first floor) of Paradise—I

*Stationery, Washington College, Hugh Moran to Cousin, February 19, 1867*

room with one Henry P. Matthews a Texan—Stonestreet VanMeter is here from Lexington Ky and rooms with Capt BM Davis Chief of the Signal Corps on E Kirby Smith's staff a splendid fellow—their room is No. 69 Paradise."[19]

In his essay, "Thoughts on Lexington," James Ward Wood gave his first impression of the town, which he wrote "contains about three thousand inhabitants, including College students, Cadets and 'Academites' . . . and is situated about one mile from the nearest point of the James River, where it crosses into the Valley . . . some fifteen miles north of the Natural Bridge . . . It possesses far more literary attainment and representation than any other town of its size with which I am acquainted."[20]

Wood then turned from the town to its institutions, "Within its corporate limits rises one of the oldest and best institutions of the Old Dominion, surmounted with the Statue of the "Father of his Country.... Just beyond this stand the ruins of the Virginia Military Institute, which we hope soon to see towering towards the skies ... on the other side rises our Sister Institution, Ann

Smith Academy; which though bearing a very common and familiar name, is by no means either a common or familiar institution. All these monuments of literature have their Faculties of learned men: and many ex-officers of the late rebellion make their abiding place with us. We must not omit the Law Class of Judge Brockenbrough nor the Freeman's School on Cross Street. We have the Franklin, Washington and Graham Literary Societies and more badges bearing greek characters than I care to enumerate."[21]

*James Ward Wood, 1866*

In November, James Wood wrote to his father about the hardships of student life, "As to Application I have done almost nothing else since I have been here. I rise at four in the morning and retire at ten at night, three hours a day are devoted to recitations and lectures and upon my three studies, Latin Greek and Mathematics, three to meals & going to and from them; one to exercise and the remained except from ten P.M. till 4 AM in study." He writes with pride about his connection to the Literary Society "We have here two literary societies, I belong to the Washingtonians. We hope in time to turn out some orators & statesmen."[22]

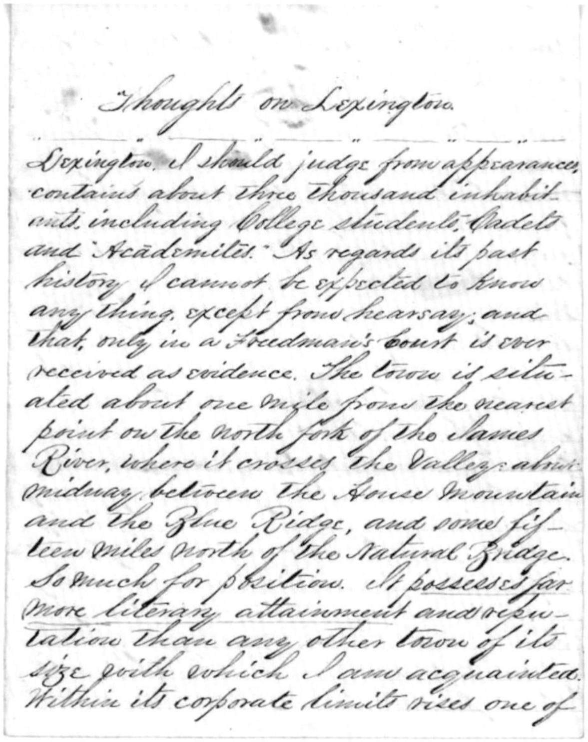

Thoughts on Lexington.

Lexington, I should judge from appearance, contains about three thousand inhabitants, including College students, Cadets and "Academites." As regards its past history I cannot be expected to know any thing, except from hearsay; and that, only in a Freedman's Court is ever received as evidence. The town is situated about one mile from the nearest point on the North fork of the James River, where it crosses the Valley: about midway between the House Mountain and the Blue Ridge, and some fifteen miles North of the Natural Bridge. So much for position. It possesses far more literary attainment and reputation than any other town of its size with which I am acquainted. Within its corporate limits rises one of

Thoughts on Lexington, *James Ward Wood*

Wood evidently found his room shortly after arriving, in an expense account that he sent to his father on November 19, about a month after he came to Lexington, he had spent close to fifty dollars furnishing the room at Paradise and he and his suite mate split all furnishing including the bed, mattress, sheets, and blankets; board for one session was $162; tuition $75; and books, paper, pens, tobacco, and lamps another $50—the total, as of November 19th about 350 dollars. His only extravagancies seem to have been tobacco, apples, joining the Washington Literary Society, and getting the dentist to "plug" his teeth.[23]

James, or Ward, as he often signed his letters, wrote his father about his classes in the first semester—Latin, Greek, and Practical Mathematics. In Greek the works to be studied were the Anabasis of Xenophon and the New Testament; he described his professor of Greek, Captain James White, as "one of the best men I ever knew. He can explain Greek so that the most obtuse mind cannot fail to comprehend it."[24] His professor of Latin he portrayed as "a very learned man having taken [his] A.M. at the University of Va. And also explains his language very lucidly." The professor of mathematics he cast in a somewhat different light. Although he thought him a "good man," he was difficult to understand by "his constant repetition" and "if you have not a perfect recollection of all the conditions you have passed over since you commenced the study of that science you will be at fault even tho you knew it ever so perfectly, to be perfect with him you must be perfect indeed."[25]

Our second soldier was Samuel Zenas Ammen, who, after his surrender to Federal authorities, received a pardon at Lewisburg and returned to Fincastle. For more than a year, Ammen spent his time at home returning to his studies and wooing the daughter of his French teacher.[26] Frustrated by the fickleness of his girlfriend, he decided that he wanted to become a physician and determined that Washington College would be the best place for him to pursue that ambition.

Thus, in early September 1866, Ammen's father sent him "with John Hoof, his sales agent to Lexington to enter Washington College."[27] In his first semester, he "boarded a half mile from town at the home of William Ruff.... Across the road... was the Imboden residence where Stern boarded during his first session."[28] Often the two would walk into town together and occasionally dined together—"I went with Rogers (a KA) up to Stern's (at Imboden's) to a lemonade supper."[29] Later Ammen reminisced, "The following year we both went into town, seeking a livelier environment and escape from the long walk."[30] Ammen moved into the Ann Smith Academy, where the Scott family lived, while teaching Latin and French to the girls of the school. Subsequent places of habitation included Fiddler's farm, a few miles from town; Bowie's College House; then to the home of Professor William Preston Johnston and, finally, to the Paradise dorm on the campus of Washington College, where so many of his compatriots resided.[31]

Benjamin Ammen had planned for Samuel to study medicine and the first winter session he attended classes in "senior Latin, senior French, and could have entered senior Chemistry had not recitation hours conflicted."[32] It was recorded in the *Kappa Alpha Journal* that Ammen had been "so well… prepared for college… that he entered Washington College with advanced standing. There were at the College in those years three classes—Junior, intermediate and Senior. Because of his unusual preparation, he became a member of the Intermediate Class, entering Senior Latin and French and Intermediate Greek and Mathematics. When the War began he was reading Latin and carried Sallust with him into battle. As he had been interested intensely for a number of years in Chemistry and Physics, and had studied them privately, he was able to enter the class in Senior Chemistry."[33]

Ammen wrote that his life "was studious, temperate, active, and regular. His daily custom was to attend classes in the forenoon, followed by recreation; to take a nap in the afternoon; to begin study at 11 p. m.; to retire at 3 a. m.; and to rise at 7 a. m."[34] But he also took interest in and was successful at other activities as Washington College: on December 19, 1866, he was elected as president of the prestigious Washington Literary Society[35]; he also won the Gold Medal for best essay in the School of English, "he was, likewise, the founder of the *Southern Collegian*, a literary paper, afterwards a magazine, which still exists at Washington and Lee University, and wrote for it many verses, sketches, and stories, including the series of *Letters of Anacharsis III*, *Mathesis Moriens*, and similar contributions both serious and humorous."[36]

In social affairs, Ammen was also accomplished. He was elected into the Kappa Alpha Fraternity on October 10, 1866.[37] He was a member of the vaunted "Ugly Club" and had been named "Lazy Man" in 1869; and was chief mourner at the Burial of Queen Math—"distinctions of no little significance in the operations of those student institutions, now obsolete: and all this in addition to his admirable standing in his classes."[38]

The third and final protagonist to land at Washington College was the precocious telegraph operator and spy, Jo Lane Stern. After Lee's surrender, Stern returned to Richmond, where he attended school from the fall of 1865 through the summer of 1866.[39] Both his connections at Richmond College and the history of the school during that time frame suggest his attendance there.

Official sources have declared that Richmond College was closed during that period, but further investigation revealed that "motivated by a grave sense of responsibility, Trustees of Richmond College met on July 24, 1865 and resolved to open at once under the supervision of President Ryland and Professor George F. Dabney, who together would offer preparation for young men recently discharged from the army."[40] A contemporary source indicated that the College was reopened as a preparatory institution, "The Richmond College, which has been suspended since the early part of the war, has, unfortunately, by the great Confederate crash, lost most of its endowment. The Trustees, deeming it impracticable, at present, to re-establish the regular courses, requested President Ryland and Professor Dabney to open a high school on the premises. The attendance is small, but pupils, we have no question, will receive through and faithful training."[41] Reuben Alley stated that in the summer of 1866 a dinner was held for alumni and graduates of Richmond College in town—implying that degrees were indeed granted that year. Whether the institution was operating as a college or a preparatory school during this time is a matter of debate, as is whether young Stern was in attendance there or somewhere else. Whatever the case, he arrived in Lexington the following fall.

Stern cut a dashing figure in Lexington because of his intriguing and charmed past, his handsome appearance, and his close connections both to the general and to his daughters. Stern was a hero to the South, a boy who had entered the perilous fray willingly, even enthusiastically, and had carried out many missions with grace and fortitude. He was, nevertheless, self-effacing and ingratiating without an ounce of superiority. He was described by his friend and fraternity brother, Samuel Ammen, as being a fellow known "by his good spirits, wit, and sound sense, dispelling the excessive seriousness to which we were prone, and introducing a bit of 'the joy of living.'"[42]

Little is known of Stern's academic career at Washington College other that he graduated with a BI degree in 1870 and attended Judge Brockenbrough's Law School at the college.[43] In a small town where there were two major schools, however, there was an abundance of males and, inversely, a paucity of female companionship. Nevertheless, to judge by letters, notes, and social engagements found in the archives of Washington and Lee, Stern was always

*President's House, Washington College, circa 1869*

in demand as an escort to church or a date to a fancy ball. Greenlee Letcher demonstrated the favored position that Stern held in the Lee household by recollecting, "Once when calling at General Lee's home, when a student, and general Lee's charming daughters were entertaining a parlor full of students, the General came in and told the girls that they must be good to his old Soldier Comrade Stern regardless of how they treated the others."[44] General Stern described those days in an article for a Richmond newspaper that was commemorating the unveiling of the Lee Monument:

> After the war, when, with hundreds of other students at Washington College, I saw a great deal of General Lee, we all learned to understand how gentle and imperturbable he was under all circumstances. General Lee's house at commencement times was always full of young ladies, visiting his daughters. The college students of that period will never forget them....It was my delight to take [one of these young ladies] to one of the commencement balls. About 2 o'clock in the morning we started up the hill to General Lee's house. He was sitting up and came down to the gate to greet us. He greeted the young lady with the greatest cordiality and kissed her. I never envied him any of his fame, but envy found a location then and there. Afterwards when I grew up and met other girls, of course—but never mind, that has nothing to do with General Lee.[45]

Stern's easy charm, his Tidewater pedigree, and his ability to transform solemn situations with optimism and vivacity made him a favor of the whole campus—an ability that he shared with James Ward Wood's friend Stonestreet Van Meter, of whom Hugh Moran wrote, "The most popular boy in College a Kentuckian [VanMeter] but he has gone home on account of his business."[46]

But it was Stern's relationship with the Lee family that made him such a sought-after companion. Stern proudly recounted the day when he rode

*General Lee on Traveller.*

General Lee's old warhorse, Traveller.

In the winter of '69–'70 General Lee went South with Miss Agnes for his health. Miss Mary sent for me one day and told me if I would go out to Dr. Ruffner's farm for some celery to be used in the salad at the Episcopal Church fair, then going on, I might ride old Traveller, the general's war horse. Bargain was never sooner made, and in a few minutes I was mounted, and with the general's saddle and bridle. When I got to the courthouse corner a lot of the students in the street saw me, and immediately gave chase in order to share in my glory, but I was selfish and Traveler was too fleet of foot for them…While the people at Dr. Ruffner's were getting the celery I was pulling out handsfull of Traveler's main (*sic*) and tail, and had pockets full when I came back. Some vandal stole it from me years afterwards, but the memory of being the only person outside of the Lee family to ride old Traveler abides with me still.[47]

All of these student warriors would soon be tied together by fraternal bonds in a story that reflects and resonates not only the story of Washington College and its future but also of the South and the nation as a phoenix rising out of the ashes.

*Notes* Chapter 4:

1 *Washington Evening Star*, April 10, 1865, p. 1.

2 Ollinger Crenshaw, *General Lee's College* (New York: Random House, 1969), 146; "I am much obliged to you for the interest you have expressed in my acceptance of the presidency of Washington College.... I have stated to the committee of trustees the objections which exist in my opinion to my filling the position, and will yield to their judgement." Robert E. Lee to John Letcher, August 28, 1865 in *Library of Southern Literature*, ed. Edwin Anderson Alderman et al. (New Orleans: The Martin & Hoyt Company, 1907): 7:3159.

3 Crenshaw, *General Lee's College*, 146.

4 William Thom to his Father, August 9, 1865, William Taylor Thom Papers, Mss 048, Archives, Washington and Lee University, Lexington, Va.

5 Douglas S. Freeman, *R. E. Lee: A Biography* (New York: Charles Scribner's Sons, 1934), 4:216.

6 Robert E. Lee to The Trustees of Washington College, August 24, 1865, Archives, Washington and Lee University, Lexington, Va.; see also Douglas S. Freeman, *R. E. Lee: A Biography*, 4:218.

7 Ibid., 225.

8 "Gen. Lee Accepts the Presidency of Washington College," *New York Times*, September 7, 1865, p. 1.

9 Robert E. Lee to The Trustees of Washington College, August 24, 1865; see also Freeman, *R. E. Lee*, 4:218.

10 "Gen. Lee Accepts the Presidency of Washington College," 1.

11 Robert E. Lee to John Letcher, August 28, 1865, in *Library of Southern Literature* (New Orleans: The Martin & Hoyt Company, 1907), 7:3159.

12 Freeman, *R. E. Lee,* 4:221.

13 Emory Thomas, *Robert E. Lee: A Biography* (New York: W. W. Norton & Co., 1995), 376.

14 Captain Robert E. Lee, *Recollections and Letters of Robert E. Lee* (New York: Doubleday, Page & Co., 1904), 185.

15 Ibid.

16 "Inauguration of Genl. Lee," *Staunton Spectator*, October 10, 1865, p. 3.

17 G. M. Branson to Branson Wood, October 9, 1865, Kappa Alpha Archives, Lexington, Va.

18 James Ward Wood to Branson Wood, October 28, 1865, Kappa Alpha Archives, Lexington, Va.

19 Ibid.

20 James Ward Wood, "Thoughts on Lexington," Kappa Alpha Archives, Lexington, Va., 1

21 Ibid., 2

22 James Ward Wood to Branson Wood, October 28, 1865, Kappa Alpha Archives, Lexington, Va.

23 James Ward Wood to Angus Wood (father), November 19, 1865, Expense Accounts, Kappa Alpha Archives, Lexington, Va.

24 James Ward Wood to Angus Wood (father), November 18, 1865, Kappa Alpha Archives, Lexington, Va.

25 Ibid.

26 William Kavenaugh Doty, *Samuel Zenas Ammen and the Kappa Alpha Order* (Charlottesville: Surber-Arundale Co., 1922), 21.

27 Ammen, My History, Typescript Copy, Kappa Alpha Archives, Lexington Va., 64.

28 Samuel Ammen, "The Founders of Kappa Alpha," *Kappa Alpha Journal* 38, No. 1 (November 1921): 20.

29 Samuel Ammen, Ammen Diary Extracts, Kappa Alpha Archives, Lexington, Va., 2.

30 Ammen, "The Founders of Kappa Alpha," 20.

31 Ammen, Ammen Diary Extracts, 2.

32 Ammen, My History, Typescript Copy, 64.

33 Ammen, "The Founders of Kappa Alpha," 19.

34 Doty, *Ammen and the Kappa Alpha Order*, 23.

35 Ammen, Ammen Diary Extracts, 4.

36 Doty, *Ammen and the Kappa Alpha Order*, 24.

37 Minutes of Kappa Alpha Session, 1866–1870, Samuel Ammen, comp., 1893, Kappa Alpha Archives, Lexington, Va.

38 Doty, *Ammen and the Kappa Alpha Order,* 24.

39 "General Jo Lane Stern," *Kappa Alpha Journal* 38, No. 1 (November 1921): 21.

40 Reuben Alley, *History of the University of Richmond, 1830–1971* (Charlottesville: University Press of Virginia, 1971), 46.

41 *Religious Herald*, Richmond, Va., November 16, 1865, p. 1.

42 "General Jo Lane Stern," *Kappa Alpha Journal* 38, No.1, p. 20.

43 Ibid., 21.

44 Greenlee D. Letcher, "General Stern," March 4, 1935, Kappa Alpha Archives, Lexington, Va.

45 Jo Lane Stern, "General Lee, Pretty Girls and Traveller," *Richmond Times-Dispatch*, January 20, 1906, p. 3.

46 Hugh Moran to Mother, February 24, 1867, Hugh Moran Papers, Archives, Washington and Lee University, Lexington, Va.

47 Jo Lane Stern, "General Lee, Pretty Girls and Traveller," 3.

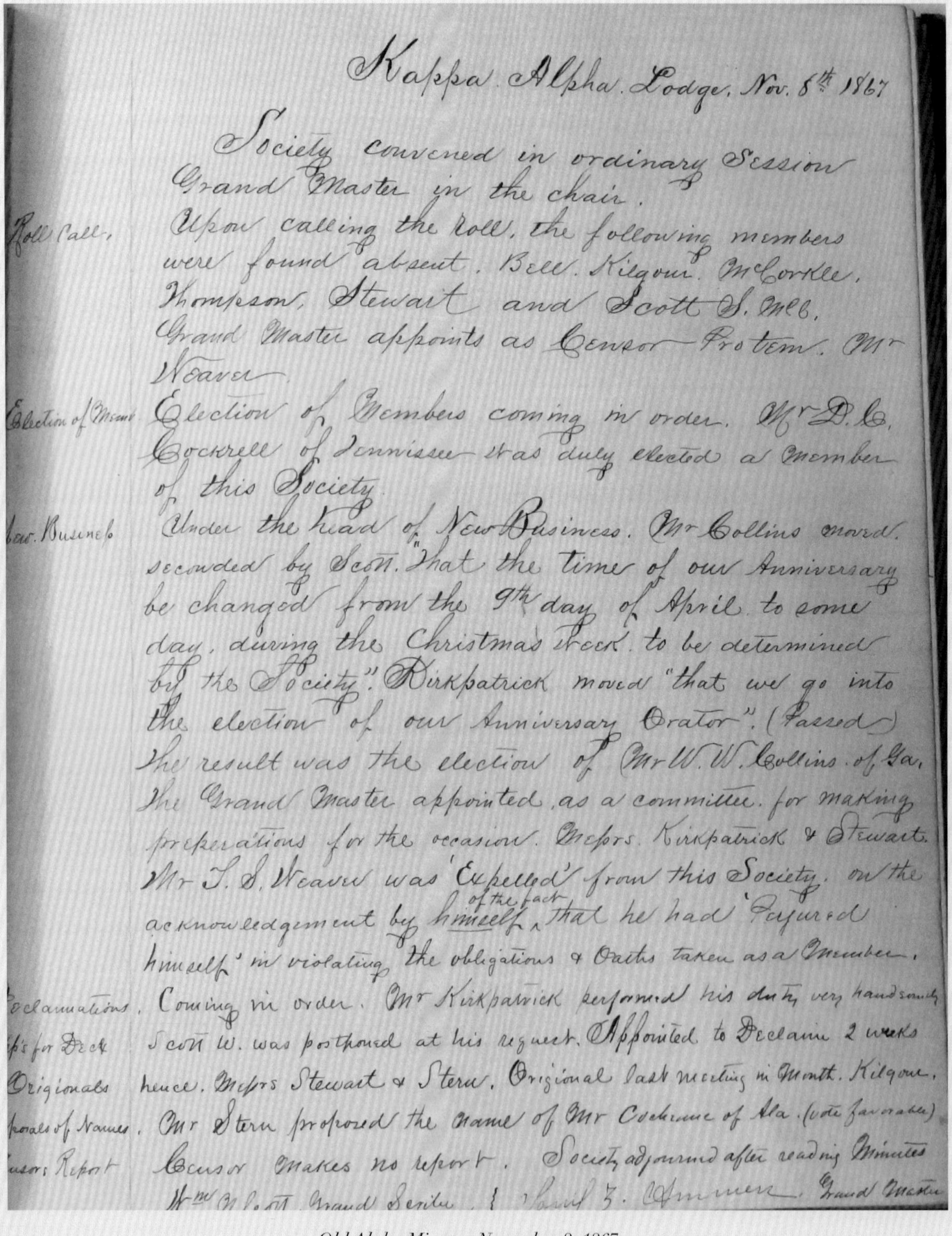

Kappa Alpha Lodge. Nov. 8th 1867

Society convened in ordinary Session
Grand Master in the chair.
Roll Call. Upon calling the roll, the following members
were found absent. Bell. Kilgour. McCorkle.
Thompson, Stewart and Scott S. McC.
Grand Master appoints as Censor Pro tem. Mr
Weaver
Election of Mems. Election of Members coming in order. Mr D. C.
Cockrell of Tennissee was duly elected a member
of this Society.
New Business. Under the head of New Business. Mr Collins moved.
seconded by Scott. "That the time of our Anniversary
be changed from the 9th day of April to some
day, during the Christmas week. to be determined
by the Society". Kirkpatrick moved "that we go into
the election of our Anniversary Orator". (Passed)
The result was the election of Mr W. W. Collins. of Ga.
The Grand Master appointed, as a committee. for making
preperations for the occasion. Messrs. Kirkpatrick & Stewart.
Mr T. S. Weaver was 'Expelled' from this Society. on the
acknowledgement by himself of the fact that he had 'Perjured
himself' in violating the obligations & Oaths taken as a Member.
Declamations. Coming in order. Mr Kirkpatrick performed his duty very handsomely
Apps for Deck Scott W. was postponed at his request. Appointed to Declaim 2 weeks
Originals hence. Messrs Stewart & Stern. Origional last meeting in Month. Kilgour.
Proposals of Names. Mr Stern proposed the name of Mr Cochrane of Ala. (vote favorable)
Censors Report Censor makes no report. Society adjourned after reading Minutes
Wm W. Scott Grand Scribe. { Saml Z. Ammen. Grand Master

*Old Alpha Minutes, November 8, 1867*

# 5

## The Founding and the Controversy

> Quae ante conditam condendamve urbem poeticis magis decora fabulis quam incorruptis rerum gestarum monumentis traduntur, ea nec adfirmare nec refellere in animo est. Livy, *Ab Urbe Condita*, Praefatio.

Perhaps the most contentious and divisive section of the history of the Kappa Alpha Order is concerned with the early years of the "Old Alpha" chapter. The reasons for the controversy of the founding have not changed in two thousand years—Livy wrote in the preface to his history of Rome, "These things which pertain to the founding of the city or even to its most remote conception are handed down having been adorned more by poetic tales than by the incorruptible accounts of actual deeds."

With the chaotic start to the Order and with the focus clearly centered on the future rather than the past, certain particulars of the founding were, and are, unclear. The result being that the true origins of "Old Alpha" are often in conflict with long-established traditions, perhaps based on faulty memory or a personal agenda. Even Ammen himself wrote, "In Old Alpha, in my day, the date of our origin was of no importance, or interest; the past was not discussed. It was our future that excited concern. I don't recall having ever had a thought about it till 1891 when I sat down to write our first history."[1]

Bitter disagreements arose in the early part of the twentieth century about the particulars of the origin of the fraternity, even among the founders or near founders. There is a part of the narrative for which there is a general consensus however—how and why James Ward Wood desired to form a society.

The story begins in the last months of the Civil War. At home for a short furlough, a young James Ward Wood decided to visit a girlfriend in the neighboring town. As he mounted his horse, he secreted a pistol in his boot, which accidently discharged and effectively ended his military career. During his convalescence, he fell into a conversation with an older man who Wood remembered as being a member of the Masonic Lodge. His new acquaintance intrigued the recovering veteran with his stories of the sacred rites, rituals, and mysteries of his society. Fascinated, Wood said that these stories inspired him with "a desire to be a member of a fraternity."[2] Thus, the seed was planted.

The following year Wood left his home to attend Washington College but he was lonely and bored as he knew few individuals that were not either in his classes or in his dormitory. Accustomed to the camaraderie of the battlefield, Wood desired to be once again in the company of friends and petitioned one of the established fraternities at the college for membership. The early fraternities of the college, however, were composed of the socially elite scions of Old Virginia families, who were often contemptuous of those who did share their common heritage. A contemporary of Wood at Washington College was a young Kentuckian by the name of Hugh Moran. He was also only too aware of the cliquishness of the native Virginians at the college. In a letter to his father, Moran wrote, "As for the Va. Boys very few of the students have any use for them. Of course, some are clever fellows. Take them as a class, however, they think themselves better than any one else. F.F.V. Aristocracy you know!"[3]

Thus, early in his first session, "Wood sought admission to the most exclusive fraternity on campus, φ.κ.ψ., Phi Kappa Psi."[4] An unfortunate event, for "at Lexington he was evidently at a disadvantage by reason of his being a country boy insufficiently prepared for College [on account of his service in the army; and] particularly unfitted to deal with the Greek Letter situation, since he was unacquainted with the niceties and taboos of fraternity etiquette."[5] As a result of which, Ammen suggested, "He was repulsed, probably, offensively; with the result of causing Wood to seek revenge. It is not unlikely that, not knowing why he was repulsed, he tried his luck with B.Θ.Π. also, with like result."[6]

Having been repelled by these organizations and still desiring to be a part of a secret society, James Ward Wood, in conjunction with William Scott, resolved to form a lodge of his own. They decided on the name of φ.κ.χ., Phi Kappa Chi; remarkably similar in sound and symbol to the organization that had rejected him so abruptly, φ.κ.ψ., Phi Kappa Psi. It was said that Wood deliberately fashioned fraternity badges to resemble closely those of the offending lodge. Samuel Ammen reported, "I was told by old members of Alpha that in 1866 that it was the sight of the φ.κ.χ. badge on the campus—similar in shape to φ.κ.ψ.'s—that caused the latter to make a row and demand the change [of the name]."[7]

Ammen suggested that it was actually Harry Estill, a member of Phi Kappa Psi, who made the request, and, in return for his cooperation, he may have helped Wood develop a ritual for his new organization.[8] An old member of Alpha, W. B. McChesney told a different version, however, "Another story that is very strongly left [with] me was that he (Wood) first called his organization Phi Kappa [Chi]. this sounded too much like Phi Kappa Si (Psi) for two members, Rob. Brockenbrough and J. Preston Cocke and they took Wood in hand and had him change it to KA, Kuklos Adelphon, a band of brothers. Excuse the Greek, [I] have not the alphabet or the knowledge that was once mine. Brockenbrough is dead but Cocke is a lawyer in Richmond and if you could get in touch with him [he] may recall the incident."[9]

A later chronicler of the Order, Leroy Boyd, stated that Colonel James P. Nelson, a fellow student of Wood at Washington College reported that "Founder Wood, failing to get into Phi Kappa Psi and Beta went to Prof. Harry Estill, a Phi Kappa Psi, and asked Estill to help him found a fraternity, and Estill did help him, and probably supplied Wood with an old Ritual of a defunct fraternity, and actually gave Wood the name of the fraternity, Kuklos Adelphon, after which Wood decided to abandon the name of Phi Kappa Chi."[10]

When asked by Leroy Boyd, in 1918, what was the derivation of the name Kappa Alpha and its meaning, Wood gave a simple answer that had the ring of truth and the naïveté of a country boy finding an alternative and in a hurry, "I saw a fraternity or college paper, don't remember what name it was, that stated that the Kuklos Adelphon Fraternity was dead & I thought it was a good name to take & Scott & others agreed, & we took it. Thought as it was dead, it would be all right."[11]

Harry Estill's assistance seems counterintuitive, for Estill was a Phi Kappa Psi, and according to Ammen, "The bitter hatred with which φ.κ.ψ. and β.Θ.π. pursued him and his fraters was due, it is believed, to his having unconsciously violated some of the unwritten laws of the College fraternity world. And hatred among the Scotch-Irish at Lexington in 1866 were of a virulence hardly known elsewhere."[12] Conversely, Ammen both proposed that Wood had "obtained the 'Papers' of a defunct fraternity which had a chapter at Wash. College before the War… and that he had [the] copy" from which Wood had crafted his own ceremony, but also asserted that Wood "got the papers through Tom Kirkpatrick of Lexington," which ceremony he described as a "pre-war ritual… sophomoric… with some good business, much of which Wood omitted."[13]

Ammen suggested that defunct fraternity might have been a chapter of Epsilon Alpha, which "was at Wash. College before the Civil War, and perished at the beginning of the War, or soon after. Some members of it may have been there as late as 1868, when, according to Jo Lane Stern, the E.A. chapter was known to be dead." Ammen may have based this assumption on a conversation from their student days; the two were walking towards town when Wood asked "what magnitudine amimi praestimus meant." The motto was reportedly used by Epsilon Alpha.[14]

This first manifestation of the fraternity was of short duration, lasting only several weeks. Ammen related that "I had a brass seal, given me by Wood in 1866, bearing the letters φ.κ.χ., for the III's use on 'official' documents. This fraternity existed probably less than one month, since Wood's receipt of May 9 speaks of 'KA' which was its successor."[15]

The precise date that Kappa Alpha came into being is not precisely known; tradition, however, claims that it was on December 21, 1865, and indeed, that may well have been the genesis, but primary source documentation indicates that an official incarnation took place on April 9, 1866.

Those who support the earlier date, December 21, 1865, allege that a mutual pledge of fidelity and friendship took place in the room of William Archibald Walsh in the South dormitory of Washington College. Conversely, those advocating for the later date, April 9, 1866, contend that the location of epiphany occurred in a dormitory room situated on the second floor of the building, unfortunately known as 'Cat-Tail,' on April 9, 1866. The countervailing claims reached their crescendo in the 1920s, when a tablet was scheduled to be erected at the site of the founding.

Greenlee Letcher, who was charged with sorting out the facts of the dispute, wrote to the Knight Commander of Kappa Alpha, Bishop Henry Judah Mikell, about the history of the dispute in 1931, "My recollection is that there were some disputes in earlier days as to whether December 21, 1865, was the proper date of the founding or April 9, 1866, the anniversary of the surrender at Appomattox and I am under the impression that these matters have been from time to time discussed and written about in earlier Journals." Letcher added the caveat, "As I wrote to Brother Crawford, Kappa Alpha Fraternity did not spring like Minerva from the Brain of Jove at a single instance, but doubtless it was some time in evolving as I recall."[16]

*Greenlee Davidson Letcher*

The most fervent supporters of the earlier date included Leroy Boyd, Bishop Mikell and, intermittently, Samuel Ammen. Boyd, who seems to have had a preestablished agenda for his version of events and attempted to marshal them into a formation that would fit his narrative, was the most fervent advocate of the December

21st date. The most consistent and insistent of this trio, Leroy Boyd, wrote to Letcher, "I have replied fully to Brother Waters of Alpha Chapter, and cited the leading references proving that KA was founded in Walsh's room in the southern-most room of the old South Dormitory, in December 1865. Wood says so, William N. Scott says so, and so does Ammen, who is our historian. I have a complete file of the KA *Journal*s from February 1879 to date and have read everything in them, and the date of 1865 cannot be changed today even if Wood and S.M. Scott would swear to it on a dozen Bibles."[17]

Boyd, however, based most of his assertions on secondhand stories and the vacillating recollections and convictions of Samuel Ammen on the matter. "Running throughout all the volumes of the *Kappa Alpha Journal* are many references to our early history, and in regard to the date of the founding of Kappa Alpha, and of its predecessor, the Phi Kappa Chi, there is ample proof that December 1865, was the month and the year. Wood told me that the Order was founded before Christmas 1865; …Wm. N. Scott, in an article in the *Journal* of May, 1898, says that the chapter had monthly meetings after December, 1865. On page 343 of the issue of the *Journal*; he says that the KA Fraternity saw its birth one evening toward the end of December 1865, in Walsh's room in a college building."[18]

He dismissed the April date by stating that it could not have been Wood's room at Washington College because he "never roomed at the college at all, but at Mr. E. S. Tutwiler's about a mile from Lexington on the road to Natural Bridge."[19] Correspondence donated recently to the Kappa Alpha Order by Wood's grandson William A. Wood and his wife, Edna Wood of Lost River, testifies that, indeed, he did live at the college from a few days after his arrival through the spring session. In a letter to his brother Branson he described his room in the Paradise dormitory and a letter to his father in April 1866 indicated that he still remained at the college.[20]

Boyd also wrote Greenlee Letcher that "after several months of consultation and preparation in which James Ward Wood bore a principal part, the constitution and ritual were evolved; and the KA Fraternity saw its birth one evening toward the end of December, 1865, in Walsh's room in a college building."[21] Were this statement accurate, it would have been necessary for Wood to have applied to the other fraternities and, having been repelled by them, to have procured, examined, digested, and reformulated the rituals and constitution of a "defunct" society into one agreeable to his own liking, consulted with others and revised the same, almost from the instant that he had departed from the Goshen stagecoach.

Ammen, by the mid-1920s, asserted that the 1865 date was correct, despite his previous positions and events in which he himself was a participant. He wrote to General Jo Lane Stern in January 1928, "Letcher has been listening to Stanhope Scott's assertions that KA was organized in Cat-Tail, whereas you & I <u>know</u> it was organized in Walsh's room, which was the end room of the South Dormitory. Letcher says my evidence is "hearsay" & Scott's is original! Stanhope, whom we in 1866 never consulted about anything, has now become an active founder at Conventions, and a source of veracious history."[22] Bishop Mikell, the reigning Knight Commander, either convinced by the scholarship of Boyd, or the indignation of Ammen, or the inconvenience of changing traditions, vetoed the concept of changing the organization's past. He wrote to Letcher in no uncertain terms, "I certainly would be most unwilling to agree to change the date of the founding of the Order from 1865 to 1866."[23]

The most vocal proponent of the April 9, 1866, date was Stanhope McClellan Scott; his

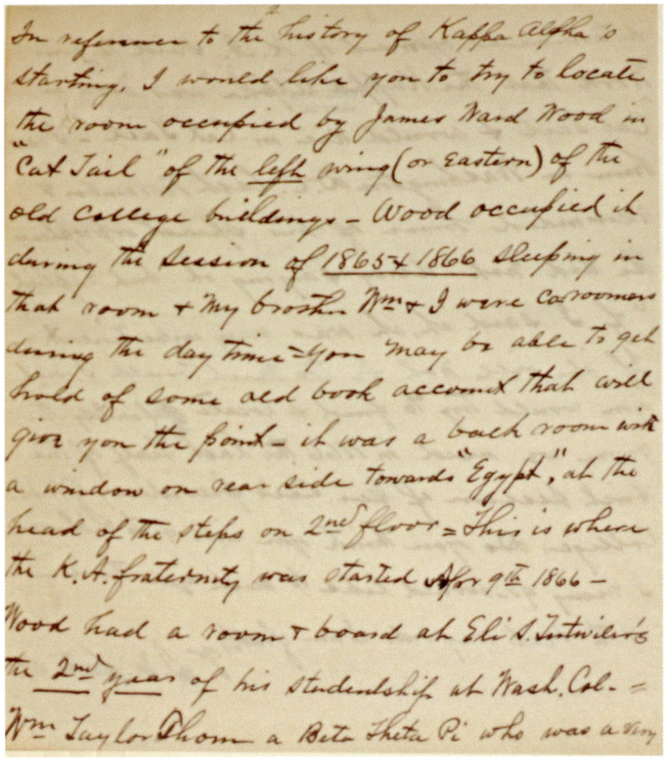
In reference to the history of Kappa Alpha's
starting, I would like you to try to locate
the room occupied by James Ward Wood in
"Cat Tail" of the <u>left</u> wing (or Eastern) of the
old College buildings – Wood occupied it
during the session of <u>1865 & 1866</u> sleeping in
that room & my brother Wm & I were co-roomers
during the day time = You may be able to get
hold of some old book account that will
give you the point – it was a back room with
a window on rear side towards "Egypt", at the
head of the steps on 2nd floor = This is where
the K.A. fraternity was started Apr 9th 1866 –
Wood had a room & board at Eli S. Tutwiler's
the <u>2nd year</u> of his studentship at Wash. Col. =
Wm Taylor Thom – a Beta Theta Pi who was a very

*Stanhope Scott to Greenlee Letcher. December 26, 1926*

conclusions were supported by Jo Lane Stern, by Greenlee Letcher, and, at times, by Samuel Ammen.

In reference to the date of the founding, Stanhope Scott informed Letcher in 1931 that "Ammen told me he had a paper turned over by Wood to him, stating that Apr. 9th 1866 was the date of the beginning of KA."[24] In turn, Scott related the exchange that he had had with James Ward Wood, in respect to the founding date and stated that Wood's reply was "we the 2 surviving founders agreed on the latter date when the 2 Scotts, Wood & Walsh met in Woods room & started the Kappa Alpha."[25]

As far as the location, Scott was again very precise and assured that the founding took place in "the room occupied by James Ward Wood in 'Cat Tail' of the left wing (or Eastern) of the old College buildings—Wood occupied it during the session of 1865 & 1866 sleeping in that room & my brother Wm & I were coroomers during the daytime = you may be able to get hold of some old book account that will give you the point ~ it was a back room with a window on the near side of 'Egypt,' at the heads of the steps on the 2nd floor = This is when the KA fraternity was started Apr 9th 1866—Wood had a room & board at Eli A. Tutwiler's the 2nd year of his studentship at Wash. Col."[26]

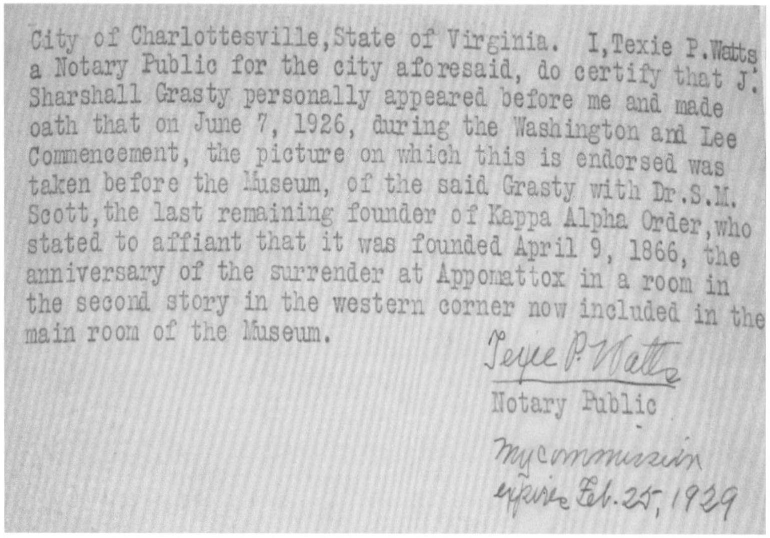

City of Charlottesville, State of Virginia. I, Texie P. Watts a Notary Public for the city aforesaid, do certify that J. Sharshall Grasty personally appeared before me and made oath that on June 7, 1926, during the Washington and Lee Commencement, the picture on which this is endorsed was taken before the Museum, of the said Grasty with Dr. S. M. Scott, the last remaining founder of Kappa Alpha Order, who stated to affiant that it was founded April 9, 1866, the anniversary of the surrender at Appomattox in a room in the second story in the western corner now included in the main room of the Museum.

Texie P. Watts
Notary Public
my commission expires Feb. 25, 1929

*Affidavit of Stanhope Scott to Notary Public, 1926*

*Scott in front of "Cat-Tail," 1926*

In 1926, Stanhope Scott, certain of his identification and anxious to have it immortalized, attended commencement ceremonies at Washington and Lee University and visited the very spot where the room in Cat-Tail had been located, in the company of a fraternal brother and witness, had a photograph taken in front of the building, issued an affidavit as to the place and its importance, and had the whole statement—testifying both as to the date and to the location of the founding of the Order—notarized.

By 1926, the appearance of the building had dramatically changed; Stanhope Scott specified that the room in question had been "in the northwestern room in the upper story of the Dormitory, now the Museum, the partitions having all been knocked out and the second floor taken out leaving a large room for the museum."[27] The only recognizable part of the room that remained at that time was the window to the rear of the upper story.

Greenlee Letcher, Kappa Alpha historian, appealed to General Jo Lane Stern to act as a mediator in the altercations between Ammen and Scott. In terms of personal memory, Stern was not a definitive voice: "Remember, that when I came into the Fraternity it was six or eight months old, and, doubtless, other men occupied the rooms about which the contention has arisen."[28]

And while Stern could not settle the matter from personal recollection, three years after the first letter and well over a decade of back and forth on the subject, he wrote to Letcher with an air of frustration, "With all respect, it seems to me this thing has been discussed full enough and long enough to be now finally settled, and there is no one living at the time, and was present, but I am relying upon the statement of Stanhope Scott, who was living at the time, was present and must have known what he was talking about when he gave his suggestions and recollections. Ammen was not a member of the Fraternity at that time, and what he said about it must have been hearsay. I can not remember to have heard the matter discussed at all while I was at College. If I ever did it made no impression on me, because I did not consider it of importance then."[29]

Ammen vacillated on the subject over a number of years and repeatedly contradicted himself about the matter. He admitted that his own personal knowledge of the true date of the founding was nonexistent and during those early days, it was the survival of the society that was of paramount interest, not its all-too-recent history. Furthermore, he initially supported Stanhope Scott's position, "In a recent Convention, Bro. S. Scott, one of the first four KAs , announced that Bro. Wood had authorized him to affirm April 9, 1866, to be the true date of the founding of KA fraternity, and the Convention accepted that date with alacrity.... [It was] also my basis for the same belief."[30]

He asserted that "that the idea that the founding was in 1865, originated in the Gulf States between 1881 and 1891, when the wish, apparently, fathered the thought…and presumably what everyone says is so."[31] After much canvassing from the southern states and with the minute books of the early years then missing and with Tazewell Hubard anxious to get a firm date for his upcoming book, Ammen said, "We cudgeled our brains, and finally agreed on a tentative date, as late in 1865 as possible (Dec 21), but recognizing the Dixie date."[32]

In 1893, the original minute book was discovered, reputedly in an attic near Ammen's hometown of Fincastle, and records revealed that, in 1867, the date of the "anniversary celebration" was denoted in Ammen's inserted brackets as April 9th.[33]

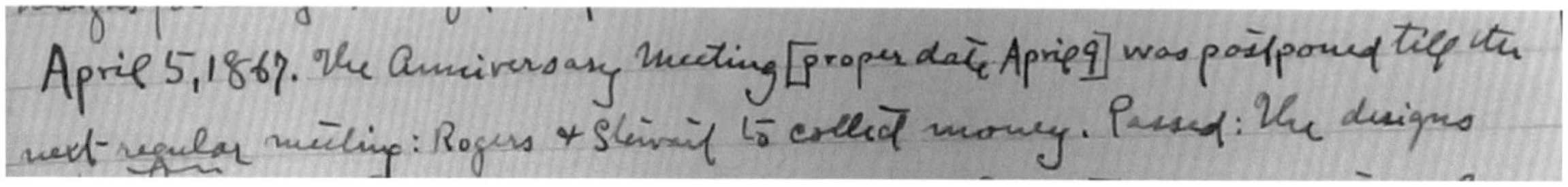
April 5, 1867. The Anniversary meeting [proper date April 9] was postponed till the next regular meeting: Rogers & Stewart to collect money. Passed: The designs

*"2nd Copy of Old Alpha Minutes" by Samuel Ammen*

Ammen later recalled that "Persons to whom, we showed the Minutes did not think 'anniversary' necessarily indicated Founding, and said that we should incur a serious responsibility if we assumed that it did. And so the discussion was spun out, and the longer action was deferred the more difficult it was. Meanwhile I felt constrained to use the Dixie Date (December 21st)."[34]

The more Ammen investigated the more he doubted the December date, "and in 1921, wrote to Crawford, the Grand Historian, [that] he was averse to "changing his books" and thought that "we needed more evidence."[35] Ammen

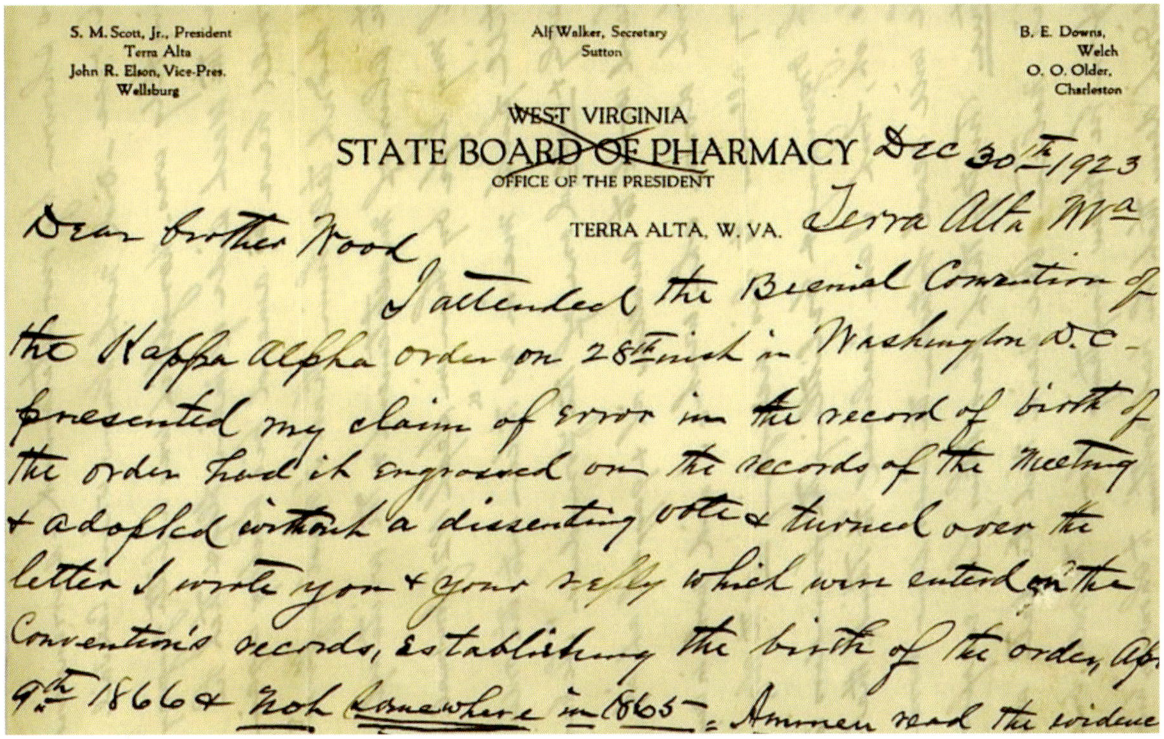
S. M. Scott, Jr., President
Terra Alta
John R. Elson, Vice-Pres.
Wellsburg

Alf Walker, Secretary
Sutton

B. E. Downs,
Welch
O. O. Older,
Charleston

WEST VIRGINIA
STATE BOARD OF PHARMACY
OFFICE OF THE PRESIDENT
TERRA ALTA, W. VA.

Dec 30th 1923
Terra Alta Wa

Dear brother Wood

I attended the Biennial Convention of the Kappa Alpha order on 28th inst in Washington D.C. presented my claim of error in the record of birth of the order had it engrossed on the records of the meeting & adopted without a dissenting vote & turned over the letter I wrote you & your reply which were entered on the Convention's records, establishing the birth of the order Ap. 9th 1866 & not somewhere in 1865. Ammen read the evidence

*Stanhope Scott to James Ward Wood, December 30, 1923*

relayed the information to Stanhope Scott, who induced the Twenty-Third Convention to accept April 9, 1866, as the official date for the founding; Ammen wrote, "I am glad the matter is settled and set right."[36]

When, how and why Ammen changed his mind on the issue is unclear. But the original minutes were available to him almost thirty years before the strident arguments once again arose. In his essay called "The Long Silence" it is apparent that he had, at one time, firmly supported Stanhope Scott's declaration of the "real" founding date of April 9th. In 1920, he wrote to Scott, "Alpha's Minutes say our anniversary was April 9, and hence I believe we date from April 9, 1866, not 1865 as most say."[37] In 1923, Stanhope Scott introduced his affidavit attesting to the 1866 date along with a letter from James Ward Wood to the Biennial Convention in Washington. Thus, the date of the founding was established as "Apr. 9th 1866 & not somewhere in 1865."[38]

By this time, Ammen had reversed his stance on the April founding date and strongly advocated for the December 21st date. Bad blood was already evident between Scott and Ammen on this matter; Scott informed Wood that although "Ammen read the evidence as shown by our statement & surrendered at once... he had hard work to swallow it & gagged at it, but down she went."[39]

In the end, however, Ammen swayed a number of authorities within the Order, including Bishop Mikell, the Knight Commander, to establish his position as the final word. In a series of letters to and from Greenlee Letcher in 1931, the outcome was determined.

On November 10, the Knight Commander wrote to Letcher, "For years 1865 has been stated as the date of our founding. Every *Journal* for years has carried 1865; every account of our Fraternity in every interfraternal publication has for years carried that date. It seems to me now much too late to change."[40]

Within a few days of receiving the instructions, Letcher composed a letter that he knew would be painful to Stanhope Scott. "I think it would be unfortunate for our fraternity under these circumstances to undertake now to change this long accepted date, nor do I think it should be done as the germination of the idea that doubtless took place in the early winter of 1865."[41] Scott's reply was immediate and bitter, "I thought that Jim Wood & I testifying the date was accepted in good faith & when they said so, I rested on it. I can see Ammen's fine hand" in the matter.[42] Nevertheless, this has been the official and accepted determination since that time.

What are the real facts and what are merely vague recollections, opinions, and interpretations based on personal beliefs or political agendas? Several primary sources have recently emerged that indicate what the Founders considered the true inauguration date. Several of the sources were previously known and dismissed, or as Stanhope Scott put it "smuggled & covered up." The first and most significant is the original minute book of Old Alpha, the second is the initiation receipt issued to William Archibald Walsh, and the third is the personal account records of James Ward Wood to his father in the fall and spring of 1865 and 1866. And, of course, there is the joke of William Taylor Thom, which is circumstantial but compelling evidence nonetheless.

It is recorded in the minutes dated April 5, 1867, "The anniversary meeting was postponed until the next regular time of meeting of the Society. A motion was passed and that a committee of two be appointed to take up a subscription and purchase delicacies for the occasion. Messrs Rogers and Stewart compose the committee. On motion a vote was taken to elect a member to address the Fraternity on the Anniversary meeting. Mr. Kirkpatrick was elected."[43] The date and the intent are unambiguous; the proximity to the original founding is certain.

The minutes of the next meeting, April 12th 1867, began, "The Fraternity met at its usual time but not with its usual appearance. For there was beaming in the countenance of every one, a pleasant smile that betoken something more than the mere formality of meeting. And so it was, that after calling the roll.... The Fraternity was addressed by Mr Kirkpatrick in a most eloquent and interesting style in commemoration of the anniversary and after being so highly entertained, the GM addressed the Society that we might enjoy each others company and partake of the sweetmeats and other refreshments prepared for the occasion and doing full Justice to ourselves in both respects."[44] There were, in the early days, a number of "feasts" or "conviviae" during the year, but only one called the "Anniversary Celebration." On June 14, 1867, the brotherhood had its "final celebration" before everyone departed for "far off homes" for vacation.[45]

After a summer break, Kappa Alpha met again on November 8, 1867, and at this meeting it was proposed, "Under the head of New Business. Mr Collins moved, seconded by Scott, 'That the time of our Anniversary be changed from the 9th day of April to some day, during the Christmas week, to be determined by the Society.' "[46] The quorum also determined that there would be an election of an anniversary orator and a committee was appointed to make preparation for the celebration. It is important to note that the request was that the anniversary date be changed "to some day during Christmas week" and that date was to be determined by the Society. The absence of a specific mention of December 21st in the minutes and the explicit reference to the date of April 9th being changed takes on added significance.

Ammen noted in his copy of the Old Alpha Minutes for the meeting of

November 22, 1867, that "under unfinished business the motion to change from 9th April to some day in Christmas week was adopted. Scott, Wm N., was appointed to find out which day in Xmas week will best suit all."[47]

If December 21st had some historic reason to replace April 9th for the anniversary celebration, it would have logically been named at once as the substitution date. It was noted in the Ammen copy for the meeting on December 13, 1867, that "it was decided, after discussion, that Monday, Dec. 23. Would be most suitable for the Anniversary Celebration. Stern was added to the Committee to prepare for it."[48] Saturday December 21st was conspicuously not designated.

And it was inscribed in the original minutes for Old Alpha on December 23, 1867,

> Society convened on this the 23rd day of December to celebrate its Anniversary.
> Upon calling the roll, a full attendance, was found present, with the single exception of Mr. Bell. Mr. Collins, then delivered the Anniversary Oration…[which] was received with much pleasure and satisfaction.... We there after a respite of a half hour or more with joyful hearts and willing hands, enjoyed the excellent delicacies provided for the occasion, the selections of which did the most credit to the Committee of three…Then after an evening fraught with perfect pleasure and enjoyment, such an evening as few ever enjoy, we parted, each on his own way rejoicing.
> Signed by
> Wm. N. Scott Grand Scribe and Samuel Z. Ammen Grand Master.[49]

A second and compelling piece of evidence for the April 9th date is a receipt presented to William Walsh in the spring of 1866. In September 1900, the *Kappa Alpha Journal* reprinted William Walsh's invitation to join Kappa Alpha and a receipt of his payment. The invitation from Wood read:

> Dear Sir—I have the honor to inform you that you have been duly elected a member of this fraternity. We would rejoice to number you as one of and amongst us if consistent with your wishes. For further information apply to me at any time. You will please keep this communication strictly confidential.
>
> Very truly yours,
> J. Ward Wood
> G.S.K.A.F.

The dated receipt:

> Received of William A. Walsh, the sum of one dollar ($1.00) as his initiation fee into the Kappa Alpha Fraternity.
>
> J. Ward Wood
> G.S.K.A.F
>
> (Signed for Grand Purser.)
> May 9, 1866[50]

The third set of tangible proofs consists of the detailed expense accounts that James Ward Wood submitted to his father. In his first report, he listed payments made from the time Wood left his father in Harrisonburg, about October 11, 1865, until the beginning of November. They included such entries as the stagecoach fare to Staunton, his bill at the Lexington House, and other expenses. He does not, however, mention either in his expense account or in his extant letters home any cash outlays for any other organization.[51]

Wood also had a more general expense account that spanned October 1, 1865, to February 22, 1866. The items for the second session included college fees, board fees, a bill for wood, payment to the dentist, a pipe, gloves, Christmas expenses, and fees to the Washington Literary Society. He contritely admitted his deficiency in accounting to his father: "There is a difference of four dollars in this bill, & the one cast up from the small items in my book but you will remember the $8 I could not a/c [account] for in my report before &

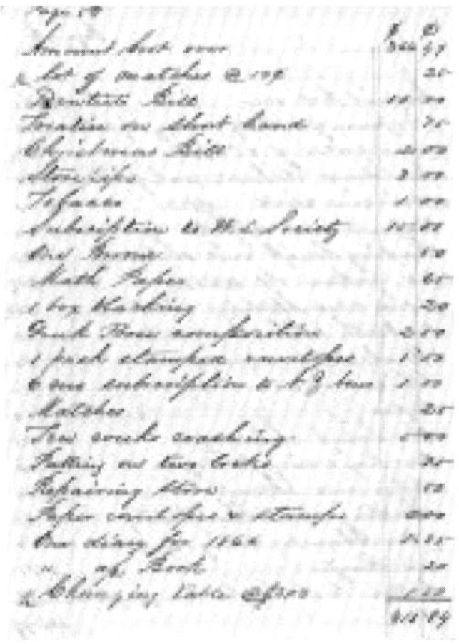

*October*

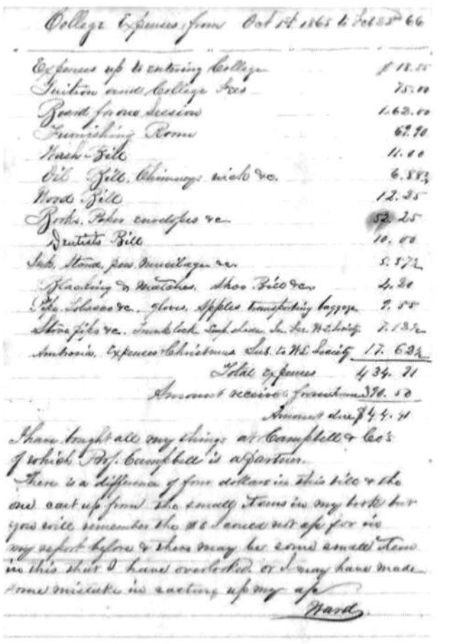

College Expenses from Oct 1st 1865 to Feb 22nd 66

| | |
|---|---|
| Expenses up to entering College | $18.55 |
| Tuition and College Fees | 75.00 |
| Board for one session | 1.62.00 |
| Furnishing Room | 67.90 |
| Wash-Bill | 11.00 |
| Oil Bill, Chimneys wick &c. | 6.88½ |
| Wood Bill | 12.25 |
| Books, Paper envelopes &c | 52.25 |
| Dentists Bill | 10.00 |
| [illegible] | 5.57½ |
| Blacking & matches, Shoe Bill &c | 4.20 |
| [illegible] | 7.55 |
| [illegible] | 7.13½ |
| [illegible] Expenses Christmas Sub. to W.L Society | 17.62½ |
| Total expenses | 434.71 |
| Amount received from [illegible] | 390.50 |
| Amount due | $44.41 |

I have bought all my things at Campbell & Co's of which Prof. Campbell is a partner.
There is a difference of four dollars in this bill & the one cast up from the small items in my book but you will remember the $4 I [illegible] in my report before & there may be some small items in this that I have overlooked or I may have made some mistake in casting up my a/c

Ward

*October–February 22*

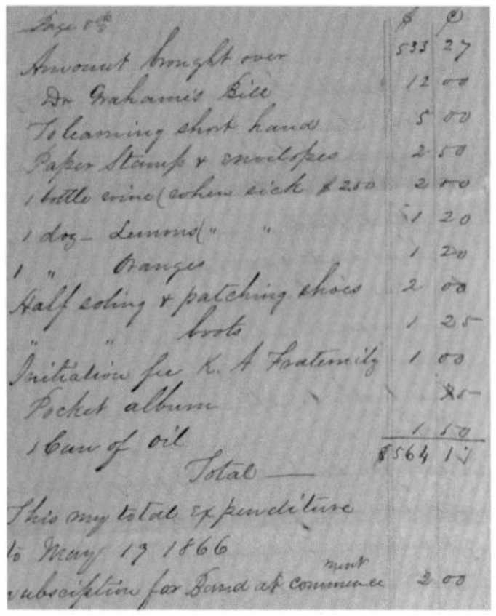

Page 8th

| | $ | ¢ |
|---|---|---|
| Amount brought over | 533 | 27 |
| Dr Graham's Bill | 12 | 00 |
| To learning short hand | 5 | 00 |
| Paper Stamps & envelopes | 2 | 50 |
| 1 bottle wine (when sick $2.50 | 2 | 00 |
| 1 doz- Lemons (" " | 1 | 20 |
| 1 " Oranges | 1 | 20 |
| Half soling & patching shoes | 2 | 00 |
| " " boots | 1 | 25 |
| Initiation fee K. A Fraternity | 1 | 00 |
| Pocket album | | 25 |
| 1 Can of oil | 1 | 50 |
| Total | $564 | 17 |

This my total expenditure to May 19 1866

subscription for Band at commencement 2 00

*February–May 19*

there may be some small item in this that I have overlooked."[52]

His third accounting extended from the end of February to May 19, 1866. This report included such extravagant items as lemons, oranges, a bottle of wine (when sick, he said), Dr. Graham's bill ($12), and an initiation fee for Kappa Alpha Fraternity ($1). It is important to note that at the top of page 8 of the May 19 report, Wood wrote "Amount brought over," which indicates that the last part of the accounting took place at the end of the billing cycle. On April 24, 1866, Wood wrote to his father, "I am sitting up for the first time in ten days. I have been confined to my bed for this length of time by the mumps. . . more tha[n] 60 of the students here have had the mumps for the past three weeks. . . . I have squared up my a/c & find the difference I have, between money received from home and money expended (including my Drs bill which I suppose will be about $15.00) to be about $89.00."[53] This time frame implies that Wood paid his initiation fee sometime in April 1866 or very early May 1866, and that he was confined to bed from approximately April 14 until at least April 24. In addition, he paid his initiation fee, which he'd never mentioned before, by May 19. All of this information supports an anniversary date of April 9, 1866.

The last supporting clue in regard to the April 9th date is circumstantial and by all accounts hearsay, but nevertheless extremely compelling. In the early days of the fraternity, when there was still a great rivalry and tempest of ill will among the societies in Lexington, a certain William Taylor Thom, a member of Phi Kappa Psi, got off what Letcher characterized a "witticism," namely that Kappa Alpha had been born in a cat's tail and that is where it will die.

The story is so pervasive and ubiquitous that it has taken on several different forms. Letcher said it infuriated Ammen to such an extent that it determined his opposition to the April 9th date. Letcher's version was a variation on the previous theme. Wood's room had been in a dormitory that "was called by the students of

Washington College 'Cat Tail' and Brother Ammen after he became a Kappa Alpha was very much incensed, he told me that Taylor Thom, a Phi Kappa Psi, perpetuated a witticism that Kappa Alpha had its birth place in a Cat's Tail [and in the heat of what then appeared to be bad feeling], [and] said that it was a very fitting place," Letcher wrote Mikell in 1931. "Ammen resented this and claimed that it was founded in the South Dormitory."[54]

Stanhope Scott had a slightly different take, writing in 1931: "Wm Taylor Thom . . . a determined opponent of KA said to Jim Wood that the Kappa Alpha 'was born in Cat Tail & would die in Cat Tail'—I saw him [Thom] in Washington D.C. last November & reminded him of his speech or prophecy. He did not deny saying it but replied 'if I said it, it was very impertinent.' "[55]

Letcher thought that the Thom story was the strongest evidence for the later date and the Cat-Tail location. He wrote to General Stern, "the very circumstance which prejudices Brother Ammen against the place, seems to me, to virtually prove that it was born in 'Cat's Tail.' " He reiterated this view to Grand Historian W. B. Crawford a year later: "A joke about the place being 'Cat Tail,' which Brother Ammen so much resented seems to me as a lawyer to give the strongest confirmation that 'Cat Tail' was the place."[56]

In 1931, five years after his visit to Cat-Tail and his notarized declaration about the April 1866 date, Stanhope Scott ironically presented to Letcher the most credible basis for the opposite and earlier date: "I have an old toast written by Jim Wood 'to the 2 Williams' Dec 21st 1865 at a supper in Walsh's room when the three were together."[57]

At the end of the controversy, Greenlee Letcher, likely the most objective observer of the founding data, having been caught between conflicting facts and traditions, had found a way to interpret the competing evidence into a plausible win for both sides of the issue.

He wrote to Stanhope Scott that the concept of the Order was likely conceived in Walsh's room in December 1865 and was born in April 1866. He concluded, with the help of Bishop Mikell, that "the fraternity was an evolution and not founded in any particular place, but the founding embraced perhaps a number of meetings at different places, the ideas being first in the minds of James Ward Wood and your brother, William N. Scott in the winter of 1865 with you and Walsh taken into the conversations."[58]

Livy concluded his statement in the praefatio—"ea nec adfirmare nec refellere in animo est—I neither intend to affirm nor refute these matters." The purpose of this chapter has been the same.

*Notes* Chapter 5:

1 Samuel Z. Ammen, "A Long Silence," Ammen Papers, Kappa Alpha Archives, Lexington, Va., 1.

2 Leroy Boyd, "James Ward Wood Interview, 1918," Question 51, Kappa Alpha Archives, Lexington, Va. According to Samuel Ammen, the inspiration for Wood's desire to "become a member of a fraternity" was a man named Van Arsdale, a Royal Arch Mason. Samuel Ammen, "Wood as Founder," June 17, 1920, Ammen Papers 45, Kappa Alpha Archives, Lexington, Va., 8; Wood, however, writes in a letter to his father (November 18, 1865, p. 4) "I will send with this letter a paper containing a long address to the Odd Fellows to Mr Vanmort as he is an old member." James Ward Wood to Father, November 18, 1865, Kappa Alpha Archives, Lexington, Va.

3 Hugh Moran to Father, February 24, 1867, Hugh Moran Papers, Archives, Leyburn Library, Washington and Lee University, Lexington, Virginia, 2.

4 Samuel Ammen, "Wood as Founder," June 17, 1920, Ammen Papers 45, Kappa Alpha Archives, Lexington, Va., 8.

5 Ibid., 7.

6 Ibid., 8.

7 Ibid., 9.

8 Ibid.

9 W. B. Brockenbrough to Greenlee Letcher, December 2, 1925, Kappa Alpha Archives, Lexington, Va.

10 Leroy Boyd to Greenlee Letcher, January 8, 1926, Kappa Alpha Archives, Lexington, Va.

11 Leroy Boyd, "James Ward Wood Interview, 1918," Questions 18 and 19, Kappa Alpha Archives, Lexington, Va.

12 Samuel Ammen, "Wood as Founder," June 17, 1920, Ammen Papers 45, Kappa Alpha Archives, Lexington, Va., 7.

13 Ibid., 8.

14 Ibid., 13, 5. "Magnitudine amimi praestimus—We excel by a magnitude of spirit"—a phrase evidently in the Epsilon Alpha ritual.

15 Samuel Ammen, "Wood as Founder," June 17, 1920, Ammen Papers 45, Kappa Alpha Archives, Lexington, Va., 8.

16 Greenlee Letcher to Bishop Mikell, October 19, 1931, Letcher Papers, Kappa Alpha Archives, Lexington, Va.

17 Leroy Boyd to Greenlee Letcher, January 18, 1928, Letcher Papers, Kappa Alpha Archives, Lexington, Va.

18 Leroy Boyd to Stanhope Scott, May 25, 1924, Kappa Alpha Archives, Lexington, Va.

19 Leroy Boyd to Greenlee Letcher, January 18, 1928, Letcher Papers, Kappa Alpha Archives, Lexington, Va.

20 James Ward Wood to Branson Wood, October 28, 1865, Wood Papers, Kappa Alpha Archives, Lexington, Va.; James Ward Wood to Father, April 24, 1866, Wood Papers, Kappa Alpha Archives, Lexington, Va.

21 Leroy Boyd to Greenlee Letcher, January 18, 1928, Letcher Papers, Kappa Alpha Archives, Lexington, Va.

22 Samuel Ammen to Jo Lane Stern, January 26, 1928, Ammen Papers, Kappa Alpha Archives, Lexington, Va.

23 Bishop Mikell to Greenlee Letcher, November 19, 1931, Letcher Papers, Kappa Alpha Archives, Lexington, Va.

24 Stanhope Scott to Greenlee Letcher, November 10, 1931, Letcher Papers, Kappa Alpha Archives, Lexington, Va., 1.

25 Ibid.

26 Stanhope Scott to Greenlee Letcher, Letcher Papers, Kappa Alpha Archives, Lexington, Va., 2.

27 Greenlee Letcher to Bishop Mikell, October 10, 1931, Letcher Papers, Kappa Alpha Archives, Lexington, Va.

28 General Stern to Greenlee Letcher, November 20, 1928, Letcher Papers, Kappa Alpha Archives, Lexington, Va.

29 General Stern to Greenlee Letcher, February 25, 1931, Letcher Papers, Kappa Alpha Archives, Lexington, Va.

30 Samuel Ammen, "The Long Silence," Ammen Papers, Kappa Alpha Archives, Lexington, Va.

31 Ibid.

32 Ibid.

33 Samuel Ammen, "Second Copy of the Minutes of Old Alpha," 1915, Ammen 66, Ammen Papers, Kappa Alpha Archives, Lexington, Va.

34 Samuel Ammen, "The Long Silence," Ammen Papers, Kappa Alpha Archives, Lexington, Va.

35 Ibid.

36 Ibid.

37 Samuel Ammen to Stanhope Scott, March 6, 1920, Ammen Papers, Kappa Alpha Archives, Lexington, Va.

38 Stanhope Scott to James Ward Wood, December 30, 1923, Wood Papers, Archives, Kappa Alpha Order, Lexington, Va., 1.

39 Ibid., 2.

40 Bishop Mikell to Greenlee Letcher, Letcher Papers, Kappa Alpha Archives, Lexington, Va.

41 Greenlee Letcher to Stanhope Scott, November 21, 1931, Letcher Papers, Kappa Alpha Archives, Lexington, Va.

42 Stanhope Scott to Greenlee Letcher, Letcher Papers, Kappa Alpha Archives, Lexington, Va.

43 Original Alpha Minutes, April 5, 1867, Kappa Alpha Archives, Lexington, Va., 29.

44 Original Alpha Minutes, April 12, 1867, Kappa Alpha Archives, Lexington, Va., 33.

45 Original Alpha Minutes, June 14, 1867, Kappa Alpha Archives, Lexington, Va., 45.

46 Original Alpha Minutes, November 8, 1867, Kappa Alpha Archives, Lexington, Va., 23. N.B: There was a new minute book, as the other had been temporarily misplaced during the summer.

47 Samuel Ammen, "Second Copy of the Minutes of Old Alpha," Entry for Novovember 22, 1867, KA Lodge, 1915, Ammen 66, Ammen Papers, Kappa Alpha Archives, Lexington, Va., 5.

48 Ibid., Entry for December 13, 1867, KA Lodge, 1915, Ammen 66, Ammen Papers, Kappa Alpha Archives, Lexington, Va., 5.

49 Original Alpha Minutes, December 23, 1867, Kappa Alpha Archives, Lexington, Va., 31.

50 J. M. Brassieux, "One of Our Noble Founders," *Kappa Alpha Journal* 18, No. 1 (September 1900): 15.

51 James Ward Wood to Father, November 19, 1865, Wood Papers, Kappa Alpha Archives, Lexington, Va.

52 Expense Account, James Ward Wood to Father, February 22, 1866, Wood Papers, Kappa Alpha Archives, Lexington, Va.

53 James Ward Wood to Father, April 24, 1866, Wood Papers, Kappa Alpha Archives, Lexington, Va.

54 Letcher to Mikell, October 19, 1931, Letcher Papers. Kappa Alpha Order, Lexington, Va.

55 Stanhope Scott to Greenlee Letcher, December 7, 1931, Letcher Papers, Kappa Alpha Archives, Lexington, Va.

56 Greenlee Letcher to Jo Lane Stern, January 27, 1930, Letcher Papers, Kappa Alpha Archives, Lexington, Va.; Greenlee Letcher to Jo Lane Stern, October 22, 1928, Letcher Papers, Kappa Alpha Archives, Lexington, Va., 2.

57 Scott to Letcher, November 10, 1931, Letcher Papers.

58 Greenlee Letcher to Stanhope Scott, November 6, 1931, Letcher Papers, Kappa Alpha Archives, Lexington, Va.; Letcher to Scott, November 21, 1931, Letcher Papers.

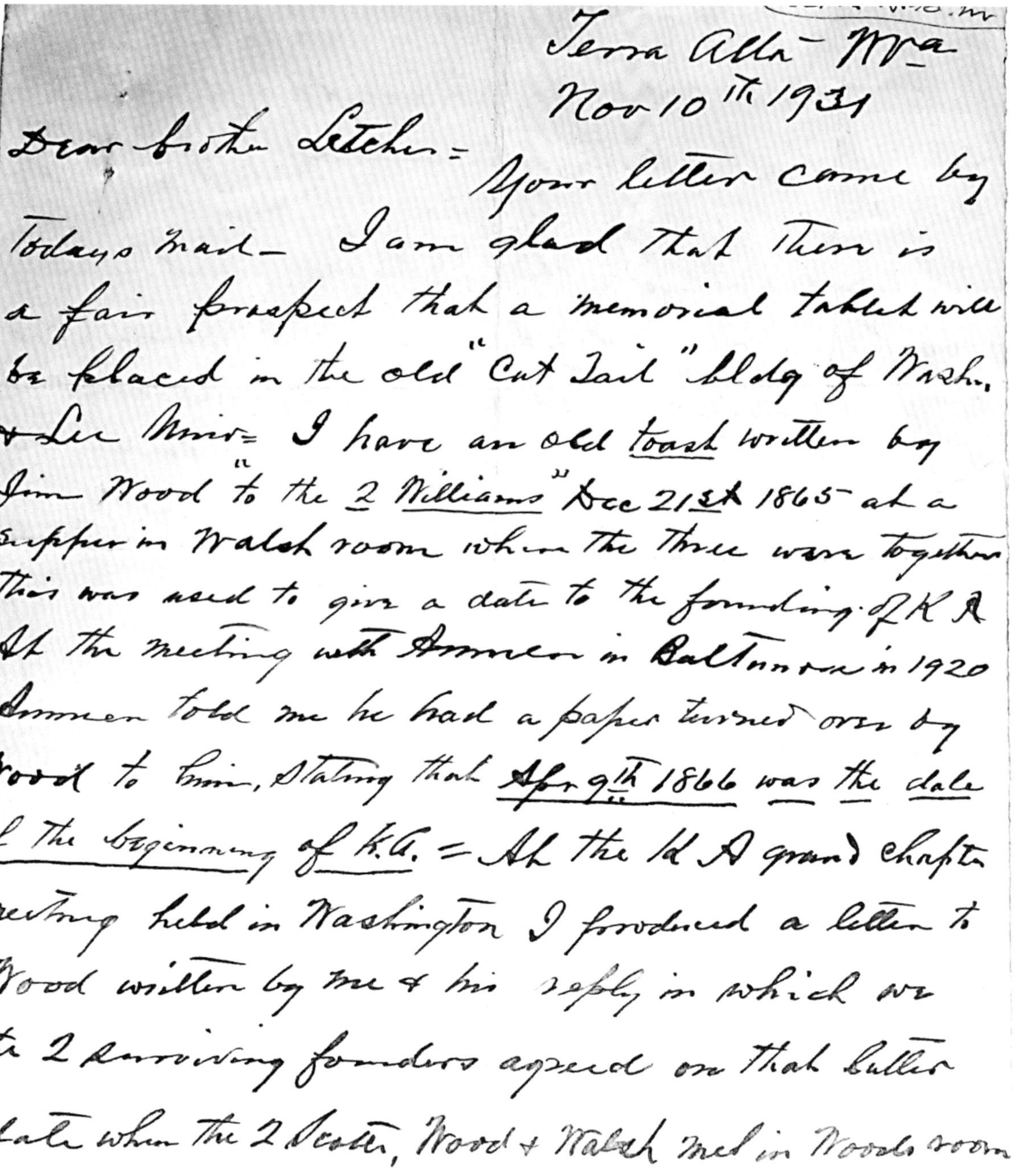

Terra Alta – W.Va.
Nov 10th 1931

Dear brother Letcher =
Your letter came by todays mail – I am glad that there is a fair prospect that a memorial tablet will be placed in the old "Cut Tail" bldg of Wash. & Lee Univ = I have an old toast written by Jim Wood "to the 2 Williams" Dec 21st 1865 at a supper in Walsh room when the three were together This was used to give a date to the founding of K A At the meeting with Ammen in Baltimore in 1920 Ammen told me he had a paper turned over by Wood to him, stating that Apr 9th 1866 was the date of the beginning of K.A. = At the K A grand chapter meeting held in Washington I produced a letter to Wood written by me & his reply in which we the 2 surviving founders agreed on that latter date when the 2 Scotts, Wood & Walsh met in Woods room

*Stanhope Scott to Greenlee Letcher, November 10, 1931*

*Gamma Chapter, University of Georgia, 1871*

# 6

# Expansion

Many of the early members of Kappa Alpha had served in the recent war and shared a special bond with their compatriots. Perhaps a fraternal organization provided a replacement for the camaraderie of former days and, as such, elicited the understanding and empathy of the new president of the college, General Robert E. Lee. The fundamental lure of a secret lodge is expressed in the old joke that maintains if three Englishmen were shipwrecked on a deserted island, two would immediately form a club—with secret passwords and handshakes—to exclude the third. Thus, the fraternal Order included both elements of inclusion and exclusion; the inclusive segment provided security and companionship, the exclusive component, an elite social status.

During Kappa Alpha's first years of existence, its founders were more concerned with the social amenities and status that came along with being a member of a fraternal organization than with creating a basis for governance and putting in place a formal structure of rituals and rules. The meetings, the feasts, the badges, the secret handshakes all provided the sense of belonging that many were seeking.

The casual nature of all this began to change in the autumn of 1866. On October 10, 1866, at a meeting of the fraternity in Room No. 6, Main Building, Washington College, it is recorded that "Mr. Ammen and Mr. Given were elected members of this Fraternity."[1] On October, 17, 1866, Samuel Zenas Ammen was initiated into the fraternity.[2] The adoption of Ammen into the organization set in motion a new direction and mission. He made it his objective to transform the organization. He later declared that the fraternity "certainly lacked all at my first entrance: bare walls, bare floors, barrenness of purpose. Then [it] was but a farce—a mere meeting. [No] By-laws, ceremonies, policies, plans. I have now given it a strength, regularity, attractiveness, and—a life & purpose which guarantee its perpetuation."[3] He maintained that "the name KA and its purpose of forming a new society originated with Wood, of W. Va.; its realization has been mostly with me."[4]

As his influence in the Order increased and he became more satisfied with the internal stability of Alpha and it structural improvements, he became more certain of the benefits of planting the seeds of Alpha throughout the South. Noting the patterns of other such organizations, Ammen thought that by exporting the fraternity he would increase both the society's prestige, influence, and finances. He wrote in his diary, "This establishment of Lodges will give us an influence of power & standing at College such as we have not yet attained."[5] As often happens, the first institution to become a target for this ambition was also the nearest.

On January 24, 1868, he noted that "Mr. Collins proposed for membership Mr. John W. Hollingsworth, Macon, Ga., cadet of VMI Permission was given Mr. Stern to take measures for establishing a Lodge of KA at Gordonsville Academy; also to Mr. Martin to take steps toward establishing a Lodge at the University of Va."[6] On March 8, 1868, after three cadets—W. S. Pearson, William M. Jerdone, and William M. Sears—were initiated into Kappa Alpha, "the GM then instructed them as to their duties in establishing a Lodge of our Order at the Virginia Military Institute."[7] On March 21st the minutes refer to Pearson and Sears as "our VMI Brothers."[8] At the same meeting it was recorded that "Mr. W. Scott laid before the Lodge the request of out Bro Mr Collins for permission to establish a Lodge of our Order at the University of Georgia, which was granted and the G.S. was instructed to furnish a copy of the Constitution, By-Laws &c. to Mr Collins."[9] Thus began the first stage of expansion for the nascent fraternity.

During the next several years, expansion was a major focus of both Ammen and "Old Alpha." Six chapters were founded throughout the South in quick succession—Beta at Virginia Military Institute in Lexington, Virginia, on March 8, 1868; Gamma at the University of Georgia in Athens, Georgia, on April 6, 1868; Delta at Wofford College in Spartanburg, South Carolina, on February 23, 1869; Epsilon at Emory University in Atlanta, Georgia, on June 4, 1869; Zeta at Randolph-Macon College in Ashland, Virginia, on November 28, 1869; and Eta at Richmond College in Richmond, Virginia, on March 18, 1870.[10]

Quite naturally, because of physical proximity and ties of consanguinity, the first campus to attract Ammen's attention, VMI, which is also located in Lexington. The two schools had a long and intertwined history. Shortly after Washington College had made its permanent move from Mulberry Hill into the town of Lexington, a bill came before the Virginia Assembly which "provided for the erections of three arsenals: ... one of these was to be situated west of the Alleghany Mountains, ...one in Richmond, and one in Lexington."[11] An early advocate for the arsenal legislation was a former patriot and Frenchman who came to America with the recommendations of the Marquis de Lafayette—Claudius Crozet. This gentleman was born in Lyons, educated at the Institute Polytechnique in Paris, served under Napoleon and Marshall Ney, and had been decorated with the Fleur de Lys. After arrival in America, he was appointed Professor of Engineering at the United States Military Academy at West Point, New York. In 1824, he accepted the post of State Engineer of Virginia and was instrumental in the development of the Kanawha Canal system.[12]

In his post as State Engineer and in his capacity overseeing the construction of the western branches of the canal project he is thought to have discussed "with some of its principal citizens the prospect of founding a military school in Lexington long ere it took tangible form."[13] The subject of military training at the state arsenal was debated in the most prominent forum in the town, the Franklin Society. It had the approval of many prominent citizens of the town and "in the summer of 1835 a series of newspaper articles, signed 'Civis,' suggested the conversion of the Lexington State Arsenal into a military institution of higher learning for worthy but indigent youth. It was argued that the students would protect the arsenal better than the existing soldier guard and "that the town could claim the title 'Athens of Western Virginia' with the additional educational faculty."[14]

The 1836 legislature passed a bill "reorganizing the Lexington arsenal and establishing a Military school in connection with Washington College." The act called for the transfer of the Cincinnati fund from the college to the new institution.[15] The *Lexington Gazette* expressed the opinion that the legislature has "assumed an authority over the Cincinnati fund and Washington College, which cannot be justified."[16] Nevertheless, a board of visitors was assembled and met in Lexington in August 1837; the trustees of Washington College, being fearful of the loss of the Cincinnati donation, appointed a contingent to meet with the newly constituted board and "to proceed with caution." [17]

In 1838, the Virginia Assembly passed an act ordering the reorganization of the arsenal and the establishment of a military school in conjunction with Washington College. By June 1839, both the trustees of Washington College and the board of visitors of the Virginia Military Institute had "accepted the articles of agreement and cooperation." Among the first articles were that "all lectures, classes, and exercises of each school were to be open to students and cadets; each faculty was to adopt regulations to keep discipline; providing for the appointment of the military professor of the Institute as their Cincinnati professor of military science & appropriate that department such portion of the Cincinnati fund as they shall deem equitable."[18]

When VMI began its first session in 1839–1840, the cadets attended classes and lectures at Washington College and the "June examinations of the cadets were held in the College's Philosophical Hall."[19] It was the custom through much of the antebellum period for the cadets of VMI and the students of Washington College to attend celebrations, holidays, and commencements together and the faculties cooperated and consulted with one another on matters of curricula and educational agenda; "several trustees of Washington College were also members of the VMI board of visitors."[20]

*Washington College, 1845*

Ollinger Crenshaw, noted historian of Washington College, declared that "formal separation of the two institutions was nevertheless inevitable."[21] Several of the underlying issues revolved around the growing fear of the trustees of Washington College that the new institution would attract many of its

*Virginia Military Institute, circa 1850*

*Colonel Francis H. Smith (1839–1889)*

prospective clientele and diminish its own status and source of income; that there existed conflicting approaches to educational traditions and methods of discipline; that the Superintendent of VMI Colonel Francis H. Smith who was a devout Episcopalian was infringing on the Scots-Irish Presbyterianism of both Washington College and the town of Lexington; and also there was the Cincinnati fund.

In 1845, George D. Armstrong, a Presbyterian clergyman and professor at Washington College, lobbied the Virginia legislature to prevent VMI 's from being converted into "an independent college open to the general patronage in Virginia." James Baldwin Dorman, who had attended both Washington College and Virginia Military Institute, and whose father had introduced the legislation to create the military school and was on its board of visitors, "summed up the history of the dispute," as follows, "The trustees & Faculty of Washington College alarmed at the rapid growth of the Institute, which together with the ambitious views of the Superintendent, seemed to bode them no good—sent Profr Armstrong to Richmond for the purpose of having its sphere of action circumscribed."[22]

Armstrong argued that the original proposition had been to transform a state arsenal into a military school, to exchange a rowdy sentry of soldiers paid in cash for a body of students compensated in education.[23] Armstrong asserted that "it was unthinkable that the legislature" would "create a rival seminary at its gates, with the unlimited power of competition, & armed with the particular facilities of military fascination, to make that competition ruinous."[24]

In defense of his institution, Colonel Smith responded that "the institute proclaimed that the limits of the institution to be its 'usefulness to the State' and argued that a public state institution should not be rendered subservient to a denominational college."[25]

In June 1845, the president of Washington College, Henry Ruffner, proposed to the trustees that Washington College and VMI merge their faculties, facilities, and student body. The plan "was promptly and decisively, yet courteously, disapproved as impracticable and inexpedient."[26] In July 1845, the College announced that "they would cease the practice of appointing a professor of military science from VMI [thus severing] the tie that had existed between the institutions through the Cincinnati professorship."[27]

Cordial relations and collaboration were renewed in 1849, when the trustees adopted friendly resolutions to VMI and its board of visitors responded in kind. "The later expressed delight in the restoration of entire harmony, and said the only rivalry they desired between Virginia's institutions was a generous emulation."[28] Thus, although the competition continued, both schools, students, and faculties resumed their symbiotic and fraternal relationship, which endured through and was strengthened by the hardships of the Civil War.

During the course of the war, both Washington College and VMI remained opened, although with diminished resources and capacity. The cadets of VMI participated in the Battle of New Market against overwhelming Union forces and fought with great valor. The youngest cadet was but fifteen years old and ten were killed, with forty-five cadets being wounded during the conflict. Less than a month later, on June 12, 1864, Federal troops, under General David Hunter, occupied Lexington and burnt the institution in retaliation for their participation in the battle.

The raid left the student barracks and faculty residences extensively damaged and the library, laboratories, and scientific equipment entirely destroyed. After the war, the cadets once again intermingled with their neighbors at Washington College in classes and shared facilities with them. The admiration for the bravery of the cadets in battle and the sympathy for the catastrophe caused by General Hunter, once again drew the two institutions into a mutually reciprocating state of friendship. It is in this environment and singular set of circumstances that the leaders of Kappa Alpha first reached out to extend its franchise.

The two earliest proponents of this expansion were Ammen and William

*VMI in ruins, barracks, 1866*

Wilson Collins. Collins was born in Macon, Georgia, in 1849 and came to Washington College after the war. He was proposed for membership in the Alpha chapter almost a year after Ammen's election on October 11, 1867, and was initiated a week later on October 18.[29] Collins became an enthusiastic supporter of strengthening and vitalizing the fraternity and Ammen noted at the Christmas celebration that we had "a very good oration from Collins."[30] It seems that he and Ammen were in agreement that the most expeditious and efficient method of making the fraternity both more stable and recognized would be to establish lodges at various institutions throughout the South.

Collins's first effort came on January 24, 1868, "Proposals of Names for Election coming in order. Mr Collins proposed the name of Mr John W. Hollingsworth of Macon Georgia a cadet at Virginia Military Institute."[31]

Following in quick succession, on February 7, 1868, "permission was granted to one brother Mr. Collins to take measures towards establishing a Lodge of our Order at the Virginia Military Institute."[32] On the same day "the name of Mr John W Hollingsworth of Ga. Was presented for Ballot. This gentleman was elected a Member of our Society.... At his request [Ammen's] permission was granted to our brother Mr Collins to take measures towards establishing a Lodge of our Order at the Virginia Military Institute" [33]

Other cadets following in rapid succession. "To-day (Sat afternoon) initiated 3 VMI's into KA All fine fellows. Of all men I ever saw Hollingsworth is the finest looking – handsomest. Our ceremony is done. What's writ is writ. All goes well. This establishment of Lodge will give us an influence and power & standing at College such as we have not yet attained."[34]

The official minutes of the Old Alpha noted, "Calling the Roll and reading the Minutes was set aside for the evening and the Society proceeded to the Initiation of the following gentlemen, Cadets W.S. Pearson of Alabama, Wm M. Jerdone of Virginia, and Wm M Sears of Virginia.... After these gentlemen had been initiated into the Mysteries of the Second Degree and had taken upon themselves the required Obligations, they were heartily welcomed into our brotherhood. The GM then instructed them as to their duties in establishing a Lodge of our Order at the Virginia Military Institute and offered the use of our Room until better arrangement could be made by them."[35] On April 4, 1868, William Pearson's younger brother was initiated into the mysteries of the Order—both brothers were to become physicians by trade and the younger brother was

*William R. Jerdone*

*William M. Sears*

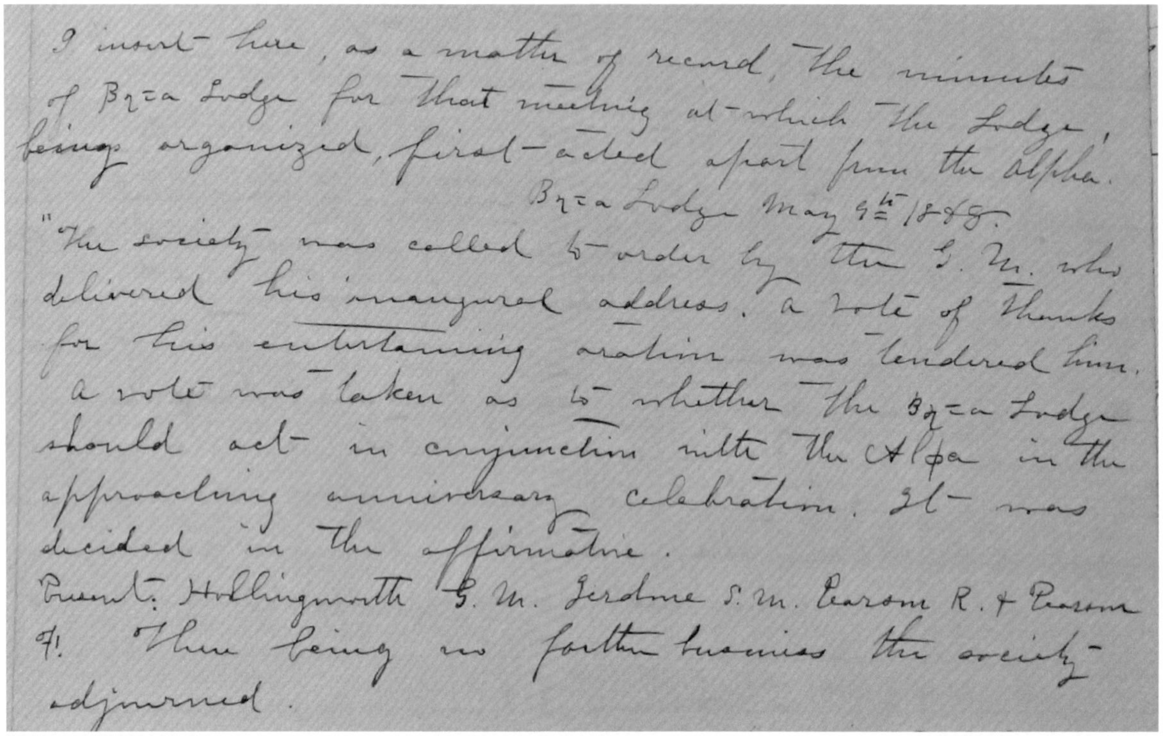
I insert here, as a matter of record, the minutes of Bη=α Lodge for that meeting at which the Lodge, being organized, first acted apart from the Alpha.

Bη=α Lodge May 9th 1868.

"The society was called to order by the G. M. who delivered his inaugural address. A vote of thanks for his entertaining oration was tendered him. A vote was taken as to whether the Bη=α Lodge should act in conjunction with the Alpha in the approaching anniversary celebration. It was decided in the affirmative.

Present: Hollingsworth G. M. Jerdone S. M. Pearson R. & Pearson F. There being no further business the society adjourned.

*First Beta meeting, May 9, 1868*

prophetically named Benjamin Rush Pearson, presumably after the noted medico of the American Revolution.[36]

On April 18, 1868, Kappa Alpha convened for the purpose "of organizing the Beta Lodge at Va. Mil. Institute." With the new initiates installed, the business of the election of officers took place: Mr. Hollingsworth was elected Grand Master, Mr. Jerdone was Second Master, Mr. Pearson as Grand Scribe. Several more cadets were slated for initiation and two more for consideration.[37] Thus, the Beta Lodge was off to an impressive beginning.

In the Alpha minutes, on May 9, 1868, Ammen recorded "as a matter of record, the minutes of the Beta Lodge for that meeting at which the Lodge, being organized, first acted apart from Alpha.[38] Ammen's notes reflected that Beta had decided to act in concert with Alpha in matters of organization and celebration, "A vote was taken as to whether the Beta Lodge should act in conjunction with Alpha in the approaching anniversary celebration. It was

*Samuel Zenas Ammen*

decided in the affirmative."[39] That season Beta met several times under Ammen's watchful eye and conjointly participated in the final convivium with Alpha before summer break on June 16, 1868. Many toasts were made "to B Lodge and may she have a child of her own! To which Stern added 'Yea, and grand-children.'"[40]

More Beta initiations ensued in the fall of 1868 and it was noted in the Alpha minutes of December 10, 1869, that a prominent member of the VMI lodge stated that "he would only initiate such men, as he could recommend for office in the "Corps" next year."[41]

As Samuel Ammen wrote in his history, however, "In the first years of the Old Alpha [we] gave no thought to the founding of additional chapters, its entire energies being employed in maintaining its own existence. In '68–'69 it lost interest even in that, making no initiations that year and at the end of '69–'70 Alpha died of inertia."[42] Kappa Alpha historian, William Sprigg Hamilton, supported this version of events in his private history of the Order noting that no initiations were made in Alpha in 1868–1869, and that only a few in the following year, and in the fall of 1869 only John Martin and Jo Lane Stern had returned to college. The last meeting of Old Alpha took place on June 2, 1870, and its executive powers were passed on to the Beta Chapter.

The primary reasons given to explain the suspension of Alpha were the departure of the two of the Founding Fathers, William and Stanhope Scott, from Lexington; the loss of the meeting hall at the Ann Smith Academy; the graduation and exodus of many of the early and energetic leaders of the society, and the crowded schedule of Ammen in his senior year.

On June 2, 1870, Charles Clemmitt, the Grand Scribe, finished his transmissions in a bittersweet note with the impending passing of Old Alpha,

"Thus endeth the Session of 1869–70, and the members of the "Alpha" Chapter part some to mingle in the active duties of life, some to repose awhile upon their hard earned College laurels, but all to carry with them, engraved on tablets of enduring memory, the virtues of their brethren in the "K.A."[43]

Hamilton wrote that "the relations with other chapters—more properly called Lodges, were kept up by the Knight Commander [Ammen], who as [Number] 1, before the creation of that office, continued to give all orders, as being the superior officer. Ammen was Knight Commander until April, 1871."[44]

Beta assumed Alpha's role as governing chapter in the fall of 1870. On November 27, 1870, Beta chapter elected Samuel Z. Ammen as Knight Commander. This office, originally proposed by Ammen on May 1, 1868, was unique to the Alpha Chapter. It was originally designated as a subordinate position to the Number I, the chief duties of the Knight Commander, or KC, were to act as a corresponding secretary, to keep records of all transactions, and, most important, to supply newly established chapters with all the pertinent information and attach requisite instructions for the Order's bylaws, rituals, and constitution. At the point when Beta elected Ammen as Knight Commander that office had transformed itself into one that was institutional rather than local, supreme rather than subordinate, initiating measures instead to reacting to requests, and having the final say on matters concerning the whole Order.

*William Wilson Collins*

After his election as KC, Ammen graduated from Washington College and took a teaching job in Millburn, Kentucky. The efficient way in which he accomplished the responsibilities of that post made it clear that it was more practical and logical to have that post independent of any particular chapter.[45] On March 31, 1871, Ammen resigned as Knight Commander. Shortly thereafter, Beta passed the governing torch over to the Gamma Chapter at the University of Georgia in 1872.

William Wilson Collins was Ammen's partner for spreading the Kappa Alpha brand throughout the South by colonization and cross-pollination. Ammen characterized Collins as "a noble, active, businesslike man."[46] The genesis of the plan to expand was likely a process of their collaboration and brainstorming. Jo Lane Stern was the peripatetic evangelist. It was Collins that both proposed John Hollingsworth as the first recruit external to the campus of Washington College and was the first to request permission toward "establishing a Lodge of our Order at the Virginia Military Institute."[47] Collins and his VMI recruit John Hollingsworth were both born in Macon, Georgia, in 1848, and it is likely that they knew one another in childhood and perhaps in war. In any case it seems that Collins's ties to his hometown were deep and strong.

It was recorded in the Alpha minutes on March 21, 1868, that "in response to the Call for New Business, Mr. W. Scott laid before the Lodge the request of Bro Mr. Collins for permission to establish a Lodge of our Order at the University of

*Lithograph of the University of Georgia, circa 1854*

Georgia, and the G.S.. I was instructed to furnish a copy of the Constitution, By Laws &c to Mr. Collins."[48]

The University of Georgia had a rich history and was similar to Washington College both in the composition of its student body, in its rich history and in its mission and sympathies. Collins found fertile ground to plants the seeds of Kappa Alpha.

The history of the University of Georgia began with the post-Revolutionary governor, Lyman Hall. Lyman Hall had been born in Connecticut in 1724 and graduated from Yale in 1742 at the age of eighteen. He first studied for the ministry but soon turned to medicine. In 1754, he moved to a town near Savannah to establish a practice and became "the leading physician" of the area. He supported the American cause during the War of Independence and was one of the three Georgians to sign the Declaration of Independence. In 1783, he was elected the governor of Georgia and made advanced education a priority of his administration. In a message to the legislators of Georgia on July 8, 1783, he encouraged them to "lay an early foundation for endowing seminaries of learning" by making grants of land and "raising revenues to support such valuable institutions."[49]

The following winter the Georgia legislature directed that twenty thousand acres be laid out in Washington and Franklin "for the endowment of a college or seminary." An act was passed for the "full and complete establishment of a Public seat of Learning" on January 27, 1785, making it the oldest chartered state-supported university in the United States. The first students arrived "at the tiny, isolated campus at Cedar Shoals on the Oconee River" in 1801.[50] In 1819, the Reverend Moses Waddel, stabilized the institution with the recruitment of qualified professors and moved to bring the curriculum in line with other institutions of the time.

"As the Civil War approached, the average age of students rose close to modern norms" but the clientele was composed of "privileged white males who faced strict codes of conduct and a rigid classical curriculum with heavy doses of Greek and especially Latin.... When the Civil War erupted in 1861, they rallied to the cause … and upperclassmen marched off to the slaughter."[51] In the spring of 1865 returning veterans were encouraged by "a mini G.I. Bill of Rights to go or return to college, and enrollment at the University of Georgia soared to almost three hundred when the school reopened in 1866."[52] It was in this time of an enlarged student body that William Wilson Collins found enthusiastic and ambitious recruits for a chapter of Kappa Alpha.

The first social fraternity, Phi Kappa Literary Society. had made its appearance at the University of Georgia in 1820. It was organized by Joseph Henry Lumpkin, who derived his concept from his experiences at Princeton. Although it was designated a literary association, it nevertheless had many attributes of a fraternal organization—the meetings were safe-guarded from intrusion, oaths were taken to "keep inviolate the secrets of the society," and the members formed an exclusive club.[53] One of the first social fraternities came into existence about 1843 and a prominent member of this group was Jabez Lamar Monroe Curry, who would later be instrumental in the establishment of the Eta Chapter of Kappa Alpha at Richmond College.[54] Curry would later write about the Greek letter societies at Georgia, "Each student was a member of one or other of these organizations. They met on Saturday mornings in their respective halls and kept their proceedings entirely secret. The competition, the rivalry was strong but gentlemanly. I must bear emphatic testimony to the value of these exercises upon my subsequent career."[55]

This secret soceity, and perhaps the one to which Professor Curry belonged, was known by the cryptic name of the Temple of the Skull and Bones. There are references made to it as early as the 1840s. It seems to have been developed from a fraternity organized in 1837 at Wesleyan College in Middletown, Connecticut, the Mystic Seven. After the Civil War several Greek Letter fraternities were

*Mystic Seven Badge, University of Georgia, circa 1843*

established at the University of Georgia, including Sigma Alpha, Chi Phi, Kappa Alpha, and Phi Delta Theta.[56]

On February 21, 1868, Collins returned home to Macon, Georgia, and by the same time the next month he had requested permission to establish a chapter of Kappa Alpha at the University of Georgia.[57] "The G.S. [Grand Scribe] was instructed to furnish a copy of the Constitution, By Laws &c to Mr Collins."[58]

On April 17, 1868, the Alpha minutes recorded that "Reports of the Committees" were ordered concerning "the prosperity of our efforts at the Virginia Military Institute and the University of Georgia."[59] In his diary dated the following day, Ammen wrote that he had heard from Collins "that he has Gamma Lodge established. Excelsior!" In the marginalia of that date he notated in red, "Gamma is older than Beta."[60]

Gamma Lodge was established on March 8, 1868, at the University of Georgia; a written charter was issued by Knight Commander J. F. Rogers on April 10, 1869.[61] The charter members of the fraternity were William Wilson Collins, Henry W. Woodruff, J. C. McMichael, R. T. Barksdale, and Thomas R. Lyon. Other early and celebrated members of Gamma were John Temple Graves, journalist and orator; Clark Howell Sr., editor of the *Atlanta Constitution;* Hugh Mason Dorsey, governor of Georgia; and, Alton Hosch, dean of the Lumpkin Law School at the University of Georgia.[62]

John Hardeman amended this list later to include others. "Sometime ago… there sprang up a new secret organization—the KA, or Kappa Alpha. Collins, Barksdale, Lyon, F. Harris, Christian, Harrison, McMichael, Brunell, Woodruff, Edwards, Jordan & Robertson are the only ones known to have belonged to it.."[63]

"She was organized, not in 1869, but April 6, 1868," noted Hardeman. "As soon as Ammen became KC he sent to us a charter written on Ladies' note paper. It was in the fall of 1868 for I know it was sent to Collins, who left Athens in the spring of 1869. When Collins became KC he at once had charters printed & sent one. The Chapter kept both, Collins thought that the printed ones looked better. He had them printed after he left college."[64]

"Early meetings were held in dormitories of members and later in a rented hall above a store on Broad Street in downtown Athens…the chapter moved to a house on Prince Street."[65] From this temporary location the lodge moved "back to an upstairs hall" and continued with its "rent and move" tradition. "Finally, a house was rented on Jackson Street and later the longtime home of Gamma on Hancock Avenue was purchased."[66]

*The Reverend Benjamin Wofford (1780–1850)*

Following fast on the heels of the almost-simultaneous emergence of the Beta and Gamma Chapters of Kappa Alpha, came the news of the founding of a new lodge at Wofford College in Spartanburg, South Carolina.

Wofford College, at the time, was a relatively new institution. The eponymous founder of the school, Benjamin Wofford, was born in 1780 close to the south bank of the Tyger River in Spartanburg County, South Carolina, the son of Joseph and Martha Wofford.[67] He attended a religious camp meeting in 1800 and was so inspired by the presiding elder, George Dougherty, that he felt the call to preach and became a circuit rider for almost sixteen years.[68] Wofford's district was the Hartford Circuit, which extended from Nashville to Cincinnati.[69] In the course of his duties, he met and married Anna Todd, the daughter of a local and wealthy planter, on July 30, 1807. Anna's father, Thomas Todd, built the couple a small house on his estate at the time of their marriage, and when the old man died, in 1809, the couple moved from their diminutive "red house" into the main building.

In 1816, Wofford secured a local post as a circuit minister in the Enoree and Reedy River Districts. When his mother-in-law passed away in 1818, the couple inherited the family property and financial interests. After several years Benjamin decided to leave the ministry and devote himself to the family businesses; by a series of shrewd investments in bank stocks and real estate,

Wofford increased the family fortune exponentially. Perhaps under his wife's influence, he also became interested in the value of higher education and contributed to Randolph-Macon College in Virginia.

Anna died in 1835, and less than a year later Wofford married Maria Scott Barron of Virginia. In 1840, the couple moved from the Todd plantation into Courthouse Square in Spartanburg. In 1844, Benjamin Wofford bought a plot of land for the purpose of building a school or college. By the late 1840s, he had acquired a substantial mass of funds and being childless and of a devote nature, he wondered how be might use his life's savings to the best advantage. At first he considered dividing his legacy to numerous Methodist charities, but a fellow cleric, Hugh Walker, convinced Wofford that the most efficacious plan was to leave his bequest for a single purpose—the establishment of a Methodist college. Thus, on February 1, 1850, Wofford signed a will leaving the then-enormous sum of $100,000 to establish "a college for literary, classical, and scientific education, to be located in my native district, Spartanburg."[70] One-half of the donation was allocated for the purchase of land and the erection

*Wofford College, Main Building, circa 1854*

of buildings, the rest for establishing an endowment. Eight months later on December 2, 1850, the Reverend Benjamin Wofford died.

A charter was obtained in 1851. In 1854 the first buildings of Wofford College were completed and, in October of the same year, the school opened. The trustees engaged noted architect Edward C. Jones of Charleston to lay out the campus. The central design included the impressive "Main Hall"—constructed in the Tuscan style—the president's home, and four faculty residences; Jones also contrived an intricate network of paths, lawns, and gardens to complement the overall effect.[71] The Main Building contained seven rooms for recitations, a handsome chapel, two large halls for the use of the debating societies, a library, a laboratory, and a museum.[72]

The first president of the college was W. A. Wightman, who had formerly been at Randolph-Macon College, and he in turn left Wofford to launch another Methodist college, Birmingham-Southern, in 1857. He was followed by Albert M. Shipp, who led the college through the desperate days of the Civil War and the hardships of Reconstruction.

"The college commenced its regular scholastic exercises on the first day of August 1854, with two classes, viz.: Freshman and Sophomore."[73] In 1854, classes started with three professors lecturing and seven students attending. By 1860, those numbers increased to 76, however, the exigencies of the Civil War decimated the student body in a spectacular manner, no new students matriculated in 1865.[74] In 1864, Professors James Carlisle and David Duncan, in order to avoid closing, organized Wofford as a high school.[75]

After the war, because of the diligence, energy, and exhortations of the president Albert M. Shipp and the faculty both the finances of the institution and the number of students either entering or returning grew steadily. By the time that William Rogers arrived and organized the Delta Lodge of Kappa Alpha at the school, the number of students had swollen to 90 and the following year the pool of recruits increased to 106.[76]

William Anson Rogers attended Washington College during the 1867–1868 session and at that time became a member of the Kappa Alpha fraternity. The following fall he transferred to Wofford College and by October was registered as a freshman at that institution.[77] He must have immediately communicated his desire to found a chapter there. A month later it is noted in the records of the Alpha chapter that "permission was granted to Wm A Rogers to establish a Lodge at Wofford College, Spartanburg, South Carolina. The KC was ordered to write out, and send him, all papers necessary for the Lodge."[78] Rogers had even made a preliminary report in which he filed the required information:

I No. of students at the College Department "75 or 80" and in the "Preparatory Department 24"
II He is acquainted with about three-quarters of the whole number of students
III At present no secret societies there.
IV He belongs to the Freshman Class. He has been at the College the required length of time.[79]

The Alpha minutes noted that the request was approved for "the Purser was ordered to give over Rogers an order for badges."[80] Rogers reported that he had already secured two seniors and a junior—"all of excellent standing."[81] On February 23, 1869, "in a retired room of the old Evans residence on Church Street," four students were initiated into the lodge.[82] "The Delta Lodge of the Kappa Alpha Order was organized, at the time and place above written, by Mr. Wm A. Rogers, a quondam member of the Alpha Lodge at Washington College, Lexington, Va., who initiated the following members:—Edwin W. Peeples and Hope H. Newton of the Senior class, and Lawrence D. Hamer of the Junior class. The following officers were then elected for the present year: W.A. Rogers, GM, E.W. Peeples, SM., H.H. Newton, G.S., L.D. Hamer, K-a-A. Mr. Jno. Woods was then elected as a suitable person to become a member of our Order." [83]

On March 11, 1869, the Grand Scribe, Hope Newton, read a letter from Samuel Ammen, "the KC of the Alpha Lodge, stating that the By-Laws, Charter, &c. would be sent. His letter was full of encouragement to the Delta Lodge."[84]

Lines of communication were also open with William Wilson Collins who inaugurated the Gamma Chapter at the University of Georgia. On March 18, Rogers heard from his compatriot, "The GM read the Lodge an encouraging letter from Bro. Collins of the Gamma Lodge."[85] Almost immediately a bracing communication was also received from Knight Commander Ammen, suggesting that Collins and Ammen were still working in concert on their project of "extension."[86] Both Collins and Rogers responded to Alpha. Ammen wrote in his abbreviated notes for the times that on April 14, 1869, that letters from "Gamma & Delta were read."[87]

The regular business of setting up the material aspects of the Lodge commenced. On April 19, a motion was made "that a Committee of two be appointed to purchase things necessary for the Lodge—lamps, curtains, &c" and also "to order half a dozen badges."[88] On April 26th Brother Gamewell, who later became a professor at Wofford and served in that capacity for sixty-five years, "entertained the Lodge with a very interesting and instructive essay… and Brother Woods reported the purchase of the necessary things for the Lodge."[89] A week later Brother Peeples deemed "our present place of meeting as being too much exposed and proposed to endeavor to get a more secret place."[90] In June, Grand Master Rogers turned his attention from pragmatic and material to the structural and philosophical matters, he made a motion "that as we are not certain about the Constitutional point, we write immediately to Alpha Lodge for information." He also asked the assembly's thought on the propriety of holding an end-of-the-year convivium and with "a majority in favor, it was determined to have one."[91]

This was the last meeting for William Rogers as Grand Master and he had accomplished much in that office: he had hatched and nursed the chapter from its inception, worked diligently to ensure it was following the proper rules and procedures, watched over the preparations and details of the physical manifestations of setting up a lodge, and, most important, recruited the cream of the crop as the chapter's members. John Wilds Shipp was the son of the president of Wofford, Albert M. Shipp; and J. Augustus Gamewell was the son of Whatcoat Ashby Gamewell, a member of the original board of trustees of Woffold College. Shortly after school reopened the next fall, on October 9, 1869, the first meeting of the session was called to order and President Shipp's son was elected Grand Master.

At Wofford, because of new blood and a relative lack of competition, Delta increased in size, reputation, and enthusiasm; at Washington College, with the departure of the old guard, the innovators, the engineers of internal governance the fortunes of "Old Alpha" waned—just as Delta was waking up, Alpha was going to sleep. In the fall of 1869, few men were initiated in Alpha; in the winter of 1870, candidates were rejected, fees were raised from two dollars to ten, and a general malaise of apathy seemed to pervade the activities of Old Alpha. Sensing an impending doom, on May 28, 1870, a meeting was held to prepare Beta to take over the leadership of the Order.[92] On June 2, 1870, a gathering was held in Lexington that Ammen termed "the last meeting."[93] The man who had done so much to ensure the survival of the Order wrote, "Alpha Chapter ceased to exist. Its exclusive authority passed then to Beta, which in April '71 elected Collins KC."[94]

The next institution that formed a chapter of Kappa Alpha was Emory College (now University) which was named for a Methodist bishop, John Emory, who died in a carriage mishap in 1834. "The real beginning of Emory was at the Georgia Methodist Convention held in Washington, Ga., in 1834."[95] A delegate from Georgia, Allen Turner, remonstrated against a plan that intended to assign all church support to Randolph-Macon College in Virginia and maintained that "Georgia Methodists needed a college of their own."[96]

Although Turner's arguments had no immediate effect, nevertheless within a year the discussions concerning an institution in Georgia gained merit among the hierarchy of the Methodist Church. Dr. Harvey Warren Cox stated, "Emory College grew out of the Georgia Conference Manual Labor School... which opened in Covington, in March 1835.... Before the school was well under way, Dr. Ignatius Few, its president, made known to the board of visitors his desire to enlarge its operations. This was the origin of Emory College."[97]

Following President Few's recommendation, the Methodist Conference gave its consent to his project and the state legislature chartered the college on December 10, 1836. The college was laid out on 1,400 acres of property in a forest near Covington, and the town that grew up around it was given the name Oxford. Fifteen students of the freshman and sophomore classes matriculated on September 17, 1838; "the course of study was in the orthodox classical mold" and the first graduation consisted of three students in 1841. In the years leading up to the Civil War the number of students grew steadily, with an average graduating class numbering about twenty students. Emory College lost the majority of its student body during the Civil War and experienced a resurgence of applicants after the soldiers returned home. Cox wrote, "Because of the war, the college closed in 1861, and did not reopen until 1866. During the conflict the campus buildings were used as Confederate hospitals."[98]

*Emory College, Oxford, Georgia. July 18, 1860*

Emory maintained, as did most other colleges, two debating societies to complement the normal course of studies. Almost every student belonged to either one such society or the other; faculty mentors and university supervision of the operations of these clubs were a matter of course. As the populations of the colleges became progressively larger and more diversified, in both social status and aspirations, "the increased size and democratization of the literary societies no doubt decreased the intimacy and status that membership in them had been able to provide" and students began to look for other outlets to accommodate those social needs. As a result, the emergence of "secret societies" on campus fulfilled the desire to belong to an intimate and close-knit group and the lure of arcane rituals fueled the imagination and more and more students aspired to become members of these exclusive clubs.

One of the first organizations of this nature established at Emory was an offshoot of the Mystic Order of the Seven, which had been "formed in 1837 by seven students at Wesleyan College in Connecticut, the members met secretly... and members used mystic symbols to communicate meeting dates and locations and selected pseudonyms... to separate themselves from the rest of the student population."[99]

The provisions of the constitution of the Mystic Order called for the establishment of lodges at other colleges, which resulted in the first chapter of the Order of Seven's being established by a transfer student. "Henry R. Branham, a member of the Original Mystic Order of Seven, transferred to Emory College in 1841 and established... the Temple of the Sword."[100] The division at Emory of the Mystic Order was known as the Irinian Society and at the University of Georgia it was called the Temple of the Skull and Bones. Thus, at Emory and the other colleges, secret societies, or fraternities, both came

*Epsilon Chapter of Kappa Alpha at Emory College, Oxford, Georgia*

about from a colonization of a mother lodge and from the social inadequacies of the debating clubs of the postbellum era. Although social fraternities were more social and secular than their immediate ancestors, they maintained, in large part, some of the ethical mission and intellectual tenor of their predecessors.

The challenges of the war had not only interrupted the academics of Emory College but also put a practical end to all societies connected with the institution. Kappa Alpha historian William Hamilton stated that a warrant was issued to Idus L. Fielder in June 4, 1869, by the Knight Commander Samuel Ammen to "organize a chapter of the Fraternity at the college."[101] In the fall term of 1869 the Epsilon Chapter emerged, its first initiates were John F. Bonnell, Howard W. Key, Charles E. Dowman, and Micajah T. Singleton. The chapter received its formal charter in 1872 through William W. Collins, Knight Commander; this charter was destroyed by the fire that consumed the Chapter Hall in 1891, but was reissued by Samuel Ammen in the same year.[102]

The last outposts of the early expansion of Kappa Alpha were both located in Virginia, in near proximity to one another, and both were produced through the efforts of one of the original members of the Order—Jo Lane Stern. Lane's first effort was to be at Randolph-Macon College in Ashland, Virginia, and the second at Richmond College. Stern may have first set his sights on Richmond College, where he likely attended classes on returning from the war, His first success was at Randolph-Macon. Although his initial proposal was made in the spring of 1868, results were not realized for more than a year.

Randolph-Macon College is the oldest Methodist college in continuous use since its date of charter. The first recorded mention of the college occurred on February 24, 1825, at the Methodist Virginia Conference, when it was proposed that "our Church consider and report the best method to consider and report the best method of establishing" a seminary.[103]

In 1830, a bill of incorporation was introduced into the Virginia General Assembly with the initial designation of Henry-Macon College, but the name was quickly changed to Randolph-Macon, leaving Patrick Henry, a former resident of Hanover, out of the picture. John Randolph of Roanoke was a

*Randolph-Macon College, Boydton Campus, circa 1860*

member of an old family of Virginia and had played an important role in the House of Representatives and as minister to Russia. Nathaniel Macon also with a distinguished career—he had been the Speaker of the House of Representatives, President Pro Tempore of the U.S. Senate, and served as a senator for the state of North Carolina; nevertheless, "he lived in remarkably humble circumstances."[104] Both gentlemen seemed to have been of eccentric and cantankerous behaviors, Randolph was given to taking opium and Macon was described as being so contrary that "if he drowned, his body would be found upstream."[105]

The campaign to raise funds for the college began in earnest in 1830 and by June of that year the board had purchased 241 acres of land. In 1836, the president of the board sold the trustees 21 acres and a house. The original campus was located near Boydton, Virginia, in Mecklenburg County, close to the North Carolina border. The school opened its doors on October 9, 1832, with the first record of matriculation's being in 1837, "with over one hundred students ranging in age from sixteen to twenty-six signing up."[106]

In 1832, the main building was completed, an impressive structure of four stories and "served many purposes: dormitory, classroom, library and chapel."[107] The central area of the building "housed the chapel, lecture rooms, a laboratory, and the literary societies."[108] Student lodging was arranged around the four stairwells and dining took place in a separate structure known as Steward's Hall. An additional building was constructed to the side of the main hall in 1834. The trustees also erected homes for the professors and a dwelling for the president—a brick house "unpretentious … of Jeffersonian simple elegance … with lovely proportions."[109]

The impact of the war had depleted the resources and student population of Randolph-Macon, which, as in other colleges transitioned into a preparatory school. The institution's former substantial endowment, having been invested in Confederate bonds, evaporated and left the college in a precarious position. After Lee's surrender at Appomatox the campus endured the occupation of Federal troops and freedmen. James Edward Scanlon quoted that "some U.S. troops and freedmen took possession of the College buildings … the occupation lasted four months and the buildings were damaged only as soldiers and freedmen know how to do." [110]

During the middle of the war, in 1863, the Virginia Conference "resolved that we recommend the Trustees of Randolph-Macon College to remove it from its present to some more eligible location."[111] Even after the college reopened, enrollment figures were dismal and most of the students attending were preparatory boys rather than college men. In August 1865, the trustees voted to eliminate the professorships at the Boydton campus, leaving only William A. Smith, who had been elected president of the college in 1846, to teach classes.

Besides the devastions of the war, the isolated location at Boydton presented an almost insurmountable obstacle to increasing the enrollment of students and attracting a qualified faculty and "one of the serious impediments to attracting students, in addition to regional economic difficulties, was transportation."[112] Roads were in poor condition and Boydton did not have a railroad. As the accustomed mode of transportation had become by train, "a carriage ride of any distance became a nuisance and a burden."[113] It was decided to abandon Boydton and relocate somewhere more accesible and commercially viable.

For these reasons, on July 11, 1866, it was resolved "that a committee be appointed to ascertain what accommodations and on what terms, and what inducements generally can be obtained for transferring R.M. College to Petersburg, Richmond, Lynchburg, or any other place."[114] The trustees of the college started discussions regarding the most suitable location for the new home of the institution. The town of Ashland, which was situated between Richmond and Fredericksburg and maintained a depot on the lines of the Richmond, Fredericksburg and Potomac Railroad, became an early contender. In addition to its location, "that town, on the railroad line, had come to the notice of the college's trustees in November 1866, when the owners of a bankrupt hotel tried to sell it to the college."[115]

The new president, Thomas Johnson, sent out inquiries to officers of the RF&P Railroad, wondering what considerations the railroad might offer to entice the trustees to settle on Ashland as the college's new home. The directors of the RF&P, believing that it would be in the company's best interest for this move to take place—as a college in Ashland would increase the population of the town, would increase property values there (and the railroad had substantial holdings in the area), and would increase the number of fares.[116] Thus, the railroad offered to move, free of charge the library, scientific apparatus,

*Lithograph of Randolph-Macon College, Ashland*

professors, and officers to Ashland; to transport food supplies to the college gratis; to convey to the college nineteen and a half acres of property in the town; and, to arrange for officers, professors, trustees, and their familities free or discounted fare on the railway.[117]

Several friends of Randolph-Macon and two of its trustees, whether for personal or philanthropic considerations, resolved to force the issue and on "May 13, 1868, purchased the defunct Ashland Hotel for $10,000." The hotel consisted of "seventeen frame buildings of varying sizes"; they ranged from two bars and a ballroom, a bowling alley, a ladies' bath, kitchens, and seven cottages of varying sizes, in addition to the hotel building convenient to the depot.[118] The center of the campus, the hotel, was a deserted establishment that, in its former life, been a pleasant retreat for the middle-class clientele of Richmond and Fredericksburg.

The hotel was transformed into a college by reimagining the buildings already extant, "The main hotel building held classrooms on the first floor and dorm rooms on the second, and many other structures were alloted to new purposes. The ballroom became the chapel and literary halls, and three buildings were used for faculty housing."[119] James Edward Scanlon described the move of the trustees and their confederates as "a coup d'etat, one engineered by the laity of the board.... By the time the full board met to ponder the future of the college, the decision was very nearly forced upon them."[120]

As was common in most other institutions of learning of the time, the absence of students occasioned by the war created both a desire and a necessity to return to the routine and purpose of normal life at the war's conclusion. In former times the major purpose for a college education was either to prepare an individual for the church and the campus was often isolated from the temptations of the city. In the postwar era, the purpose shifted from the sacred to the profane; a majority of the new students sought to improve their economic situation rather than to elevate their souls; they were looking for a job rather than a calling. Most had little desire to be sequestered in the countryside, but rather wanted to be in an evironment that was urbane, exciting, and accessible.

The urge to find a higher purpose in life, to secure a reliable way of making a living, to advance one's social status—all compelled the returning veterans, and those coming into adulthood, to seek a more-advanced education. In addition, many colleges transitioned from a religious concentration in an isolated location. They were founded, or were moved to sites that were more accessible, more urban, and more exciting, with missions that were more pragmatic, secular, and focused on securing employment. The changes attracted a larger and more diverse group of students. Many of the new matriculates were middle class and boosted populations that had previously been restricted to the sons of elite families—thus increasing the student bodies, the competition for grades, the rigor of the professors, and the wish to belong.

The new Ashland campus opened for business on October 1, 1868. In the first year, 60 students enrolled; the next year, 100. The burgeoning population, coupled with the absence of competition, made the new Randolph-Macon a favorable place to establish a new fraternity. On July 9, 1870, the General Assembly declared, "The removal of the aforesaid college is hereby ratified and confirmed, and there be and is hereby established in Ashland, in the county of Hanover, in this commonwealth, a seminary of learning for the instruction of youth in the various branches of science and literature, the useful arts, agriculture, and the learned and foreign languages."[121]

In the early nineteenth century, the fraternity was a new and novel type of organization and the population of colleges and universities was restricted to the scions of wealthy families. The democratization of the 1830s brought the common man, to a degree, into the fold of the educated elite. The mission of institutions of higher learning transformed from instilling character, duty to God and country, and performing the activity expected of one's social status into a more practical quest of preparing oneself for an occupation. Particularly, after the war, encouraged by funding and subsidies, the introduction of the middle class into higher education swelled the matriculation rolls of colleges. The exigences of the Civil War had eliminated or diminished the exsistence of social clubs, but with a resurgence of students also came a desire, or even a need, to become a member of a brotherhood. Students routinely belonged to the literary societies, which were present on any campus worth its name and usually existed in competing pairs for spurring intellectual rivalry. But many were seeking a more relaxed and symbiotic setting—one that also carried with it an intense sense of loyalty and comraderie.

When Jo Lane Stern arrived at Ashland with a letter from Robert E. Lee, there were no fraternal organizations at Randolph-Macon. Historian James Scanlon noted the limited number of these societies persisted until the end of the nineteenth century and that the ones that existed had small memberships, possessed no houses of their own, and that the fraternity brothers did not live together as a social unit but were scattered all over campus. In the decades following the Civil War there were five fraternities established at Randolph-Macon; Kappa Alpha (1869), Phi Kappa Sigma (1872), Phi Delta Theta (1873), Sigma Chi (1874), and Kappa Sigma (1889).[122]

The first mention of the Zeta Chapter at Randolph-Macon College appears in the minutes of Old Alpha in the fall of 1869: "Mr Stern made a very interesting report, in regard to the Zeta Lodge at Randolph-Macon; the establishment of which, is owing, mainly to the energy and zeal of the above-mentioned gentleman. He stated that he had initiated two (2) of the best men at the College, and that he had received a letter from them, saying that they were fully organized."[123]

The first gentlemen conscripted by Stern were Edward Scott Johnson and Frank M. Anderson. The excitement generated by the new and novel type of "secret" organization and the independent nature of being a society not directly controlled by the authorities of the school and the enthusiasm for becoming a member of an exclusive club, led to a rush to sign up and be accepted. Within five weeks of the first initiations, and before the end of the year, seven more students had joined: Philip N. Sanderson, Bernard Briel, John Hannon, John Wilson Jr., Herbert E. Weisiger, Jefferson W. Duffy, and H. L. Newbill. By the end of spring term the number of brothers had expanded to twenty.

The first records for Zeta were not meticulously recorded. At the first

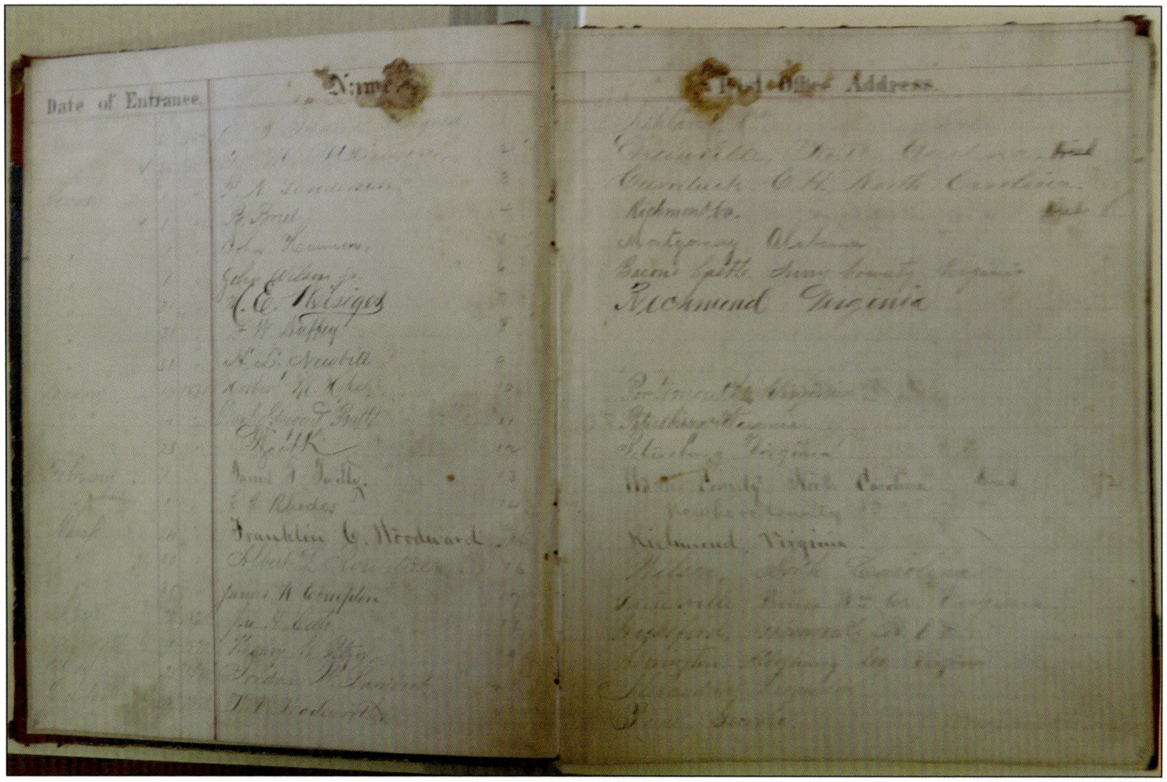


*Zeta Lodge Log Book, Randolph-Macon College, 1869*

recorded meeting it was noted: "Owing to the unsettled condition of the new chapter and the consequent irregularity in the time and place of meetings, there were not definite minutes kept until April 12 but from December to that time… John Hannon, John Wilson Jr., J. W. Duffey, H. L. Newbill, H. E. Weisiger, D. G. Butts, H. H. Hope, G.W. Scott, F. C. Woodward, C. C. Rhodes, J. F. Twitty, J. W. Compton, and A. L. Roundtree were initiated."[124]

In the following year, 1870, the chapter planned a building in which to hold meetings (very likely the one in the photograph opposite), the fulfillment of which was accomplished by the "generosity and energy" of one of the brethren. Years later, because of a fall in revenues, the young band was forced to give up their hall and rent a room from one of the literary societies. The rigorous examination of candidates in the 1882–83 session caused membership to fall to four, but by the spring of the year it was back at normal levels.[125]

*Zeta Chapter, Randolph-Macon College, March 8, 1871*
*Several of the earliest members are included in this photograph: Daniel G. C. Butts, Frank M. Atkinson, P. N. Sanderson, John Hannon, H. L. Newbill, Herbert H. Hope, W. W. Wadsworth, S. G. Ferguson, Jas. R. Humphrey, J. F. Twitty, F. C. Woodward, Dabney Price, J. W. Compton, J. H. Cato, and J. W. Lambert.*

In Lexington, on the day following the first initiations in Ashland, in a meeting of the Old Alpha, Stern informed the members of the fraternity that Zeta Lodge had joined the fold. The next year, 1870, Zeta showed a greater propensity for attracting new members than for creating an internal infrastructure. Presumably, the vast majority of the constitution, bylaws, officer designations, grips, badges, and ceremonies were adopted directly or with modifications of those handed down by Ammen and Alpha.

One of the most interesting traditions about the founding of Zeta, and later the Eta Chapter at Richmond College was the personal involvement of Jo Lane Stern's former commander, the concurrent president of Washington College, and personal benefactor—General Robert E. Lee. It must be remembered that Stern had been a telegraph operator for General Lee during the war, that he had been a family favorite of Lee's daughters and a frequent visitor to his residence in Lexington, and, as his greatest mark of favor and trust, the only known person outside of the family to ride Lee's trusted steed—Traveller.

It has been long told that when Stern arrived at Randolph-Macon (and later at Richmond College), that he carried with him a letter of introduction for the bearer and a recommendation for his purpose for the authorities of the aforementioned institutions. In 1922, William Doty wrote in his work *Samuel Zenas Ammen and the Kappa Alpha Order* that General Stern had personally told him that "he [General Lee] gave me permission to go to Randolph-Macon College to establish a Kappa Alpha Chapter."[126] This book was published during Jo Lane Stern's lifetime and it is unlikely that he would have let such a statement, had it been inaccurate, go unchallenged.

A longtime member of Kappa Alpha and keeper and collector of fraternity lore, whose father was the governor of Virginia during the Civil and who has been said to have broached the subject of the office of president with General Lee, Greenlee D. Letcher, wrote to Randolph-Macon authorities in 1934, "I understood General Jo Lane Stern to tell me … that when he went to Randolph Macon about 1869 to found a Kappa Alpha Chapter, he carried a letter from General Robert E. Lee and as soon as the authorities learned that he had a letter from Gen'l Lee, they at once gave him permission for the Chapter, saying that anything that Gen'l Lee approved would be approved by them."[127]

Captain Letcher even attempted to retrieve the letter from General Stern's sister-in-law, Mrs. Cary Ellis Stern, for it had been rumored that the self-same letter had become a sacred shrine in the home of the Reverend Ellis, having been placed on display in a glass case in the parlor.[128]

Unfortunately, Mrs. Stern no longer had the letter, if, indeed, it had ever made an appearance in her home on Grove Avenue in Richmond. Apparently, the original had been kept in the archives at Randolph-Macon. Following requests, an extensive search was made by the archivist at Randolph-Macon.

The catalog showed that no such letter was to be found. A more-exhaustive investigation was promised, however, with the tantalizing response:

> Dear Dr. Clagett,
> I went to talk to my boss Laurie Preston and explained your request. She nodded seemingly with understanding of the topic. Laurie said that at some point in the 20th century the college did have this letter but unfortunately it was probably taken by someone. It has been missing for at least 40 years. What a shame! I am sorry to report this news to you.
>
> My best to you in your continued research,
> Mary Virginia Currie[129]

It, of course, would be a wonderful find, if the letter itself ever makes another showing. Multiple statements by General Stern himself to various persons and the confirmation by authorities at Randolph-Macon of its existence, if not its tangible presence, however, give great credence to an important and engaging tale. General Lee, who was seen in an almost divine light in the South, was even was so well considered in the North that the *New York Herald* had proposed his name as the Democratic candidate to run against his old foe, Ulysses S. Grant.[130]

The imprimatur of his name and the weight of his reputation made a request to the college administration by General Lee almost impossible to reject. Thus, *verbum sapienti satis est*, and it was done. Lee is said to have written a second letter on this subject to the head of the faculty at Richmond College.

Jo Lane Stern's intention to found a chapter at Richmond College preceded the reality by almost two years. In the minutes of the Alpha Chapter in the summer of 1868 it was recorded, "Permission was granted to Bro Stern to take steps towards establishing a Lodge of our Order at Richmond College in this state."[131] Perhaps Stern's early interest in Richmond College stemmed from his immediate history after the war.

*Ryland Hall, Richmond College, circa 1909*

Stern, who had at the age of twelve began his career as a telegraph operator for the Confederate army and had been under General Lee's command at Jericho Mills, was paroled in Richmond on May 2, 1865, and returned to school.[132] He mentioned that he went to school in Richmond following the war; he may have resided with his brother who resided at 1700 Grove Avenue, very close to the then-campus of Richmond College, a convenient walk to lectures.

Richmond College officially closed during the war and college records say that it did not reopen in 1865. In his history of Richmond College, however, Reuben Alley noted, "Motivated by a grave sense of responsibility, Trustees of Richmond College met on July 24, 1865 and resolved to open at once under the supervision of President Ryland and Professor George F. Dabney, who together would offer preparation for young men recently discharged from the army."[133]

Although official records are not presently found at the University of Richmond concerning this time frame and the reference librarian asserted that classes did not reconvene until 1866, she said Reuben Alley, the author of the *History of the University of Richmond,* was also the editor of the *Religious Herald*, a Baptist newspaper of the day, and was the final word on the matter. Alley's book cited the *Religious Herald* for November 16, 1865, which detailed the school's activities in the immediate aftermath of the war, "The Richmond College, which has been suspended since the early part of the war, has, unfortunately, by the great Confederate crash, lost most of its endowment.

The Trustees, deeming it impracticable, at present, to re-establish the regular courses, requested President Ryland and Professor Dabney to open a high school on the premises. The attendance is small, but pupils, we have no question, will receive through and faithful training."[134] Alley also noted that in July 1866, there was a meeting of "number of alumni and fourteen graduates."[135]

The combined statements give a good indication that Richmond College opened in July 1865, with the specific mission of educating "young men recently discharged from the army." Noting that Jo Lane Stern was probably living in Richmond in close proximity to Richmond College, and his early desires were to implant a chapter of Kappa Alpha there, it is plausible that he attended Richmond College before he went to Lexington. Seeing that there were fourteen graduates at Richmond in the summer of 1866, it is also logical to assume that college-level courses were being offered.

Richmond College, like Washington College and the other institutions that acted as homes to the early chapters, had a religious affiliation. As early as 1820, the Goshen Association, an organizational unit of the Baptist Church of Virginia, appointed a committee "to study the question and solicit churches for contributions to support a program of ministerial education."[136] On June 8, 1830, an assemble of Baptist ministers met and decided that "it is expedient that the Baptists of this state form an Education Society for the improvement of the ministry," and to that purpose wrote a constitution and elected a board of officers.[137] In a subsequent meeting of the group in August of that year the planning committee drew up a plan to found an institution with a regular course of study, to employ appropriate teachers, to find a suitable location, and to divide the school into literary and theological departments.[138]

On March 31, 1832, the society agreed to purchase property, known as Brook Tavern, as the site of the first manifestation of the college, but it was soon decided that the plan was impracticable and the location should be closer to Richmond. That location, Spring Farm, was in operation for two years when it, too, was found to be an inopportune site for a seminary. In 1834, it was decided to move the college to the Haxall property, which lay about a mile beyond the then borders of Richmond. Its location was described as "in a neighborhood of the first intelligence and respectability ... nearly equi-distant from two public roads without exposure to interruption from either."[139] The property included a main house, three stories high "finished in the most elegant and durable style"; accompanied by three smaller buildings—also with three stories; in addition, there was a greenhouse and an icehouse.[140]

Alley wrote that the move was advantageous in that the property possessed fine buildings and a location that had "easy access to Richmond with its many opportunities for the intellectual and social development of students."[141] In December 1834, the seminary moved its furniture and equipment to the property, "which had been improved to accommodate sixty students."[142] In 1839, the Education Society appointed thirty-eight trustees for Richmond College and on March 4, 1840, "the act of incorporation for Richmond College had been passed by the General Assembly."[143]

In the period intervening between the incorporation and the beginning of the Civil War, the trustees of the college had laid "a sure foundation for the future development of a quality education," and it was a period of slow but steady growth.[144] Until 1842, there were two preparatory classes, a freshman and a sophomore class; in 1848, a junior class was added and in 1849, a senior class. It was in that year that the first Bachelor of Arts degree was awarded.[145] In 1859, the college enrolled 114 students and launched two literary societies—Mu Sigma Rho and the Philologian, which were provided rooms for their meetings.[146]

As the threat of war approached, bellicose rhetoric was heard and financial support for the cause was raised. In November 1859, "a large and enthusiastic group of students met and resolved to form themselves into a military company. The resolution was supported by the faculty and arms were supplied by Governor Henry A. Wise, who "thought the step highly commendable in the students."[147] The student volunteers became known as the "Richmond College Minute Men" with J. M. Binsford elected as captain.[148]

As elsewhere, the trials of war weighed heavily on the college and its location in the capital of the Confederacy made its struggle all the more difficult. After the fall of the city, Federal troops occupied the campus buildings to which they did considerable damage. "Stripped of most of its resources by circumstances of war, the college depended for survival upon friends who themselves were in distress."[149] Nevertheless, many made what contributions that they were able to make and funds were made available from sources out of state as well. "Although the condition of the school seemed quite hopeless in 1866, yet within less than five years ... of public distress and destitution ... the college has not only regained the position held in its best days but also won new laurels."[150] These changes came about at the end of Reconstruction and the improvement in the national economy.

By 1870, Richmond College had almost doubled the enrollment of students, from 90 before the war to 160; between 1849 and 1870 the college conferred degrees on 71 students; the faculty had grown from five to nine with a corresponding expansion of courses; buildings had been repaired and two brick structures housing eight dormitories were constructed; and, a law school had been established.[151] Similarly to Randolph-Macon, by the time of Stern's intercession, Richmond College had become a thriving community and its most influential professor, later to be chairman of the board, was an old comrade of General Lee, J. L. M. Curry.

*Jabez Lamar Monroe Curry*

William Doty noted in his history of Samuel Ammen and Kappa Alpha the following, "General Stern's own account of these matters is of interest: 'he [General Lee] gave me permission to go to Randolph-Macon College to establish a Kappa Alpha Chapter. He subsequently gave permission to James S. Iverson, of Macon, and me to go to Richmond to establish a chapter at Richmond College.'"[152] Stern recalled, "Our friends claimed, particularly at Richmond College, that the Fraternity must be well vouched for as General Lee had given permission to Iverson and me, and it was the talk at the time that the Honourable J. L. M. Curry, a Confederate congressman from Alabama, who had married in Richmond, and was a professor at Richmond College, stated at a faculty meeting, when it was considering the question of permitting a fraternity to be established at Richmond College, that if General Lee had permitted two of his students to come to Richmond for that purpose, he was satisfied to vote for admitting it."[153] Stern later in life wrote to Greenlee Letcher that although "the organization of the chapter at Richmond College is accredited to the Randolph-Macon KAs. Iverson and I had authority from Alpha to establish that chapter and associated the Randolph-Macon fellows with us."[154]

Stern may have had reason for concern for the Eta minutes reflected a more self-congratulatory account, "on the night of March 18th AD 1870, Messrs J.F. Twitty and D.C. Butts of Randolph Macon College, assisted by J L Stern and J S Iverson of Washington College met and initiated into the mysteries of the Kappa Alpha Order Messrs J.E.L. Holmes, of Franklin, Southampton County, Va., Henry J. Barnes of Barnesville, Charlotte County, Va., J.T. Walker of Eufaula, Barbour County, Ala., and Taylor N. Cox of Enon, Bullock County, Ala., students of Richmond College."[155]

Little more than three weeks later, on April 22nd, the four initiates met and "set about immediately to organize a Lodge at aforesaid College and held their meeting on the night of March 30th in Mr. Holmes' boarding house room on the corner of 3rd and Carey Streets, Richmond,

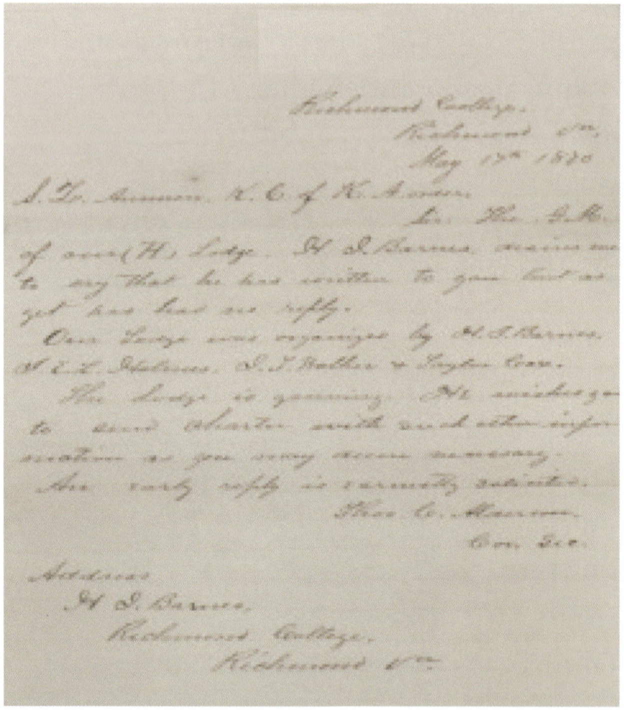
Richmond College,
Richmond Va,
May 17th 1870
S. Z. Ammen K. C. of K. A. [illegible]
[illegible]
of our (H) Lodge. H. J. Barnes desires me to say that he has written to you but as yet has had no reply.
Our Lodge was organized by H. J. Barnes, J. E. L. Holmes, J. T. Walker & Taylor Cox.
The lodge is growing. We wish you to send charter with such other information as you may deem necessary.
An early reply is earnestly solicited.
Thos. C. Alderson
Cor. Sec.
Address
H. J. Barnes,
Richmond College,
Richmond Va.

*Thomas C. Alderson to Samuel Ammen, May 17, 1870*

Va.; and voted upon the following names for membership viz. Alex Fleet, James B. Cox, and N.W. Roberts. No other business demanding their attention. They adjourned."[156]

The group quickly requested instructions from Alpha in an urgent manner, the "the GM of our Eta Lodge, H.J. Barnes, desires me to say that he has written to you but has yet has had no reply. Our Lodge was organized by H.L. Barnes, J.E.L. Holmes, J.S. Walker & Taylor Cox. The Lodge is growing, He wishes you to send charter with such other information as you may deem necessary. An early reply is earnestly solicited. Thos. C. Alderson."[157]

By the end of May, Robert Fleet of the committee to secure rooms for lodge meetings reported that "the Faculty granted us the choice of two rooms," which indicates that not only did the professors not have any objections to the establishment of a fraternity at the College but even supported it.[158]

Fraternal lodges at Richmond College, like other colleges in the second half of the nineteenth century experienced phenomenal growth; "faculty and trustees gave encouragement by a friendly attitude when a group of students sought to organize a chapter of Kappa Alpha in 1870."[159] As with the Zeta Lodge at Randolph-Macon College, the Eta Chapter of Kappa Alpha was the first fraternity on the campus of Richmond College. By 1878, the Eta Lodge had initiated sixty-seven members.

Even as Old Alpha faded in the mountains, her progenies prospered in Virginia, South Carolina, and Georgia. Her alter ego, or other self, the Beta Chapter at VMI took over the leadership of the Order, "which in April '71 elected [W. W.] Collins K.C...; then Beta ceased to exist and passed its authority to Gamma."[160]

In 1873, the Order had grown to such an extent that individual lodges were advocating for a infrastructure in which all the chapters participated and a single executive position was established to look out for the good of the Order as a whole. Thus, Gamma yeilded her power to the convention and "made the KC an officer of the Convention, outranking all other officers."[161]

## *Notes* Chapter 6:

1 Minutes of KA Sessions '66–70, "Second Copy of Minutes of Old Alpha made by S.Z.A. for Alpha." The ledger notes that "the original was lost some 20 years, found in 1893 in a garret in Virginia, near Fincastle, examined by Hubard, 1893; lost again or borrowed." Ammen 63, Kappa Alpha Archives, Lexington, Va., 1.

2 Ibid.

3 Samuel Ammen, "Diary Notes: 1893," Kappa Alpha Archives, Lexington, Va., 9.

4 Ibid., 10.

5 Ibid., 6.

6 Minutes of KA Sessions '66–70, 5.

7 Original Alpha Minutes, March 8, 1868, Kappa Alpha Archives, Lexington, Va., 71.

8 Ibid., 75.

9 Ibid.

10 The founding dates for the respective lodges are derived from: Beta at Virginia Military Institute (Original Alpha Minutes, March 8, 1868, p. 71); Gamma at the University of Georgia (John Hardeman to G. L. Snowden, February 26, 1895, Tazewell Hubard Correspondence Book, No. 2, Kappa Alpha Archives, Lexington, Va., 1895, p. 112); Delta Lodge at Woffold College ("Our Fraternity at Wofford," *Kappa Alpha Journal* 3, No. 8 [May 1891]: 436); Epsilon Chapter at Emory (William S. Hamilton, "History of the Epsilon Chapter," Memoranda of the Kappa Alpha Order, Kappa Alpha Archives, Lexington, Va. See also "Epsilon Chapter," *Kappa Alpha Journal* 7, No. 5 [February 1890]: 201; Zeta Lodge at Randolph-Macon College, The Alpha Minutes date the founding from November 27, 1869. See Original Alpha Minutes, November 27, 1869, p. 103. The Zeta Lodge Book provides notes and signatures for E. S. Johnson, from Ashland, and F. M. Atkinson, from Greenville, North Carolina, on November 26, 1869; see Kappa Alpha, Zeta Lodge, Randolph-Macon College, 1869, Vol. 1, Mss4 K1422 b, Virginia Historical Society, Richmond, Va., 1; Eta Lodge at Richmond College. Kappa Alpha Minutes, Eta Chapter: 1869–1899, RG 26.5.1.2, University of Richmond Archives, administered by the Virginia Baptist Historical Society.

11 Jennings C. Wise, *The Military History of the Virginia Military Institute* (Lynchburg, J. F. Bell Co., 1915), 30.

12 Ibid.

13 Ibid., 31.

14 Ollinger Crenshaw, *General Lee's College* (New York: Random House, 1969), 59.

15 Ibid., 60.

16 Ibid.

17 Ibid.

18 Ibid.

19 Ibid.

20 Ibid., 61.

21 Ibid.

22 Ibid., 63.

23 Ibid., 62.

24 Ibid.
25 Ibid.
26 Ibid., 64.
27 Ibid.
28 Ibid., 65.
29 Samuel Ammen, "Notes, Alpha Minutes, 1867–1868," Kappa Alpha Archives, Lexington, Va., 40.
30 Ammen, "Diary Notes, 1893," 4.
31 Original Alpha Minutes, January 24, 1868, p. 35.
32 Original Alpha Minutes, February 7, 1868, p. 53.
33 Ibid., 51.
34 Ammen, "Diary Notes, 1893," 6.
35 Original Alpha Minutes, March 8, 1868, p. 71.
36 Original Alpha Minutes, April 4, 1868, p. 77.
37 Original Alpha Minutes, April 18, 1868, p. 81.
38 Original Alpha Minutes, May 9, 1868, p. 97.
39 Ibid.
40 Ammen, "Diary Notes, 1893," 8.
41 Original Alpha Minutes, December 10, 1869, p. 105.
42 S. Z. Ammen, *History of the Kappa Alpha Order and Its Institutions* (Charlotte: Queen Printing Co., 1903), 19.
43 Original Alpha Minutes, June 2, 1870, p. 131.
44 William S. Hamilton, Memoranda Book of Kappa Alpha Order, Kappa Alpha Archives, Lexington, Va., 6.
45 "History of Alpha Chapter," *Kappa Alpha Journal* 69, No. 1 (November 1952): 44.
46 Ammen, "Diary Notes: 1893," 10.
47 Original Alpha Minutes, February 7, 1868, p. 57.
48 Original Alpha Minutes, March 21, 1868, p. 75.
49 Thomas W. Reed, *History of the University of Georgia* (Athens: University of Georgia, 1949), 6.
50 B. F. Boney, "The Rising Hope of Our Land: University of Georgia Students Over Two Centuries," *Georgia Historical Quarterly* 74, No. 1 (Spring 1990): 117.
51 Ibid., 118.
52 Ibid.
53 Reed, *History of the University of Georgia*, 786.
54 Ibid., 786.
55 Ibid., 787.
56 Ibid., 792.
57 S. Z. Ammen, "Ammen 40 - Gist of Kappa Alpha Minutes," Kappa Alpha Archives, Lexington, Va., 2.
58 Original Alpha Minutes, March 21, 1868, p. 75.

59 Original Alpha Minutes, April 17, 1868, p. 79.

60 Ammen, "Diary Notes, 1893," 7.

61 "The Minutes of the Alpha Chapter state that Rogers was elected KC by that chapter on May 1, 1868, and that his successor, Ammen, was elected as his successor on February 8, 1869.... Gamma Chapter was established on March 8, 1868, two months prior to the creation of the office of Knight Commander, Rogers was considered the proper official to issue the charter, and he dated it at the time of signing, 'April 10, 1869,' which was, of course, after his retirement from office and during the reign of his successor, Samuel Zenas Ammen." See William S. Hamilton, History of Kappa Alpha, "Gamma Chapter," Kappa Alpha Archives, Lexington, Va., 1.

62 Hamilton, History of Kappa Alpha, "Gamma Chapter," 1.

63 John Hardeman to G. L. Snowden, February 26, 1895, p. 112.

64 Ibid.

65 Hamilton, History of Kappa Alpha, "Gamma Chapter," 1.

66 Ibid.

67 J. B. O. Landrum, *History of Spartanburg County* (Atlanta: Franklin Press, 1900), 238.

68 Colyer Meriwether, *History of Higher Education in South Carolina*, Circular of Information, No. 3, 1888 (Washington, D.C.: Government Printing Office, 1889), 98.

69 "Our Fraternity at Wofford," *Kappa Alpha Journal* 3, No. 8 (May 1891): 432.

70 Colyer Meriwether, *History of Higher Education in South Carolina*, 98.

71 Personal Communication, Phillip Stone to Martin Clagett, June 19, 2014.

72 "Our Fraternity at Wofford," 433.

73 *Catalogue of Wofford College*, June 26, 1872 (Charleston: Walker, Evans & Cogswell, 1872), 20.

74 Ibid., 6.

75 Ibid., 20.

76 Ibid., 6.

77 Joseph S. Chick, *History and Catalogue of the Kappa Alpha Fraternity* (Nashville: Kappa Alpha Order, 1891), 55.

78 Original Alpha Minutes, N.D., November 1868, p. 95.

79 Ibid.

80 Ibid.

81 Original Alpha Minutes, May 9, 1868, p. 97.

82 "Our Fraternity at Wofford," 436.

83 Delta Chapter Minutes, February 23, 1869, Wofford College Archives, Spartanburg, S.C., 5.

84 Delta Chapter Minutes, March 11, 1869, p. 7.

85 Ibid., 8.

86 Delta Chapter Minutes, April 1, 1869, p. 9.

87 Samuel Z. Ammen, "Gist of Session, 1869–1870," Kappa Alpha Archives, Lexington, Va., 4.

88 Delta Chapter Minutes, April 11, 1869, p. 11.

89 Delta Chapter Minutes, April 26, 1869, p. 12.
90 Delta Chapter Minutes, May 3, 1869, p. 12.
91 Delta Chapter Minutes, June 1, 1869, p. 14.
92 Ammen, "Gist of Session, 1869–1870," 4.
93 Ibid.
94 Ibid.
95 Franklin M. Garrett, *Atlanta and Environs* (Athens: University of Georgia Press, 1969), 2:641.
96 Ibid.
97 Ibid.
98 Ibid.
99 Richard Rose, "The Emergence of Secret Societies in Antebellum Georgia Colleges," *Georgia Historical Quarterly*, 70, No. 1 (Spring, 1986): 55.
100 Ibid.
101 William S. Hamilton, "History of the Epsilon Chapter," Memoranda of the Kappa Alpha Order, Archives Kappa Alpha, Lexington, Va., N.P.; see also "Epsilon Chapter," *Kappa Alpha Journal* 7, No. 5 (February 1890): 201.
102 Hamilton, Memoranda, "History of Epsilon Chapter," N.P.
103 James Edward Scanlon, *Randolph-Macon College: A Southern History* (Charlottesville: University Press of Virginia, 1983), 23.
104 Ibid., 32.
105 Ibid.
106 Ibid., 41.
107 Ibid., 45.
108 Ibid.
109 Ibid., 47.
110 Ibid., 117.
111 Ibid., 119.
112 Ibid.
113 Ibid.
114 Ibid., 125.
115 Ibid., 126.
116 Ibid.
117 Ibid., 137.
118 Ibid., 128.
119 Virginia E. Young, *Randolph-Macon College* (Charleston: Arcadia Publishing, 2011), 7.
120 Scanlon, *Randolph-Macon College,* 128.
121 Ibid., 137.
122 Ibid., 167.
123 Original Alpha Minutes, November 27, 1869, p. 103.

124 Kappa Alpha, Zeta Lodge, Randolph-Macon College, 1869, Vol 1, Mss4 K1422 b, Virginia Historical Society, Richmond, Va., 1.

125 Chick, *History and Catalogue of the Kappa Alpha Fraternity*, 95.

126 William Kavanaugh Doty, *Samuel Zenas Ammen and the Kappa Alpha Order* (Charlottesville: Surber-Arundale Co., 1922), 44.

127 Greenlee Letcher to Randolph-Macon College, August 22, 1934, Kappa Alpha Archives, Lexington, Va.

128 Greenlee Letcher to Eva Stern, August 22, 1934, Kappa Alpha Archives, Lexington, Va.

129 Personal Communication, Mary Virginia Currie to Martin Clagett, January 29, 2014.

130 H. W. Crocker III, *Robert E. Lee on Leadership* (New York: Three Rivers Press, 1999), 167. "Others had higher aspirations for him, including political office. Despite his being barred from voting… Lee was considered as a possible gubernatorial candidate and even as a possible presidential candidate. For the latter office, he was endorsed by the *New York Herald*, which advocated that if it had any hopes of electing a former general who could defeat Republican Ulysses S. Grant in the coming election, it should nominate General R.E. Lee… making no palaver or apology."

131 Original Alpha Minutes, June 16, 1868, p. 89.

132 Greenlee Letcher, "Stern Biography," March 4, 1935, Kappa Alpha Archives, Lexington, Va., 2.

133 Reuben Alley, *History of the University of Richmond: 1830–1907* (Charlottesville: University Press of Virginia, 1971), 46.

134 *Religious Herald*, Richmond, Va., November 16, 1865, p. 1.

135 Alley, *History of the University of Richmond*, 47.

136 Ibid., 5. The boundaries of the Goshen Association, established in 1791, extended from Fredericksburg, up the Rappahannock River to Three Notched Road, down to the James River. Robert Semple, *A History of the Rise and Progress of the Baptists in Virginia* (Richmond: John Lynch Printer, 1810), 139.

137 Alley, *History of the University of Richmond,* 10.

138 Ibid.

139 Ibid., 23.

140 Ibid.

141 Ibid., 24.

142 Ibid.

143 Ibid., 32.

144 Ibid., 38.

145 Ibid., 42.

146 Ibid., 45.

147 Ibid., 44.

148 Ibid., 45.

149 Ibid., 46.

150 Ibid., 54.

151 Ibid.

152 Doty, *Ammen and the Kappa Alpha Order*, 44.

153 General Stern to William Doty, July 16, 1921, Kappa Alpha Archives, Lexington, Va.

154 General Stern to Captain Greenlee Letcher, February 12, 1930, Kappa Alpha Archives, Lexington, Va.

155 Kappa Alpha Minutes, Eta Chapter, 1869–1899, RG 26.5.1.2, University of Richmond Archives, administered by the Virginia Baptist Historical Society.

156 Ibid.

157 Miscellaneous Letter 14, Thomas C. Alderson to S. Z. Ammen, May 17, 1870, Kappa Alpha Archives, Lexington, Va.

158 Kappa Alpha Minutes, Eta Chapter, 1869–1899.

159 Alley, *History of the University of Richmond*, 77.

160 Ammen, "Gist of Session 1869–1870," 4.

161 Ibid.

*John Francis Rogers*

# 7

## Conventions and Knight Commanders

Even as the size and strength of the Kappa Alpha Order was expanding and strengthening, the Old Alpha Chapter was contracting and dying. In the 1868–1869 session at Washington College, only five members of Old Alpha were still present, and they conducted no initiations. Of the remaining five, the Knight Commander, J. F. Rogers, soon left Lexington. In 1869–1870, it had initiated only three candidates—Charles W. Clemmitt, R. Cloughton, and James S. Iverson—"so that its extinction, which occurred in 1870, was already imminent." Samuel Ammen described the decline: "After this meeting [September 28, 1868] there were in the session 1868–69 but few meetings. One in Oct. [5th]; 1 in Nov.; 1 in Feb. '69 – are recorded. There were probably not more than 5 or 6 altogether. There were no convivia, no initiations."[1] At the October 12, 1869, meeting of the Alpha Lodge, they had "no quorum present [and] the GM of the last session officiated and the regular order of business was suspended." Nevertheless, as we have seen in the previous chapter, the lack of activity so pronounced in Lexington did not extend to the efforts of its members, and former members, to expand the franchise throughout the South.[2]

The Beta Chapter fell under the direct instruction of the officer known as the Grand Master (GM), and they worked so closely with the mother chapter that it was difficult to distinguish the two. In the early years, the GM of Alpha presided over Beta Chapter meetings, Beta often used Alpha's hall, the two lodges joined together in celebrations and photo opportunities, and Ammen even recorded early Beta meetings in the Alpha minute book. As late as 1867, an Alpha was still holding court in Beta's meetings—"January 1st 1876 – Alpha and Beta met together at 2 ½ o clock P.M. Brother McCorkle of the Alpha occupying the chair."[3] At one of the first meetings of Beta, "the GM then instructed them to their duties in establishing a Lodge of our Order at the Virginia Military Institute, and offered them the use of our Room until better arrangements could be made by them." The relationship between Alpha and Beta was close and hands-on. Therefore, the members of Beta did not have a great need for written instructions and manuscript guidance from Alpha.[4]

As members of Alpha moved on to other institutions, however, and established their own lodges, it became important for the Order to have explicit documentation for matters relating to the Order's constitution, bylaws, rituals, badges, grips, and official garb. The uptick in the number of new chapters; the constant demand for more precise information; questions relating to those instructions; requests for advice; all this, along with the paralyzed state of the mother chapter, made the existence of an officer to transmit instructions and information to all chapters of central importance to the survival of the Order. At first, an officer called the Grand Scribe (G.S.) handled the task.

In the spring and summer of 1869, Delta and Epsilon joined the fold, and in the fall, Zeta and Eta. "Alpha Chapter now virtually suspended its corporate functions for the session. If there were meetings—they are not remembered or recorded. The members, however, were interested in Beta, Gamma, Delta, and Epsilon, and conferred informally about their affairs."[5]

At a meeting of the Alpha chapter on March 21, 1868, a request to establish a lodge "of our Order at the University of Georgia" was received and the "G.S. was instructed to furnish a copy of the Constitution, By Laws &c to Mr Collins."[6] On May 8, 1868, "The G.S. read an official communication from the Gamma Lodge and was instructed to reply to it."[7] In the following session, permission was granted to establish Delta at Wofford and the officer "was ordered to write out, and send him, all papers necessary for the Lodge."[8] The cavalcade of requests for detailed information—all of which had to be copied out by hand—became too much for the already overtaxed officers of Alpha Lodge, and like all good administrators, when in doubt—delegate.

This odious task was foisted on the Number III, who initially "made no complaint when the first set of papers" was ordered, "but, when the new chapters multiplied, his loud lamentations caused Ammen ... to propose [the creation] of a new officer to do this work." He was "to copy papers, do the number I's correspondence with the new chapters and supervise the new chapters."[9]

Thus, on May 1, 1868, a resolution was put forth concerning the new official, grandly entitled the Knight Commander: "The matter of having an officer in Alpha Lodge to take a general supervision over the other Lodges of this order & make reports to the same was brought up and passed. Upon motion the Soc'y went into the election of this Officer which resulted in the selection of our Bro Mr J S [F.] Rogers of Ga."[10] In the beginning, the Knight Commander was a chapter officer of Alpha subordinated to the Number I and he was elected by the chapter with "multifarious duties and powers." Initially and essentially, the post was a corresponding secretary who communicated with the newly formed lodges and transmitted to them all the papers necessary for conducting business in the proper fashion according to the constitution and bylaws of the Alpha Chapter. Within a short time, however, the KC, was responsible for all the tedious responsibilities that no one else wanted; he became "the General Supervisor of its affairs, the dispenser of charters, the collector and spender of the General Fund, the statistician, historian, publisher and judge."[11]

At this time the KC was exclusive to the Alpha Chapter and he resided in Lexington. Moreover, in the early stages, the duties of the KC were so light and insubstantial, according to Kappa Alpha historian, William Sprigg Hamilton, that "at this time we find no mention of the title of this office, nor of the origin of one adopted, nor have any mention of the duties assigned to him. In later minutes, however, we find him mentioned as the KC, and in the report of the election of officers we find that his name appears in order after that of the second chapter officer."[12]

Until the time that Old Alpha became extinct in 1870, the absolute control of new lodges resided in Alpha and was "exercised by the number I of that chapter through the Knight Commander."[13] After being elected Knight Commander, Ammen attached some of the responsibilities to that office that he had held as the Number I, writing "who as (I), before the creation of the office of Knight Commander, had directed affairs, and after the creation of that office, continued to give all orders, as being the superior officer."[14] In the waning years of Alpha the members felt that "the strenuous efforts of the previous years had given them the right... to rest [and] to hand fraternity toil over to the younger chapters."[15] At the same time it was the consensus that Alpha's control over her children was inspired "not by vanity, but by the sincere conviction that young chapters, without practical experience, require the guidance of their elders."[16]

The first Knight Commander, John Francis Rogers, was born in Macon, Georgia on July 10, 1847. As a teenager he had been a courier for General Thomas Reade R. Cobb, First Battalion, Georgia Reserve Cavalry. After the war he enrolled at Washington College and became a member of Old Alpha on March 18, 1868. Less than two months later he was elected as the first Knight Commander, and, on October 5, he was reelected. He retained that post until he left Lexington the following spring.[17] On February 8, 1869, "Mr Ammen was elected KC *vice* Mr Rogers who has returned home."[18] Despite assertions to the contrary, that the title "Knight Commander" did not appear in early Kappa Alpha documents, it was used less than six months after the creation of the office.

Ammen, through whose efforts Kappa Alpha had established a stability and an order by the use of a well-formulated and articulated set of bylaws, rituals, and constitution that made it an organization rather than a mere gathering, and he took on the position of KC in addition to the office of Grand Scribe. After graduating from Washington College, Ammen left Lexington to accept a position at Milburn Academy in Kentucky. It became apparent to all, however, that the office of Knight Commander was essential to the survival of the Order and that

Ammen's effectual participation in that role was necessary to its success. "So well had he attended to duties of his first term, and so essential was his aid to the young Order, that the Alpha reelected him to this office on November 27, 1869, in spite of the fact that he was living apart from the chapter, and this office was supposed to be a chapter office."[19]

Thus, on November 27, 1869, having left Lexington for his post in Kentucky, Samuel Ammen was reelected to that office. Ammen must have considered it a sacred duty to continue in that post.[20] During his time at Milburn Academy, he not only efficiently performed his duties as KC, but also completed his First Degree, revised the Ritual and had the Kappa Alpha Constitution printed "with additions and changes at Columbus, Kentucky."[21] At the end of the year, he left Milburn for a position at Dr. Atkinson's School for Boys in Baltimore, Maryland, where he taught Latin, Greek, and Chemistry.[22]

Ammen's physical removal from Lexington was a portent of things to come—namely that the Order had crossed the line from being a local organization into a regional institution; that an officer could be independent of the parent chapter and that "the fact that this official could function independently of any one chapter" introduced the concept of equality among the newer and more prosperous offspring. Indeed, it also anticipated the momentous and transformational changes that took place in the Convention of 1873.

The fundamental impetus for diversification, however, came from the number of lodges established both in Virginia and throughout the South. It also became evident that the children had grown larger and possessed greater energy and passion than the parent. Ammen even commented the "the Gamma, the Delta, and the Epsilon frightened their poor old mother nearly out of her wits by their rapid growth."[23] By 1874, the Gamma Chapter at the University of Georgia had initiated eighty-four, by far the most students in their lodge; followed by Epsilon at Emory College with sixty-four, Eta at Richmond claimed fifty; Delta Lodge at Wofford had forty-eight, Zeta at Randolph-Macon enlisted forty-one; Old Alpha numbered twenty; and Beta at VMI came in with the smallest number, at seventeen.[24]

"The subjugation of the other chapters to Alpha was not agreeable to the younger chapters, and they soon began to seek a position of equality and self-government, through representation in a sovereign body composed of delegates from the several chapters," Hamilton noted. "Alpha was of the opinion that new chapters, by reason of their youth, were unfit for self-government. However, to mitigate discontent, Alpha inserted in the Code of 1870, Article XVI, which provided for a meeting of delegates."[25] The conditions set forth in Ammen's constitution of 1870 were explicit and restrictive in regard to changing the basics of doing business.

The major concessions that were made to mollify the new lodges included: "The Alpha Chapter yields to the General Council of the Order the power of making additions to the Constitution; that the KC shall annually convene a Council (convention) with one representative from each chapter; that the members of the convention 'shall deliberate upon the means of extending and strengthening the Order; and, suggest such additions to the Constitution as may seem for the good of the Order.'" The limitations almost cancelled out concessions, however, for it was advised that; while Alpha would entertain suggestions made by the General Council, that it "may not change or abrogate anything already contained therein; that the suggestions of the convention would not have the force of law until the KC submitted them to all the chapters for ratification; and, that a majority of two-thirds in each chapter would be needed for the KC to declare them adopted.[26]

On March 10, 1870, the Alpha records reflect that in regard to a place of holding a convention that a "motion was made and seconded that the cities of Macon, Charleston and Richmond be submitted to the KC; so that he may decide in which of the three, the July Convention shall be held."[27] Two weeks later on March 24, further plans were made in which "a Committee of three (3) be appointed to confer with the G.S. of each Lodge, be requested to send to the G.S. of Alpha, a complete history of their several Lodges. Motion carried."[28] And on May 6 "Mr. Stern suggested that we appoint delegates to the Convention as soon as practicable; also moved that in our next letter to each of the Lodges, we request them to send us notice what business of importance they intend to bring forward at the Convention, in order that our delegates may find out the spirit of the Alpha upon it, and give their votes accordingly."[29]

Hamilton described the representation at the 1870 convention as follows, "Alpha Chapter had ceased to exist for a time in 1870, but was represented at the convention by S. Z. Ammen, Jo Lane Stern, and C.W. Clemmitt; Beta—W.M. Jerdone, Gamma—W.A. Broughton, Delta and Epsilon—[not of record], Zeta—D.G.C. Butts, Eta—R.D. Wortham."[30] He notes, however, that the 1900 catalog names Charles William Clemmitt as the delegate for Alpha.[31] And the minutes of the Zeta Lodge at Randolph-Macon College report that on May 23, 1870, "Brother Butts moved that we act to make an election of a delegate to represent us in the Convention to be held at Richmond Va., 11th July 1870. Bro F.C. Woodward was elected."[32] Woodward evidently attended as the lodge book notes, "Under the head of Report of Committees Mr Woodward, delegate to the General Convention of last July, stated the actions of that body and gave a written report of the same, which was turned over to the G.S."[33]

The convention was held in the capital of Virginia and extended for three days beginning on July 11, 1870. The delegates met in a hotel, presumably arranged by members of the Eta Lodge of Richmond College, around a table and "its proceedings were uninterrupted by excursions or banquets."[34] The Order of Proceedings included an opening by the GM of Eta or the KC, an

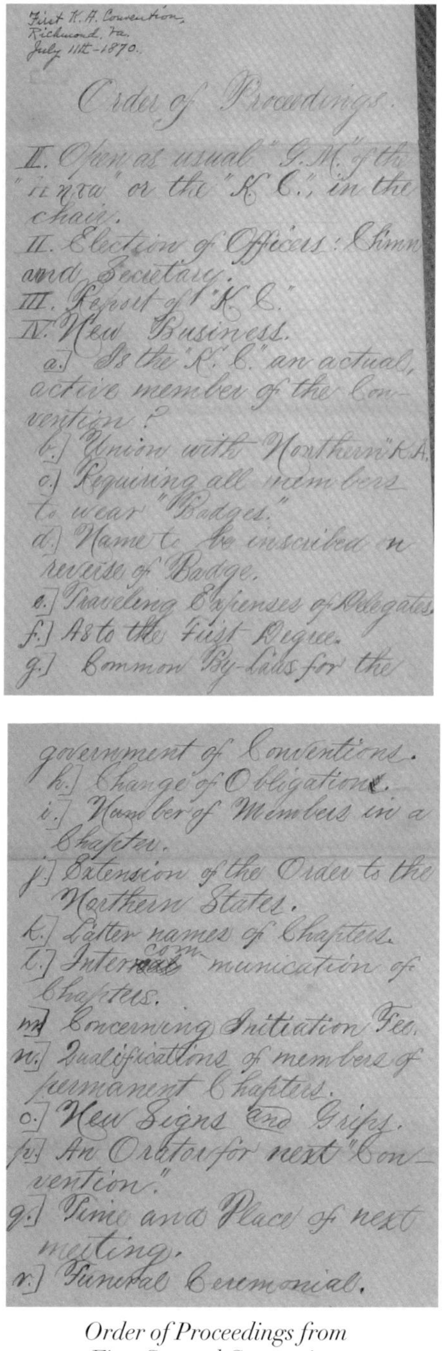
First K.A. Convention,
Richmond, Va.
July 11th - 1870.

Order of Proceedings.

I. Open as usual "G. M." of the "ητα" or the "K. C.", in the chair.
II. Election of Officers: Chmn and Secretary.
III. Report of "K. C."
IV. New Business.
a.] Is the "K. C." an actual, active member of the Convention?
b.] Union with Northern "K.A.
c.] Requiring all members to wear "Badges."
d.] Name to be inscribed on reverse of Badge.
e.] Traveling Expenses of Delegates.
f.] As to the First Degree.
g.] Common By-laws for the government of Conventions.
h.] Change of Obligations.
i.] Number of Members in a Chapter.
j.] Extension of the Order to the Northern States.
k.] Letter names of Chapters.
l.] Intercommunication of Chapters.
m.] Concerning Initiation Fee.
n.] Qualifications of members of permanent Chapters.
o.] New Signs and Grips.
p.] An Orator for next "Convention."
q.] Time and Place of next meeting.
r.] Funeral Ceremonial.

*Order of Proceedings from First General Convention, July 1870* elections of officers, particularly the chairman and secretary, the report of the KC, and new business. Some of the fundamental discussions evolved around whether the KC was an "actual and active" member of the General Council; if a union with the Northern KA was advisable; the common bylaws for the governance of conventions; new obligations of chapters, members, and officers; number of members, in a chapter; intercommunications between chapters; and, the time and place for the next meeting.[35]

The major results of the meeting were: there was to be no union with any other fraternity, no chapters were to be established in a northern state, the first section of the ritual was adopted, the Knight Commander was made an ex officio member of the convention, and alumni chapters were granted the power to initiate.

Ammen asked the chapters to send their individual data to him. He knew that documentation of the earliest history of Old Alpha was fragmentary at best, that the anecdotal information was often contradictory, and that he did not want the same pattern to repeat itself with the newer lodges. His frustration was clear in the letter of resignation that he sent to W. F. Pearson of Beta on February 22, 1871:

> I regret the inconsistences of these reports arising partly from the fact that the Corresponding Secretaries of the various chapters did not all last year furnish reports of their numbers, proceedings, &c., and partly this year. . . . Nothing has been heard from any chapter but Gamma with regard to the recommendations made by the Convention held in Richmond. . . . Indeed the Chapters all the while pervaded with enthusiasm for the Order, and devotion to its local interests have shown a general and lamentable apathy in regard to the general interest of the Order. Form has been neglected, reports are not sent in, everything is done in a loss way. This is greatly to be regretted as it is impossible to compile a Catalogue without the data to be obtained from Chapter reports.[36]

After Alpha's passing, Beta became the senior chapter and "it devolved upon the Beta Chapter to elect a Knight Commander. The chapter was rather slow about doing this," which resulted in a protracted and unwelcome extension for Ammen. He favored Collins, however, as the most logical choice for his replacement, as he was a cohort in the early stages of the campaign to extend the Kappa Alpha franchise, and noted that he sent to Collins "four KA books, reports, letters and an order for rituals [Greenbooks, edited by me & printed by Robt. Summers, Winter 1869–70 at Columbus, Ky.], and a letter."[37]

In an aside to himself, Ammen wrote:

> I am done with KA, I hope. I made its Constitution, by-laws, Ritual, Symbols, explanation of Symbols, Lectures, policy, some of its officers, customs, dress, grip, chief motto—all in effect. . . . I made the Society, sustained it at College, governed it directly, or indirectly ever since. I filled all its highest offices—it is my creation <u>in</u> <u>toto</u>.... One blue spot is the fact that the name "K.A." and the idea of forming a new society originated with ... Wood, J.W., of W.Va.; the rest [is] all mine.... Done with it, I commit all to Collins, a noble soul—active, practical, If I've been the brain, so far, of the Order, Collins will be the muscle.[38]

William S. Hamilton wrote, "Collins was the first to start the movement of extension. He it was that brought together Ammen and Hollingsworth. And made possible the establishment of Beta."[39] In the winter session of 1868, Collins transferred from Washington College to the University of Georgia, and began to recruit fellow students for a Kappa Alpha Lodge that he wished to establish there. He obtained permission from the Alpha Chapter to organize the Gamma Chapter on April 6, 1868, "and by his efforts, soon placed this chapter on a firmer basis than the Alpha itself."[40]

During Collins's administration as KC, the Iota Chapter at Furman University in Greenville, South Carolina, was founded and he "prepared and issued charters to all the chapters that were then living."[41] Reflecting the growing influence of the Georgian lodges, the second convention was held in Macon, Georgia, in July 1872.

When the first convention met in Richmond, four out of the seven chapters were in Virginia. Now that Theta Prime was established at Oglethorpe University in Atlanta, early in 1871, the state had the three of the largest chapters. So, it was natural for the second convention to be held in Macon. Moreover, the president and the secretary of the convention were two future Knight Commanders—William Walter Wadsworth of Epsilon and John Lumsdale Hardeman of Gamma. The Third Convention was held in Spartanburg, South Carolina; little of importance was accomplished during either convention.

Seismic changes, however, took place at the Fourth Annual Convention, which has been considered, by many, the most important in Kappa Alpha history. Some called the impact of the Convention of 1873 "revolutionary" and indeed it was. It transformed the Order from a provincial and insular institution into one with the capacity to adapt and change and to a position of strength and focus. There was already discontent among the younger lodges; Gamma had recently been one of the most vocal in regard to the subjugation of other chapters to a senior chapter and "they soon began to seek a position of equality and self-government."[42] Although Gamma had inherited the position of senior living chapter, she did not forget her former sentiments on the matter.

*Knight Commander John L. Hardeman*

Likely one of the most contentious issues was that the Constitution of 1870 had provided for an annual convention of limited powers, with its acts not becoming law until they had been approved by each chapter with a two-thirds majority. This gave the KC the power to decide when and if to present the suggestions to the separate chapters; it then was necessary for the individual lodges to pass the measures. This process must have seemed both cumbersome and almost futile to the separate chapters, and therefore, "the chapters usually neglected to act on the convention's proposals, so that the system was as unsatisfactory."[43]

Also, having the Number I of the senior chapter being the final authority on all matters must have been at variance with the innate American sense of representative governance. In order to rectify this situation timid steps taken during the previous conventions and the cautious nature of the leadership effected little change but the events of the Convention of 1873 proved to be momentous. "Up until this time the Order was governed by the Senior living chapter, under the guidance of the Knight Commander, who was subordinate to the (I) of the Senior chapter. This form of government, by a senior chapter, was as unsatisfactory as it was inequitable."[44] Ammen followed J. F. Rogers as the second KC while he was still at Washington College, "but [he] continued in that office after he had left college, and even after the death of Alpha. So members became thus familiarized with the idea that the Knight Commander need not be a member of the senior chapter, or subject to the chapter's supervision in the performance of his duties."[45]

John L. Hardeman served as both the presiding officer of the Fourth Convention and the Knight Commander. "I was KC when the convention met in Athens in '73," he wrote to Paul Murrill in 1900. "At its first meeting I decided that the power was in Gamma. I then got the [Number] I of Gamma to call a meeting of that chapter, I then introduced a resolution in Gamma that she yield to the convention the power she had, and ask the convention to accept it. At the next day's session of the convention, the convention accepted it. I, as KC, then decided that the power was in the convention."[46]

The result of the valiant and selfless act of Gamma and Hardeman was that both the legislative and the executive branches of the Order were transformed in a profound and pragmatic manner. The deliberative body of the Order changed from relying on the autocratic decisions of the senior chapter and did away with the restrictions that the Constitution of 1870 had placed on the powers of the convention, and it abolished the referendum. In short, the shift allowed that for the conventions "the power of changing, as well as adding to, the constitution was assumed, and the acts of the Convention were made immediately operative."[47]

In regard to the executive function of the Knight Commander, previously he had been subservient to Number I of the senior chapter and selected by his lodge, now, he was elected by, and responsible to, the delegates of the convention—a tectonic shift. The vote of the convention enlarged the authority of the Knight Commander and "gave him rank above all other officers, and provided for his election by the convention. In the interval between conventions he was to be the supreme and only executive. The effect of the change was to give the Order a strong government, unlike any other fraternity."[48]

"The Convention ... became at once ... the active, governing body, and was no longer the merely consultative assembly that it was originally designed to be."[49] Now, individual members and chapters were not all a relevant part of the process, but they were invested in the success of the Order, not only during their college days but also throughout their lifetime. In essence, the impact of the work of this convention changed profoundly the nature and mission of the Order.

For more than the next decade the conventions produced little legislation or innovation of worth. The Fifth Annual Convention held in Ashland, Virginia, elected Jo Lane Stern the Grand Historian and resolved that he should "accumulate documents to preserve the history of the Order."[50] The Sixth Annual Convention met with the Epsilon Chapter at Emory College and addressed the prospect of establishing alumni chapters; the Seventh Annual Convention in Richmond found no new lodges had been established and that those extant were lax in their responsibilities; the Eighth Annual Convention suggested founding noncollegiate lodges and a resolution was put forth to change the annual meetings to biennial.[51]

At the Ninth Annual Convention members authorized the publication of the *Kappa Alpha Journal*, which was to be devoted to the "literature and the welfare of the Fraternity"—mirroring the prewar publications of the debating societies. Also there were suggestion on regalia, a coat of arms, and simplifying collars. It was determined that after 1879 conventions would be held every two years.[52]

No business of note occurred at conventions until the Twelfth Biennial Convention in Richmond in June 1883. At this gathering it was decided, "The Order shall be divided into Commanderies, subject to rearrangement by subsequent conventions, as the growth of the Order may require."[53] The districts included one for Virginia and West Virginia; another for Georgia, Alabama, and Tennessee; a third for North and South Carolina; and the last for Louisiana, Mississippi, and Texas – reflecting the move toward the Southwest. Each division was to have a Knight Visitor who would check in on each chapter at least once a year—the plan did not pan out and was abolished at the following convention.

The new attitude of vitality and energy that made a timid appearance at the Twelfth Biennial Convention reappeared with more conviction and vigor at the Thirteenth Biennial Convention, which was held in October 1885, in Nashville, Tennessee. "This convention was one of the most important that had been held. It was composed of men who were determined to build the Order up on a substantial foundation. Until this convention the laws had been, more or less, temporary… and that they had not been carefully studied. The Order was having solid growth… and set the member to thinking, the result of which was the rapid development in every part of the organization."[54]

Other signal actions of this convention included a plan to put the Order on a more linear and stable financial basis by creating the office of Grand Purser, making the *Kappa Alpha Journal* more relevant and marketable, and producing a catalog—"published in the best paper, well-bound, and that it should contain a complete history of each chapter from its organization to that time…published out of the general fund and furnished free to all active members and sold to alumni."[55]

The Fourteenth Biennial Convention was held in Columbia, South Carolina, in September 1887. The headquarters of the convention was the elegant Jerome Hotel. It was reported in the Columbia newspaper that "the Hotel Jerome was all day yesterday marked by being the headquarters of numerous groups of good-looking young men, too modest to be drummers and too lively to pass for ministers of the gospel."[56] The following article reported that on the second day reports were given by various chapters that now numbered twenty-seven and were situated throughout the South and Southwest. It was also recorded that "during the interval of two years between the meeting of the present and last conventions there have been nearly three hundred initiations."[57] On the last day of the convocation the newspaper noted that "plans are on foot for immediate establishment in the universities of Florida, Mississippi and California."[58] The ambitions for a westward expansion to the Pacific were becoming more pronounced.

On the last evening of the convention, the combined attendees sat down to an elaborate meal consisting of "a Claret Punch, and Ox Tail Consomme a la Royal, a combination of Ribs of Mountain Beef, New York Turkey, Ferris' Ham, Smoked Beef Tongue, Bone Turkey, Chicken a la Mayonaisse, Potato Salad, Wine Jelly, Currant Jelly, Cholate [*sic*] Blanc Mango, Italian Ice Cream, Lemon Sherbet, Orange Cake, Almond Cake, Cream Cake, Cocoanut Layer Cake, Grapes, Oranges, Apples, Bananas, Layer Raisins, Assorted Nuts, Oolong Tea or French Coffee" followed by cigars and conversation.[59]

William Sprigg Hamilton declared that the "new Order" really came into being at the Sixteenth Biennial Convention in September 1891. The convention established an advisory board, which acted in conjunction with the Knight Commander as the arbiter of expansion. In regard to the composition of this group, it was resolved that the convention should select five members at large, who should "vote on the establishment of all new chapters."[60] Previously Kappa Alpha had long been "the only fraternity to confide to one man the authority to extend or not."[61] The autocratic rule of the Knight Commander was slowly evolving into governing by consensus.

The Sixteenth Convention also was marked by the return of the Old Guard—Samuel Z. Ammen was elected Knight Commander and Tazewell Taylor Hubard was named Grand Historian. The selection of these officers signaled a return to past principles and visions and a new determination in direction.

The opening of the Seventeenth Convention was described in the *Richmond Dispatch:*

> The seventeenth biennial convention of the Kappa Alpha Fraternity will convene this morning at Murphy's hotel. A good many of the delegates have already arrived and the convention promises to be unusually well attended, and one of special interest and importance as many matters affecting the vital interests of the fraternity will be brought up and acted upon....The Kappa Alpha Fraternity...has strengthened and grown from one chapter and four members to its present roll of thirty-four chapters and 2,768 members. This signal growth has brought about the necessity of a revision of the old constitution and a perfecting of the administration. A new constitution and ritual, prepared at a great cost of time and labor by Mr. S.Z. Ammen, the present KC will be submitted to the convention for adoption.[62]

The changes in the constitution indicated the aspirations of the author, Samuel Ammen, to return the centralized control of the Order into the hands of the Knight Commander. According to the amendments, "petitions for charters must be presented to him" and "a power of veto was granted to the KC Also the Advisory Board was exchanged for a council to the Knight Commander consisting of the Grand Historian, Grand Purser and the editor of the *Journal*; a unanimous vote of these three officers can stop the issuance of a charter."[63] With these enhanced authorities the Knight Commander could exercise his discretion concerning what areas and how fast the Order should expand.

Tangential to the locus of authority in regard to "extension" of the Order into certain geographic sections of the country was the issue of northern chapters and the controversy concerning the merger of northern and southern orders of Kappa Alpha—this subject, as it had been from the first convention, was a source of prolonged and heated discussion, with adherents and detractors from both sides. "The idea of Northern expansion was broached and an animated discussion followed. This quest has been regularly presented to every convention for the past twenty years, but has always met with the same fate."[64] Ammen's statement in the article suggests his own viewpoint on the matter, and while the Knight Commander was aggressive in his ambitions for the growth of the Order, instead of directing his attentions to the North, he followed the dictates of Horace Greeley and Manifest Destiny – Go West, Young Man!

The period from 1870 through 1893, in terms of the Order's history, was a period of growth and change. Both of these aspects were the result of the reforms and modifications within the framework of the society itself. As Old Alpha's grip on control was weakened by atrophy within its own lodge, the more recent arrivals, many of whom were founded by original Alphas, began to demand an equal say in the governance of the Order. Deeming itself more sophisticated in the ways of the world, the Old Guard in Lexington, was reluctant to let loose the reins of authority; the writing, however, was on the wall that the participation of the younger lodges was crucial to the perpetuation of the Order, and, little by little, bit by bit, adjustments and concessions were made. The two areas in which this change was most greatly effected was the agreement to hold regular conventions in which all the lodges would have a voice, if not the say, in the decision-making process; the second was the centralization of the executive power into one person, the KC, or Knight Commander.

The evolving relationship between Old Alpha and her progenies was a combination of the changing nature of the centralizing authority of the Knight Commander caused by the adjustments and growing influence of the new lodges through progressive innovations made in successive conventions. Even as Alpha died, she sought to retain the tradition of the power remaining in the hands of the senior chapter and the power passed to Beta, which, in turn, passed the torch on to Gamma.

John Hardeman, the Knight Commander from Gamma, at the 1873 Convention brought about a fundamental change to the nature of the Order relying on an ethical and pragmatic principle, namely, that the authority in the

Order should lie in the aggregate decisions of the convention and that the office of the Knight Commander should be elected by the Order at large through its delegates at the convention, thus transferring the legislative authority of his own lodge and subordinating the executive function of the Knight Commander to the wishes of the convention. "Such an officer, was admitted, on all hands, to be indispensable, but this conception of duties was from the first objected to by the Gamma, which was always much more muscular than the mother chapter... insisting that, the chapters being co-equals, the officer should be their joint representative, selected by delegates of the various chapters, from the entire membership of the Order, and not from the Alpha alone."[65]

The impact and presence of the conventions undulated for the next two decades, energetically implementing new plans and dejectedly abandoning them. In the late 1880s, with a growth of the chapters, a more-sustainable financial basis, and a restructuring of administrative platform—the Order was reinvigorated. The Conventions of 1891 and 1893 saw the return of a number of the early members of the Order and of Old Alpha in particular. Samuel Z. Ammen, who had played a central role in transforming Kappa Alpha from a social clique into an organization of substance and purpose, and Taylor Tazewell Hubard, who hailed from Alpha and Beta, were prime movers in the attempts to make Kappa Alpha an institution of one heart and one mind. Ammen desired to turn the position of Knight Commander into one that was both stronger and more directive than ever before and one that would be able to drive the Order's ambitions forward with a concerted focus.

The perennial question that had dominated conventions from 1870 and was still recurrent in 1893—expansion and growth. Two pivotal elements of that issue were a merger with the northern branch of Kappa Alpha, the Kappa Alpha Society, and the geographic and sectional limitations of "extension"—in other words, what states or even territories were desirable for the purpose of establishing new chapters and whether the new lodges would be restricted to academic campuses. These are questions to be addressed in the next chapter.

## *Notes* Chapter 7:

1 Samuel Z. Ammen, "Ammen Diary Extracts," Kappa Alpha Archives, Lexington, Va., 4.

2 Minutes of Alpha Lodge KA Order, 1869–70, Miscellaneous Folder 26, Kappa Alpha Archives, Lexington, Va., 101.

3 Beta Lodge Minutes, 1876–1882, Kappa Alpha Archives, Lexington, Va., 1.

4 Beta Lodge Minutes, 1876–1882, 1; Alpha Minutes, March 8, 1868, Kappa Alpha Archives, Lexington, Va., 71.

5 William Sprigg Hamilton, Chronological History of the Kappa Alpha Order, Kappa Alpha Archives, Lexington, Va., 5.

6 Alpha Minutes, March 21, 1868, p. 75.

7 Alpha Minutes, May 8, 1868, p. 78.

8 Alpha Minutes, November 1868, p. 95.

9 W. B. Crawford, *Directory of the Kappa Alpha Order* (St. Augustine: The Record Co., 1929), 8.

10 Alpha Minutes, November 1868, p. 85.

11 Joseph Chick, *History and Catalogue of the Kappa Alpha Fraternity* (Nashville: Kappa Alpha Order, 1891), xxxi.

12 William Sprigg Hamilton, Biographies: General Officers, Kappa Alpha Order, 1868–1936, Kappa Alpha Archives, Lexington, Va., N.P.

13 Crawford, *Directory of the Kappa Alpha Order*, 9.

14 Hamilton, Chronological History of the Kappa Alpha Order, 6.

15 Ibid.

16 Crawford, *Directory of the Kappa Alpha Order*, 9.

17 "Minutes of the Alpha Lodge KA," Miscellaneous Folder 26, October 5, 1868, Kappa Alpha Archives, Lexington, Va., 93.

18 "Minutes of the Alpha Lodge KA," February 8, 1869, p. 98.

19 Tazewell T. Hubard, "The KC-ship and the KCs," *Kappa Alpha Journal* 11, No. 3 (April 1894): 328.

20 Crawford, *Directory of the Kappa Alpha Order*, 10.

21 William Kavanaugh Doty *Samuel Zenas Ammen and the Kappa Alpha Order* (Charlottesville: Surber-Arundale Co., 1922), 37.

22 Ibid.

23 Mary Westheimer, *The History of the Kappa Alpha Order* (Phoenix: Heritage Publishers, 1994), 17.

24 Biennial Catalogue: 1873–1875, Miscellaneous Folder 28, Kappa Alpha Archives, Lexington, Va., 2–10.

25 Hamilton, Chronological History of Kappa Alpha Order, 7.

26 Ibid.

27 "Minutes of the Alpha Lodge KA," October 5, 1868, p. 113.

28 Ibid., 115.

29 Ibid., 125.

30 Hamilton, Chronological History of Kappa Alpha Order, 7.

31 William Sprigg Hamilton, Synopses of the Conventions, 1870–1937, Kappa Alpha Archives, Lexington, Va., 8.

32 Zeta Lodge Book, May 23, 1870, Mss4 K1422 b2, Archives, Virginia Historical Society, N.D., 8.
33 Ibid., 13.
34 Hamilton, Synopses of the Conventions, 1870–1937, p. 8.
35 First KA Convention, Richmond, Virginia, July 11, 1870, Miscellaneous Folder 20, Kappa Alpha Archives, Lexington, Va., N.D.
36 S. Z. Ammen to W. F. Pearson, February 22, 1871, Kappa Alpha Archives, Lexington, Va., 1.
37 Ibid., 6.
38 Ibid.
39 Hamilton, Biographies: General Officers, Kappa Alpha Order, 1868–1936, "William Wilson Collins."
40 Ibid.
41 Ibid.
42 Hamilton, Chronological History of Kappa Alpha Order, 7.
43 Hamilton, Synopses of the Conventions, 1870–1937, p. 2.
44 Hamilton, Chronological History of Kappa Alpha Order, 10.
45 Hamilton, Synopses of the Conventions, 1870–1937, 2.
46 J. L. Hardeman to Paul Murrill, June 23, 1900, in S. Z. Ammen, *History of the Kappa Alpha Fraternity* (Charlotte: Queen City Printing Co., 1888), 5.
47 Chick, *History and Catalogue of the Kappa Alpha Fraternity*, xxxv.
48 Ammen, *History of the Kappa Alpha Fraternity*, 5.
49 Chick, *History and Catalogue of the Kappa Alpha Fraternity*, xxxv.
50 Hamilton, Synopses of the Conventions, 1870–1937, p. 3.
51 Ibid., 4.
52 Ibid., 5; see also Chick, *History and Catalogue of the Kappa Alpha Fraternity*, xxxvii.
53 Hamilton, Synopses of the Conventions, 1870–1937, p. 9.
54 Ibid., 11.
55 Ibid.
56 "Kappa Alpha Convention," Columbia, S.C., September 20, 1887, Miscellaneous Folder 30, "Newspaper Clippings," The Daily Report, Kappa Alpha Archives, Lexington, Va., N.D.
57 "Kappa Alpha Convention," September 21, 1887,"Newspaper Clippings," The Daily Report.
58 "Kappa Alpha Convention," September 22, 1887, "Newspaper Clippings," The Daily Report.
59 "Kappa Alpha Convention," September 23, 1887, "Newspaper Clippings," The Daily Report.
60 Hamilton, Synopses of the Conventions, 1870–1937, p. 15.
61 "The Greek Press," *Kappa Alpha Journal* 9, No. 1 (October 1891): 88.
62 "The Kappa Alpha Convention," *Richmond Dispatch*, September 15, 1893, p. 3.
63 Samuel Z. Ammen, "The Convention of Ninety-Three," *Kappa Alpha Journal* 9, No. 1 (October 1893): 6.
64 Ibid., 8.
65 Samuel Z. Ammen, "The Early History of Alpha," *Kappa Alpha Journal* 1, No. 3 (April 1884): 5.

*University of California, Berkeley Campus, circa 1900*

# 8

## Manifest Destiny

From the 1870s through the 1890s, recurrent and separate yet interrelated issues affected the geographical and social aspects of expansion. The earliest and most contentious of which showed up as early as 1870, as a proposition that a merger between the Northern Kappa Alpha, or Kappa Alpha Society, and the Southern Kappa Alpha, or Kappa Alpha Order take place. The later and more organic conversation involved the propriety and pragmatism of implanting fraternal lodges in the Western states and was, in many ways, a continuation of the initial conversation.

The merger, however, was the more complex issue. On one side, there remained the residual feelings of animosity because of the Civil War and Ammen's stated mission of preserving southern tradition; but, on the other hand, a credible historical link existed between the two institutions and the practical advantage of combining resources and human capital.

The subject of a union between the two separate of Kappa Alphas became a topic of discussion on the agenda list at the First Convention of 1870. Ammen noted that he presided over this first meeting and presented the Council with "a list of questions sent me from the several Chapters."[1]

The second and third questions submitted by the chapters were: "Shall we enter Northern States? and Shall we affiliate with Northern KA?"[2] Since the affiliation question was neither explicitly rejected nor accepted, it became a matter of investigation. It was determined, at this time, that the Order should not extend into the northern states and no affiliation would be made with the northern branch.

The debate gave way to needs more critical and immediate and fell into abeyance until 1883, when the Committee on the Propriety presented the following recommendation to the Richmond Convention: "We are in favor of uniting with the Northern KA and recommend that steps be taken to bring about a reconciliation.... A second committee was appointed to find out all possible information about Northern KA and whether it would be willing to unite."[3] At the Twelfth Biennial Convention in 1883, a committee of three was appointed to determine if a union with Northern Kappa Alpha was feasible and asking all chapters to vote on this question.[4]

In January 1884, James Morris of the Lambda Chapter revealed in an article in the *Kappa Alpha Journal* that he had discovered in the minutes of the Lambda Chapter that H. P. Cooper of that lodge had been contacted by a member of the Northern Kappa Alpha "desiring to know our views on the question of a union," which demonstrated that "Northern Kappa Alphas desire a union, and in approaching them on this subject we are seeking no favor of them, but simply complying with their known wishes."[5]

Morris thought it an idea worth exploring. He argued that "in the first place the Northern Kappa Alpha is the oldest college fraternity in the country. It has the prestige that always adheres to venerable institutions. Its membership includes some of the most distinguished men of New England. Its organization has that stability and dignity which inhere in age and make it superior to youth."[6] The perspective of the prestige that accompanies old age must have resonated with the Virginia delegations.

Morris's second pitch was likely foremost in the minds and hearts of his audience and commanded greater attention. "Again, the Northern Kappa Alpha is a wealthy organization. There is no use evading the matter: we all know that we need money. Had we been in possession of the necessary means we had long ere this planted our standard in every State in the South."[7] Conversely, argued Morris, the incentive for Northern Kappa Alpha is that since "Northern colleges are full of fraternities, it is obliged to look South. With the immediate gain of a large accession to its active membership, and an infinite capability for extension in the future, it cannot but regard the union as an end to be attained at any cost."[8]

The symbiotic benefit to both the Northern and Southern Kappa Alphas would be that "the union of our energy and enthusiasm with their solidarity and strength must make a fraternity that will outstrip in active work all others."[9] William Sprigg Hamilton encapsulated Morris's position as "Southern Kappa Alpha would receive the prestige and wealth acquired by them in their long career in return for a goodly list of first class chapters they could add to their roll. One large fraternity, the peer in quantity, the superior in quality, of any in the land would result."[10] And as late as 1895, three of the most prominent leaders of Kappa Alpha Order—John Temple Graves, John S. Chandler, and Greenlee D. Letcher spoke to the convention in favor of a merger.[11]

The initial reaction to Morris's arguments for a union, however, was a cacophony of opposing voices, loudly countering his most persuasive arguments—point by point. The area that engendered the most fervor was any apparent similarity between the two fraternities. The respondents claimed that in terms of spiritual consanguinity the organizations were at odds in fundamental ways and the only point of convergence was in name. One editorial noted the longevity of the controversy, "For a number of years past the subject of union of our own Kappa Alpha and the so-called Northern Kappa Alpha had been agitated with some ardor in certain quarters. Every convention for the last eight or ten years has considered this subject.... I, for one, am opposed to this union." The author, Walter Brown, also maintained that "By some coincidence, two fraternities, formed at different times, in different places, and under different circumstances, have agreed upon the same name.... The entire machinery—symbols, secrets, objects, principles, and purposes—of the Northern KA is as different from our own Kappa Alpha as the tropics from the polar regions."[12] Another member posted an opinion in agreement reflecting that the two societies were as different as "east and west," instead of "North and South," thus, avoiding the elephant in the room.[13]

In the ways that are most conspicuous and reaffirming to the identity of the Order, there was again a disconnect with the northern branch, "It is essential that its forms, secrets, symbols, principles, purposes, etc., be the same throughout its extent—that its membership be as nearly one as possible in feelings, sympathies, and associations."[14] The consequences of such an unnatural marriage, according to one correspondent, would be that whenever "there is an attempt to unite by harmonizing and compromising principles and opinions, particularly where these are radically different, the results are almost sure to be disastrous."[15] The historian of the Southern Kappa Alpha, William S. Hamilton, gave his opinion that "these figures go to prove that the makeup of the membership of a chapter is determined by its geographic location and that the inevitable tendency of 'Northern Extension' would be to change completely the complexion of our membership and bring about two diverse factions, disunited by geographic position, inherent sentiment, and lack of sympathetic principle.... Northern extension offers no hospitable home to us, and should not be sought."[16] Echoing Hamilton's position, another's concern was that when "two societies may be so dissimilar that they cannot be united without the loss of some great principle; then will either side be willing to be the loser?"[17]

Morris's assertion that Northern Kappa Alpha was seeking this accommodation and that to respond would only be to comply civilly with its wishes, was countered by a reply from Charles Avery, a senior member of the Cornell chapter of Kappa Alpha. He took issue with the assertion that the northern organization desired a union with the southern branch. "While there are among us some who would favor the union, I may safely say that a large majority are strongly opposed to it. During the fifty-nine or sixty years of our existence as a small society there has grown up to considerable strength a sentiment of conservatism, which now colors, if not regulates, all official acts.... and it would be difficult to remove it."[18] The northern branch expressed the same concern as the southern branch had. "By joining so large a body as yours we should certainly be 'swallowed up' and our independence lost. To speak plainly, I cannot see that any advantage would accrue to either by tying together with a merely formal bond two societies whose only common subject of interest is two Greek initials."[19] And in regard to practical application, Mr. Avery noted "For this reason any such radical change in the social government and make-up, as proposed, would undoubtedly meet with great opposition."[20]

Ammen responded to Avery's dismissive letter to the *Journal,* "Brother Boyd rightly assumes that combination with Northern KA is an indispensable condition of going North.... If we are so wanting in self-respect as to ask Northern KA to combine with us, we shall be snubbed for our want of delicacy. We shall get a harvest of insults and jeers, but to no profit. There has been an unofficial correspondence already... on this subject which ended in a polite snub. We deserved it and we got it. It would be a shame for a powerful fraternity like ours to go on its knees for favors."[21]

At the same time, Ammen synopsized the main points against joining with the Northern Kappa Alpha. He specified that were a merger to occur that chapters in the North and West would soon outnumber those in the South by virtue of number, wealth, and political influence and, therefore, would be able to determine the character and direction of the institution; that the *Journal* would be compiled and composed by an unsympathetic northerner; that the administrative infrastructure would be quickly dominated by northern and western interests; and, the Southern KA would be forced to surrender its rituals and ideals.[22]

The most objective and clinical argument for union proposed from the first convention in 1870 was the Southern Kappa Alpha Order that had descended from the Northern Kappa Alpha Society. If so, a merger would be in fact a reunion; if not, a sham. Thus the question took on more than an academic importance.

The two elements that argued against such a coalition were the antipathy by many of the older members against anything connected to the north and a fear that the southern values, which was a key factor of Ammen's mission for the Order, would be diminished and corrupted by an association with the northern branch. In order to undercut the arguments of the prounion contingent it was crucial to maintain that there was no credible evidence to suggest that there was a kinship, however remote, between the two.

The advocates of those wishing to effect a united Kappa Alpha was to establish a common bond, a common history. There was some reason for this early supposition, namely, the perennial rumor that James Ward Wood had found both the name, the inspiration for Kappa Alpha in the vaults of the library of the University of Virginia, which contained the "papers" of an antebellum chapter of the Northern Kappa Alpha. It was a story of such circulation among the members of Old Alpha that it has the ring of truth. James Ward Wood, having been rebuffed by two of the established fraternities at Washington College, founded one of his own, Kappa Alpha. It was reported in the early lore of the Order that "Wood got an old ritual from the University of Virginia, from which he copied portions for use by KA. He would not let the chapter use the entire ceremony."[23] Jo Lane Stern wrote as a student in 1870 that he thought the connection to the Northern Kappa Alpha was genuine—"for we may be an illegitimate daughter of the old lady, and cannot find our mother."[24] Stern also wrote to John Hardeman that a Mr. Griffin, of Princeton, the parent of the University of Virginia chapter, had been tracing the reputed connection between his lodge of the Northern Kappa Alpha and the one established in Charlottesville before the war. Stern noted that "Griffin seems to think a delegate will come to Richmond (for the First Convention in 1870). I presume we can see what kind of kin we are if any."[25]

This organization was said to have been chartered by a branch of the Northern Kappa Alpha. Ammen not only disputed that claim but also asserted the Northern Kappa Alpha was a stepchild of a society founded at the College of William and Mary in 1812.[26] Ammen noted, "Brother Boyd has inquired for many years to discover whether the KA which began in Lexington Va. [in] 1866 [and] derived its existence for the older KA; from the Northern KA, or from the Older Southern KA. From the similarity of the symbols of the two fraternities and other circumstances it is inferred that the Northern KA is an offshoot of the Southern KA."[27]

The Northern Kappa Alpha was one of the first-established fraternities in the United States, "The Society had its origin … in Union College, Schenectady, N.Y., in the fall of the year 1825."[28] Its appearance followed the disbanding of "an organized company of about sixty students for out-door exercise and military drill." In November 1825, one of the founders, Thomas Hun, suggested "the idea of a new secret society for literary and social purposes" and John Hart, Isaac Jackson, Charles Clark, and Andrew Knox were united in that purpose.[29] Charles C. Young recounted that "on the 26th day of the same month" that the five passed through "some very quiet but impressive ceremonies' and the name Kappa Alpha was adopted. Afterwards, there was "some talk about future action [and] an adjournment was had to the well-known dining room at Knight's boarding house."[30] The author noted that the proceedings were concerned with "the definite objects of the Association;… no care or attention [was] given to the minutes of the earliest proceedings; and its long life must have been well assured before the Key came into use."[31] Boyd remarked that the Union College division of Kappa Alpha did not have badges but only keys. The evidence of this account dispels the version that claimed the pedigree of the northern branch descended from William and Mary in the South.

There was also a prolonged debate about the origin of the ritual for the fraternity and the actual name—Kappa Alpha. Ammen insisted that Wood had obtained the rite from a Lexington lodge—Epsilon Alpha."[32] He maintained that Wood developed the origins of fraternity from his freshly minted association with Epsilon Alpha and thereby dismissed a contemporary consensus that, in fact, the name and ceremonies came from a branch of the Northern Kappa Alpha Society that had been established at the University of Virginia.

In spite of suspicions of fraternal fiction, in fact, the chapter of the Kappa Alpha Society founded at Union College in 1825, soon spread throughout the Northeast and even crossed the Mason-Dixon Line. John Peter Jackson of the Princeton lodge wrote in 1855, "We propose to establish another chapter (of K.A.) in the University of Virginia. A committee of one was appointed from each chapter to canvass the subject."[33]

Joseph Hobson, who graduated from Princeton, traveled south to attend the Law School at the University of Virginia. It was during the winter of 1856 that Hobson "approached Alexander Duncan, John Kennard, William Zachary Meade and Charles Goolrick upon the subject of founding a chapter at the University of Virginia. The suggestion was favorably received and a charter was asked for and obtained ... on January 8, 1856."[34]

The history of Kappa Alpha Society in Charlottesville was brilliant but brief. "Her members carried off more college honors than those of any other secret society at the time;... lodge meetings were held, for some time, in the second story of a brick house which was on the left side of the road leading from the University. At the outbreak of the Civil War many members left the University and joined the Confederate army...The suspension of the Chapter was due to the war [and] the lodge meeting became less frequent, until, in 1861, the Chapter was given up and the papers and books stored in the Library of the University of Virginia." [35]

In his later years, Wood was vague about the early years of the fraternity and the actions that he may have taken. He could not remember from where the name and first rituals of Kappa Alpha derived, only that he knew that there was once a Kappa Alpha chapter at the University of Virginia, although he consistently referred to the society as Kuklos Adelphon, and "that it died & we took its name."[36] Absent Wood's definitive statement on the matter, whether the University of Virginia legend is the actual origin or whether Wood had come across its "papers" by happenstance rather than by purpose is anybody's guess, but the argument was persuasive to those who wished to join together with the northern branch. Moreover, the UVA connection was more logical than the other hypotheses offered on the matter. Even Ammen had reported that "if Wood got the 'the Papers' of the Northern K.A. in the Library of the University of Virginia, that was one additional reason for the name K.A."[37]

The more probable solution is that Wood, being in a tight position, cast around until he found a ritual that had "some good parts" and some allure and a name "that nobody was using" and appropriated it for his own group. Both sides used the "evidence" as a way of either bolstering support for a merger with the

Northern Kappa Alpha or for undercutting it. Even to this day nobody can say if the story is certain.

Having put the merger controversy more firmly behind them, however, the Order turned its expansionistic tendencies to the south and west rather than the north. But even here there was substantial opposition. At the Fifteenth Biennial Convention in 1889, it was announced that "the establishment of chapters in several Northern and Western Colleges was recommended by the committee, but the convention, by an overwhelming vote, refused to consider the recommendation."[38]

At the Sixteenth Convention, in 1891, two conflicting events occurred that had a nullifying effect on the process of merger and expansion to western states. First, the convention abolished the board of directors and replaced it with an advisory board that was appointed by the covention at large and was to be from different states. "This Board should vote on the establishment of all new chapters."[39] This innovation may well have provided an avenue for an accommodation with Northern Kappa Alpha and increased the likelihood of establishing new chapters in northern and western states. The second factor was the election of Samuel Z. Ammen as Knight Commander, who was adverse to accommodating any extension into the North.

During the Seventeenth Convention in 1895, the convention abolished the Advisory Board and restored the control of charter chapters back to the Knight Commander. Thus, Ammen again became controller of the geographic direction in which the Order would proceed.[40] Depite some opposition, expansion in the South, Southwest, Midwest and West continued apace.

Despite all the *Sturm und Drang* associated with the merger controversy, nevertheless, the Order made substantial headway in its extension program. Until late in the 1870s, all of the institutions courted and won were, territorially, in the South—Virginia, Georgia, and South Carolina produced the first children. The early chapters were mainly planted in southern colleges, but even in the first days Jo Lane Stern had proposed to establish a lodge at Gordonsville Academy, a military school near Charlottesville.[41] His proposal for the school at Gordonsville never materialized but there are two instances of noncollegiate chapters—both in the early history of expansion before they were outlawed by the conventions. The first was established at Gordon Military Institute in Barnesville, Georgia, on April 18, 1879. The institute had existed as a high school for both boys and girls prior to 1873, when Charles Lambdin opened the doors of Gordon Institute. By January 1873, the school had been enlarged and restricted to males being prepared for a collegiate career.

The second chapter was nearer to Lexington, established in October 1878 at Bethel Academy, in Fauquier County, Virginia. The school was established as a military academy by a Confederate veteran Major Albert G. Smith in 1867. It began as a small and "rough hewn" log cabin called Hawk's Nest and during the next decade expanded dramatically. During the 1870s the size and sophistication of the school grew exponentially and by 1873, enrollment reached 113 students, with 96 from Virginia. Both chapters were ultimately short-lived.

The Convention of 1870 prohibited northern extension and union with Northern Kappa Alpha, but these restrictions were wiped out by the Convention of 1873. Twenty years later the Convention of 1893 reversed that fiat with the provision that no chapter could be established in the North without the unanimous consent of all the chapters. And, counterintuitively, some of the earlier chapters and proposed chapters were located in the North—some were successful and situated at renowned colleges, others the reverse.

Because of the enthusiasm of a former member of Beta, John H. Campbell, "a chapter was established at the Philadelphia College of Dental Surgery in 1877."[42] Campbell recruited and initiated George Carlton Brown of New York; Alfred Hough Scofield of Elizabeth, New Jersey; and Charles P. Gilpin of Elkton, Maryland. The lodge was fined when it neglected to send a delegate to the 1879 Convention and the Convention of 1883 recalled its charter, not knowing that the lodge was already expired.[43] About 1880 a group at Marietta College in Ohio "secured permission to become a chapter of Kappa Alpha, but for reasons unknown the matter fell through."[44] In 1886, Knox College at Galesburg, Illinois, was even considered for a candidate for incorporation.[45]

The first chapter of the Order established at major northern university was at Johns Hopkins in Baltimore. The institution was founded at the behest of the childless millionaire, Johns Hopkins, in 1876, who gave what, at the time, was the largest donation to a college in American history. The university was founded on the German model of scientific research and quickly rose to academic prominence among American institutions.

The Alpha Lambda Chapter of Kappa Alpha was installed on its campus on October 21, 1891. W. A. Harris, John McNeel, James Ray, W. A. Montgomery, W. C. Bell, W. H. Kirkpatrick, and Julius Blume were the founders. "These were all graduate students and were quick to see the opening for a chapter. They had the additional advantage of the presence of Bro. Ammen, who personally gave the charter to the new chapter and has remained a true friend and wise counselor."[46] The first decade of its existence was one of ups and downs, but by the turn of the century the lodge had stabilized itself in membership and prominence.

In 1893, Kappa Alpha alumni gathered in the nation's capital and discussed the prospectus of founding an active chapter at Columbian University, now

*Hopkins Hall, Johns Hopkins University, circa 1885*

*1931 K Street Northwest*

*2011 Columbia Road*

George Washington University. The concept of a national university had been promoted by George Washington himself and the seed money to start the institution derived from the same fund of stocks that had provided the genesis of Washington College. In 1819, John Quincy Adams, William Crawford, John C. Calhoun, William Wirt, the Reverend Luther Rice, and thirty-two members of Congress contributed to a fund to purchase forty-seven acres for the project. Congress chartered Columbia University on February 9, 1821. By 1822, the main building was opened and the first commencement was held on December 15, 1824, with President James Monroe and the Marquis de Lafayette in attendance.In 1873, Congress officially changed the name of the institution to Columbian University. [47]

In the spring of 1894, "a motion was made that the Alumni Chapter petition the KC for a charter for an active chapter to be established at Columbian University."[48] Several of the alumni secured a charter within a few weeks and after its arrival John Carroll Goodfellow, Ormesby McCammon, Robert Campbell Kelton, and Horace Hampton Wescott were introduced into the sacred rites. "Brother Ammen, the then KC and charterer of the new chapter, was likewise present, lending much valuable service in enthusiasm, suggestions and in other ways."[49]

In the same year the son of the Chilean ambassador, Alfredo Ganna, was inducted into the lodge and rooms were obtained at the old Wormley Hotel for meetings. The chapter room changed to meet the needs of the expanding lodge from a room on the third floor of the Arts Club on 17th Street to 1931 K Street, Northwest, where it remained for many years. In later years the chapter moved from its elegant dwelling on K Street to the more utilitarian abode on Columbia Road.

Finally the Beta Epsilon Chapter of Kappa Alpha was founded at the University of Delaware in Newark, Delaware, on April 29, 1904. The initial attempt to found this chapter began in 1895, when Paul Berghaus campaigned for a chapter there. Ammen noted in his KC's diary, "I wrote to President Rauls, Del. College, whether he has anti-frat law. Sent off all facts to W.S. Hamilton."[50] The following week he sent a message to Berghaus that he would charter a lodge at Delaware if "it [was] not *sub rosa*; if he had 10 men approved by 3 K.A.s; if it was name[d] Mu; and, if it were chartered before September 20."[51] A week later Berghaus replied that "he is pleased with my assent to Chartering Del. Under Conditions: the name[d] Mu will be acceptable."[52]

The founders included Warren McBryde and Kappa Alpha chronicler Leroy S. Boyd. Ammen had his trepidations about the northern pedigree of this lodge as well, while it was south of the Mason-Dixon line, nevertheless he wrote "I will enter Oct 20… on application for charter (University of Delaware)…. White wrote that the Order considers Del. A Northern state and many objections have developed…. There was grumbling when Johns Hopkins was entered."[53]

Beta Kappa at the University of Maryland was established in 1914, and Beta Nu was founded at St. Johns College in Annapolis in 1916, but these were, more or less, the interesting aberrations. The general trend of colonization, however, was within the linear concepts of geographic proximity and philosophical mandates—first to the deep South and fringes of the Midwest, then to the southwestern states and Indian Territories, and finally to the Pacific states.

The two principles that determined expansion in the late nineteenth century among the leaders of Kappa Alpha were practicality and sectional identification.

The pragmaticism of the fraternal manifest destiny extended in a direction that would allow for the largest number of new chapters, and thereby new members, with the least opposition, in the shortest period of time—more members, more money, more prestige and power. During the Civil War the fraternal system of Southern institutions fell into abeyence and was nearly destroyed, some of the old lodges were able to limp back, but many failed. The Southern landscape was one that was lacking in competition and fertile ground for planting new fratenities. In Northern colleges many of the old associations were maintained and, after the war, expanded. It is certain that attempts to "head north" would have met with great resistence and acrimony.

The harsh realities of attempts to expand northwards, however, fit in nicely with the Ammen's vision of the Order's mission, namely to perpetuate the history and culture of the old South lest it be destroyed by deliberate intervention or the passage of time. Thus, from the beginning, with a few aberrations, the movement was to the South and West.

The first fifteen chapters were all located in the Southeast. By natural progression, in the early 1880s Kappa Alpha expanded into the Deep South, lodges were raised at Tulane University in New Orleans (1882); Southern University in Greensboro, Alabama (1882); Vanderbilt in Nashville, Tennessee (1883); Centre College in Danville, Kentucky (1883), Alabama Polytechnic Institute at Auburn, Alabama (1883); University of Tennessee at Knoxville, Tennessee (1883); University of Alabama in Tuscaloosa (1885); and Louisiana State University at Baton Rouge (1885).

The Midwest and the Southwest were in the direct pathway in the march to the Pacific coast. The two major tests for Ammen, and presumably a majority of the southern members, was a test of congeniality and a geographic equation. The test of congeniality was based on "territories peopled by folks not hostile to the South in general sentiment[54]"; the geographic considerations restricted expansion to "all that region south of the Mason & Dixon's line (extended to the Pacific) as is possible and desirable."[55]

The Knight Commander elaborated, "'Going West' is the same as going

North, if regard be had either to the test of congeniality or to the geographic test. Every Western State is 'north' of some Southern State, in sentiment as well as latitude. There can be no objection to entering Oklahoma, Arizona, New Mexico, or Indian Territory, when they develop suitable colleges ... but 'West' includes such rankly antipathetic States as Ohio, Indiana, and Kansas. California is not a 'Western' State, but a 'Pacific' State, peopled from the South, and never having shared ... the feeling which characterizes the attitude of Northern and Western people toward the South."[56]

The initial thrusts forward were in the Deep South—Louisiana, Mississippi, and Alabama—and in those states tangential to the Southeast—Kentucky, Tennessee, Arkansas, and Missouri. The next incursion was into Texas, long regarded as southern both in location and in sympathies, and finally out to the Golden West—California.

One of the earliest of the midwestern fringe state institutions was the William Jewell College located in Liberty, Clay County, Missouri. It was initially funded by physician William Jewell in 1849. Throughout the Civil War most of

*Jewell Hall, William Jewell College, circa 1890*

the Clay County residents sympathized with the South as many had migrated from Virginia. During the war the campus was twice occupied by Union troops.

After the war there little appetite among the students for fraternal orders; there was also little opposition and the Zeta Phi Chapter of Phi Gamma Delta plugged along. But in 1886, a group of antifraternity agents, nicknamed "barbs" mounted a crusade against secret societies and were determined to root out the "fraternal pest." These barbs called themselves the Invincible Twenty-Three and pursued a study to prove the deleterious impact of secret organizations. Their study concluded, however, that a fraternal organization was really a good thing and that the Kappa Alpha chapter best exemplified the type of society that was most beneficial.

Induced by the results of this work, on January 26, 1887, a charter was granted by the Knight Commander to the Alpha Delta Chapter and on February 5, 1887, the charter members met at the Arthur House for their first session. Following a difficult year, the lodge grew in strength and numbers. The members exemplified the wholesomeness of the Midwest and the tradition of Old Alpha.[57]

Tulane University in New Orleans serves as an exemplar of the type of institution that the Order was seeking out. Founded as the University of Louisiana in 1834, it began its history as a medical school. In 1845, the university modified its scholastic identity to that of a liberal arts college.

*Tulane University, 1909*

Because of the war, the university closed its doors in 1861, and when it reopened it operated with a reduced schedule and faculty. In 1882, the institution's fortunes improved when a local merchant, Paul Tulane, who was childless, decided to adopt the school as a substitute daughter. He added to his substantial endowment by tirelessly campaigning among other sympathetic supporters to amass a sum of one million dollars, in 1880s money, to reinvent the institution. Money is the paper fertilizer that makes things grow. And, indeed they did. In gratitude, the school was renamed Tulane University by an act of the legislature in 1884. While still under the aegis of the University of Louisiana in 1882, however, John S. Chandler, along with four other students had gained a charter and were initiated into the sacred rites of Kappa Alpha. So was born the Psi Chapter of Kappa Alpha, very much at home in the South.

It was only a short distance, both in terms of geography and sentiment, from Louisiana and Mississippi to the Southwest. The state of Texas was founded mainly by southerners and many settlers came from Virginia, for example, Sam Houston was from Lexington. Two of the earliest sites to plant the Kappa Alpha

*Southwestern University, Georgetown, Texas*

Order were the University of Texas and Southwestern University and the lodges were founded almost in the same month. In the fall of 1883, the University of Texas at Austin opened its doors. On October 8, 1883, Phi Delta Theta established a lodge at the university and one week later, on October 18, 1883, the Omicron Chapter of Kappa Alpha was founded there. The following month, on November 28, 1883, Alexander Stuart Walker and Frederick Cocke Procter, both of the newly formed Omicron Chapter at the University of Texas, returned to Georgetown and founded the Xi Chapter at Southwestern University.

The only secret organization that had been at Southwestern, the Duke Viola Chapter of the Rainbow Fraternity, had closed its doors because of faculty opposition and university regulations. Therefore, for three years the Xi Chapter operated in secret, or sub rosa, meeting irregularly, in constant fear of discovery and suppression. In 1887, the faculty voted to repeal antifraternity rules and Xi thereafter flourished in the sunlight.

In 1893, Kappa Alpha was granted the privilege of escorting young ladies to parties and the first official event occurred in 1896, when "Southern Gentlemen" of the Xi Chapter escorted young ladies to an entertainment at Mrs. Mood's home. "The affair was heavily chaperoned, and the woman students were escorted to and from the affair by a teacher." The society grew rapidly in reputation, popularity and numbers and by 1895 had constructed and occupied a chapter house.[58]

The expansion fever became absolutely incandescent and many in the Order were anxious to extend Kappa Alpha's reach all the way to the Pacific Ocean. Thus, one of the most interesting and exhilarating segments of fulfilling the ambition of the Order's own version of Manifest Destiny began. Not that it was accomplished without the reservations and trepidation of some members of the Order.

Initially, Samuel Ammen hesitated and considered the southern *bonae fides* of California to be questionable at best. He stated that "I have never regarded California as a Northern state in the sense that Pennsylvania is."[59] In applying his criteria for establishment of new chapters—the geographic and affinity test—he begrudging acknowledged that "Univ Cal [is] not in 'the South', tho it is the same latitude as Lexington,"[60] and that "two-thirds of California are south of the Mason and Dixon's line extended."[61]

In respect to a test of affinity, Ammen admitted that California was "peopled by folks not hostile to the South in general sentiment… and is perhaps mixed or neutral in this regard."[62] He also conceded that "on the main point of congeniality between chapters in California and the South the situation [is] believed to be satisfactory."[63]

Despite these tepid approvals, Ammen confided to Hubard that "it is with some reluctance that I go to California—a new departure. Only the exceptionally good prospects & the southern latitude reconcile me—imperfectly—to it[64]"; moreover, "My heart is not in it—a sentimental halt."[65]

Hubard, on the other hand, was an enthusiastic supporter of the move to the Pacific coast and Ammen noted to himself that he had received a "Letter from Univ Calif Berkeley asking charter… write to Hubard for advice & vote, sending petition in my name, tho' I tell him it does not imply I favor it."[66] Within a short time the KC accepted the aggregate thoughts of his closest associates, "Hubard favors chartering California! So does W.S. Hamilton & Penick & other men of Alpha Lambda… Benners favors California… all favor it but me."[67] Ammen slowly began to reconcile himself to the prospect of entering the institutions of the Golden State into the ranks of the Order 'All the Council favors it & all members I consulted.'" Still he added, "I hesitate much."[68]

One of Ammen's greatest concerns, other than the ambiguous geographic and sentimentality tests, was that fraternities "in the West" lacked the seriousness of purpose and moral compass, and that they "tend to large and promiscuous masses immersed in college politics."[69] Although at the very same time these ethical issues were being raised about the California colleges, Ammen noted the peccadillos of various lodges nearer to home. He viewed the actions of a chapter in Baltimore with a great deal more understanding and leniency, "I warned A-λ… it must stop gambling in 1st floor rooms "[70]; and the following week he reiterated and expanded, "Alpha Lambda . . . there should be no more imbibition of spirits or play for $ on the 1st floor."[71]

In a short time, however, Ammen's concerns about the University of California were mollified. Perhaps, this change in attitude was caused by the unanimous consensus of his compatriots on the council or perhaps to the growing realization of the benefits that might accrue to the Order by the addition of these lodges, and, likely, his reconciliation was a combination of the two factors.

The true story about Kappa Alpha at the University of California actually started in January 1895, when a group of students wrote to John Keeble expressing their interest in inaugurating a chapter of Kappa Alpha at the university. "There being a group of students out here who are earnestly desirous of establishing your Fraternity in the University of California at Berkeley, it becomes my purpose to make enquiry as to the steps necessary to be taken on application for a charter. . . . We have become thoroughly imbued with the idea

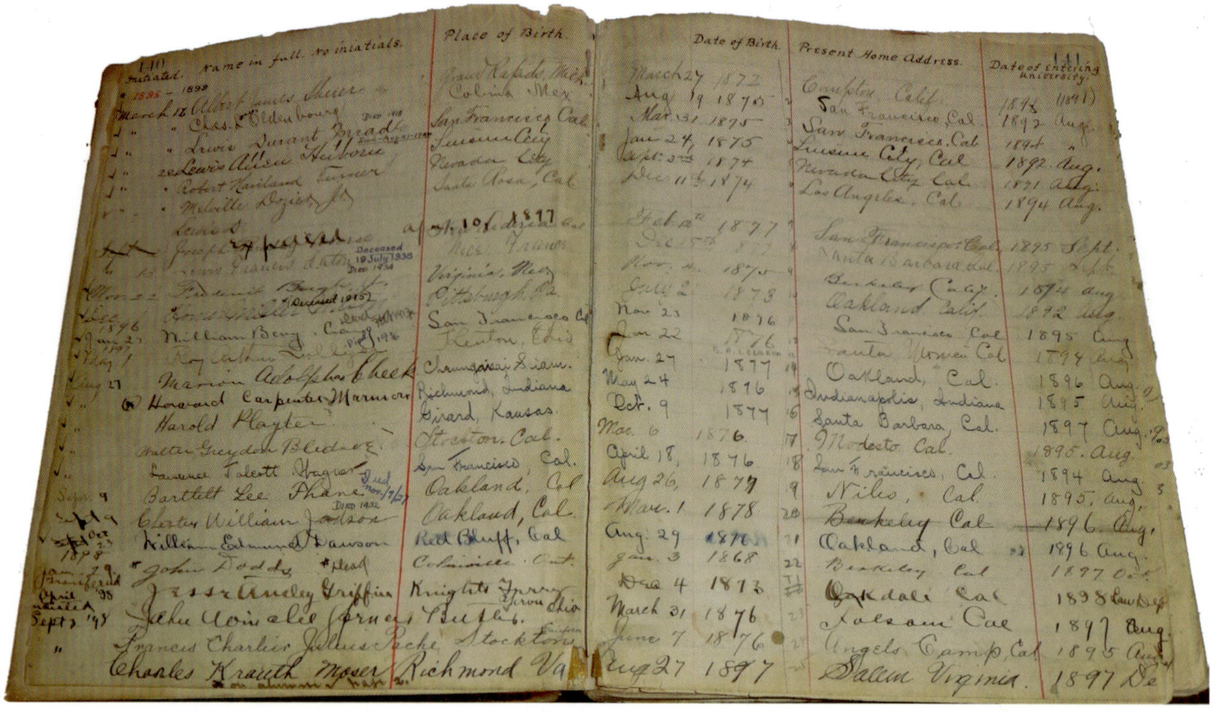


*Alpha Xi Member Roster, 1895–1898*

that in our University the Kappa Alpha would find an excellent field wherein to grow and flourish. It is beyond conjecture that a chapter could advantageously be placed on the Pacific Coast."[72]

The request was forwarded to Ammen, who followed up in February by finding a Kappa Alpha in the area to assess the situation, "Thro' W.S. Hamilton I found Mr Bonta, Chi, in San Franciso, and have had a letter saying he would take the Berkeley matter in hand: had written to Sherer to come and see him."[73] Evidently, the meeting took place and it was reported that "Bonta kindly visited the 8 men & recommends them & the place."[74]

From this point forward, matters proceeded quickly. In early March, Ammen instructed Tazewell Hubard to "please send at once to Mr W.S. Bonta (attorney at law), No. 39–40, 5th Floor, Mills Building, San Francisco Rituals, CS & Pursers blank-books, copy minutes '93, Annual Catalogues, alumni circulars, pads, CH report blanks, charter and what else (with advice) you think necessary."[75] The letter continued that Bonta went to the campus to interview the men "of whom I have detailed accounts, individually, and whom I find men of good standing and character. [Bonta] warmly commends these men & the prospects."[76] He also commended the eight saying, "There are many frats there now & our 8 have been sought, but stood apart and sought us. I believe A-Xi will be a good chapter and enter us into California creditably."[77] In addition to the positive news about the situation at Berkeley and the content of the character of the applicants, Bonta also reported, "The men assure me we shall have a chapter house!"[78]

Enthused by the report, on March 9, Ammen "sent Keeble an account of University of Cal. & first steps of a A-Xi."[79] About ten days later a letter came to Ammen in Baltimore, "Letter from Bonta (of 15th) saying my letter (of 6$^{th}$) was rec'd 'some days ago' and the ritual was on the 15th & he will 'without delay' proceed to create A-Xi." The hesitation had completely dissipated and on the first of April Ammen confided in his diary, "I am anxious about hearing from California....Bonta failed?"[80] But his fears were soon put to rest, "Hubard writes A-Xi was organized with 6 men & I sign charter."[81]

The University of California was the result of the ambitions of a group New England clerics who came to California in the days of the great gold rush, when the Bay Area was known more for sin than sensibility. Its first incarnation was as a preparatory school located in a former fandango dance hall in Oakland, California. In 1868, the state legislature established the institution as the University of California and the campus was moved to a site in Berkeley, four miles from Oakland. "Here it now is overlooking the beautiful Bay of San Francisco and the Golden Gate, commanding one of the finest of the... marine views of the world."[82] The physical orientation of the university is towards the Pacific and the East, reflecting the mandate of the eponymous Bishop George Berkeley and Manifest Destiny, "Westward the course of empire takes it way."[83]

By the time that Alpha Xi was chartered, the university encompassed more than a thousand acres "facing the Golden Gate and bounded on the rear by the foothills of the coast range."[84] The situation of the university "is all that could be desired, standard of instruction high, number of students large, and a faculty to be proud of."[85] The two major buildings of the university were the North and South Halls and the Bacon Library with its "60000 volumes and art gallery."[86] At the time of Alpha Xi's founding, the university was the home to more than 1,600 students and, even though it was thought that the founding of Stanford would diminish the numbers at Berkeley, surprisingly they increased to the extent of overcrowded classrooms and a spate of construction. The expansion of the campus and the student body seemed to be insured as the university "is so handsomely endowed that there seems no danger of it ever being in want."[87]

And the prospects for the fraternity were also as favorable as they were for the institution, while in the first year the members of the lodge thought it "best not to increase the membership" and to rely on the incoming class for more pledges.[88] The author of the article estimated that "from the present indications the next Freshman class will have between three and four hundred members; from them we should gain sufficient numbers to put us on so firm a footing that we can hold our own against the oldest established fraternities here."[89]

One of the greatest draws to Berkeley was an active social life and the fact that tuition was free. Another incentive was that there were "innumerable clubs organized for various purposes; student newspapers and magazines, debating unions, [and] athletic organizations."[90] But, in particular, the University of California was a good fraternity college, for which there are several reasons: first there were no dormitories which made the prospect of a chapter house very appealing; second, as antifraternity laws were unknown the number of "frats" was constantly on the increase, and, third, they had in their numbers representatives from the best families in the state.[91]

For most of the eastern lodges, especially in the first years, chapter meetings were held at a member's family's home, or a hotel, or a hall at the college and, occasionally, at a building that the fraternity had constructed. But, in California, "All the frats have their own Chapter Halls."[92] The chapter house at Berkeley was functional, since there were no dormitories and since lodging was limited, it was used residentially as well as socially. And the members of the fraternity were often those that came from affluent families. As could be expected, having been exposed to the progressive and liberal life style of San Francisco in the Gilded Age and without financial worries, the brothers of Alpha Xi lived an entertaining existence.

The first chapter house of Alpha Xi was about two blocks from campus and was often the center of drama laced with a fair dose of comedy. A note to historian Tazewell Hubard reported that one day a "Chinese laundry-man came in violent protest, simply because his account was some five months in arrears, and to this house came the ruling of the National Order forbidding such racy performances as using Brother Hussey as a suspended tackling bag."[93] The high jinx continued at the next residence where athletics was the chief focus of college life, but a change began to occur when the chapter moved to its residence on Ridge Road, where athletics and also student affairs became prominent. "Here, also was a distinct advance of bookkeeping and financial management, and a regard for scholarship that placed the chapter near the top of the campus. It was in this house that the war came [WW I]."[94]

As the influence and the presence of the chapter increased, so did the

*University of California, Berkeley, Alpha Xi House, circa 1928*

elegance of the chapter houses. In 1922, with financing made available by the alumni of the chapter and the Alpha Xi Building and Loan Association, the lodge bought a residence on Piedmont Avenue, "The property was exceedingly choice . . . and without question one of the finest fraternity houses in Berkeley and the whole West. At the time of the purchase the chapter house appeared in the *House Beautiful* and *American Home* magazines."[95]

Elements from Berkeley soon were supporting a move to establish a chapter at the newly founded and neighboring Stanford University. On February 20, 1896, James A. Griffin wrote to Tazewell Hubard that he had, by chance, met a member of the freshly minted Alpha Xi from the nearby University of California, who persuaded him that a branch at Stanford would be a good thing. "The chapter had its origin in the following way: last summer Chas. L. Oldenbourg [Alpha Xi] met me in Angels Camp of this state where we both were stopping. We became friends and I told him that I intended to join a certain frat on returning to college in the fall. He then confided to me as follows: Alpha Xi wants a chapter at Stanford and wants a man at the lat[t]er place to work it up for him in the early fall. I at last consented to be that man. Immediately after returning to college for this year I began to look for fraternity material and out of a dozen or so who appeared favorable to me"[96]

After seeking out appropriate candidates and sizing up both their character and their abilities to contribute to the fraternity he wrote to Ammen in August requesting to be made familiar with the next steps, "Aug 16 1895 Letter from Stanford Unity Cal J.R. Griffin asking about a charter."[97] Several days later Ammen noted, "Wrote to Griffin to see A-Xi & be guided by them, sending list, petition & catalogue."[98] Griffin informed Hubard that he had petitioned for a charter and the "KC and Council acting favorably, we were initiated and organized into Alpha Pi under the auspices of Alpha Xi at San Francisco on Nov 20, 1895."[99] After only a short time in operation, Griffin boasted, "We now have a membership of eleven, are domiciled in a chapter house [residence] and, on the whole, I consider that we are in very flourishing condition."[100]

The Leland Stanford Junior University was founded by Leland and Jane Stanford in 1885, in memory of their son who had died of typhoid fever. They decided that their institution would be something practical and universally useful for the future—it would be nondenominational, coeducational, and pragmatic, with a mission to create not only cultured but also effective citizens. The Founding Grant stated the university's objective was "to qualify its students for personal success, and direct usefulness in life" and its purpose was "to

*Leland Stanford Junior University, 1905*

promote the public welfare by exercising an influence in behalf of humanity and civilization."

Stanford University is located in Palo Alto, California, about thirty miles south of San Francisco on a large tract of land that the Stanfords had formerly used for breeding and training horses. Stanford opened on October 1, 1891, with a class of 555.

Stanford was an impressive campus from the beginning, stylized with stone rectangular buildings that were linked by semicircular archways and red roof tiles. Leland Stanford recruited some of the finest educational talent in the country for his institution as well and offered the presidency to Andrew White, then president of Cornell. A number of buildings on campus were destroyed by the Earthquake of 1906, but the university was rebuilt and expanded during the following decades.

Alpha Pi of Stanford, the kid brother of Alpha Xi of the University of California, grew in leaps and bounds as did the college. Otto Van Norden wrote to Hubard not long after their chapter was launched, "Our chapter has been doing splendidly the last year, we have moved into a new house and furnished it nicely. This has been an exceptionally hard year on fraternities and two have gone under. However, with a magnificent new Library and Assembly Hall completed the University attendance ought to pass the fifteen hundred mark next year and as the building goes on the growth will continue."[101]

The Alpha Pi House was an early product of the financial planning work done by the national Order and the alumni. The university forbade the fraternities from owning lots or raising mortgages, so the work was done by the Kappa Alpha House Association and the Kappa Alpha Fraternity—the first being a corporation existing under ordinary business conditions and the second a secret fraternal organization.[102] The structure was an imposing edifice attesting to the prestige of the organization—it was in the style of an English Tudor mansion, three stories, with the first shingled and the upper two half-timbered on stucco. There is a large porch and an impressive stairway greets one entering the front door, to the left is a massive living room with a limestone mantle piece. For the members' pleasure a billiard room was constructed adjoining the living room and the first floor is completed by a library, a dining hall, and a gourmet kitchen accompanied with pantries and wine closets.[103]

In regard to the policy of extension, it was noted that "when Leland Stanford, Jr., University was entered there was another step taken in that direction that clearly demonstrates the fact that hereafter only the question of practical results is to be considered. That it is wise to enter the West, we do not hesitate to affirm. All bridges are, burnt away; we cannot now go back."[104]

A statistical analysis from the 1900 catalog revealed "it will be found that our

*Alpha Pi Chapter House, Stanford University, circa 1900*

total membership taken in round numbers is about five thousand. Of this nearly ninety-five percent are men born in the South. Of the remaining five percent only two hundred and fifty—one percent—are Western born, one percent foreign born, and three percent Northern born. Alpha, Beta and Gamma [in Virginia and Georgia] count three and one-quarter percent Northern and 1 percent foreign born members; while Alpha Rho, Alpha Pi, Alpha Lambda and Alpha Nu, our extreme border chapters, have 33 percent of their enrollment Northern born men....Since the publication of the Catalogue Beta Beta [West Virginia] and Beta Epsilon [Delaware] have been established, with 80 percent of Northern born membership."[105]

The Order, which now extended from the Atlantic to the Pacific Oceans, was on the precipice of transitioning from a regional power to a national institution.

*Notes* Chapter 8:

1 S. Z. Ammen to W. K. Doty, March 18, 1920, Kappa Alpha Archives, Lexington, Va., 2.

2 Ibid., 3.

3 Leroy S. Boyd "A Summary of the Efforts of the Kappa Alpha Fraternity of the Southern States to Extend North and West for the Union with the Kappa Alpha Society of the North," Kappa Alpha Archives, Lexington, Va.,3.

4 William S. Hamilton, Hamilton, Synopses of the Conventions, 1870–1937, Kappa Alpha Archives, Lexington, Va., 9.

5 James W. Morris, "Union with Northern Kappa Alpha," *Kappa Alpha Journal* 1, No. 2 (January 1884): 1.

6 Ibid., 2.

7 Ibid.

8 Ibid., 3.

9 Ibid.

10 W. S. Hamilton, "Merger of Northern and Southern Kappa Alpha," Memorandum 17, Kappa Alpha Archives, Lexington, Va.,

11 Boyd "A Summary of the Efforts of the Kappa Alpha Fraternity," 1.

12 Walter Brown, "Against Union with Northern Kappa Alpha," *Kappa Alpha Journal* 1, No. 4 (June 1884): 2.

13 R. L. Parks, "Union with Northern Kappa Alpha," *Kappa Alpha Journal* 1, No. 3 (April 1884): 10.

14 Brown, "Against Union with Northern Kappa Alpha," 2.

15 Ibid., 3.

16 William Sprigg Hamilton, Memorandum 9, Kappa Alpha Archives, Lexington, Va., 30.

17 Parks, "Union with Northern Kappa Alpha," 10.

18 Charles Avery, May 25, 1884, in Joseph S. Chick, *History and Catalogue of the Kappa Alpha Fraternity* (Nashville: Kappa Alpha Order, 1891), xxxix.

19 Ibid.

20 Ibid.

21 S. Z. Ammen, August 28, 1904, "Northern Extension," *Kappa Alpha Journal* 22, No. 1 (October 1904): 11.

22 Ibid.

23 Boyd "A Summary of the Efforts of the Kappa Alpha Fraternity," 1.

24 Leroy Boyd to S. Z. Ammen, May 18, 1916, Ammen 13, Kappa Alpha Archives, Lexington, Va., 17.

25 "A Letter from Judge Hardeman," Jo Lane Stern to John Hardeman, April 27, 1870, in *Kappa Alpha Journal* 19, No. 2 (November 1901): 175.

26 Ammen Pamphlet, "Origin of Kappa Alpha" Kappa Alpha Archives, Lexington, Va., 1.

27 S. Z. Ammen, "Wood as Founder," Kappa Alpha Archives, Lexington, Va., 16.

28 Charles C. Young, "The Origin of Kappa Alpha," in *A Record of the Members of Kappa Alpha Fraternity* (New York: Kellogg Press, 1892), 7.

29 Ibid.

30 Ibid., 8.

31 Ibid.

32 Ammen, "Wood as Founder," 8.

33 "History of KA at the University of Virginia," in *A Record of the Members of Kappa Alpha Fraternity*, 203.

34 Ibid.

35 Ibid.

36 "Origin of Kappa Alpha: Questionnaire submitted to James Ward Wood by Leroy Boyd," July 3, 1918, Question 8, Kappa Alpha Archives, Lexington, Va.

37 Ammen Report 63, Kappa Alpha Archives, Lexington, Va., 41.

38 Hamilton, Synopses of the Conventions, 1870–1937, p. 13.

39 Ibid., 15.

40 Ibid.

41 Kappa Alpha Minutes, January 24, 1868, Kappa Alpha Archives, Lexington, Va., 35.

42 Boyd "A Summary of the Efforts of the Kappa Alpha Fraternity," 3.

43 Ibid.

44 Ibid., 4.

45 Ibid.

46 W. A. James, "Alpha-Lambda and Johns Hopkins University," *Kappa Alpha Journal* 19, No. 4 (March 1902): 356.

47 *Washington Evening Star*, November 29, 1893, p. 8; William S. Hamilton, "George Washington University," Kappa Alpha Archives, Lexington, Va., 8.

48 Ibid., 4.

49 Ibid., 5.

50 S. Z. Ammen, entry August 14, 1895, Diary of the K.C.'s Office, 1891–1897, p. 14, Ammen 64, Kappa Alpha Archives, Lexington, Va., 182.

51 Ammen, June 22, 1895, Diary of the K.C.'s Office, 1891–1897, p. 181.

52 Ammen, June 27, 1895, Diary of the K.C.s Office, 1891–1897.

53 Ammen, June 15, 1895, Diary of the K.C.'s Office, 1891–1897.

54 S. Z. Ammen to Tazewell T. Hubard, February 5, 1896, Correspondence Book No. 6, November 18, 1895, to June 13, 1897, Kappa Alpha Archives, Lexington, Va., 5.

55 Ibid.

56 S. Z. Ammen, "Northern Extension," *Kappa Alpha Journal* 22, No. 1 (October 1904): 9.

57 Chick, *History and Catalogue of the Kappa Alpha Fraternity*, 324.

58 Ibid., 190–192; see also Gary Scott, Williamson County Historical Commission Report, http://www.williamson-county-historical-commission.org/GEORGETOWN_TEXAS/Xi_Chapter_Kappa_Alpha_Order_Southwestern_University_Georgetown_williamson_county_Texas.html (viewed April 29, 2015).

59 Ammen to Hubard, February 5, 1896, Correspondence Book No. 6, November 18, 1895, to June 13, 1897, p. 5.

60 S. Z. Ammen, February 1, 1895, Diary of the K.C.'s Office, 1891–1897, p. 14, Ammen 64, Kappa Alpha Archives, Lexington, Va., 174.

61 Ammen, "Northern Extension," 8.

62 Ammen to Hubard, February 5, 1896, Correspondence Book No. 6, November 18, 1895, to June 13, 1897, p. 5.

63 Ammen, "Northern Extension," 9.

64 S. Z. Ammen to Tazewell T. Hubard, March 6, 1895, Correspondence Book No. 5, September 1894–November 1896, Kappa Alpha Archives, Lexington, Va., 115.

65 S. Z. Ammen to Tazewell T. Hubard, February 27, 1895, Correspondence Book No. 5, September 1894–November 1896, Kappa Alpha Archives, Lexington, Va., 109.

66 S. Z. Ammen, entry February 1, 1895, Diary of the K.C.'s Office, 1891–1897, p. 14, Ammen 64, Kappa Alpha Archives, Lexington, Va., 174.

67 Ibid.

68 S. Z. Ammen to Tazewell T. Hubard, March 9, 1895, Correspondence Book No. 5, September 1894–November 1896, Kappa Alpha Archives, Lexington, Va., 114.

69 S. Z. Ammen, February 10, 1895, Diary of the K.C.'s Office, 1891–1897, p. 14, Ammen 64, Kappa Alpha Archives, Lexington, Va., 174.

70 Ibid.

71 S. Z. Ammen, February 16, 1895, Diary of the K.C.'s Office, 1891–1897, p. 14, Ammen 64, Kappa Alpha Archives, Lexington, Va., 175.

72 Albert J. Sherer to John Keeble, January 16, 1895, Correspondence Book No. 5, September 1894–November 1895, Kappa Alpha Archives, Lexington, Va., 105.

73 S. Z. Ammen to Tazewell T. Hubard, February 27, 1895, Correspondence Book No. 5, September 1894–November 1896, Kappa Alpha Archives, Lexington, Va., 109.

74 Ammen, March 6, 1895, Diary of the K.C.'s Office, 1891–1897, p. 176.

75 S. Z. Ammen to Tazewell T. Hubard, March 9, 1895, Correspondence Book No. 5, September 1894–November 1896, Kappa Alpha Archives, Lexington, Va., 114.

76 Ibid., 115.
77 Ibid.
78 Ibid.
79 S. Z. Ammen, March 9, 1895, Diary of the K.C.'s Office, 1891–1897, p. 14, Ammen 64, Kappa Alpha Archives, Lexington, Va., 176.
80 S. Z. Ammen, April 1, 1895, Diary of the K.C.'s Office, 1891–1897, p. 14, Ammen 64, Kappa Alpha Archives, Lexington, Va., 176.
81 Ibid.
82 "University of California History," *Kappa Alpha Journal* 19, No. 2 (November 1901): 150.
83 Ibid.
84 "At the University of California–Berkeley," *Kappa Alpha Journal* 12, No. 4 (June 1895): 336.
85 Ibid., 337.
86 Ibid.
87 Ibid., 336.
88 Ibid.
89 Ibid.
90 "University of California History," 150.
91 "University of California–Berkeley," 340.
92 Ibid.
93 Robert W. Stevens to Tazewell T. Hubard, March 21, 1949, Correspondence of William S. Hamilton, Kappa Alpha Archives, Lexington, Va., N.P.
94 Ibid.
95 Ibid.
96 James A. Griffin to Tazewell T. Hubard, February 20, 1896, Correspondence Book No. 7, January 23, 1897, to December 15, 1897, Kappa Alpha Archives, Lexington, Va., 40–41.
97 S. Z. Ammen, August 19, 1895, Diary of the K.C.'s Office, 1891–1897, p. 14, Ammen 64 Kappa Alpha Archives, Lexington, Va., 182.
98 S. Z. Ammen, August 19, 1895, Diary of the K.C.'s Office, 1891–1897, p. 14, Ammen 64, Kappa Alpha Archives, Lexington, Va., 183.
99 Griffin to Hubard, February 20, 1896, Correspondence Book No. 7, January 23, 1897, to December 15, 1897, p. 41.
100 Ibid.
101 Otto Van Norden to Tazewell T. Hubard, January 8, 1897, Correspondence Book No. 7, January 23, 1897, to December 15, 1897, Kappa Alpha Archives, Lexington, Va., 239.
102 "Alpha Pi," *Kappa Alpha Journal* 23, No. 3 (February 1906): 329.
103 Ibid.
104 "Stanford," *Kappa Alpha Journal* 13, No. 1 (October 1895): 85.
105 "Sectionalism," in William S. Hamilton's Memoranda Books, No. 9, Kappa Alpha Archives, Lexington, Va., 30.

*Convention of 1923, Washington, D.C.*

# 9

## A National Order

By the late nineteenth century, Kappa Alpha had already laid a foundation of expansion and common identity, but the leadership was beginning to envision a grander plan—one in which the Order would become national entity rather than a local or even regional organization. The surprisingly swift success of moving from the Southeast to the Deep South, to the Midwest, into the Southwest and to the Pacific coast of California led to ambitions beyond the earlier scope.

William Hamilton characterized the Convention of 1885 as follows, "[It] was one of the most important that had been held. It was composed of men who were determined to build the Order up to a substantial foundation. Until this convention the laws adopted had been more or less temporary.... The Order was having a solid growth; it was building up inwardly and becoming stronger in every way."[1]

The metamorphosis was more than growing ambition, a codification of bylaws, and a desire to expand; it was a synthesis of mission, a synchronization of action, a standardization of rules, an evocative integration of symbolic imagery and rituals, and the laying of a foundational structure—all to the effect of marshalling a cacophony of dissonant and discordant murmurs into a single and unified voice. And this voice was articulated through a defining and a refining of the internal infrastructure of the institution, which began in a reactive and almost intuitive manner.

In order to manage the often-tangled web of competing agenda within the rapidly expanding institution, the frequently overwhelmed KC depended on subordinates to supervise the various areas of activities and to manage them in an increasingly specialized fashion. A national identity evolved through the consensus of conventions, the regular publication of catalogs, the synthesis of diverse traditions into a common core of shared history and mythology, the establishment of communal body of literature and records, and the efforts to found a cultural and administrative Mecca that personified the ethos of the Order.

The first and most pragmatic steps came from the rapid growth of the Order itself. Even in the early stages "Old Alpha" was amazed by the swift extension of the society throughout the Southeast, but nothing prepared the leadership for the blitzkrieg of advancement that spurred expansion all the way to the Pacific Ocean. It was self-evident that the simplistic and casual template of managing the affairs of Kappa Alpha had outgrown the model of a single executive governing all aspects of the fraternity with little or no supporting staff. Following the military dictates of Caesar—divide and conquer—or, in this case, divide and survive.

Judge Philip Hamer, in 1913, described the early evolution as follows, "Thirty five years ago [1878], when my connection with Kappa Alpha began, the fraternity was a very different affair from the powerful machine-like organization we know today. At that time there were only eight chapters in active existence, and of these four were in Virginia, three in Georgia and one in South Carolina at Wofford College.... The active chapters were little more than independent local clubs. They operated under the same general name and used the same ritual, but the relationship between them practically began and ended with that. They knew nothing of one another; personal communication of any kind between them was practically unknown, and even correspondence was infrequent and brief."[2]

Hamer recalled that the period between 1880 and 1890 was remarkable in that twenty-one new lodges were added to the rolls and "for the first time, began to take on the form and semblance and substance of a real [organization]."[3] He explained that previously the fraternity had been too obsessed with 'extension' and 'we lost sight of our underlying reasons and motives for existence.'"[4] The first expression of the desire for a hierarchical design through delegation of power came during the Twelfth Biennial Convention in 1883 when it was resolved that the Order "shall be divided into Commanderies, subject to rearrangement by subsequent conventions, as the growth of the Order may require."[5] The divisions were named the First Commandery that consisted of Virginia and West Virginia; the Second Commandery included North and South Carolina; the Third Commandery embraced Georgia, Alabama, and Tennessee; and the Fourth Commandery comprised the newest territories, Louisiana, Mississippi, and Texas.[6]

It was determined that each sector would have a sectional officer known as a Knight Visitor, who would be an assistant to the KC. It was his responsibility to visit each chapter within his district at least once a year for inspection and to report his results to the Knight Commander. This plan, however "was not at all satisfactory" as neither the chapters within the districts nor the appointed Knight Visitors took their positions seriously and at the next convention the system was abolished.[7]

A serious attempt to return to the Knight Visitor System of provincial command did not take place until the twenty-third convention in 1905, when Verner Jones proposed an act "to improve the governmental efficiency of the Order," which replicated, in essence, the old Knight Visitor System of 1883.[8] The recommendation, however, died in committee "owing to the lack of legislative quorum."[9]

The question was not brought up again until the convention in 1911 when the prototype for the current Province System was established.[10] The new code required the Knight Commander to divide the Order into provinces, to include both active and alumni chapters, along such geographic boundaries to ensure "a moderately large convention." The provinces were organized with representatives of the chapters within a province meeting biennially to consider Kappa Alpha interests, both locally and generally, and with each council's electing a president who would organize the district and collect facts and reports for the Knight Commander. The Province Commander was charged with bringing members and chapters into closer contact and training local talent for the higher offices of the Order. The minutes of the meeting were transmitted to the Knight Commander for review and comment.[11]

In 1911, the Knight Commander, Samford C. Fullilove, rejected the proposal of some to reorganize according to state boundaries for a more elastic model. He decided to organize the Order into seven provinces and, through private correspondence, "find some one man in each province and charge him with the duty of organizing that province."[12] Since the code permitted drawing boundaries at the Knight Commander's discretion, he affirmed that he would entertain requests from individual chapters to be moved to another jurisdiction.[13]

The new designation of the redrawn districts were the Samuel Zenas Ammen Province, which included Virginia, West Virginia, Maryland, Delaware, and the District of Columbia; the Edward Chambers Smith Province—North and South Carolina; the John Slaughter Candler Province—Kentucky and Tennessee; the John Lumsden Hardeman Province—Alabama, Florida, and Georgia; the Horace Henry White Province—Louisiana, Mississippi, and Texas; the Philip Bascomb Hamer Province—Arkansas, Missouri, and Oklahoma; and the Daniel Rowell Neal, Jr., Province, which was solely devoted to California.[14]

Fullilove praised the Convention of 1911 for having the wisdom to frame the provisions of the system in such a way as to allow for flexibility in modifying the points of implementation and he noted that although "only a bare outline of the province organization was made," the outline will be "filled in by experience" and "be completed within a few years."[15] Keeping in mind the short-lived efforts of the Knight Visitor System of 1883, he added that the success or failure of the new plan was in the hands of the Province Commanders, who could either produce results large and fruitful if they were diligent or put an end to it by neglect. Moreover, the duties of the office were numerous and time consuming and included keeping in touch with the active chapters in his province, learning their conditions, "with special reference to difficulties which they encounter," advising the alumni chapters, and awakening their enthusiasm in order that they grow.[16]

An editorial in the same issue of the *Kappa Alpha Journal* in which Fullilove's article appeared pointed out "there is now established a school of efficient and trained laborers in command of restricted fields with which they are peculiarly acquainted. A live visitation and supervising organizer is about all that is now needed to render the organization machinery of the highest possible efficiency."[17]

According to the minutes of the 1915 Convention the newly defined duties of the Province Commander were articulated in a more-specific and accountable manner. He was to preside at the meetings of the Province Council; visit each chapter at least once a year and, spending at least two days at each visitation, was to investigate the chapter and its members and, time permitting, question members of other campus fraternities as to the actions and reputations of the Kappa Alpha brothers; advise the chapters; and, to report his findings to the Knight Commander.[18]

From this time forward, the Knight Commanders and the central administration began to rely increasingly on the input of the Province Commanders and expanded their role from visitations, inspections and advisors also to collect information and looking into and making budgetary recommendations. The Province System provided the administration with a linear hierarchy of the military mold and served as an organizational skeleton on which to hang the flesh of a cohesive national community.

While the Province System made more efficient and united the scattered and disorganized elements of the Order, the leaders of the institution also sought to create a more-regulated and cohesive organization by drawing together the diverse elements of the fraternity with a common values, traditions, history, and core of literature. The primary instrument to accomplish this end was a common core of literature—catalogs and a fraternity magazine. The catalogs provided a record of the Order's accomplishments and a proud roster of its members and their lives. The *Kappa Alpha Journal* was the vehicle of collective visions and current events and wisdom. It allowed members, active and alumni, to weigh in on heady issues of the day that affected the fraternal community, to keep abreast of the doings of their comrades and former friends, and give everyone the opportunity to contribute.

Former Knight Commander Dr. Idris R. Traylor, Jr. wrote in his "History of the Kappa Alpha Journal" that the publication was founded with the express intent to "bind together the scattered chapters, sustain the interest of alumni, and promote" the initiatives of the Order.[19] The *Journal* was conceived in the months directly preceding the Ninth Convention and was "a subject which had occupied" the attention of many delegates who attended the meeting."[20] Their enthusiastic support for the actualization of the publication made it one of great import for passage.

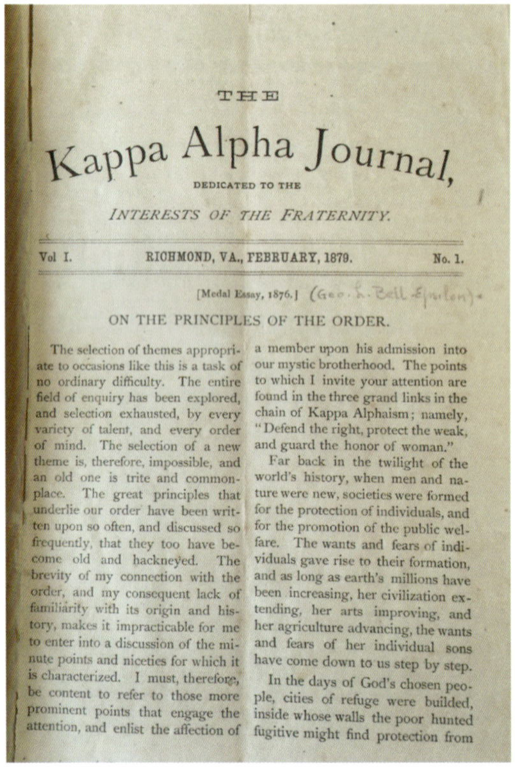

THE

Kappa Alpha Journal,

DEDICATED TO THE

*INTERESTS OF THE FRATERNITY.*

Vol I. RICHMOND, VA., FEBRUARY, 1879. No. 1.

[Medal Essay, 1876.]

ON THE PRINCIPLES OF THE ORDER.

The selection of themes appropriate to occasions like this is a task of no ordinary difficulty. The entire field of enquiry has been explored, and selection exhausted, by every variety of talent, and every order of mind. The selection of a new theme is, therefore, impossible, and an old one is trite and commonplace. The great principles that underlie our order have been written upon so often, and discussed so frequently, that they too have become old and hackneyed. The brevity of my connection with the order, and my consequent lack of familiarity with its origin and history, makes it impracticable for me to enter into a discussion of the minute points and niceties for which it is characterized. I must, therefore, be content to refer to those more prominent points that engage the attention, and enlist the affection of a member upon his admission into our mystic brotherhood. The points to which I invite your attention are found in the three grand links in the chain of Kappa Alphaism; namely, "Defend the right, protect the weak, and guard the honor of woman."

Far back in the twilight of the world's history, when men and nature were new, societies were formed for the protection of individuals, and for the promotion of the public welfare. The wants and fears of individuals gave rise to their formation, and as long as earth's millions have been increasing, her civilization extending, her arts improving, and her agriculture advancing, the wants and fears of her individual sons have come down to us step by step.

In the days of God's chosen people, cities of refuge were builded, inside whose walls the poor hunted fugitive might find protection from

Kappa Alpha Journal
*Vol. 1, No. 1, February, 1879*

In fact, William Hamilton considered the establishment of the *Journal* to be the most important accomplishment of the Ninth Convention. With the recommendation of delegates, the matter was referred to the Committee on New Business, which was comprised of "R. L. Honiker (Epsilon), R. T. Daniel (Epsilon), and W. T. Gaulden (Kappa), [who] reported favorably on a proposal to establish a K.A. Fraternity Journal."[21] These gentlemen declared that they approved the resolution "and suggested that a committee of five be elected, two of which committee shall act as editors and three as canvassers for subscriptions, and that the five be invested with discretionary powers to establish said *Journal* or not as they see fit."[22] According to historian Idris Traylor, "The recommendation was received with noisy approval and was unanimously passed."[23]

The *Kappa Alpha Journal,* founded in 1879, was

in the forefront of fraternal publications; the first successful edition of these journals was the *Beta Theta Pi*, which had first appeared in 1872, and several other periodicals west of the Appalachians followed. The first fraternal magazine that appeared in the East was Phi Upsilon's *Diamond* at Cornell in 1878, and the *Kappa Alpha Journal* of 1879 was "the first permanent publication of a fraternity of southern origin."[24] The vernacular conception took place when the fraternity was little more than a dozen years old, "had only eleven functioning chapters, a total of 562 active and alumni brothers, and its finances were in a constant state of depletion."[25]

The first editors were Herbert Clay Hill of Macon, Georgia, who had been a member of the Epsilon Chapter at the University of Georgia, and Mortimer Austin Turner of Richmond, Virginia, erstwhile brother of the Eta Chapter at Richmond College. Three publications were slated for publication for the first year; in the first issue it was stated "That the *Journal* will be the means by which a lively interest will be created, a bond of union established between the alumni and active members, and consequently a more united feeling with regards to what concerns the Order in general."[26]

The initial plan was to publish the first number at Richmond as soon as enough financial aid to warrant the venture could be obtained. There were to be forty pages-size octavo, double columns, to be published "once every three months during the scholastic year."[27] The subscription and distribution proposal was to divide the South between three canvassers, "who sent letters or circulars to all Kappa Alphas in their respective territories, asking active and alumni members to subscribe to the *Journal* which was referred to as 'A Golden Link that will serve to bind us together after we have left our Kappa Alpha Halls.'"[28] The price of subscription was one dollar per year and "it was *optional* with both active and alumni members whether they should subscribe for the JOURNAL or not."[29]

Unfortunately, the editors decided to follow the classical model of the publication of the old literary societies, which included items of short articles of elevated prose, poetry, literary criticism, biographies, and essays. Ironically, one of the articles in the first edition was entitled "Tempora mutantur et nos mutamur in illis" (The times are a-changing and we are being changed in them). But the editors harked back to the classical mold of their youth and did not change with the times. This was hardly the stuff that young college students were anxious to read, much less purchase, and it did not even hold much charm for the older and more erudite alumni. What both audiences were looking for was news about themselves, their old friends, events that might be of interest, and disparaging remarks about other Greek organizations.

The editors optimistically projected in the final (December 1879) edition of the first manifestation of the *Journal* that "the Kappa Alpha Journal has been a delightful surprise to the Fraternity. It has indicated in the Order more strength than many of us had been wont to suppose existed: it has developed strength which all of us desired. It has the 'promise and potency' of still greater things."[30]

In spite of the rosy predictions of December, even at the Convention of 1879 in the preceding July, the handwriting was already on the wall; although the financial gap was not great—the *Journal* had expended $161 in its production costs and taken in $131 in subscriptions. In order to rectify this deficiency, the members of the committee on the Good of the Order determined that each member "be assessed 25 cents for the support of the JOURNAL; that the money usually paid for the printing of the minutes be given to the JOURNAL, and that to any brother securing twelve subscribers one subscription be given."[31] Alas, in addition to a reluctance to change direction and take a more sustainable journalistic approach, the resolution was too little, too late.

In the December 1879 issue, with a great deal of finger-pointing in all other directions, the editors noted, "With the present issue of the JOURNAL, the highest hopes of those who actually wished for its success will end in consummation. After much perseverance, the editors and canvassers saw their plan assume a shape that was practicable and tangible, and at last the result of their work was seen in the appearance of the first and subsequent copies; and now they have to announce with this number the completion of the first volume." Thus, the first foray into fraternal journalism lasted but three issues. Simply put, "The purpose was correct, the motivation commendable, but the method chosen proved to be inadequate for the intent."[32]

Out of sight, however, was not out of mind in this endeavor; it was the consensus of active and alumni members that a common source of communication should be maintained. "Therefore, many delegates came to the Eleventh Convention in Richmond in 1883 with instructions to take action to revive the publication."[33] It was noted in the minutes of the convention that the delegates fulfilled their duty: "Whereas the growth of our Order… [necessitates] some means of binding together the chapters more closely in fraternal feeling to preserve our unity…we conceive that a suitable journal, not solely literary, but of the fraternity… shall serve [as] a means of both informing the members of the chapters' conditions, and also of spreading and preserving such knowledge of the Order… we hereby establish a fraternity journal."[34] The convention also determined that "a suitable man be elected every two years, that is shall be located in a central place and be supported by a subscription list and a fund for that purpose." The following day it was further resolved that the magazine be called the *Magazine of Kappa Alpha*, to be published quarterly, that the price of a subscription would be one dollar a year to be collected by the Knight Visitor, and that the support of the magazine would be determined by the finance committee.[35]

One of the editors made clear that the emphasis and the content of the new publication would leave behind the pretentions of a literary journal and would concentrate on expressed interests of the member—"Now that our fraternity has an organ, we should avail ourselves of this opportunity of discussing what we think will be of interest to the Order. To be a means of interchange of opinion is the aim of our MAGAZINE and the MAGAZINE will succeed just so far as we occupy its columns with discussion of pertinent questions. As our worthy and able editor has remarked, we do not want a literary journal; we want a journal devoted primarily to Kappa Alpha interests, and secondarily to the interests of the "Greek world" at large."[36]

The motion was carried to establish the *Magazine*, further that it was to be published quarterly, an editor and assistant were to be elected very two years, and a committee would be established to determine the finances. In July 1883, one of the elected editors passed away and the other resigned. P. B. Hamer was named as the successor and his first issue was published in Charleston, South Carolina, in November 1883.[37]

The articles were essentially devoted to discussions about expansion, the early history of the fraternity, "reprints from other fraternity magazines, and news from the "Greek World," which often contained humorously written articles about rival fraternities. The *Magazine* also published news and gossip of individual chapters, making personal observations—unhappily not married, with numerous children, still in Biloxi, a lawyer of many words and little note—all meant to entertain but not demean.

At the Thirteenth Convention in 1885, the magazine was again named the *Journal* and a step was taken "which for the first time gave the Order a full treasury and made possible the regular publication and constant development of the *Journal*. The annual contribution per member per session to the General Fund was quintupled, and it was decided to support the *Journal* out of the General Fund, voluntary subscriptions being no longer relied upon. A 'Grand Purser' was created to collect the General Fund from the Chapters, and the Chapter Pursers were required to pay dues to this officer monthly. The work of collecting and editing was placed on a strictly business basis by giving the Grand Purser a commission of 5 per cent on his collections, and by creating the office of Editor-in-Chief and establishing the principal of paying him for his services."[38] The changes taking place in respect to the fraternity journal presaged those to be taken in administrative and financial areas in the near future.

At the Fourteenth Biennial Convention, in 1887, the specifics of the *Journal* were expanded and refined—it now became a bimonthly publication; it had a staff of three—an Editor-in-Chief, a Business Manager, and a third to be determined by the first two; it contained sixty-four pages of reading material published five times during the collegiate year; chapters were fined for failure to send in a chapter letter to the editor, the magazine could be sold to non-KAs; and, Chi Chapter would publish the magazine.[39]

Previously the content, layout, and presentation of the *Journal* relied on the discretion of the editors; now much of this was prescribed by the fiats of the convention; formerly the publications were determined in a random fashion and now they were to be distributed at predetermined intervals; in the early years the financing of the *Journal* was left to the energy and diligence of the canvassers and the generosity of the readers; at this present juncture the marketability of the product was enhanced by both a central oversight in member purchases and a willingness to expand the marketplace to beyond the limits of the initiated—in other words, to anyone who would buy it. All of this reflected a concentration of authority, a linear approach to administrative methodology, and a more businesslike approach—the American Factory Model of the Gilded Age.

The Fifteenth Biennial Convention in 1889 modified the previous edict concerning the *Journal* in several respects; firstly, that the number of pages be reduced from sixty-four to fifty, secondly, that the journal be published monthly from October to June, and, thirdly, that the Chi Chapter be in charge of the *Journal* and that the editors were to be selected from "active or alumni members of the chapter now living in or near Nashville."[40] John Bell Keeble was named editor and "from this time the traditions and patterns for the *Journal* really began. In the first issue Keeble established regular features entitled the 'Greek Press' and 'Official Notes' and 'Personals' which Keeble assigned [to designated] places in the Journal."[41]

The Sixteenth Convention of 1891 introduced an expanding vision of administrative professionalism by consolidating the management of the *Kappa Alpha Journal* into the hands of the editor in chief and paying him a salary of three hundred dollars per year.[42] In 1895, the convention voted to appoint an assistant editor with an annual salary of one hundred and fifty dollars, thus reflecting the growing importance of the journal and the professionalism that was beginning to pervade the mindset of the administration.[43]

The transition that took place in the *Journal* was indicative of what was happening on a larger scale throughout the Order—a reorganization that made for an administration that was more professional, efficient, and responsive; a staff that had transitioned from often reluctant volunteers into a group of paid professional employees who regarded their work as a duty fulfilled rather than a favor imposed; a system of communication that was inclusive and increasingly necessary because of the exponential explosion of chapters and members and the burgeoning cadre of alumni; and a central location to conduct business. This modus operandi of linear restructuring became a characteristic that extends down to the present day.

Another facet of this organic effort to pull together all the members throughout the nation was the semiregular production of a fraternity catalog. The esoteric purpose of the publication was to instill a sense of pride and ownership among all the brothers, to act as an instrument of unity and coalescence, and to establish a common history and pedigree. On a more pragmatic level, it allowed members to connect with old friends, to locate former brothers of their own chapters or other chapters for business or social purposes, and to enable alumni to connect or reconnect with other Kappa Alphas in a society that was becoming progressively more mobile and transitory.

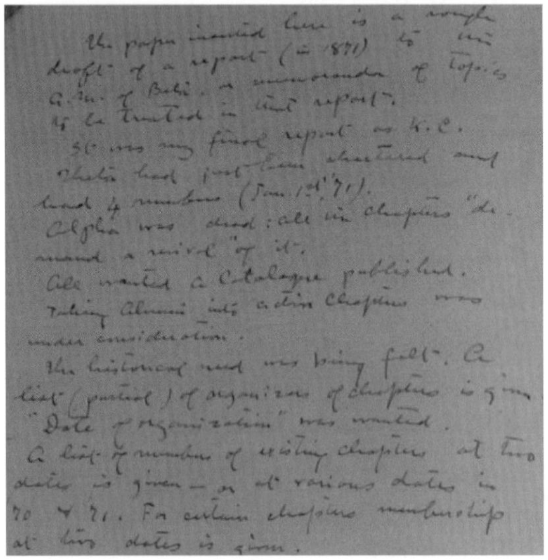
The paper inserted here is a rough draft of a report (in 1871) to the G. M. of Beta, a memoranda of topics to be treated in that report.
It was my final report as K. C.
Theta had just been chartered and had 4 members (Jan 1st '71).
Alpha was dead; all the chapters "demand a revival" of it.
All wanted a Catalogue published.
Taking Alumni into active Chapters was under consideration.
The historical need was being felt. A list (partial) of organizers of chapters is given.
"Date of organization" was wanted.
A list of members of existing chapters at two dates is given—or at various dates in 70 & 71. For certain chapters membership at two dates is given.

*Ammen's notes to the Original Alpha Minutes (206)*

As early as the Convention of 1870 the subject of establishing and financing of a fraternity catalog was first discussed.[44] Samuel Ammen reported in a rough draft of the First Convention, "All wanted a Catalogue published … the historical need was being felt. A list (partial) of organizers of chapters is given. Date of organization was wanted. A list of members of existing chapters at two dates is given—or at various dates in '70 & '71. For certain chapters membership at two dates is given."[45]

The 1870 Convention made it the duty of the Knight Commander "to compile and have printed statistics and Catalogues, showing the general condition of the Order" and took precedence in commitments from the General Fund.[46]

No concrete steps were taken, however, until three years later, in 1873, when the official history of the Kappa Alpha Catalogues began; a General Catalogue was compiled and issued by Knight Commander J. L. Hardeman. The volume was 16 pages in length, contained 297 names and included nine chapters – six active and three inactive. Two years later, in 1875, a second edition was completed by Hardeman and had grown to twenty pages, contained 392 names and covered twelve chapters.[47]

The Third Catalogue was compiled in 1878 by Knight Commander D. R. Neal Jr. The size had expanded to twenty-eight pages, it contained 562 names, with twelve chapters represented.[48] It also enjoyed "the distinction of having suggested and made possible the publication of the first volume of the KA Journal, which appeared in 1879. Supplying an up-to-date mailing list, this Catalogue enabled the official canvassers to collect money required for that enterprise."[49]

After the 1879 edition, the publication of the Catalogue on a predetermined basis "was for many years neglected."[50] With the rapid expansion of the Order in the next decade, the task of compiling a new directory became daunting and the Knight Commanders who immediately succeeded Neal "fought shy of the task the law imposed upon them, so it had ultimately to be arranged by the convention."[51] The Convention of 1885 concluded that the most expedient path for producing the much needed new catalog was to assign it to the most industrious and enthusiastic lodge – Rho Chapter was selected for the work. Nevertheless, Rho struggled with the task for four years "without making great progress."[52]

In 1889, the endeavor was next delegated to the Chi Chapter, which "in two years completed it, the finished catalog being presented to the Convention… in 1891."[53] Between 1879 and 1891, the Order was without an up-to-date listing of its members.[54] In the 1880s, the Knight Commander "received no reports, except such as might be made informally in private letters."[55] In 1891, Samuel Ammen was "amazed to find himself entirely out of touch with the Chapters and General Officers.... To bring the Chapters and Officers again into proper relations with the KC, [Ammen] prescribed a system of reports which had the effect of restoring the general organization."[56] Chapters were required to report certain facts to the Knight Commander monthly and to submit names and addresses to be used in compiling an annual catalog.[57]

Joseph Chick was the compiler and editor of the *History and Catalogue of the Kappa Alpha Fraternity of 1891*, which "was a handsome volume, printed on good paper in the best style of modern catalogue making, including, besides a history of the Order and each of its Chapters, full indices, statistical tables and numerous illustrations."[58] The publication was underwritten partially by an assessment on active members, partly by alumni subscriptions, and also by a draft upon the General Fund.[59] Although there existed the Hardeman Catalogues of 1873 and 1875 and the Neal Catalogue of 1878, along with the "scrappy and unsatisfactory" histories of individual chapters, until the 1891 publication there was little reliable data for members and officers of the Order.[60]

The prototypes of earlier editions had included a brief rendition of the founding of the Alpha Chapter and a listing of the members of the various chapters with abbreviated information about their progress in life and their current address and location. From the time of the 1878 Catalogue, the number of listings for members had ballooned from 562 to 2,303; the number of pages jumped from 28 to 431; the number of chapters (active and inactive) had almost tripled—from 12 to 32; and the cost of publication from $75 in 1878 to $1,770 in 1891.

But even Chick's monumental effort, as the editor admitted openly in the preface, had its deficiencies of inaccurate data—misspelled and omitted names, defective and incomplete histories, dates gone wrong, and most disconcerting to those affected, members who were alive and kicking being reported as dead. The Grand Historians, Tazewell Hubard and, subsequently, William S. Hamilton, put in place procedures to rectify the process of collecting data. Hubard procured register books in which to enter the names of all the members and asked alumni to assist in providing accurate information about each chapter. William Hamilton "conceived the idea" of compiling and publishing annual catalogs as "an excellent means of obtaining correct chapter lists for use in future General Catalogues."[61] By breaking down the process into annual increments, Hamilton set up a format by which the editors of the General Catalogues were relieved of the odious necessity of gathering together, from sources far and wide, in a limited amount of time—the names, addresses and up-to-date information of the members of the various chapters, and instead, for the most part, relied on data already-collected and categorized.[62]

*The Catalogue of 1900* was almost exclusively the work of Paul Murrill, who was appointed in 1899 as the editor of the Decennial Catalogue, "wisely giving him entire control of the formidable task of compiling and verifying the biographical data of a catalogue of four thousand five hundred names."[63] The whole task was completed within eighteen months—including the printing of the book.

Murrill encouraged members and alumni to subscribe to his new work and advertised the upcoming publication in the January 1901 issue of the *Kappa Alpha Journal* with the following description of the work: "The General Catalogue of the Kappa Alpha Order of the year 1900 will be completed and be ready for distribution about November 24th, and a copy will be sent to you on receipt of price. Prices are as follows: Bound in full red cloth, $1.75; bound in half Morocco and cloth, $2.00; full red leather, $2.50. Special bindings will be furnished if desired, and at a reasonable charge. The catalogue will be a volume of about 500 pages, printed on best quality of book paper, and will be complete and accurate up to date of August, 1900. It will contain a concise history of the fraternity, from the pen of S. Z. Ammen, ex Knight Commander, and also full alphabetical and geographical indexes to all members."[64]

The product of Murrill's labors lived up to his promises and Samuel Ammen praised both the style of writing and the terse utility of the volume, "Certain interesting facts in regard to each chapter are concisely stated. There are no pictures of persons or places, these being unnecessary in a practical band-book. The Order's Coat of Arms is the only illustration. As for the typographical execution, it is all that can be desired. The size and shape of the book and the paper are just right. Bro. Murrill brought to his task good judgment and taste as well as infinite patience and tact."[65]

The last General Catalogue before the Convention of 1923, which marked the end of the Old Guard of Alpha, was W. B. Crawford's *Directory of 1922*. An article in the *Kappa Alpha Journal* approved of the "use of India paper (which) give[s] us a book that can be carried in the coat pocket, a very desirable advantage, and although there are 1335 pages, it is not cumbersome in the least."[66] A rival fraternity, Alpha Tau Omega, reviewed the *Directory* in its own journal and while agreeing with its quality, disputed its convenience, "Kappa Alpha Order has just published a new directory, its third, edited by Grand Historian, W.B. Crawford. It is a very neat and well printed volume in what doubtless was meant to be pocket size, since the pages are small; but 1560 pages, even on very thin paper, give a bulk that would bulge the most capacious pocket."[67] New information seems to have been added in the intervening years of the articles as the size grew by 225 pages—a substantial amount but not large enough to discount Alpha Tau Omega's comment—but, perhaps, fashion diminished the size of pockets in the intervening years.

Sanford Fullilove also noted that, "The printing and binding are good. This makes a handsome, complete, and convenient volume."[68] Alpha Tau Omega agreed with this assessment and stated that the volume "was well-printed."[69] But Crawford's edition was not only praised for its convenience and quality but also, like the evolution of the Order itself for the effective organization, "There is our history, then our Chapters, then our members geographically arranged, and finally alphabetically arranged. A member desiring to look up a single individual, or to see what K A lives in a certain town or city has a quick answer right at hand."[70]

Foreshadowing the controversies that would dominate much of the Convention of 1923 and cause such friction among various factions and individuals of Old Alpha concerning the true origins of the founding, Fullilove stressed that "in addition to its eloquence there is a wealth of detail in this History. Facts that, at the time, were considered trivial, but now are of vast importance."[71]

Ammen from the first realized the significance of both the journal and the catalog "for the various important improvements of organization."[72] Both publications served as a catalyst, a sustaining influence, a unifying mechanism, and an enduring literary testament to the past, present, and future of the Order. The *Journal* allowed members, past and present, to keep abreast of issues and events in the fraternity's daily life and express their own viewpoints—promoting a feeling of community, the gratifying impression of involvement and that sense of purpose that often defines the awareness of self-importance. On a practical level, the catalog's main value was that "it enables members to communicate readily with each other, thus promoting intercourse and unity. It is at once a directory, mailing-list and a memorial."[73] In short, one of the most effective means of promoting a well-oiled and finely tuned business model for the Order was the promotional encouragement of its literary apparatus.

In a fascinating codicil, a book was recently brought to Kappa Alpha's current archivist, Sergeant Major E. Kent McMichael, who received a note written in 1952 by Miss Roberta Browning informing the fraternity of the discovery of a long-lost directory of the Alpha Chapter. The brief volume, in its primitive state, was rediscovered by a friend of the family among the effects of her father in the process of moving Miss Browning to a retirement home. The old catalog of the Alpha Chapter may have been the first attempt to record Kappa Alpha member information.

Miss Browning wrote more than a half a century ago, "Recently while looking through my late father's possessions, I discovered an old notebook belonging to your chapter in the 1860s, containing data on the first charter members, I believe, and also the history of the chapter."[74] Why Miss Browning did not send the letter and the notebook at the time is unknown. Her father, Edward Parry Browning, had been a Number I in Alpha and she supposed the tome had been entrusted to him before World War I.

*Frontis Plate, Alpha Chapter Catalogue, circa 1884*

The catalog contains a brief history of the Alpha Chapter. The handwriting abruptly changes in 1884 as does the subject matter; before this juncture the writer concentrated on a history of the chapter as it was being disseminated at that time, with the change in penmanship also came a shift in emphasis—the scribe concentrated specifically on the details of badges and dates of photographs. The historical section abruptly stops at this time. At the end of the catalog, in the 1890s, a brief recounting of the minutes of the chapter are inscribed. The date reflected was October 7, 1899. A new century must have required a new notebook. The catalog in and of itself is valuable as a relic of the earliest times of the fraternity and includes names and data not listed elsewhere.

The evolution of the fraternity into a national Order manifested itself not only in the changes to the internal structure and the nurturing of the literary traditions by which it defined itself, but also in the transformations that took place in its laws, the redefining of the roles of its officials, and the expansion and refinement of its bureaucracy.

When the fraternity was first founded, the rules and the officers were quite simple as suited the situation—every member an officer—the Grand Master, the Grand Scribe, the Second Master. The rules were uncomplicated and almost innocent—attend the meetings, be loyal to your comrades, pay your dues. Naturally, as the organization grew, the rules, rituals, and officers became more numerous and complex. As the early extension of the franchise took place, the leadership of Old Alpha tightly held onto the reins of authority, believing that the young chapters were like young children and lacked self-discipline and maturity. Indeed, the first child, the Beta Chapter at VMI held joint meetings, took group photographs with Alpha, the Betas shared the Alpha Hall, and celebrated conjointly the convivia and anniversaries. Even with their own officers and insignia, Beta remained under the wing of Alpha. The recently acquired Alpha Catalogue of the 1880s still included the names and information of Betas nestled in among the Alpha members.[75]

The extension of the Order, from the beginning, necessitated change and accommodation to emerging circumstances and the new voices joining the conversation. Thus, in addition to innovations, there were modifications and adaptations to rules already in place. The two areas most visibly affected were in the laws, particularly in the constitution, and the administration of the Order, most notably organizational structure and the evolving nature of the officers, especially the Knight Commander.

The changing nature of the office of Knight Commander began almost immediately after its inception. First the position was more or less a recording secretary for the Number I, created to sustain communications with newly formed lodges. As this function became more crucial to the survival and extension of the Order, the office became more essential and important. When he was elected Knight Commander, Samuel Ammen made the authority of the KC all powerful. When the new lodges demanded change at the First Convention, and Alpha yielded, she still inserted a restriction that impeded any swift changes and protected the hegemony of the Knight Commander and Alpha; namely that any proposals "may not change nor abrogate anything already contained" in the constitution and any additions "shall not have the force of laws, till the KC submits them to the various chapters for ratification, that a two-thirds majority in each chapter was necessary for a change to be effected, and the KC must declare them adopted."[76]

A profound shift in the constitutional nature of the Order took place at the Fourth Convention in 1873, removing the supreme power from the senior chapter and the Knight Commander and giving it to the delegates of the convention. The actions taken at that convention changed the dynamics of the Order making it more responsive and inclusive to the needs of the whole Order.

Kappa Alpha Historian, William S. Hamilton, called the 1885 Convention "one of the most important" in the history of the Order. He maintained that up until this time the laws had been adopted on a "more o[r] less temporary" basis. But, inasmuch as the Order "was having solid growth … it set the members to thinking" about a more effective way of orchestrating matters between the different lodges and branches of administration, which resulted in deliberate changes, resulting in the "rapid development of every part of the organization."[77] One of the most consequential outcomes was the creation of the Office of Grand Purser for the Order, who would direct the financial affairs of the Order in a systematic manner. The first man to hold the post was the same individual that proposed it, James Allen Williams.

Williams had held the post in the Fifth Commandery previously and perceived that the same post should be extended to the whole Order. In an article, Williams noted that "No organization, association or order, can exist without money ... that a college secret fraternity derives its rank in the Greek world, not from the number of her chapters or men, but rather from the quality of her men, the size and rank of the colleges in which her chapters are formed, and above all from the character of her printed *journal*, catalogue, chapter buildings, etc."[78] The Grand Purser, in the beginning, concentrated primarily on the collection of funds to support the literary efforts of the fraternity, but would come to encompass the duties of a chief financial officer—to collect fees, dues, fines, assessments; keep the financial records; be responsible for the safeguarding of property; and report his findings on a regular basis.

The finances of the Roman Empire were, until the time of Augustus, in the hands of the various generals, who accumulated great masses of wealth in various spoils of war and distributed them according to their own purposes; local officials sent to Rome not the entire amount of taxes collected but only what was demanded. This process made for a confused and fractious government. One of the first reforms of Augustus was that all taxes and monies that were collected were to be sent to Rome for an official accounting and that a redistribution of the funds would occur according to the best interests of the empire. The result was a linear and rational administration that benefited the entire realm and introduced a period of peace and stability and expansion that lasted for two centuries.

The office of Grand Purser operated in the same manner and with like results. It was one of the first steps to a reasoned and structured format for conducting the affairs of the Order. As it developed, as it progressed, the evolution of scientific methodology in administration grew with it.

A further realignment took place at the Fifteenth Convention in 1889, when it was resolved to establish a Board of Directors whose duty it was to "fill by appointment all general offices left vacant by death, resignation or disability."[79] Although the concepts of the office of Grand Purser and the Board of Directors were fine in theory, they were, at the time, lacking in execution.

When Ammen was reelected, after so long an absence, as Knight Commander in 1891, he found that "there was a lack of control throughout the whole fraternity; the Chapters were, if at all, but loosely articulated. The KC of 1891 received no reports, and had to apply to the Grand Purser for the addresses of the Chapters."[80] In 1893, Ammen wrote to Tazewell Hubard about the process of rewriting the fraternal constitution, "the work on [our] new Constitution, &c. is immense in volume—so much reflection, so much writing.... I feel that if I do again now in '93 the work I did in '68–'70, but better, I'll gain the lasting good will of our Fraternity. I work for that.... This is about the only ambition that I have. So I work to perfect our machinery."[81]

Eleven sections of the new constitution dealt with changes in the procedure by which new chapters were established. For "up to that time the power of granting a charter rested absolutely in the Knight Commander; nor was it necessary for him to take any steps toward satisfying himself as to the fitness of the institution."[82]

Some of the major changes included "no chapter shall be established *de novo* at any institution where there are less than sixty-five students of collegiate grades."[83] Also it was "prescribed that no chapter shall be established at an institution that has no academic department."[84] In order for a charter petition to be considered, the applicant needed to provide "sufficient information" in regard to the number of faculty, males in the collegiate department, and "the endowment; the income; the religious denomination, if any; the fraternities then established there; and information as to the men to whom it is proposed to commit the charter."[85]

If the substance of the report met with his approval, once the Knight Commander had garnered all of the necessary information, he would present the information, with whatever comments the Knight Commander thought appropriate, lay it before the chapters of the applicant state, and request their advice. If there was agreement, the Knight Commander met with his Council, the Grand Historian, the Grand Purser, and the Editor of the *Journal* as "these officers are in constant communication with the active and alumni members of the fraternity, and are generally prepared to easily decide upon the advisability of issuing a charter."[86] If the Council disapproved of the applicant's qualifications, the matter was ended; if it did approve, the final decision was in the hands of the Knight Commander. Thus, the ultimate power of accepting or rejecting a new application for chapter membership was effectively taken away from the local chapters and put back into the hands of the Knight Commander and his Council.

The thrust of these new bylaws was to ensure that chapters were established in larger and well-regarded institutions, that new members would be men of quality and consequence, and that the Order would grow in such a way as not only to enhance its coffers but also to reflect a reputation of dignity and respect. By this action the bar was raised for incoming lodges and the status of the Order elevated.

But Ammen's new constitution and the events that took place in the Convention of 1893, were more than procedural changes concerning chartering new lodges, they reflected a fundamental shift in emphasis and organization. A column in the *Journal* recognized the import of the new constitution and the work of the convention even in the moment of occurrence. "In the first place there was a sifting of all laws of general enactment and of constitutional nature. Everything of chaff was winnowed out. There was a reconciliation of apparently repugnant principles. There was a careful arrangement of the law in a convenient manner. All the new methods adopted of volition by the executive officers for the past two years were made a part of the constitutional duties of these officers.... All of the machinery was put in good condition; within a few years the fraternity should be almost automatic."[87] While a consensus of opinion and advice was advocated in Ammen's new constitution, it also provided for a reconcentration of authority in the hands of the Knight Commander, thus enabling, like Augustus, a nexus of power and decision making. These changes manifested themselves over the coming decades in the transition of the organizational structure and the progression from an ad hoc bureaucracy scattered about the country into a cadre of professional administrators situated in a central and permanent location.

The Twenty-Second Convention in 1903, made a proposal that presaged the establishment of a professional administrative bureaucracy within the Order. This small beginning would have profound implications for the growth of the Order following the end of the First World War. The resolution read, "We believe that the Order has grown to such proportions that it is unjust to require a Knight Commander to devote his time to the details of the office, which could be properly performed by a clerk. We therefore recommend that three hundred dollars be appropriated to be used as a salary for such a clerk."[88]

At the 1905 Convention, former Knight Commander, John Hardeman, made an address comparing the Knight Commander to a general, "The Knight Commander accordingly has the authority of a military officer to direct the movements of the force under his command. The other officers of the Order being members of his staff and the heads of chapters, captains of companies—all are, in fact, sworn to obedience and in theory, discipline is enforced."[89] So while a ramification of duties was coming into force, the determining factor, the *primus inter pares*, remained the Knight Commander. Ammen had not short-changed himself or the office.

But the bywords of the new era were method and competence. In addition to a revision of the old Knight Visitor System, the 1905 Convention also proposed a bill to provide a "fund for the building of chapter houses and the supporting of the *Journal*."[90]

The Knight Commander, Edward Chambers Smith, advocated that the necessary steps be taken to incorporate the Order and copyright the fraternity pin.[91] The Certificate for the Act of Incorporation of the Kappa Alpha Order was presented to Judge S. H. Letcher on April 1, 1907, in the Circuit Court of Rockbridge County. The purposes of the incorporation was

> to maintain and establish Active Chapters at educational institutions in Virginia and elsewhere, and in towns and cities Alumni Chapters; to buy, erect, or receive by gift, devise, contract, conveyance or otherwise, property real or personal, at Lexington, Virginia, or elsewhere, within or without the state of Virginia, with grounds and appurtenances to be used as places for meetings or depositories for archives, records and papers, of the Kappa Alpha Order, or any Chapter or officer thereof, and for such other purposes as the hereinafter named Trustees or their successors may deem proper under suitable rules and regulations to be made by them under the authority of the Convention, constitution or by-laws, of the Kappa Alpha Order, the said property and franchises are to be held and used solely for fraternal, benevolent, charitable and literary purposes, according to the principles, usages and teachings of the Kappa Alpha Order.[92]

At the next convention, in 1909, Knight Commander Smith proposed to adjust the administrative schema of the previous convention. He noted that it ought to be clear to everyone paying attention that "our governmental system needs reconstruction. It is crude and lacks systematic arrangement. In many cases the duties are not placed in the hands of the proper officers, and in some cases duties pertaining to the same subject are divided among several officers. In my opinion we should divide the work as at present under four general heads, the Executive, Financial, Historical, and Publication."[93] The administrative articulation begins in earnest with this resolve.

Knight Commander Smith, preparing to depart from office, also advocated for the beginnings of a clerical staff to assist the top official of the Order, "The

Executive, Knight Commander, should have charge of all executive work, hampered as little as possible, and should be allowed a sum sufficient for office expenses and to employ a first rate secretary, competent to do all the general work under his supervision, leaving to the other officers only those duties pertaining to their special departments."[94]

In 1911, the Convention further refined the Province System from operating along geographic lines according to state demarcations and making more pragmatic clusters of authority. The country was divided into seven provinces, each named for an influential member of the society and each was to be governed by a Province Commander, a position and a title of responsibility and respect to this day.

In other matters the Knight Commander, although he had appointed a "committee of three for the revision of the constitution," agreed with the other members of his council, that, for the time being, "there was no necessity for haste, as the present Constitution met fairly well with present conditions."[95] In 1913, the Twenty-Seventh Biennial Convention authorized the Knight Commander to "appoint a General Secretary at a salary not to exceed $1,500 per annum, to raise and collect money for an endowment fund; to visit active and alumni chapters," to promote the circulation of the *Kappa Alpha Journal* and "to do such other things as may be considered advisable and to the best interest of the Order."[96]

The exigencies of World War I turned the attention of the delegates from the local interest of the fraternity to those of the country and, for the most part, the status quo was maintained. With the conflict over and the nation back on safe and solid ground, however, the Order once again turned its attention to the growth and refinement of the fraternity. Two such initiatives were the establishment of regular and professional salaries for the officers of the Order, and the founding of a national headquarters.

The professionalization of the Kappa Alpha bureaucracy continued apace and a number of resolutions were passed in this regard: the Grand Historian was allowed to "appoint one or more assistants … to aid him in his work," the Business Manager of the Journal was to receive $200 a year in salary and 10% of the subscription monies, the Journal's editor $300 per annum, the Grand Historian $500 per annum, the Grand Purser 'shall receive ... $200 per year ... and a commission of 5% on all moneys collected by him,' and the Knight Commander—$500 yearly."[97] In 1927, it was resolved to establish the post of the Travelling Secretary at an annual salary of $3,500, "who would give his entire time to the work of the Order" and carry out the instructions of the Knight Commander and the other General Officers.[98]

At the Thirty-Seventh Convention of 1933, the office of Travelling Secretary was abolished and replaced by the Executive Secretary, who was to be paid $4,000 per year and was to carry out the Orders of the General Officers as well as the executive decisions of the Knight Commander.[99]

The Thirty-Eight Convention of 1935, took into consideration the findings of the Constitutional Committee and resolved that the Constitution of the Order be amended "by repealing in toto all of the existing constitutions ... together with all amendments" and adopting the recommendations of the Committee.[100]

The Committee after "a thorough study of the history of the Order's government and the systems used by other leading social fraternities" prepared "a clear, concise, and forceful statement of the ideal form of government for the Order and its subordinate units."[101] The Constitutional Committee advocated that laws of Kappa Alpha be coordinated with respect to the ideals of the present administration; that it retain the fundamental principles of the Order; that the material be presented "in a logical form tending to greatest simplicity of its use"; that the changes made were to be restricted only to the existing provisions "where experience of the Order or of other leading fraternities has shown a change to be wise"; and, it has set out "in a distinct manner" the various offices and units of the Order for the greatest efficiency.[102] The final result of the Committee's work, according to the article, was to state "in a very concise statement the fundamental law of the Order" and projected that "this Constitution should require few amendments in the future."[103]

After a roll call it was determined that the requisite number of votes had been cast and the new constitution was adopted "without a dissenting vote being cast against it."[104] The new constitution provided that the Administrative Office in New Orleans be continued; the duties of the Knight Commander remain the same; the duties of the Grand historian, Grand Purser, Editor of the *Journal*, and Chief Alumnus will "be administered by a full-time Executive Secretary, located at the Administrative Office"; the advisory capacity of the four General Officers was replaced by an Executive Council who would work in conjunction with the Province Commanders "thereby giving a flexible, small working organization to deal with the current affairs of the Order; and a slightly larger deliberative body… to advise and consent in the more important matters, including the granting of charters."[105]

"In lieu of the old these old offices," the creation of the office of the Executive Secretary and the Executive Council composed of four councilors and the Knight Commander, fundamentally changed the nature of the administrative function of the Order and streamlined the decision-making process while at the same time making it more inclusive.[106]

The four councilors of the Executive Council served as the Knight Commander's cabinet, in effect, as his eyes and ears providing perspective and experience. They were ubiquitous and omnipresent—showing up for a Province Meeting in New Orleans, making an appearance at a smoker at Wake Forest, observing a football rivalry at UCLA, unveiling a memorial tablet in Robinson Hall, visiting the Lambda Chapter in Charlottesville, attending an alumni banquet at the Jefferson Hotel in Richmond, installing the Mu Chapter at the University of Tulsa, officiating at a ceremony of Wood Province officers at St. John's College, lecturing at the convention in Jacksonville, assisting in the establishment of the KA Scholarship Advisory Board—the duties and obligations were varied and numerous, but all making a presence known and joining together the dispersed elements of the Order.

While the economic conditions were gaining ground at home and the financial conditions of the Order were slightly improving, ominous rumblings in Europe were beginning to cause concern. The economic difficulties of the

Depression were reflected in the financial conditions of fraternities but Kappa Alpha soldiered on. Chapter and Province Meetings were held at more or less regular intervals; conventions took place under more austere conditions but attended to new and old business much in the accustomed fashion.

Franklin Roosevelt had signaled his intentions of involving the United States in the expanding conflict in Europe as early as 1939, with the Fourth Neutrality Act, which allowed American companies to supply armaments to belligerents provided that they were paid in cash. In 1941, the president geared up American industry to mass produce armaments to the Allies and raise a stockpile of weapons and machinery to defeat the Nazi threat, which led Congress to pass the Lend-Lease Act of 1941; after the USS *Greer* was fired on by German U-boats, Roosevelt issued a shoot on sight order for American vessels. On December 7, 1941, "a day which will live in infamy," Japanese planes attacked the American Fleet at Pearl Harbor. America entered the war, and for all intents and purposes, American fraternities ceased to exist. And while the chapters, bereft of their active members, slept, the administrative team did their best to keep up the spirits of their brethren, both at home and abroad, with news of the accomplishments and acts of heroism of their members overseas and personal stories and items of their families and friends at home

The Forty-First Convention in August 1941 was the last to take place until the end of the war. When the Executive Council met in Louisville, Kentucky, in October 1943, the conventions were officially postponed; chapter after chapter depleted of members old and new—closed; the only news that William S. Hamilton had to report for his chronology of Kappa Alpha for the year 1943 was that John McKissick had died.[107]

With the advance of American, British and Soviet troops through German territory and a light at the end of the tunnel being seen, Americans in general and the Kappa Alpha Order in particular, set their sights on rebuilding and welcoming home old comrades. The Executive Council met as the Postwar Organization Committee in February 1945, "to study the general situation respecting all chapters arising out of the national emergency and to propose a plan of reactivation."[108]

Less than ten weeks later the Postwar Organization Committee met in conjunction with the Province Commanders, and the Reactivation Committee for the Kappa Alpha Order was established. The Servicemen's Readjustment Act of 1944, better known as the GI Bill, provided for low-cost mortgages, low-interest business loans, one year of unemployment compensation, and as cash payments for tuition and living expenses to attend universities, was already in place; it was self-evident that the college ranks would swell with far more students than had ever been able to afford an education before and these students would have money to spend.

The prospect for growth of the fraternal orders seemed assured, and the same desire to belong to a circle of friends that impelled many veterans to want to become fraternal brothers after the Civil War, would also compel the returning veterans to seek out a band of brothers in a similar manner. Moreover, these new recruits to the Order were bound by a far more profound purpose than those who, in peacetime, were seeking recreational and business opportunities. Thus not only the ranks of lodges would soon burst but also there would be a deeper appreciation and sense of belonging with their generation.

All the efforts, whether deliberate or unconscious, which had taken place since 1891 within the Order, to reorganize, to restructure, to refine, to redefine, to become a tighter, more unified, and more dedicated society would pay unintended dividends in the organization that would arise like a phoenix, from the ashes of war, just as the founders of Kappa Alpha had risen from the surrender of Lee at Appomattox.

Another aspect of this consolidation and restructuring was an impetus for a common core—both pragmatically and emotionally—that eventually, joined together, and would lead the Order back to Lexington. The practical application had to do with a central location in which the various officers and support staff members could work together under one roof to improve communications between all the various branches of the administration. The emotional component was an expression of identity and belonging, a common place to remember and honor the past—a Memorial Hall. Likely because of the locations of the various officers of the Order and their hometowns and the difficulty of commuting to faraway headquarters, often a particular branch of the Order was located in the place most convenient to the head official—the central office might be in New Orleans, the *Journal* offices in Nashville, the historian's archives in Norfolk—depending on the official in office at the time. When the convention elected a new official, the headquarters for that division of the administration probably would also change. Thus, it made the location of the central office tenuous and the potential of a permanent home impractical.

It was not reasonable to expect individuals to uproot their families and neglect their own affairs in order to attend to matters that were voluntary and often either poorly paid or paid not at all. Even with these factors, being self-evident, however, efforts began to establish a permanent home for the Order in the early twentieth century and one for a Memorial Hall even earlier.

Like the early tribes of Israel, the ark and covenant of Kappa Alpha journeyed back and forth on an odyssey of more than one hundred years until it reached its own Jerusalem in the mountains of Virginia and the place of its birth. The details of this trek, however, will be investigated fully in a later chapter. But for now, it is important to know that the establishment of a central and permanent home, both in terms of efficiency of operation and confluence of affection, was essential to the Order's continuing growth and sustainability.

*Notes* Chapter 9:

1 William S. Hamilton, Synopses of the Kappa Alpha Conventions, 1870–1937, Kappa Alpha Archives, Lexington, Va., 15.

2 P. B. Hamer, "Kappa Alpha Development," *Kappa Alpha Journal* 29, No. 2 (January 1913): 169.

3 Ibid., 170.

4 Ibid.

5 Hamilton, Synopses of the Kappa Alpha Conventions, 1870–1937, p. 8.

6 Ibid.

7 Ibid., 9.

8 Ibid., 29.

9 H. T. Burnley, "The Convention of 1905," *Kappa Alpha Journal* 23, No. 1 (October 1905): 11.

10 Hamilton, Synopses of the Kappa Alpha Conventions, 1870–1937, p. 34.

11 W. B. Crawford, *Directory of the Kappa Alpha Order, 1865–1922* (Atlanta: Index Printing Co., 1922), 45.

12 Sanford Fullilove, "Knight Commander's Opening Address," *Kappa Alpha Journal* 28, No. 3 (February 1912): 37.

13 Ibid.

14 William S. Hamilton, The Chronological Record of Kappa Alpha Order, 1866–1940, Kappa Alpha Archives, Lexington, Va., 34.

15 Sanford Fullilove, "From the Knight Commander," *Kappa Alpha Journal* 30, No. 2 (January 1913): 202

16 Ibid.

17 "Editorial," *Kappa Alpha Journal* 30, No. 2 (January 1913): 301.

18 *Minutes of the Twenty-eighth Biennial Convention* (Kissimmee, Fla.: Kissimmee Valley Gazette Press, 1915), 34.

19 Idris Traylor, "The Kappa Alpha Journal: A 100-Year History," *Kappa Alpha Journal* 96, No. 1 (Winter 1978): 2.

20 Ibid., 3.

21 "The Kappa Alpha Journal," *Kappa Alpha Journal* 18, No. 2 (November 1900): 74.

22 Hamilton, Synopses of the Kappa Alpha Conventions, 1870–1937, p. 7.

23 Traylor, "The Kappa Alpha Journal: A 100-Year History," 3.

24 Ibid., 2.

25 Ibid., 3.

26 Ibid.

27 "The Kappa Alpha Journal," 75.

28 Ibid.

29 Ibid.

30 Traylor, "The Kappa Alpha Journal: A 100-Year History," 4; "A Plan and a Plea for the KA Review," *Kappa Alpha Journal* 1, No. 3 (December 1879): 101.

31 Hamilton, Synopses of the Kappa Alpha Conventions, 1870–1937, p. 7.

32 Traylor, "The Kappa Alpha Journal: A 100-Year History," 2.

33 Ibid., 4.

34 Hamilton, Synopses of the Kappa Alpha Conventions, 1870–1937, p. 9.

35 Ibid.

36 E. B. McGilvary, "A few voluntary remarks," *Kappa Alpha Journal* 1, No. 3 (April 1884): 7.

37 "The Kappa Alpha Journal," 80.

38 Ibid., 81.

39 Hamilton, Synopses of the Kappa Alpha Conventions, 1870–1937, p. 12.

40 Ibid., 14.

41 "The Kappa Alpha Journal," 84.

42 Hamilton, Synopses of the Kappa Alpha Conventions, 1870–1937, p.14.
43 "The Kappa Alpha Journal," 85.
44 Joseph Chick, *History and Catalogue of the Kappa Alpha Fraternity* (Nashville: Chi Chapter, 1891), xxxvi.
45 Alpha Minutes with Commentary by S. Z. Ammen, Kappa Alpha Archives, Lexington, Va., interladen before page 29.
46 Crawford, *Directory of the Kappa Alpha Order,* 31.
47 Samuel Z. Ammen, "The General Catalogue of 1900," *Kappa Alpha Journal* 18, No. 3 (January 1901): 259.
48 Ibid.
49 Ibid., 256.
50 Ibid.
51 Ibid.
52 Ibid., 257.
53 Ibid.
54 Crawford, *Directory of the Kappa Alpha Order*, 31.
55 Ibid.
56 Ibid.
57 Ibid.
58 Ammen, "The General Catalogue of 1900," 257.
59 Ibid.
60 Ibid.
61 Ibid., 258.
62 Ibid.
63 Ibid., 256.
64 Paul Murrill, "From the Catalogue Editor," *Kappa Alpha Journal* 18, No. 3 (January 1901): 149.
65 Ammen, "The General Catalogue of 1900," 259.
66 Sanford Fullilove, "The New Directory," *Kappa Alpha Journal* 39, No. 1 (November 1922): 46.
67 "Kappa Alpha Directory," *Palm of Alpha Tau Omega* 49, No. 2 (May 1929): 202.
68 Fullilove, "The New Directory," 46.
69 "Kappa Alpha Directory," *Palm of Alpha Tau Omega*, 202.
70 Fullilove, "The New Directory," 46.
71 Ibid., 47.
72 Ammen, "The General Catalogue of 1900," 258.
73 Ibid.
74 Roberta Browning to President of the Kappa Alpha Fraternity, November 29, 1952, Kappa Alpha Archives, Lexington, Va., 1.
75 Alpha Catalogue of 1884, Kappa Alpha Archives, Lexington, Va., ad passim.
76 William S. Hamilton, Chronological History of Kappa Alpha, Kappa Alpha Archives, Lexington, Va., 7.
77 Hamilton, Synopses of the Kappa Alpha Conventions, 1870–1937, p. 11.

78 James Williams, "Official Communication," *Kappa Alpha Journal* 3, No. 4 (January 1886): 13.

79 Hamilton, Synopses of the Kappa Alpha Conventions, 1870–1937, p. 14.

80 William Kavanaugh Doty, *Samuel Zenas Ammen and the Kappa Alpha Order* (Charlottesville: Surber-Arundale Co., 1922), 46.

81 Samuel Ammen to Tazewell Hubard, March 9, 1893, Tazewell Hubard Correspondence Book, No. 2, Kappa Alpha Archives, Lexington, Va., 64.

82 "The New Plan," *Kappa Alpha Journal* 11, No. 1 (October 1893): 32.

83 Ibid.

84 Ibid.

85 Ibid., 32.

86 "The Convention of 1893," *Kappa Alpha Journal* 11, No. 1 (October 1893): 6.

87 Ibid.

88 *Minutes of the Twenty-Second Regular Convention of the Kappa Alpha Order* (Raleigh: E. M. Uzzell, 1903), 12.

89 Hamilton, Synopses of the Kappa Alpha Conventions, 1870–1937, p. 27.

90 *Minutes of the Twenty-Third Regular Convention of the Kappa Alpha Order* (Raleigh: E. M. Uzzell, 1905), 16.

91 Ibid., 20.

92 *Minutes of the Twenty-Fourth Biennial Convention of the Kappa Alpha Order* (Jackson: Tucker Printing House, 1907), 28.

93 *Minutes of the Twenty-Fifth Biennial Convention of the Kappa Alpha Order* (Jackson: Tucker Printing House, 1909), 8.

94 Ibid.

95 *Minutes of the Twenty-Sixth Biennial Convention of the Kappa Alpha Order* (Jackson: Tucker Printing House, 1911), 14.

96 Hamilton, Synopses of the Kappa Alpha Conventions, 1870–1937, p. 35.

97 *Minutes of the Thirty-First Biennial Convention of the Kappa Alpha Order* (Orlando: W. Crawford, 1921), 18.

98 Hamilton, Synopses of the Kappa Alpha Conventions, 1870–1937, p. 49.

99 Ibid., 55.

100 Ibid., 56.

101 "Constitutional Committee Makes Report," *Kappa Alpha Journal* 52, No. 1 (November 1935): 9.

102 Ibid.

103 Ibid.

104 "The 38th Biennial Convention," *Kappa Alpha Journal* 52, No. 1 (November 1935): 92.

105 Ibid.

106 William S. Hamilton, "Kappa Alpha Chronology," *Kappa Alpha Journal* 62, No. 2 (January 1946): 12.

107 Ibid., 6.

108 Ibid.

*Funeral Cortege of Franklin Delano Roosevelt: A Changing of the Guard*

# 10

## Vertical Integration: A New Model for Progress

The stock market crash of October 1929 abruptly brought an end to the boom times of the twenties, and a new and stark reality to a nation of vibrant and optimistic men and women. The status quo had suddenly been stood on its head, and many suffered a substantial reversal of fortunes and a totally unwelcomed change of perspective.

The Depression brought on by the crash affected not only the financial state of Americans but also psychologically shook to the core their system of values and perspectives on what was true. Affluent citizens were broke, middle-class families were on the streets, and the scions of wealthy families were forced to quit college and take on whatever work they could find. That new reality also left diminished the ranks of the fraternities that inhabited the campuses.

In 1932, Franklin Delano Roosevelt was swept into office as president on a promise of a New Deal meant to restore the nation. The programs Roosevelt proposed were known as the three Rs—relief, reform, and recovery. Desperate times called for desperate measures, and some of the solutions that FDR found necessary and appropriate upset the conservative elements of the population, particularly with respect to elastic interpretations of the Constitution and the division of powers between the state and federal governments.

In the financial arena, the president created the Securities and Exchange Commission, the Federal Deposit Insurance Corporation, and the Social

Security Administration. These entities formed the initial basis for a sound financial system. The immediate problems of unemployment and displacement were addressed by the Federal Emergency Relief Act (FERA), the Civil Works Administration, and the Civilian Conservation Corps. FERA supplied jobs to employable citizens on the welfare rolls; the Civil Works Administration provided short-term employment for unskilled laborers on the nation's infrastructure—building dams, roads, and bridges; the Civilian Conservation Corps not only put to work thousands of unemployed men repairing roads, establishing national and state parks, and fighting fires, but also provided shelter, food, and vocational training in armylike CCC camps.

The result of these combined efforts was to produce a national government more responsive to the needs of the country with a more cohesive decision-making process—thus, reducing, combining, or eliminating many of the departments and forcing the various agencies to work together in a more systematic fashion.

On December 7, 1941—a day that will live in infamy—the Japanese air force bombed the American Fleet at Pearl Harbor, Hawaii. Now the efforts that had been in play to make life better for the individual and then society became consolidated in a patriotic struggle to defend the nation. Roosevelt called for the country to defeat the enemy by outproducing them "overwhelmingly." Americans responded and the results were startling—in 1941, American shipping launched more vessels in that one year than Japan did during the entire war; in 1944, the United States produced more planes than Japan did from 1939 to 1945, and, by the end of the war, America was responsible for more than one-half of all industrial production in the world.

The fate and actions of the Kappa Alpha Order, like that of any other organization in America, followed the collective path of the nation. During the 1930s many chapters of the fraternity either were seriously reduced or closed up altogether because of the failure of families to be able to send their sons to college or the ability of members to maintain their dues. Once hostilities commenced and America entered the war, young men in college and those intending to attend school quickly joined the armed services. The last convention before the war was held in Virginia Beach in August 1941, and another one did not take place until 1947.

The *Kappa Alpha Journal* took on a patriotic utility during the war years. Gone were the articles about fraternity houses, examinations of methods of expansion, and news from the provinces; more conspicuous were themes and content modified to support the war effort and of interest to Kappa Alphas both at home and abroad. The various chapters proudly advertised their members and the branches in which they served in the "Legion of Honor" column; a new segment entitled "Campus Chatter" relayed news of the accomplishments and promotions of the enlisted men; chapter letters were devoted to stories about members in the services; "Military Notes" presented letters from brothers across the seas—somewhere in England, somewhere in Africa—the letters often noted; "Stars-Bars-Chevrons" featured photographs of heroic members in uniform; "Military Sketches" gave accounts about various members divided into the separate branches of the armed services; "Cenotaph" provided obituaries of those who had made the ultimate sacrifice for the country; Kappa Alphan George Patton was a frequent target of praise and example; the pages were even littered with semihumorous cartoons depicting KAs as soldiers. The domestic news was demoted to a segment known as "KAKA News"—whether this was Kappa Alpha doubled up or related to the Greek sense of the word is a matter for conjecture. The contents of the *Journal* were, no doubt, an accurate reflection of the hearts and minds, hopes and prayers, of both the Order collectively and of individual members on a more personal level.

The mindset and the policies of the Order's administration in many ways mirrored that of the American people and government. In the 1930s, pessimism prevailed and just as the country seemed to be turning the corner and spirits rose—the war abroad intervened. The quiet desperation and cautious anticipation of better things to come, turned to resolution and an iron will of determination. Although the national situation had not returned to normal, the uncertainty and malaise of the Depression was replaced with the self-satisfying steadfastness of a commitment to a mission undertaken for the greater good.

As the war pressed on, the clouds began to lift and the optimism brought about by the light at the end of the tunnel energized and emboldened the outlook of the nation. The triumph of good over evil was predicted, but even as late as 1945 the Executive Council decided to postpone, again, the convention under the rationalization that there were "restrictions on transportation and the difficulties in obtaining hotel accommodations."[1]

*Knight Commander John Berryman*

Nevertheless, the Knight Commander in 1945, John Berryman, shortly issued a positive note in the *Journal* proclaiming that "now that the events of the war have taken a favorable turn, surely everyone will become more enthusiastic as to the future."[2] He predicted that the war in the Pacific would soon be completed and "the sooner this feat is accomplished the sooner we can get back to the normal way of life and dig in."[3] Plans were already afoot for the reactivation of the Order. Berryman apprised his readers that not only was the Order interested in those chapters "who have been forced to suspend due to war activities, but also in the ones that have been able to remain open and operate on a somewhat curtailed basis. The plan that has been devised and thoroughly discussed at a recent meeting in the Administrative Office can well be made a realization with hard work and cooperation from all connected with our organization."[4]

The first meeting of the Reactivation Committee took place in Washington, D.C., on February 17, 1945, and was comprised of Kappa Alphas who were members of either the legal community in the Capital or the federal government. Many of those advising the Executive Committee on this matter had also been consulted by the government on programs and policies connected with correcting the economic situation of the 1930s and the war effort of the 1940s. This reevaluation and rehabilitation of the national framework, of simplifying and making the flow chart of business into a more-streamlined and efficient template was at this point in time also being applied to the Order and its policies and activities. Once again the history of Kappa Alpha Order mirrored the history of the nation.

The Executive Council, taking its cues from FDR's popular reforms, began to refine, revise, and reconstruct the governance of the Order. The committee explained its mission and the importance of cooperation in the preamble to the Reactivation Program, "Never before in the history of Kappa Alpha Order has there been a greater need for the interest and cooperation of every member of the fraternity than at this moment. We have but one objective—the restoration of active chapters which have been temporarily closed by the national emergency and the strengthening and rebuilding of the active chapters that are still in operation."[5] The Council explained that the Reactivation Program provided a unique opportunity "to strip our fraternity system of its nonessentials and past bad practices."[6] By revamping and consolidating the structure and policies of the institution the Order could return to the fundamentals and reaffirm the "aims, purposes and precepts of Kappa Alpha."[7]

One of the first reforms was to be the installation of new officers to coordinate and consolidate the reactivation process. The three officials included a National Liaison Officer, whose duties included meeting and talking with younger active members and the alumni on fraternity problems of administration and operation, and contacting and discussing "fraternity values and aims with college administrators" in order to enlist their support for the reestablishment of fraternity chapters on their campuses. In anticipation of a large influx of incoming applicants, the second set of new administrators were classified as Reactivation Officers and their primary goals were "to aid in active rushing, instruct in chapter operation and the initiatory observances, and train pledges."[8] The third branch of the reactivation initiative were the voluntary Reactivation Committees. They were to maintain a general oversight of the individual chapters and to assist veterans returning to college; to rush, pledge, and initiate new members; to direct the election of new officers, if needed; to solicit funds from alumni and other sources; and, supervise the finances of active chapters. In addition, the committee was charged with communicating the needs of individual chapters "in the work of restoring and rebuilding the chapter."[9]

The Reactivation Committee established a Chapter Loan Fund for the purpose of refurnishing and rebuilding existing chapter houses, or renting chapter houses with the approval of the Committee. It committed itself to hiring and paying the salaries of the necessary officials to carry out the business of the Order. The said officers were to inform the college administrations of the aims and ambitions of Kappa Alpha in order to solicit their support and to communicate with the returning members the plans of the Reactivation Committee.[10] The Committee produced a list of expectations of behavior for returning and new members, a rigorous plan of training for new pledges, and the abolition of hazing in any form.[11]

One aspect of the new plans that commanded extended consideration was the establishment of new chapter houses and the expansion of the scholarship program. When the Servicemen's Readjustment Act, or GI Bill, was passed on June 22, 1944, it became evident that the student population would increase dramatically at the conclusion of the war, and with this development new applicants to fraternities would also materialize.

*Howard P. Locke*

Howard P. Locke, a member of the Executive Council, who was instrumental in the postwar agenda, was at the time an executive attorney in the federal government, who had written authoritative articles on the workings of the Tax Division of the Department of Justice for the American Bar Association.[12] Locke, a federal employee during the Roosevelt administrations, was a keen advocate for reform and, at the critical time of the reactivation, an enthusiastic supporter of the expansion of the Fraternity Housing Corporation, the development of the Regional Advisor System, and the establishment of the Officers Training School, which became the National Leadership Institute and today is the Number I's Leadership Institute. He also wanted to promote a more-aggressive Interfraternity Conference as a proactive vehicle for a change in federal tax laws regarding donations to fraternal orders, particularly in relation to scholarship funds and issues of housing.

Foreseeing the financial difficulties of the returning veterans, the Reactivation plan called for an accelerated chapter house program to accommodate incoming students. The proposal maintained that "every active chapter shall maintain and operate a Chapter House, where finances permit and housing accommodations are available, or Chapter rooms, where a house is not practicable."[13] The committee would also see to it that every chapter house or meeting room be provided with appropriate "furniture and furnishings" and have a separate chapter room to "be set apart, to be used solely for meetings and initiations, and be furnished in dignity and good taste."[14] Perhaps the most-inviting prospect to potential pledges was the instruction that "a table shall be maintained in every Chapter House where the members can be furnished meals, as required, at reasonable prices."[15] And to make certain that everything was on the up-and-up, the Reactivation Committee requested that a "House Mother" be appointed to preserve the decorum and cleanliness of the chapter house, monitor the morals of the inhabitants, and ensure the domestic stability of the house and the kitchen. Other amenities to be offered were various facets of entertainment: a chapter library to be furnished with "music and Victrola records as well as books and magazines," and the formation of intramural sports competitions, "chapter plays and shows, etc." and discussion groups for the intellectual improvement of the members.

Alumni chapters were also encouraged to play an active role in the readjustment process by including the Order in their wills to help the returning servicemen, writing articles for the *Journal* explaining the mission and the values of the Order, visiting active chapters in their community, referring names of college-age Kappa Alpha legacies, and offering advice and encouragement to returning veterans.

The impetus for all this activity at the administrative levels of the Order was the overwhelming response to the GI Bill. The day of its passage President Roosevelt told the nation that the bill "gives servicemen and women the opportunity of resuming their education or technical training after discharge, or of taking a refresher or retraining course, not only without tuition charge up to $500 per school year, but with the right to receive a monthly living allowance while pursuing their studies." The president's seminal plan, however, for the GI Bill began two years earlier—November, 13, 1942, when he signed into law an amendment to the Selective Service Act lowering the draft age to eighteen. With the social and financial consequences of an economic depression fresh in the minds of all Americans and with Congress fearing a mass of returning veterans without jobs, Congress passed the GI Bill with the "educational reforms functioning as another form of unemployment relief."[16]

Prewar attitudes indicated that a college education had little relevance to the average man, "A 1937 *American Magazine* survey ... found that 70 percent were not particularly concerned with college degrees, believing they guaranteed no useful" advantages.[17] The general consensus at the time of the passage of the act was that "college going was associated with the consumption of the upper-middle class, something aspired to by some but often resented or dismissed as frivolous by many."[18]

Congress was of the same mind and believed that only a handful of returning servicemen would take advantage of the educational portion of the program. The war and the technological advances that had intervened, however, brought about a "refashioning of the perceived value of a college education [that] occurred while Americans adjusted to a new era, one dominated by corporate organizations, a mass media and an evolving consumer ethos."[19]

Almost no one expected the veterans to enroll in college in such large numbers. In three surveys conducted between 1943 and 1945, one found that 7 percent planned to return to school full time, another predicted 8 percent, and the last concluded that "a minimum of 8 percent and a maximum of 12 percent of all veterans would attend school or college."[20] Nevertheless, by the time the GI Bill's education title officially ended, 37 percent of all veterans had used its benefits.[21] During the peak enrollment year of 1947–48, the Director of Higher Education for New York State wrote, "When the G.I. Bill was made a law of the land it is probable that no one in his wildest flight of imagination anticipated that veterans would attend college in such numbers."[22]

According to educational historian Keith Olson, the story of the GI Bill was that of an unqualified success. *Time Magazine* classified it as the "most ambitious educational experiment" in the nation's history.[23] The measures of the GI Bill allowed "2,232,000 veterans to attend college at a cost of 5.5 billion dollars. For half a decade following the war veterans dominated the nation's campuses by their numbers and their academic superiority over nonveteran classmates. Aware of their opportunity, veterans tolerated with general good will crowded classrooms, inadequate housing, crammed libraries and overworked professors."[24] The postwar enrollments for American colleges and universities was 75 percent greater than the prewar matriculations and in many schools the numbers doubled.[25]

World War II had acted as a catalyst for the democratization of Americans—men from all levels of society had fought together and unlike in previous conflicts the sons of the aristocrats were not sequestered in the officer's quarters but fought side by side with the teacher's son, the mechanic's son, and the farmer's son. In battle one's reputation was determined by one's actions not by one's relatives. This led to an unanticipated change in attitude toward higher education after returning, a change that created a mass of applicants to the nation's most formidable institutions, thus, making for not only a larger class size but also a higher bar for entrance requirements, competition for grades, and expectations of faculty and staff.

Contrary to the conventional wisdom, the returning veterans "astonished educators with the quality of their academic work and general decorum as students," wrote Olson.[26] "Contrary to the substantial, but not universal, fear that veterans would be liabilities as college students, the veteran generation established perhaps the most distinguished record in the history of higher education."[27] And they even earned the resentment of the elite underclassmen at Stanford who referred to them as "D.A.R.s," or Damn Average Raisers, who by their ambitious drive for high marks and their diligent hard work, ruined the standard curve. "The almost unanimous conclusion of the many studies comparing grade-point averages of veteran and nonveteran students was that veterans not only earned higher grades, but earned higher grades relative to their ability."[28]

Advertisements—for men's clothes, for automobiles, for executive positions—all reflected the growing affluence and expanding middle-class that was a consequence of a college education. It also demonstrated the change in perceptions of the nation. America's favorite illustrator, Norman Rockwell, fashioned a number of covers for the *Saturday Evening Post* from 1941 to 1946 on a fictional character named Willie Gillis. Readers saw the war experience

*"Willie Gillis in Convoy"*

*"Willie Gillis as College Joe"*

and its aftermath through the eyes of the young freckled-faced country boy. In a progression of covers from the *Post* Gillis makes his journey from inductee, to combatant, to a transformed young man returning to attend college on the GI Bill—an opportunity that would have been unthinkable without the war and its unintended, but advantageous, consequences.

From contemporary covers of the *Post*, the public saw Willie riding in a convoy, sitting pensively in a church pew—making amends and asking favors—honorable, decent, yet afraid. His postwar persona depicts an individual transformed from an awkward and anxious youth into a self-confident young man relaxed in his own skin.

In war and innocence, Willie's eyes looked out from the rear of a jeep toward heaven as if saying "It is all in your hands." By contrast, his relaxed demeanor in the college portrait reflects a comfort, a stability, a purposeful enterprise of useful study mixed with the pleasures of a nice pipe and the anticipation of a competitive game of golf. The pensive young man venturing into dangerous territory with a future fraught with doom and destruction makes a startling transformation into one of security, hope, and optimism. "Willie's symbolic transformation captures both the myth and the reality of the GI Bill.... The GI Bill has become a mainstay of political rhetoric—a shorthand term for any government program that seems to provide expansion of opportunity and social uplift."[29]

Nor was the Greek community unaware of the potential windfall of applicants from the corps of returning military. In the issue of the *Kappa Alpha Journal* directly following the passage of the GI Bill appeared a full-page announcement from the Chairman of the Interfraternity Conference. H. Seger Slifer, the Chairman, estimated that at least a million soldiers will return to the classroom (actually it was more than twice that number) and that the "N.I.C. has asked that all fraternities, through their offices and magazines, give wide publicity to the educational benefits under the law so that there should not be any ignorance as to the plan and opportunities in the mind of any undergraduate now in service."[30] In his broadside Slifer provided the information concerning both the necessary qualifications to receive the benefits of the act and the amount of support that the government would supply—both of which categories were later expanded. The chairman ended his message with the recommendation to all the various fraternal orders that they should "keep the members of your fraternity advised of their opportunities so that your postwar chapters may have as many as possible members of pre-war fraternity training.[31]

The Executive Council of Kappa Alpha was quick on the uptake and concentrated its Reactivation Program in several specific areas, all with the purpose of being prepared to recruit the greatest number and the best quality of the returning servicemen. At its genesis, Kappa Alpha had been originated by veterans and veterans who were seeking the comradeship to which they had become accustomed during the campaigns of the Civil War and the Order and discipline that was attendant to the military way of life. In short, the founders sought an organization, leadership structure, and society that was quasi-militaristic—to provide that environment to veterans returning, much in the same way that the founders had returned to Lexington—made older, wiser, and more mature by the travails of war than the typical young man matriculating at college; this ethos was in the Order's blood and breeding.

The immediate area of activity was the aggressive recruitment of applicants that ramified into a number of parallel and interlocking programs. The foremost initiative was aimed at increasing membership by a series of direct and indirect incentives, the second focused on setting the Order on financial terra firma by raising and employing fraternal income in the most sensible and linear way possible, and the third aimed at creating an institution of a highly defined and efficient chain of command—all, in one way or another, reflecting the aggregate experience of the "Washington Cabal."

The so-called "Washington Cabal" was a concoction of Kappa Alpha alumni who lived in the capital and maintained positions of power and influence in political, legal, and financial circles. Several had been advisors and consultants to the Roosevelt administration and been instrumental in the development and execution of programs that led the nation out of the Depression and to victory in World War II. Two of the most crucial figures in these endeavors may well have been Frank Myers, who was a Judge of the Municipal Court for the District of Columbia and concurrently the Chairman of the Reactivation Committee, and Howard Locke, also a member of the Reactivation Committee and the president of the Fraternity Housing Corporation.[32]

The first stratagem was direct, to contact all former members who had joined the armed services and invite them to return to the fold, and specifically, "To set up a committee on postwar aid and counsel for returning Kappa Alpha World War veterans for the purpose of effectively offering encouragement, understanding, advice, and actual assistance to these men in their period of readjustment from war service to civilian capacity, and especially to urge their return to university or college for the completion of scholastic courses in preparation for the future."[33] A second feature of the direct approach was to encourage alumni to "to promptly advise the Executive Secretary with respect to the births of Kappa Alpha sons and the names and addresses of good prospects for membership in the Order coming to the universities or colleges from their home towns or elsewhere."[34]

The indirect approach involved a series of incentives to entice old members back to the fraternity and attract new members. The first and most sincere approach was to appeal to the bond formed between soldiers fighting for a cause—this involved a desire to belong to an organization with a clear and defined structure; to create a society dedicated to decency, patriotism, and fair play; and, provide an environment that nurtured academic excellence and professional growth.

A more tangible avenue that appealed to individual concerns rather than the more ethereal was connected with financial and logistical considerations. Although the estimations of matriculants to college was vastly underrated, nevertheless, early on the expectation was that campuses and resources would be overtaxed in the postwar period and it would be an opportune moment to revitalize the organization that had been dormant during the war. The two areas of greatest concern were the financial restraints of the returning veterans and housing on campuses that had been deserted for the duration of the war and underutilized for ten years prior to the outbreak of hostilities during the Depression.

The Convention of 1947 represented a watershed moment in the history of the Kappa Alpha Order in respect to the very nature of the institution and the approach to accomplishing its mission. The country had endured two events of biblical proportions—the economic apocalypse and World War II. In response to these events the United States government, led by the executive branch, radically changed both its composition and its way of conducting business. Rules, regulations, and representations of the law, which, by their very nature, seemed to fly in the face of nineteenth-century interpretations of the Constitution were amended; programs that resembled incipient socialism were instituted; opposition to these issues were softened. Necessity, once again, was the mother of invention.

In fact, one of the most important resolutions of the 1947 Convention was a constitutional amendment that redefined the executive branch of the Order. "Constitutional Amendment no. 11. Amend Section 1-401 to read as follows: 1-401. The General Officers as a body shall constitute the Executive Council of the Order and the Executive Council shall be the executive body of the Order."[35] The duties of the Executive Council were redefined "to advise the Knight Commander in the exercise of his office; shall decide upon, appoint, prescribe the duties and fix the compensation of officers and employees which it shall deem necessary for the interest of the Order, where not otherwise provided for in this Constitution; and shall designate the general headquarters of the Order and effect any change therein which is in the best interest of the Order."[36]

In addition to these fundamental obligations the Convention allowed that "the Executive Council may exercise generally the powers of an executive body, and shall have authority to act in the interest of the Order as it may consider advisable and appropriate in any matter for which there is no provision in this Constitution, the By-laws or the actions of the Convention."[37] Other features of this provision that had important implications for the exigencies of the anticipated influx of new and returning members and a revitalization of the Order included: the employment of special counsel; the establishment of a National Training School for Chapter Officers; the establishment of loan funds and regulations governing their distribution; and the "inauguration and effectuation of any plan, program, fund or project in line with the purpose and operation of the Order and not inconsistent with this Constitution or any provision."[38] The final provision of the amendment that so strengthened the position and purpose of the Executive Council touched on interregnum powers. "The Executive Council shall also have the authority, upon a majority vote, to appropriate available monies in the General Fund of the Order to specific uses and purposes in the interim between Conventions."[39] The amendment reinvented the internal structure of the Order. Two programs that concentrated on these issues were the Scholarship Fund established by the 1947 Convention and the establishment of the Fraternity Housing Corporation.

The dictates of the 1947 Convention also included the requirement that all "installations of chapter officers, whether by the chapter or at a Joint Installation shall be subject to the satisfactory completion of a course of training at the National Training School for Chapter Officers by those officers whose attendance is required or directed by the Executive Council and any installed officer who fails to complete that course satisfactorily shall not thereafter take office."[40]

This last major area of priority for the postwar strategy was intended to have all new and incoming pledges on the same page following the same standards—in short, to have a unified and uniform set of regulations, officers to oversee the implementation, and a well-informed and trained corps of pledges. Two programs connected with this agenda were the Officers Training School and new rules for the instruction of applicants. The Reactivation Committee felt that because of the early and prudent planning and in light of the great number of anticipated returnees, and especially because of the benefits and the strong incentives that Kappa Alpha was offering—the fraternity should be selective in its choice of the candidates vying for a place in the society.

These various arrangements and preparations fed into a master plan of modernizing, simplifying, and making more responsive the structure of the Order and the discipline of its members. Probably the most surprising aspect of the plan was the various strategies for improvement and expansion and the smorgasbord of benefits for new and returning members in that it was constructed in such a way as not only not to bankrupt the Order, but actually, by its inventive construction would bring monies into the organization to further strengthen and to expand programs already in existence—at a profit.

In an article entitled the "Benefits of Fraternity Life," the Chairman of the Reactivation Committee, Frank Myers, put forth the philosophical tenets of the Order that would speak to those contemplating a return to college and their place within that community at an emotional and psychological level; namely, that being a part of a fraternal organization resembled in many ways the security and comfort that they derived from being a part of a group during combat, that somebody always had your back, and that every member of the group would be attentive to your viewpoints. This new environment of trust and support was on an intellectual and emotional plane that would provide comfort to shell-shocked veterans. Myers concluded that "man is necessarily a gregarious animal and will seek his intimates upon a basis of congeniality of spirit and character. That the fraternities have exerted a powerful influence for good in the lives of their members is attested by the brilliant accomplishments of the early American statesmen, scholars and writers who received much of their youthful training from the keen, yet friendly, criticism of the companions with whom they were closely associated in the fraternity chapters."[41]

Myers added that "book learning is only a part of the educational process" and that fraternities "supplement classroom instruction with social experience and prepare their members to take their places in the world as well-rounded men."[42] Almost as an aside and perhaps intended for a different audience, Myers also noted that college authorities recognize "that the fraternity serves as a useful adjunct to college discipline and organization."[43] This was likely a statement of optimism that was more wishful than deliberately considered. All the points made for a good hook, however.

On a more tangible level, there was a conscious effort by the new leadership to employ all the resources at their disposal by careful investment and deployment of funds that have become a hallmark of the Order down to the present day. Whereas before much of the operation of Kappa Alpha came from the heart and, while sincere and heartfelt, was not always prudently nor systematically executed. In the postwar period the men in charge, and in particular Howard Locke, were tempering the hot enthusiasm and quick response of previous times with the cold logic and premeditated calculations to accomplish the intended goals and at a profit.

Perhaps the most conspicuously pressing problem facing those returning from duty was that of housing. Many letters from the different chapters relating to this appeared in the *Kappa Alpha Journal* in 1946, following the first wave of returnees from the war; they were full of horror stories concerning the unavailability of accommodations at the various institutions. The Phi Chapter at Birmingham-Southern College noted that "the housing problem remains the big headache at the moment."[44] Iota at Furman looked wistfully to the future, "Due to the housing shortage here in Greenville, we haven't been able to return to our house, but we are looking forward to the time when we can occupy it again."[45] The Omicron Chapter at the University of Texas used humor to draw attention to the situation there. "As has been the custom for many years, festivities were launched with a fifty-three float parade. Omicron entered a comic float featuring an antique outhouse complete with a half-moon cut in the door, set on a foundation, and occupied by several of the brothers. Adding to our University of Texas housing shortage theme, we spotlighted Earle Freeman in a tub taking a bubble bath."[46] At Auburn, one returning vet used his ingenuity to supply himself with temporary housing there. "Although turned down by the "sorry, no rooms available" replies of landlords in Auburn, young Bennett returned to the home of his sister… and built quarters for himself"… .He "constructed a one-room frame building, 16′ by 7′, equipped with two built-in bunks, as well as a folding desk and book case, and transported it to Auburn by truck. The temporary quarters were put up in the back yard of a residence on College Street."[47]

The fall of 1946 saw the first full year of college for the servicemen and the problem of finding suitable accommodations became even more acute as higher education became the preferred option of the government benefits. Beta Kappa at the University of Maryland revealed how its chapter was dealing with the shortage, "to make room for all of the brothers who wanted to live in the house, we doubled up and now have 36 members living here."[48] At the campus of Leland Stanford University, where the Kappa Alpha House had been patriotically billeting army personnel for three years, it "again has Kappa Alphas living in it—in fact, more Kappa Alphas than it has ever had before. Most of the Brothers living in the house are former Alpha Pi men who have returned from the service to their books. However, our number includes several transfers and several pledges."[49] Perhaps the most extreme testimony came from Beta Psi at the University of California at Los Angeles, "The growth of the University to over 14,000 students, makes such a problem a difficult one. Many students are living in trailers, tents, and even cars."[50]

In August 1946, when it became apparent that a horde of veterans would soon descend on the campuses of America, and that fraternities would provide the answers to many of their social and economic needs, the Executive Council realized that "it had to do something" to help the Order and the country. Besides housing, the most urgent problem was additional funding for the vets. Howard Locke later remembered that the council passed a resolution that the Order would issue "such loans as are recommended by the Province Commanders and are found to be supported by satisfactory evidence of necessity and ability to repay them."[51]

The problem of supplying adequate housing for returning servicemen was brought up at the Savannah Convention of 1947, where it was noted that "some chapters have acquired and then lost, not one house, but two, three, or even four. These harsh economic shocks to the undergraduate chapters were especially prevalent in the Depression Thirties and during the campus-emptied war years."[52] The concept of a fraternal corporation to supply Kappa Alpha Order with appropriate lodging for both its present and future members had its beginnings here and the corporation's prime objectives were to provide a stable basis to ensure that a mortgage would be paid and thereby secure a reasonable loan rate for the various chapters wishing to build a chapter house. The basic premise for the loans was classified into two major divisions: "One is loans to active chapters for purchase or acquisition of personal property, furniture and equipment and the like for a chapter house. The other class respecting loans to alumni corporations ... for the acquisition of chapter houses." [53] The decision was made at the Savannah Convention that the minimum goal for a base would be $250,000.[54]

In response to this crisis and as an opportunity for recruiting a confederation of prominent members of Washington's legal, financial, and political community, the use of their aggregate legal and financial expertise garnered from their collective experience in policy making—which navigated the country through the Depression and WWII—was instrumental in forming a new platform of operations for the Kappa Alpha Order.

Taking direct action, under Howard Locke's guidance, the Order created the Fraternity Housing Corporation on June 17, 1948.[55] Members of this group included Howard Locke, who was a special assistant to the Attorney General and had a long history as a tax expert for the Department of Justice; Frank Myers, architect of the Reactivation Program and a Washington Municipal Court Judge; Geoffrey Creyke, a partner in the Washington law firm of Hudson, Creyke & Lipscomb; Alvin Aubinoe, a well-respected Washington architect; and John E. Moore, the Director of Personnel at the Department of Defense.[56]

Although the creation of the Fraternity Housing Corporation was new, the concept was not. Almost from the beginning of Kappa Alpha, Samuel Ammen had advocated for the establishment of residential lodges and considered chapter houses essential to fraternal association. In 1905, the alumni of Alpha Gamma organized the Kappa Alpha Chapter House Company "with the purpose of building a new chapter house at Louisiana State University ... in order to perfect and to strengthen the ties of affection and esteem formed during college days ... and erect ... a suitable home for the fraternity."[57] In the same year, the Alpha Pi chapter at Stanford University organized the Kappa Alpha House Association to issue $10,000 worth of stock to construct a three-story home in the half-timbered architecture of Tudor England.[58]

Both active members and alumni in the early years of the twentieth century devoted of their collected energy and funds to enabling local chapters to rent or build their own facilities. This concept was resurrected to meet the exigencies of the post-war housing shortage. The FHC allowed Kappa Alpha to be a resource for the returning members, but also provided a strong incentive for those entering college for the first time to join the swelling ranks of the Order.

After its formation in 1948, the officers of the FHC took a survey to determine which chapters most urgently needed assistance: there were eleven; which chapters were not allowed to own properties: thirteen; which chapters were renting adequate quarters: ten; and which chapters owned or were in the process of purchasing houses: thirty.[59] Using this rationale, they were able to decide the best way to allocate funds to accomplish the greatest good and this was done "in the practical manner" by having a plan to reconcile the need with the best financial means to achieve their goals. In some cases the FHC enabled chapters to build new homes, in others "to acquire better houses at reduced monthly outlays," and in other instances the FHC "provided funds for improving or refurnishing properties already owned by chapters."[60]

The FHC had a three-pronged strategy: it pooled the ownership of as many Kappa Alpha properties as possible into a single corporate entity administered by the Washington brain trust—men who were recognized as being among the most capable administrators; it leveraged the assembled funds in such a way "as to assist the maximum number of chapters by obtaining the maximum loans through conventional financing and utilizing the minimum amount of Fraternity Housing Corporation's funds in each case"; and it conducted the process at the minimum cost to the Order.[61]

Having ascertained the needs of the individual chapters, the Corporation employed several different plans to best utilize available resources. If the chapter already had some funds or equity in a house and wished either to purchase another house or to refinance the building that they already were in, the FHC would lend the chapter "sufficient money, on a second or third mortgage or trust, to make up the difference between the sum that could be obtained on a conventional loan and the amount the chapter" already possessed.[62] In a second scenario, the FHC would outright buy the house and hold the titles in the name of the Corporation.... "With Fraternity Housing Corporation's substantial assets and permanent corporate structure, it has then been able to place loans on these houses on better terms and in larger amounts than the local group could have done, and thereby tie up as little money as possible in each chapter house."[63] Customarily under this arrangement, the corporation would buy "a house for an active chapter, hold the title for the chapter's exclusive use, and rent it back to the chapter at the lowest rental possible, sufficient to cover financing costs."[64]

More specifically, the FHC made loans to the chapters at 4 ½ percent interest, "which is, of course, greatly below the prevailing second trust interest rates anywhere in the country, and lower than many first trusts. In turn, it is paying the Order 3 per cent interest, and pays what expenses it has out of the difference."[65]

In the first three years of FHC's operations twenty loans were made to chapters and "some of them [had] been paid off in full [within four years]. In addition, the Corporation had bought houses for ten chapters."[66] By 1953, after four years of operating, the Fraternity Housing Corporation had assisted twenty-seven chapters financially and five chapters built their own new lodgings.[67]

By the tenth anniversary of the founding of the FHC, the institution had "assisted or bettered the living facilities of 35 chapters of the Kappa Alpha Order. This is an incredible accomplishment when one realizes that this number amounts to nearly 50% of the Kappa Alpha chapters."[68]

The Fraternity Housing Corporation continued in its capacity of buying and maintaining chapter houses in like fashion until 1983, when it was determined that the institution would no longer act in the capacity of an owner-manager agency but would continue to act as a lending institution for the Order's housing needs. The FHC Committee issued an advisory that "by June 30, 1983, all existing houses owned by FHC will be transferred to local housing corporations. Locally owned houses have stronger alumni groups because it provides a central point of interest, involvement and need for alumni help and this benefits the local chapter."[69] The reason for the change in operating procedures was ostensibly given that "existing chapters will be better served" by local housing authorities that would be better able to "exert proper control of the house operations and assure preventive maintenance." But the real reason may have been more closely aligned to the insurance issues of risk-management and the collateral legal entanglements. Having molted the skin of an owner, the FHC explained that it could better serve more undergraduate chapters and that it would continue to offer reasonable terms for the attendant purposes of housing, but offered the caveat that "it was not the FHC's purpose to become a primary source of funding for large projects."[70]

While the Fraternity Housing Corporation was brainstorming the funding of chapter houses, another arrangement was being made to supplement the income of those returning from the war. Thus, on November 18, 1948, "an endowment was incorporated as the Kappa Alpha Scholarship Fund, Inc."[71] It was officially described as "a non-profit corporation, without capital or stocks, existing and operating solely and exclusively for beneficent, charitable, literary and educational purposes. Its objects are to solicit, receive, hold, use and invest money or other contributions from KA alumni and others for scholarship awards, and [provide] aid and assistance to needy and deserving students, among members of the Order and other students in colleges and universities on the campuses of which active chapters of the Order are chartered."[72] The Executive Council considered that it was the duty of the Finance Committee "to invest the contributions made to the Fund so as to produce income for scholarship awards and student loans and to this end it is empowered to make specified investments under the Fund's by-laws."[73]

Howard Locke and other members of the council contrived to have the

Internal Revenue Bureau declare the Kappa Alpha Scholarship Fund to be tax exempt. The status was granted on April 29, 1949, in a letter in which the Bureau ruled "that Contributions to it were deductible in the computation of individual taxes."[74] The Washington Cabal believed "that benefit to individuals will be an added incentive to contribute to the Fund and that in some instances it may attract a larger gift than would have otherwise been made."[75]

Despite the incessant exhortations for contributions and the incentives of tax-deductions, the Kappa Alpha Scholarship Fund got off to a slow start and it was not until the later part of the 1950s that substantial donations were made. Over the years, the Order tried to encourage contributions through direct appeals in the *Journal*, through the purchase of life insurance, by the incentives of tax deductions, and by memorial contributions.

In successive editions of the *Kappa Alpha Journal* appeals were made in the Knight Commander's Message, in any number of articles, and on subscription sheets on the inside covers of the magazine urging readers to donate to the cause.[76] In 1954, James Randolph came up "with an Incentive Funding Plan, tying life insurance with scholarship."[77] The basic scheme was that for "every $1,000 of insurance purchased on this special plan the Scholarship Fund receives a total benefit of $50."[78] Another means of attracting funds to the KASF was the Memorial Fund. A notice of the contribution together with the name of the departed brother was listed in the *Journal* with the following sentiment introducing the notice, "Flowers are a beautiful conveyance of Love and Sympathy, but wither, Love and Sympathy expressed through our Scholarship Fund, is Life."[79] But perhaps the greatest draw were the appeals that preceded the Centennial Celebration. These were very successful and brought in a number of large, what the Scots call, "mortifications," or bequest left in one's last will and testament.

In 1957, an anonymous contribution of $50,000 was made from a California alumnus; in 1958, a gift of $52,000 was donated by Verner McCall and his wife Mildred.[80] In 1956, the KASF had barely $2,000 in assets, by 1962, after distributions, the corporation had more than $50,000 in reserve.[81] In a statement of contributions for the Centennial Fund in 1957, out of $13,279.50 collected—$3,132.50 was designated for the Scholarship Fund and $20 for the Fraternity Housing Corporation, while the rest of the money, $10,147 came from dues.[82] From this point forward the Scholarship Fund became a significant magnet for voluntary contributions.

On another academic front, the Order devised a plan to offer cash incentives to chapters in order to raise the aggregate grade-point average, and therefore the reputation, of the Order. In 1947, Dr. John Rohrer was appointed as the first National Scholarship Officer.[83] The duties of the position were directed towards recruiting the most academically capable candidates for pledging, creating a scholastic index for each chapter to quantifiably evaluate both the status and the progress of the individual chapters and the Order as a whole, to create an atmosphere and assist active members in using their time and academic talents to the optimal extent, and publically to recognize and reward outstanding scholarship.

The second National Scholastic Officer, Dr. Carl Rees, maintained that the selection of unmotivated pledges not only seriously affected the overall average of the local chapter but that a large majority of those men ultimately dropped out of college. He reported that "at Louisiana State University during the first semester of 1947–48, Kappa Alpha reported 46 pledges. Of this number, only 37% were initiated and 63% failed to attain the mandatory academic standards."[84]

Rees advised that it was essential to establish a scholastic index for each chapter and for every chapter to maintain individual records for each member. Besides the fact that the index was the directive of the National Interfraternity Conference, Rees advocated its usage for a variety of more pragmatic reasons: it was needed to compare the average of the Kappa Alpha chapters with other fraternities on campus, to weed out undesirable pledges, identify those brothers in need of tutoring services and motivation, and to encourage academic competition between fraternities on campus. It was also crucial to develop an environment conducive to good study habits—quiet periods at certain hours of the evening, an isolated and separate part of the chapter house for study, tutorial assistance, and having graduate students live in the house as mentors and inspiration.[85]

And the last step was to encourage success by recognition. At the local level this was done by awarding citations to the members whose grade-point average boosted the chapter's scholastic rating by the greatest extent and holding a public ceremony to present an intercollegiate scholarship cup. At the national level both public recognition and cash awards were presented to the most outstanding students.[86] Conversely, those chapters that performed poorly were defamed in *Wilson's Blame and Shame Club;* unfortunately, in the immediate postwar period many of Kappa Alpha's chapters made an appearance in that publication.[87]

In an effort to boost academic ratings, in 1953 the National Scholastic Officer began to include in his articles to the *Journal* the fashion of a carrot or a stick. The carrot segment of his article included an Honor and Fame Club, recognizing those chapters that "achieved special distinction" by improving their academic averages, the rankings by province, and the ten highest chapters. On the stick side were the ten lowest-ranking chapters and the scholarship resolutions that placed restrictions and imposed penalties on those chapters that continued to underperform.[88] The active members, however, proved themselves to be recalcitrant and reluctant catechumens.

In 1955, with much fanfare, the *Journal* proclaimed that the scholarship index demonstrated that half of the Kappa Alpha Chapters were above the All-Men's average—it failed to mention, however, that half were not—likely assuming that at least 50 percent of the active members would be able to figure that out for themselves. In November 1955, the editors of the *Journal* sought to incentivize academic standards by developing the "star system" for the Chapter Letters section of the magazine, with three stars being the highest rating. Each star indicated a year period in which the chapter "was above the All-Men's Average."[89]

Too little, too late for 1955 though. In the first edition of the *Journal* for 1956, the Knight Commander, James Duncan, wrote proudly about the accomplishments of the previous year, "Many encouraging things are taking place in the Order," he reported, "The first has been the improvement in the scholarship of the active chapters."[90] The piece was likely written before the article on the "Final Scholarship Report" was composed and published on the very next page, under the subtitle of "More Decline than Improvement from 1953–54."[91] There was a very bright note, however, "The brothers in Graves Province continue to lead the Order… for three straight yea[r]s every chapter in the Graves Province has been above the all-men's average."[92] By 1957, real academic progress seems to have been made by a combination of more-selective recruiting and the implementation of the fraternity's initiatives.[93]

In 1957, two donors contributed more than a hundred thousand dollars to the KASF within months of each other. From that time forward, contributions began to pick up quickly—thus ensuring not only the survival of the mission but also portending the expansion to come. By 1967, in spite of the fact that KASF was dispensing funds almost as soon as it took them in, but because of a series of prudent and well-considered investments, the Fund had "grown from a small organization with very little capital to one with a net worth at this time of approximately $100,000."[94] The KASF continued in its work and expanded both the number of scholarships awarded and the monetary value of the prizes involved until 1992 when the foundation was subsumed by the newly created Kappa Alpha Order Educational Foundation.

The third area in which the Reactivation Committee concentrated its efforts was a throwback to the Order's roots in the aftermath of the Civil War—a return to a highly delineated infrastructure with a membership trained in the industrial-military tradition. The Officers Training School, specifically designated as an obligation of the Executive Council in the Constitutional Amendment of 1947, was at the time described as "a tremendous step forward in our national progress and that the Convention was wise in establishing the School as an annual project. It should assure us of two things: qualified chapter leaders trained in the work of supervision and operation of their chapters and standardized and uniform practices and procedure in the government of our active chapters."[95]

In the course of its development and execution, the format of the Officers Training School changed its mission, nature, and format best to suit the needs and the restrictions of the times. In its earliest manifestation the Officers Training School was held in conjunction with the conventions, usually after the convention programs had been completed. Under the direction of Senior Councilor Frank H. Myers and others, "It was organized as a method by which the Order could reorganize and coordinate its methods of operations, which had been drastically curtailed during World War II."[96] In 1946, the first Officers Training School was held at the Hotel Seelbach in Louisville, Kentucky, "where three or four officers of each chapter [attended] a three-day school, at the expense of the Order. For better organization in operating the chapters, the committee plan was recommended so that every member would have a job to do."[97]

During the second Officers Training School, there were seventy-seven students enrolled, who were required to be present for the purpose of qualifying as delegates to the convention, and before registering that they had both completed the course and taken the necessary examination. The following session the number of candidates increased to ninety-four.[98] At the Fourth Officers Training School every active chapter had an official delegate for the entire session.[99]

In 1950, the session was held at the Pinnacle Inn in Banner Elk, North Carolina, a rural and secluded retreat in the mountains of western North Carolina and it was a radical departure from former officer training schools. A new, diversified and more-sophisticated agenda was adopted; the first day was dedicated to the inspirational aspects of Kappa Alpha, the second to a series of lectures concerning Kappa Alpha Laws, specific duties and requirements, and the fundamental of better and more effective chapter administration. The third day became an open forum on a variety of topics—rushing, chapter officers, chapter organization, pledge training, finance and alumni relations—with the participation of both faculty and students.[100] Another significant change for the 1950 Officers Training School was that the Executive Council ruled that "only the Chapter Number I's expenses [were] to be paid by the Order."[101] This, in many instances, made the participation of other officers financially impossible.

By the mid-1950s, the lodging expenses had become so great that the Order resorted to coopting vacant college facilities as a cost-effective alternative to conducting the sessions at the pricey hotels of the convention. As the boundaries of the chapters expanded geographically, the cost of travel was also prohibitive for many candidates. In 1958, the Training Schools were held in three different geographic locations at separate times. The eastern session met in Columbia, South Carolina, in the early part of June; the western session at the Alpha Xi Chapter House at the University of California at Berkeley in mid-August; and, the central session in Memphis, Tennessee, at the end of August. This allowed the faculty to be present at all three and to deliver a consistent program.[102]

The subjects addressed were again progressively expanded and refined; the lectures included: "A Brief history of the Order, Regional Advisor Program, Scholarship, Kappa Alpha Laws, Rushing, Alumni Relations, Active Chapter Administration, Active Chapter Finances and Reports, Pledge Training, Fraternity Housing Corporation, and Active Chapter Public Relations."[103]

It was also during this time frame that the training sessions began to use the breakout session technique, where after lectures or lessons, the students would meet in smaller classrooms for more-inclusive and in-depth discussions about both the lectures and new ideas. In the 1960s, progressive education and more-responsive relationships between establishment figures and the young were shifting the style of management both in business and in government; accordingly, the format of the Training School was changing from a lecture and learning agenda into a comprehensive and cooperative workshop.[104]

The military-industrial model for the Order that had been in place since the onset of the Second World War started to fade, and the process adopted by the Order, much like that of the nation, began to modify into a more-corporate and progressive standard. The chain of command of the administrative team was headed, as always, by the Knight Commander, but developed a whole team strategy that included a growing and more-specialized staff to advise and assist him in the rapidly expanding arenas of interest and concern. Business, legal, and risk management issues were subrogated to specialized committees, councils and advisors. Aspects of the post-WWII business side of the Order were expanded, while the communal spirit of the active members was adapting itself to the times.

The early 1960s until the present have been a roller-coaster ride for both the nation and the Order. The 1960s and 1970s created an atmosphere of anti-establishment and rebellion, which in turn made the recruitment of pledges and the sustaining of an active chapter a difficult task. With the advent of Ronald Reagan and during his two terms as president, however, there was a return of optimism, a flexing of military muscle, and an outpouring of patriotic fervor—all of which created a generation concerned with education and securing a place in the business world and longing for the sense of community only a fraternal organization could supply.

Economic prosperity and the fall of the Soviet Union provided a boon time for college going and fraternity joining; the chaos caused by the collapse of the housing market in 2007 has left the administration of the Order in a more-cautious and deliberating state. These changes will be investigated in the next chapter.

*Notes* Chapter 10:

1 "Convention," *Kappa Alpha Journal* 62, No. 1 (November 1945): 4.
2 J. R. Berryman, "From Me to You," *Kappa Alpha Journal* 61, No. 4 (May 1945): 1.
3 Ibid.
4 Ibid.
5 "Reactivation Program," *Kappa Alpha Journal* 61, No. 4 (May 1945): 2.
6 Ibid.
7 Ibid.
8 Ibid., 3.
9 Ibid., 4.
10 Ibid.
11 Ibid., 5.

12 Howard P. Locke, "The Tax Division of the Department of Justice: Its Function and Operation," *American Bar Association Journal* 30, No. 6 (June 1944): 319–325, 363–366.

13 "Reactivation Program," 6.

14 Ibid.

15 Ibid.

16 Daniel A. Clark, "The Two Joes Meet—Joe College, Joe Veteran: The GI Bill, College Education, and Postwar American Culture," *History of Education Quarterly* 38, No. 2 (Summer 1998): 173.

17 Ibid.

18 Ibid.

19 Ibid., 167.

20 Keith W. Olson, "The G. I. Bill and Higher Education: Success and Surprise," *American Quarterly* 25, No. 5 (December, 1973): 601.

21 Ibid., 602.

22 Ibid.

23 Ibid., 596.

24 Ibid.

25 Ibid., 608.

26 Ibid., 602.

27 Ibid., 604.

28 Ibid.

29 Daniel A. Clark, "The Two Joes Meet," 168.

30 H. Seger Slifer, "Postwar Education," *Kappa Alpha Journal* 60, No. 5 (August 1944): 2.

31 Ibid.

32 "Howard P. Locke," *Kappa Alpha Journal* 68, No. 1 (November 1951): 2; see also Geoffrey Creyke, "Fraternity Housing Corporation Story," *Kappa Alpha Journal* 69, No. 3 (March 1953): 21.

33 "Reactivation Program," 7.

34 Ibid.

35 Ransom Bassett, ed., *Proceedings of the Forty-Second Convention of the Kappa Alpha Order* (Louisville: KA Administrative Office, 1947), 65.

36 Ibid.

37 Ibid.

38 Ibid.

39 Ibid.

40 Ibid., 74.

41 Frank Myers, "Fraternity to College," *Kappa Alpha Journal* 63, No. 4 (May 1947): 8.

42 Ibid., 9.

43 Ibid.

44 "Chapter Letters: Phi, Birmingham-Southern College," *Kappa Alpha Journal* 62, No. 3 (March 1946): 24.

45 Ibid., 20.

46 Ibid., 34.

47 "Kaka Talk," *Kappa Alpha Journal* 62, No. 3 (March 1946): 8.

48 *Kappa Alpha Journal* 63, No. 1 (November 1946): 48.

49 Ibid., 40.

50 Ibid., 41.

51 Bassett, *Proceedings of the Forty-Second Convention,* 15.

52 "Does Your Chapter Need a House," *Kappa Alpha Journal* 68, No. 3 (March 1952): 12.

53 Bassett, *Proceedings of the Forty-Second Convention*, 16.

54 "Does Your Chapter Need a House," 12.

55 Bassett, *Proceedings of the Forty-Second Convention*, 18.

56 Creyke, "Fraternity Housing Corporation Story," 21.

57 "Kappa Alpha Chapter House Company," *Kappa Alpha Journal* 23, No. 1 (October 1905): 48.

58 "Alpha Pi Chapter House," *Kappa Alpha Journal* 23, No. 3 (February 1906): 327. "The fact that our house is new and admirably constructed, is all that saved us from a most severe loss; but as it is, she shows many a scar." —"Alpha Pi Reports," *Kappa Alpha Journal* 23, No. 5 (June 1906): 611.

59 Creyke, "Fraternity Housing Corporation Story," 16.

60 Ibid.

61 Ibid.

62 Ibid.

63 Ibid.,17.

64 "Does Your Chapter Need a House," 12.

65 Creyke, "Fraternity Housing Corporation Story," 17.

66 "Does Your Chapter Need a House," 12.

67 Creyke, "Fraternity Housing Corporation Story," 16.

68 R. T. Feller, "Fraternity Housing: A look at the Fraternity Housing Committee after Ten Years," *Kappa Alpha Journal* 74, No. 3 (March 1958):11.

69 "FHC to take new approach," *Kappa Alpha Journal* 74, No. 3 (Summer 1982): 18.

70 Ibid.

71 Ransom Bassett, ed., *Proceedings of the Forty-Third Convention of the Kappa Alpha Order* (Louisville: Kappa Alpha Administrative Office, 1949), 17.

72 Ibid.

73 Ibid.

74 Ibid.

75 Ibid., 18.

76 "Scholarship Fund," *Kappa Alpha Journal* 65, No. 4 (May 1949): 2.

77 "Want to Help the Scholarship Fund and Be Insured Too," *Kappa Alpha Journal* 71, No. 1 (November 1954): 3.

78 Ibid.

79 "Memorial Contributions to Scholarship Fund," *Kappa Alpha Journal* 74, No. 1 (November 1957): 19.

80 "Centennial Program Makes Strides," *Kappa Alpha Journal* 74, No. 1 (November 1957): 18; "McCall Donation." *Kappa Alpha Journal* 74, No. 4 (May 1958): 12.

81 "The Knight Commander's Message," *Kappa Alpha Journal* 79, No. 1 (November 1962): 21.

82 "Statement of Contributions," *Kappa Alpha Journal* 74, No. 1 (November 1957): 19.

83 "John Rorher," *Kappa Alpha Journal* 64, No. 1 (November 1947): 5.

84 Carl Rees, "Scholarship," *Kappa Alpha Journal* 65, No. 1 (November 1948): 11.

85 Ibid., 13.

86 Ibid.

87 Ibid.

88 John Nowell, "The Record Could be Much Better," *Kappa Alpha Journal* 71, No. 2 (January 1955): 2.

89 "The Star Chapters," *Kappa Alpha Journal* 72, No. 1 (November 1955): 36.

90 "Knight Commander's Message," *Kappa Alpha Journal* 72, No. 2 (January 1956): 1.

91 Ibid., 2.

92 Ibid., 3.

93 "Scholarship Report," *Kappa Alpha Journal* 74, No. 1 (November 1957): 2.

94 "KASF Awards Irwin Scholarships," *Kappa Alpha Journal* 84, No. 3 (Summer 1968): 8.

95 "Second Chapter Officers School," *Kappa Alpha Journal* 64, No. 1 (November 1947): 8.

96 *Kappa Alpha Journal* 62, No. 2 (January 1946): 15.

97 *Kappa Alpha Journal* 76, No. 4 (May 1960): 10.

98 "Third Chapter Officers School," *Kappa Alpha Journal* 65, No. 1 (November 1948): 2

99 "4th Chapter Officers School," *Kappa Alpha Journal* 66, No. 1 (November 1949): 8.

100 "5th Chapter Officers School," *Kappa Alpha Journal* 66, No. 2 (January 1950): 3.

101 "5th Chapter Officers School," *Kappa Alpha Journal* 66, No. 4 (May 1950): 5.

102 "12th National Training School," *Kappa Alpha Journal* 75, No. 1 (November 1958): 14.

103 Ibid., 16.

104 "Officers Training School Will Be Held in Memphis," *Kappa Alpha Journal* 77, No. 4 (May 1961): 9.

*Kappa Alpha, University of Kentucky, 1947*

*First Officers Training School, Louisville, Kentucky*

# 11

## Transition and Adaptation

During the postwar era, a combination of factors brought about the stunning expansion of students' attending institutions of higher learning and the burst in fraternity membership. Americans, having overcome the dire economic conditions of the Great Depression, were imbued with a sense of self-confidence and a can-do attitude; having defeated a powerful enemy and force for evil through the Second World War gave Americans a tremendous sense of pride in their country, their military, and themselves and a feeling of optimism and destiny; having been enticed by the GI Bill and the prospect of a brighter life, the returning veterans flooded campuses across the county to obtain that passport to opportunity—a college degree.

College enrollments and membership in fraternal organizations remained constant through the 1940s and 1950s, to be a Greek was not only a by-product of the desire for a system of support and a feeling of belonging, but, according to many anecdotal sources, it was the best way to meet girls. Joe College sported a Greek letter jacket, had a special handshake, wore the pin, and was a part of the social elite of the school. He was not only Joe College, he was also Joe Cool. The years of "Give 'em hell Harry" and "I like Ike" still reflected a nostalgia for the upbeat sentiments of a triumphant America.

Between 1962 and 1969, however, changes in student values were sweeping and universal. Much of the change was brought about by opposition to the

Vietnam War and animosity toward the traditional elements of society and government. "Student values in the 1960s reflected the following trends: a drop in church attendance and the need for religion; interest in careers in corporate business declined; fear of a Communist threat weakened; emphasis on and involvement in college extracurricular activities and fraternities dropped; and an alienation from the military and national ideology rose."[1]

It was a difficult time for Greek organizations across the nation and for Kappa Alpha as well. The backlash against conservative politics and on-campus organizations, fraternities included, became, endemically, more virulent as American involvement in Vietnam increased and resistance to conservative norms and politics became more strident.

Many college students of the era "regarded fraternity membership as thoroughly inconsistent with their interests in civil rights, student rights, antiwar activism, feminism, racial equality, and independence from institutional constraints."[2] In 1966, "30% of all college students belonged to Greek letter societies; by 1976, however, this figure dropped to only 19% nationally. In fact, fully two thirds of colleges had experienced declining enrollments. During the 1970s, on some campuses across the country, fraternities completely disappeared."[3]

In response to the changes taking place in society, the administration of the Order adapted to the new environment, both in terms of policy, internal structure, and finance. The shifts in policy were adapted in respect to membership qualifications, ethnic sensitivity, public relations efforts, a reconfiguration of internal administrative hierarchy, and installing more-efficient and objective financial planning and development.

In the Kappa Alpha Order, the shift in policy in regard to "race, religion and national origin" actually started earlier than was the general trend in the nation. A resolution of the Thirty-Ninth Biennial Convention, in 1937, called for restrictions to be lifted from the recruitment of those candidates "of the Jewish blood."[4] The caveat to this decision being that the member be actively practicing his religion. The comradeship in arms and the alteration in attitudes brought

*Knight Commander John W. Nowell*

about by fighting side by side in a common cause and the recognition of the general public about the sacrifice, gallantry, and noble character of all servicemen who struggled against a common enemy created a new reality in postwar America. Shortly after the end of hostilities, universities across the nation "began questioning the propriety of fraternity and sorority constitutional membership restriction clauses."[5]

By 1948, a number of fraternities affiliated with the National Interfraternity Conference (NIC) had already acted to discourage exclusionary clauses in their bylaws. In 1959, "the Chancellor of the University of California announced that by action of the Board of Regents a deadline for the removal of restrictive clauses had been set for September 1, 1964."[6] In 1961, when the Order's California chapters "were threatened with the loss of institutional recognition for non-compliance with 'state statutes and university policies' regarding prohibitions of membership due to 'race, religion and ethnic descent,' the leadership of the Order was compelled to reexamine the exclusion policy."[7] In addition, it was required that "all chapters of national fraternities at institutions in the University system would be required to sign a statement to the effect there were *no rules or policies* that would inhibit their members from accepting students without discrimination on account of race, religion or national origin."[8] Statements from the various fraternities were required to be signed annually and any "violation of it would result in the withdrawal of University recognition and privileges."[9]

The debates of the Forty-Ninth Convention of the Kappa Alpha Order in 1961 were devoted almost exclusively to "the discussion and consideration of the problems which the Order faces on several campuses where the duly constituted authorities have adopted policies banning student organizations which have constitutional or other provisions restricting membership based on race, creed or ethnic origin."[10]

The deliberations of the Convention produced more heat than light, however, and the following September, Knight Commander John W. Nowell appointed a Special Advisory Committee to look into the matter. Even within the Committee there were spirited and sometimes "volatile" negotiations. There was also intense pressure from "various individuals and groups [who had] taken it upon themselves to badger and abuse several members of the Committee."[11] Nowell advocated that "those who have sent abusive communications to individual members of the Special Advisory Committee" ought to be censored for their actions.[12]

Despite the passionate objections of those opposed to lifting restrictions on membership, the Committee, the Executive Council and the Knight Commander expressed their "convictions and intent" regarding the matter. The Executive Council in an open letter, reminded the collective circle of the Order about the importance of Kappa Alpha's maintaining its high position in the Greek world, the wisdom in continuing the expansion of the fraternity, and the necessity of continuing "the heritage and traditions and teachings of our Order [that] are of the highest caliber and deserve to be offered and perpetuated on all campuses."[13]

Nowell admonished his audience that the "votes taken at the recent Memphis Convention showed that a great majority favored a change of policy" and the decision to lift restrictions on membership was unanimously endorsed by the Special Advisory Ccommittee who considered it "a moral obligation."[14] Nevertheless, many of the Alumni Chapters sent resolutions indicating that "that the feeling of their memberships [was] opposed to any consideration of… changes in membership clauses."[15]

The disgruntlement of many of the alumni, while not devastating in the boom times of the 1960s, would have serious implications for the poor economic conditions of the 1970s. Nevertheless, the pragmatic choice of the moment was either adhere to federal and local regulations concerning an elastic approach to membership or face being shut down altogether.

Based on the Special Advisory Committee's recommendations, the Advisory Council "passed a provision that would permit an active chapter" to waive any restriction. By the following year "three quarters adopted the provision… and

[by] 1971, 97 percent of the active chapters were operating under the waiver."[16] According to Mary Westheimer, "That same year Delta Lambda proposed and the fifty-fourth Convention in Tulsa passed an amendment to discontinue the sections of the constitution with the restrictive membership provision."[17]

With the issue of membership having been put to rest, the Order turned its attention to other areas that caused fraternities in the 1970s to be seen in a negative light. In reaction to the popular conception that fraternities were collections of narcissistic individuals and coinciding with the zeitgeist of altruism of the sixties, the Kappa Alpha Order and many other fraternities combated negative publicity by expanding their efforts to be of assistance to local and national philanthropic campaigns; thus, not only ramifying the original mission of the Order to be of service to one's fellow man, but also, in the process, presenting an engaging and positive image to a candid but skeptical world.

The Upsilon Chapter at the University of North Carolina "employed its willing and able pledge class in a campus clean-up program ... and participated in a Thanksgiving Basket donation program to many needy families in the Chapel Hill area."[18] Gamma Rho at East Carolina College, reported that it "had 20 brothers who participated as orientation counselors at the start of school ... then staged a simulated train robbery, in the manner of Jesse James, for benefit of underprivileged children in Greenville ... contributed 24 pints of blood to the Red Cross Blood Bank ... and donated 7,500 pints of milk to UNICEF ... sponsored a Little League Football Team in Greenville, which won first place ... also gave a Thanksgiving basket to a local needy family."[19] At the time the letter was being written, Gamma Rho also was in the process of "sending Christmas cards to some of the servicemen serving in Vietnam ... collecting clothes for Vietnamese children."[20] Finally, the chapter "planned to collect cigarette packs which [would] be redeemed in the form of a wheel chair for a local church" and to join with the Chi Omegas' in a Christmas toy drive.[21]

The individual chapters of the Order went from primarily local charities and causes to collaborating with one another in order to launch national campaigns into its schema of service projects. In the 1960s, various lodges raised money for the March of Dimes, the Cancer Fund, and the Heart Fund, among other worthy causes. In 1976, the Executive Council and the Committee on Undergraduate Programs adopted the Muscular Dystrophy Fund as the Order's primary philanthropic cause. The administration of the MDA, which had more than 150 district officers across the country, promised to help local chapters to organize and promote fund-raising events. Each chapter was encouraged "to choose its own project" such as a dance marathon, and the funds raised were to "go to support MDA's worldwide research programs; to provide extensive patient services at the local level and numerous other services in connection with MD."[22]

As a positive legacy of the social activism of the 1960s, Kappa Alpha has continued its role as a leader in the Greek world as an enthusiastic leader in fraternal philanthropy. Since 1976, the Order has raised more than 2.7 million dollars in support of the Muscular Dystrophy Association. Also the Order has developed Operation Crimson Gift, a project close to former Knight Commander David M. Warren's heart because of his mother's illness, which encourages fraternity members to donate blood to the American Red Cross during the year. The Order, under the umbrella designation of Project Outreach, also participates in various other charities and projects of local and national interest, including the American Humane Society, the March of Dimes, the American Cancer Foundation, Goodwill Industries the Salvation Army, local churches, YMCAs, clean-up and restoration projects for schools and clubs, Thanksgiving and Christmas donations for the needy, and repairing and building homes for veterans and other worthy individuals.

The fraternity system in the 1960s and 1970s faced other challenges that affected membership and public perception. Even as the political activism of the 1960s abated when the Vietnam War wound down, nevertheless, the shift in demographic, economic and political realities had a profound impact on the perspectives of Americans in general and college-age students in particular. These factors also had serious implications for the number of college men who wanted to belong to fraternal organizations and their reasons for it.

Demographically, the growth rate in the United States during the 1970s was one of the lowest in history, divorce became more commonplace, and single parent households became prevalent. In other words, there were fewer college-age students in America and less expendable money in the average household. These conditions translated into fewer students attending institutions of higher learning and the ones who did, did so with a more serious purpose.

Politically, following the fall of Saigon, the focus of the nation turned to the transgressions of the Richard Nixon administration and the debacle of the Watergate affair, the pardon of the disgraced president by his successor, and the Iranian hostage crisis. In the 1970s Americans felt demoralized by the loss of the Vietnam War, scandalized by Watergate and Nixon's resignation, anxious about Soviet expansionism, and incandescent about the condescending pronouncements of Third World dictators.

Economically, OPEC had raised the price of a barrel of oil from $3 a barrel in 1973, to $30 a barrel in 1979. During President Jimmy Carter's administration, the high rate of inflation, the increase in unemployment, and dismal prospects of securing jobs dissuaded millions from seeking a postsecondary education. "The academic scene of the seventies [was] very different. Gone [was] the optimism in the face of the 'steady state,' [there were] declining enrollments, and the loss of confidence by public authorities in higher education. Fewer young people [were] entering the universities, and there [was] a severe recession in most academic fields at the level of graduate education."[23]

Because of these factors, among others, those students who did matriculate during the seventies were more serious and focused on their future job prospects. Fraternities "regained some strength on campus in the seventies" as students sought out "a sense of community."[24] The resurgence of membership also had pragmatic aspects to it that reflected a general shift in purpose for the incoming student population. Insulation from the draft became a nonissue, parents and students reacted to the increasing demands of the economic situation, and the incoming matriculants were more interested in future income than political and philosophical purity. In short, collegiate students of the post-Vietnam era differed from their carefree and gregarious predecessors of the 1940s and 1950s and were the antithesis of the revolutionary firebrands of the 1960s and 1970s. The refuge from chaos and disorder is order, stability, and conformity. For the goal-oriented student of the 1970s, the chapter house was a better choice for support, structure, and an active social and academic lifestyle.

Rick H. Schrager conducted a sociological study in the mid-eighties that concluded that students who chose to live in the dorms and those who elected to join fraternities had both different motivations and experiences.

> "The [study] indicates that Greek and non-Greek units have substantially different social environments.... Greek living groups, relative to non-Greek living groups, are characterized by high involvement and emotional support and low independence. This press towards involvement, social support, and conforming behavior is consistent with the aims of social fraternities. They tend to be highly cohesive and supportive groups that actively engage their members in a wide range of social and extracurricular activities.... A fraternity is more than just a place to live. It functions, in many respects, as an organization. In comparison to resident hall groups, fraternities have more well established norms, have a more clearly defined status hierarchies, and foster a stronger identification among group members."[25]

During the 1980s, in the process of integrating the institutional forms of the past with the political and philosophical sentiments of the times and the needs of a new and more serious generation of fraternal candidates, the leaders of Kappa Alpha began to align the policies of the past with the realities of the present and anticipated the growth of the future.

In 1946, the Kappa Alpha Order established the Officers Training School originally designated the "National Training School," which was described as a three day session where "where three or four officers of each chapter [would] attend a three-day school, at the expense of the Order… for better organization in operating the chapters."[26] The subjects covered in the school were Kappa Alpha Laws, Pledge Training, Chapter House Operations, Rushing, Chapter fiscal Operations, Chapter Officers Duties, Reports and Records, Chapter Meetings, Scholarship, and Model Initiations.[27] By May 1949, the name of the program was changed to the Officers Training School.[28] Its organization, internal structure, and mission—even its name—had a military and patriotic aura.

In reaction to the sentiments of the sixties and the needs of the Order, the Officers Training School was renamed the National Leadership Institute and it "came to life on August 13, 1972, at Vanderbilt University, Nashville, Tennessee."[29] The new manifestation of the program not only retained many of its former areas of emphasis concerning the operations of the chapters and reports to the national office, but also incorporated into its agenda elements touching on the personal growth and leadership qualities that would sustain the candidates who attended in their postgraduate personal and professional lives—reflecting the need for relevance that became a ubiquitous practice at colleges in the career-oriented seventies. The revamped program also stressed stratagems for social interaction with the community, risk management programs, and academic achievement.

The core curriculum of the National Leadership Institute was succinctly described as "a new approach to problem solving" and stressed the five major areas of emphasis for the Order—leadership, scholarship, brotherhood, finances, and Kappa Alpha programs.[30] The goals of the institute were to instill certain personal, professional, and technical characteristics into the chapter leaders, as well as a knowledge and expertise in the Order's history and the operation of Kappa Alpha both on a local and national level.

Personal characteristics included a sense of humor, optimism, fairness and honesty, tolerance of disagreement, courage to fail, and self-confidence. Professional characteristics embraced experience, planning, and knowledge in the business of one's organization. Technical characteristics invaluable to a leader included the ability to listen attentively, to speak effectively, to write clearly and precisely, to make decisions in a linear fashion, and to set priorities.[31] In addition, the Institute covered the traditional areas that had been presented in the past for the more efficacious and standardized operation of the chapters. It was announced that "there will be seminars of a topical nature that will cover rush, finances, pledge education, customs, KA Laws and parliamentary procedure, scholarship, alumni relations, and university-community relations, as well as a model initiation ceremony."[32]

Increasingly the subjects of the Institute's session came to include risk management, public relations concerns, and legal liabilities. Several of the new issues added for discussion were alcohol and drug abuse prevention strategies, the legal liabilities of the individual chapters and its impact on the national organization, and what was termed "social survival," or public relations.[33] An innovation of the National Leadership Institute was to make many of the educational programs available to the Province Councils, who were encouraged to orchestrate "mini-workshops" on the covered subjects.[34]

In the summer of 1981, in order to facilitate this expansion of the Institute's outreach program, the Executive Council approved the inauguration of a video production and storage campaign. Tapes were made of the selected lectures and discussions that took place at the Institute's meetings, stored at the national headquarters in Atlanta, and made available to the Province Councils on request. "The National Leadership Institute was the site for the first series which included 30 minute to one hour tapes on Rush, KA Laws, and Scholarship. This has been followed with additional filming on Pledge Education and Chapter Image."[35] The second stage of production included Leadership, Chapter Management, and Ritual, which was to be followed by a series revolving around Alcohol Abuse Prevention. Also prospective topics of interest were Alumni Relations and the History of the Order.[36] This endeavor to expand both the scope of topics discussed and the number of participants involved was emblematic of the change that was occurring in all sectors of the Order's administration and infrastructure—an inclination toward consolidation and standard procedures, a centralization of decision making based on experience and expertise, and the changes made necessary by both economic factors, social pressures, and legal imperatives. The trend to integrate and update programs and streamline the internal structure of the Order continued throughout the seventies and up to the present time. To this day, the Number I's Leadership Institute, initiated by future Knight Commander J. Michael Duncan in 2002, continues its mission of educating chapter presidents in the tradition of the Officers Training School.

The sobering realities of the times also encouraged the leadership and the members of Kappa Alpha to rethink their administrative modus operandi. It was imperative to streamline and integrate vertically the various internal components of the administrative team into a more-cohesive and responsive unit. There was no room for miscommunication, internal bickering, and working at cross-purposes given the realities of the fragile economy and diminished pool of recruits. In addition to these factors, the social fiats of the past two decades had imposed an increased burden on the responsibilities of the Order in maintaining the positive image of the organization and restricting its actions in terms of legal and insurance issues.

In the 1980s, Ronald Reagan's campaign of optimism, of patriotism, of administrative reform spilled over from politics into the spirit of the nation. Americans were tired of self-deprecation, the fractious and destructive nature of foreign and domestic policies, the condescending and exploitive posturing of foreign governments and peoples. The rebellious and antiestablishment zeitgeist of the sixties and seventies virtually disappeared in college classrooms—Marxism was out, Capitalism was in.

Moreover, the disappearance of college fraternities on campuses was a short-lived phenomenon and, in the early eighties, a major resurgence of interest in fraternal societies blossomed. "By 1981, almost one half of all colleges and universities had already reported seeing growth in fraternity enrollments…In some southern schools, fraternity membership reached 80%."[37]

As the economy improved, spirits lifted, and foreign policy issues faded into the background, the pragmatic value of a college education became more self-evident. One of the more-pressing reasons for the dramatic increase in the collegiate population was a reemphasis on the importance of a postsecondary education to secure a stable and lucrative job; the chances of landing such a situation increasingly depended on the candidate's level of education and academic success. Students were also more willing to attend distant schools if it improved their marketability in a certain field.

The same trend that was occurring nationally also took place in respect to Kappa Alpha. An article in the *Kappa Alpha Journal* in 1983, reported that the researchers had culled information from 285 institutions and 60 percent of those colleges had chapters of Kappa Alpha. The report noted that there was substantial growth and a "widely observed strength" in Greek activity on those campuses, and emphasized that "93 institutions had added 278 fraternity chapters and 58 had re-chartered chapters during 1981," also the mean chapter sizes had risen to "38.5 for fraternities and 46.8 for sororities. These [statistics] obviously represent a sound basis for continued growth of the Greek system."[38] The number of students pledging for Kappa Alpha "rose from 1933 [pledges] in 1972 to 2609 in 1982; the number of active chapters in the same period rose from 93 in 1972 to 112 in 1982."[39] Kappa Alpha followed, or led, the national trend.

The process of synchronizing and coordinating between the separate entities within the Kappa Alpha Order as a response to the reversals of the 1960s and 1970s produced an unexpected benefit in the more prosperous 1980s and beyond. In May 1980, then Knight Commander Loren Hanson conceived and fertilized an organ of the Order that was to have profound implications for the future of Kappa Alpha with the gift of a single dollar. This embryo of an idea and a dollar became a squalling brat at the Fifty-Ninth Convention in 1981, when the Kappa Alpha Order Educational Foundation was established for "the purpose of financing and supplementing various programs of an educational nature for Kappa Alpha Order."[40]

With an eye to the future, KAOEF, was to be "a publicly supported organization with gifts and bequests being deductible for income and estate tax purposes, will have goals including the education of undergraduate and graduate students in scholarship, leadership, alcohol and other drug abuse prevention, and other general education areas at colleges and universities where chapters of the Order are located."[41] Hanson, who would become the president of the KAOEF, stressed the importance of the organization, "It is our belief that this endeavor is of critical importance to the future of Kappa Alpha Order and its continued existence."[42]

The concept was to create a tax-deductible foundation that could serve as an omnibus entity for a multiplicity of purposes. The projected incorporation could at the same time entice donors with the lure of tax savings, eliminate duplication in staff and administrative cost, align diverse programs to complement one another, mollify friction and infighting between individuals and committees, and establish a national headquarters. Knight Commander Hanson prophesized that "since the activities of the Order are limited by our financial resources, this Foundation may provide [a] guarantee to each of us that KAO shall be the leader in the fraternity world, always improving its goals and attainment."[43]

The new organization was following in the footsteps and, for a decade, was in competition with the Kappa Alpha Scholarship Fund, which had a similar mission and agenda. In 1949, Knight Commander Berryman had announced the creation of the fund, in his column in the *Kappa Alpha Journal* "From Me to You."[44] The concept of the fund was approved by the 1947 Convention in Savannah, Georgia, and came to fruition in 1948. It was defined as "an incorporated organization, separate and distinct from the Order, and *will* operate under its own Board of Trustees headed at all times by the Knight Commander."[45] The three major initiatives of the newly formed foundation included ensuring "support for existing chapters and the ability to develop new chapters will be perpetuated, [increasing] the Order's capacity to provide meaningful educational programs and scholarships for undergraduate members, and [locating] a national office in surroundings compatible with the Order's proud traditions and history."[46]

The overlap in purpose and execution between the newly founded KAOEF and its prototype the KASF, was soon apparent to many of the executive staff members. As early as 1988, at an Executive Council meeting, Knight Commander Idris Traylor reported that the subject of merging KASF and the recently formed KAOEF was being discussed—"the Trustees of KASF agreed to consider combining the scholarship programs of KASF and KAOEF subject to obtaining competent legal advice as to whether the scholarship activities can be legally combined."[47]

The leadership of the KASF vacillated back and forth for several years about the melding of the separate foundations; the main concern of the trustees of the Scholarship Fund was that there were "no unnecessary liabilities on the books of KAOEF" and that they wanted to make sure "that the funds of KASF are not 'at risk' and [that] 80% of the income [would] be available for scholarships."[48] The concerns were addressed, an agreement was made, and, at a meeting of the Executive Council, Executive Vice President William Forester reported that "the merge[r] between the Kappa Alpha Scholarship Fund and the Kappa Alpha Order Educational Foundation will be complete when the assets of KASF are transferred following the audit for the year ending December 31, 1991."[49]

The two foundations were combined on the following day, January 1, 1992, and the event was described as a historic merger that "allows for sweeping changes in streamlined administration, endowment management, funding drives, and the scholarship application process."[50] At the time of the merger the Kappa Alpha Scholarship Fund had been in existence for forty-three years and had served as "a catalyst for the Order's approach to education in a variety of innovative ways."[51] Some of its innovations were requirements for a minimum GPA for initiation, a Freshman Scholarship Citation for the individual, and a Chapter Scholarship for the lodge with the highest aggregate GPA. All these factors encouraged competition and inspiration for members of Kappa Alpha to achieve excellence in scholarship. In addition, at the time of the merger, "approximately 280 young men [had] benefitted from over $623,000 in scholarships awarded by KASF"[52]

The KAOEF was also more aggressive and promotionally savvy in its approach to fund-raising and its scope extended beyond the academic to include activities that promoted leadership enhancement, funding for the National Leadership Institute, and Province Councils. The "Campaign for KA," assisted with funds for the purchase, renovation, and furnishings of the permanent headquarters in Lexington.

In the 1920s, the Knight Commander, Bishop Henry Mikell, had decided that the Order's constitution, which had been amended in a constant and fragmented way since its inception, had developed into a "complex instrument, inconsistent and difficult to interpret" and realized that, as the Order grew, the "divided responsibility and a lack of a central coordinating agency bred inefficiency which even the most competent staff could not combat successfully."[53] Bishop Mikell recognized that the old constitution lacked the functionality of a vehicle for progress and would, if continued, frustrate the efforts to make clear and objective decisions.

The death of Bishop Mikell in 1929, however, delayed this process. In the years that followed "worthy progressive amendments were defeated by a well-meaning and conscientious minority who feared that any change might alter the fundamental traditions and customs representing the basic principles of the Order."[54]

Nevertheless, Province Commanders and General Officers requested that W. Elliot Dunwody and Clarence W. May, Commander of the Hardeman Province and Grand Historian respectively, collaborate to bring forth a new set of rules and to propose to the Convention of 1933 "a concise and complete change" to the fundamental law of the fraternity that would create a centralized administration.[55] The resolution was put forward and defeated by 53-to-19 vote. Nevertheless, a temporary amendment was adopted to create an Executive Secretary and establish a central administrative office.

A committee was formed to rework the provision and it was adopted at the 1935 Convention. The Executive Council was created at that time. Under Article I-410: "The General Officers as a body shall constitute the Executive Council of the Order... and shall advise the Knight Commander... [and] shall appoint, prescribe the duties and fix the compensation of officers and employees...[and] shall designate the general headquarters of the Order and effect any change therein which is best to the interest of the Order."[56]

In addition, the Executive Council was given the authority in any matter that it deemed appropriate and necessary and for which there was not already a restriction in the constitution. The Council could establish loan funds and the regulations pertaining to those funds, inaugurate and effectuate any plan, program, fund, or project it considered consistent with the aims and purposes of the Order, and appropriate monies from the General Fund to specific uses in the interim between conventions. The new laws declared that the Executive Council would be ex officio and Trustees of the Order under its articles of incorporation.[57]

An Advisory Council was also established that was composed of the General Officers and Province Commanders and it met once a year to deliberate on common objectives of the Order. The precursor to the Executive Director was the Executive Secretary who was "a full time paid officer, a member of the Order holding no other office therein, and [one who] shall act directly under the supervision and direction of the Knight Commander."[58] His duties included the collection of all incomes and obligations to the Order, keeping the Seal of the Order, reporting to the convention the state of affairs of the Order, and any other such duties as directed by the Knight Commander or the Convention.[59]

Thus, at the "1935 Memphis Convention... new laws were adopted and the offices of the Grand Historian, Grand Purser, Chief Alumnus, and Editor of the *Journal* were replaced by an Executive Council composed of the Knight Commander and four councilors, which together acted as a board of directors."[60] This consolidation was the beginning of the corporate model and vertical integration within the Order; perhaps its conception was influenced by the successes of the Roosevelt administration to marshal resources, eliminate waste, and use the collected funds in the most efficient and productive way possible.

The corporate structuring of the Order in the area of development, or tax-deductible charitable donations, began with the establishment of the Kappa

Alpha Scholarship Fund as an independent educational entity with a separate board of trustees in 1948. The success of this venture led Knight Commander Loren Hanson to advocate for the establishment of a foundation that would be publically supported by gifts and bequests with enhanced provisions for income and estate tax deductibility. The initial goals included educational loans and scholarships, and programs promoting leadership, community services, and substance abuse control.[61] Hanson started the ball rolling with his own contribution in 1981.[62] The Kappa Alpha Order Educational Foundation differed from the Kappa Alpha Scholarship Foundation in that in addition to awarding scholarships, it also provided support for KA educational programs such as the National Leadership Institute, travel funds for KA consultants, funding fraternity publications such as the *Varlet*, and, by 1986, raising money to establish a national headquarters in Lexington.[63]

To this end KAOEF launched the "Campaign for KA" in 1987, with a goal of raising an unprecedented five million dollars to support its service and educational programs and also to build a solid basis for founding a permanent administrative headquarters in the birthplace of the Order—Lexington, Virginia. The Kappa Alpha Scholarship Fund and the Kappa Alpha Order Educational Foundation merged on January 1, 1992, creating an expanded instrument for raising funds and allocating resources to the areas that would have the most benefit.[64] With a united front and the combined experience and creative energy of the two cooperating foundations, new avenues were found for development, which included cash, publically traded securities, closely held securities, real estate, tangible personal property, mortgages, notes, copyrights, royalties, bequests, pooled income funds, annuities ($10,000 or more) life estate gifts, life insurance, finder's fees, and professional fees.[65]

New techniques in reaching a target audience were expanded to include mass mail appeals, telemarketing, and personal solicitation. Merging the two foundations into one eliminated competition for alumni dollars, thereby updating addresses and cutting postage costs. The promotion of a national headquarters and administration gave active and retired constituents a project that they had been long wanting and were willing to support. That enthusiasm was not only beneficial to the headquarters initiative but also boosted support for the many other aspects of KAOEF's agenda.

The merger of the two foundations also resulted in a merger of officers. Three former KASF officers now became members of the KAOEF's board: Frank Asbury, John Nowell, and Tim Adams, thus complementing the creativity and enthusiasm of the KAOEF board members with the depth of experience of the KASF officers. The improved condition of the Order, both in terms of administrative unity and financial stability, instilled in many the long-deferred desire to go home.

The dream of returning to Lexington stretched back to the late nineteenth century when an arrangement was worked out for a Memorial Hall to be established on the Washington and Lee campus. Finances and internal rivalries, however, prevented that vision from becoming a reality. Other attempts were made during the intervening years. The frustrations of an almost-accomplished end brought about a feverous ambition to complete the original intent—the more that you cover a boiling pot, the hotter it burns. In the history of the Order there has been an underlying and recurring theme of returning home—and even with the many false starts, detours, and thwarted ambitions—will the circle be unbroken?

*Notes* Chapter 11:

1 Dean Hodge, "Changes in College Students' Value Patterns in the 1950's, 1960's, and 1970's," *Sociology of Education* 49 (April 1976), 155.

2 Jack Levin, ed., *Sociological Snapshots 5* (Thousand Oaks: Pine Forge Press, 2008), 78.

3 Ibid.

4 William S. Hamilton, Synopses of the Kappa Alpha Conventions, 1870–1937, Kappa Alpha Archives, Lexington, Va., 58.

5 Mary Westheimer, *The History of Kappa Alpha Order* (Phoenix: Heritage Publishers, 1994), 56.

6 Herbert Brown, "Do Fraternities have Social Rights," *Kappa Alpha Journal* 77, No. 4 (May 1961): 13.

7 "Syndicated Story Outlines a Major Fraternity Problem," *Kappa Alpha Journal* 77, No. 3 (March 1961): 39.

8 Brown, "Do Fraternities have Social Rights," 13.

9 Ibid.

10 John Nowell, "An Open Letter," *Kappa Alpha Journal* 78, No. 3 (March 1962): 20.

11 Ibid.

12 Ibid.

13 Ibid.

14 Ibid.

15 Ibid.

16 Westheimer, *The History of the Kappa Alpha Order*, 57.

17 Ibid.

18 John Brewer, "Chapter Letters," *Kappa Alpha Journal* 82, No. 1 (January 1966): 23.

19 Dani Guepper, "Gamma Rho Stresses Service," *Kappa Alpha Journal* 82, No. 1 (January 1966): 40.

20 Ibid.

21 Ibid.

22 "KAO Endorses Muscular Dystrophy as Its National Philanthropy," *Kappa Alpha Journal* 93, No. 3 (Spring 1976): 1.

23 Philip Altbach, "From Revolution to Apathy: American Student Activism in the 1970s," *Higher Education* 8, No. 6 (November 1979): 622.

24 Ibid., 620

25 Rick Shrager, "The Impact of Living Group Social Climate on Student Academic Performance," *Research in Higher Education* 25, No. 3 (1986): 274.

26 *Kappa Alpha Journal* 62, No. 2 (January 1946): 15.

27 *Kappa Alpha Journal* 65, No. 1 (November 1948): 2.

28 John Berryman, "From Me to You," *Kappa Alpha Journal* 65, No. 4 (May 1949): 2.

29 "NLI stresses Big Five," *Kappa Alpha Journal* 89, No. 3 (Fall 1972): 1.

30 Ibid.

31 Ibid., 2.

32 William Hubard, "Undergraduate Committee Plans National Leadership Institute," *Kappa Alpha Journal* 91, No. 2 (Spring 1974): 7.

33 "NLI," *Kappa Alpha Journal* 99, No. 3 (Summer 1982): 2.

34 Ibid.

35 Richard Barnes, "Lights, Camera, Action," *Kappa Alpha Journal* 99, No. 1 (Winter 1981): 7.

36 Ibid.

37 *Sociological Snapshots 5*, p. 78.

38 Robert Shaffer, "Status of the Greek System," *Kappa Alpha Journal* 100, No. 3 (Summer 1983): 6.

39 "Year End Statistics, 1981–1982," *Kappa Alpha Journal* 99, No. 3 (Summer 1982): 23

40 *Minutes of the 59th Convention of the Kappa Alpha Order* (Nashville: Kappa Alpha Order, 1981), 27.

41 "KAOEF," *Kappa Alpha Journal* 99, No. 3 (Summer 1982): 1.
42 Ibid.
43 Ibid.
44 John Berryman, "From Me to You," *Kappa Alpha Journal* 66, No. 2 (January 1950): 1.
45 "Scholarship Fund," *Kappa Alpha Journal* 65, No. 4 (May 1949): 2.
46 John W. Stephenson, "A Decade of Development," *Kappa Alpha Journal* 109, No. 1 (Spring 1992): 8.
47 "Minutes of the Executive Council Meeting, April 1988," Kappa Alpha Archives, Lexington, Va., 5.
48 "Minutes of the Executive Council Meeting, 1990," Kappa Alpha Archives, Lexington, Va., 6.
49 "Minutes of the Executive Council Meeting, April 1992," Kappa Alpha Archives, Lexington, Va., 6.
50 John W. Stephenson, "A Decade of Development," 8.
51 Ibid.
52 Ibid.
53 Ransom Bassett, ed., *Kappa Alpha Laws* (Louisville: Kappa Alpha Order, 1947), 1.
54 Ibid.
55 Ibid., 2.
56 Ibid., Section 1-401.
57 Ibid.
58 Ibid., Section 1-501.
59 Ibid.
60 Westheimer, *The History of the Kappa Alpha Order*, 44.
61 "KAOEF," 1.
62 Westheimer, *The History of the Kappa Alpha Order*, 51.
63 "KA Celebrates 125 Years of Excellence," *Kappa Alpha Journal* 107, No. 2 (Summer 1990): 11.
64 William Garner, "Merger Benefits Order," *Kappa Alpha Journal* 109, No. 1 (Spring 1992): 8.
65 "KAOEF Board of Trustees Meeting, 1996, Attachment D, Gift Acceptance Policy," Kappa Alpha Archives, Lexington, Va.

*Jerry Lewis Labor Day Telethon, 1980*

*National Administrative Offices, 1252 West Peachtree Street, Atlanta, Georgia, 1961*

# 12

## Will the Circle Be Unbroken?

Almost as soon as the mantle passed from Old Alpha to Beta and Beta to Gamma, a desire began among the Founders and earliest members to return home to Lexington. The first efforts to have a central home for all the far-flung offspring of the Order took place in the last decade of the nineteenth century. Historian Greenlee Letcher described the emotional pull of this desire as "the Japanese worship their ancestors; the Mohammedans have their Mecca. A land without monuments is a land without history."[1]

When Samuel Ammen reprised his role as Knight Commander in 1891, he promoted and advocated for a central and permanent headquarters for the Order to be called Memorial Hall. On December 29, 1896, Ammen convinced the trustees of Washington and Lee University to allow the Order "the privilege of erecting this building on the Washington and Lee campus."[2] Ammen advised the entire Order that the university had not only given the Order the sanction to erect such a building on the campus but had compounded the honor with incentive—the plot on which the Hall was to be erected was to be donated by the college—"relieving us of the cost of a lot. It remains only to raise the money to Build."[3]

The enthusiastic Knight Commander exhorted all loyal KAs to support the effort as the hall would "commemorate the founding of the Kappa Alpha Order" and be a "visible token to or success."[4] Ammen made the argument that the hall would be open to all KAs—a Mecca of the Kappa Alpha World.

In an open letter in the *Journal*, he wrote, "I have a special desire to see Alpha, the Mother Chapter, living in a Memorial Hall, on College Hill, at Lexington, Va., under circumstances, significant of the present dignity, power and resources of the Order." He reiterated the compliment paid to the Order by the trustees of the university.

The Knight Commander believed that it was imperative to have a secure repository for the Order's archives, as in the past many important documents of the Order had been lost in the peregrinations of the administrative sites and that, at any one time, parts of the collection might be scattered among several of the General Officers in various locations. He pointed out that many precious documents would certainly have disappeared except for the ardent efforts of Tazewell Hubard, the Grand Historian, who gathered together as many papers as possible and placed them in his own office in Norfolk. Ammen warned that "his successor (Hubard's) may not possess like facilities."[5] Ammen asserted that a Memorial Hall with a safe and fireproof vault would prevent such a calamity and serve as a sure holding place for other records from the past and those of the future.

Ammen appealed to the alumni, who would assuredly provide the bulk of the needed revenue, that funds collected "may be placed in charge of Alumni, who will serve as trustees, select a site and control the property—and for the mere cost of several thousand dollars."[6] Toward the end of his sermon the Protestant Ammen inserted a very catholic message to that group, "It is hoped, [that the alumni will] see in this work a welcome opportunity for the exercise of their zeal."[7]

The cagey Knight Commander, however, may have unintentionally shot himself in the foot with his opening salvo, by exalting the Alpha Chapter above all others, and in a somewhat deprecating and self-important manner, "Alpha will, doubtless, co-operate to collect the needed funds. I made the suggestion without consulting her, but not, I trust, without her concurrence."[8] Ammen admitted that "Alpha Chapter will be greatly benefitted, doubtless, by the erection of a hall which it will occupy, in part, as a Chapter House, at a moderate

*Proposed Memorial Hall, circa 1896*

rent."[9] He continued that with Alpha occupying such a prestigious address that her influence will be increased and she will "find the task of rushing much facilitated."[10]

One author explained the idyllic projections of the surroundings of the intended hall as "a handsome structure of pleasing design, distinguished from the adjacent residences of the professors of the university by our coat of arms" situated on a quiet avenue between the campus of Washington and Lee and VMI that "looks out upon the beautiful grounds of the University, bright with verdure and the leafy wealth of innumerable trees."[11] Another envisaged the interior of a house of two stories—"on the first floor are the reception room, parlor, 'Library' and the large room in which the chapter meets; on the second floor are the bath room and rooms occupied by members as lodgings"; the author also imagined the library that would contain many treasures, which "every year some chapter, or well-to-do member, enriches the hall with a bust, relief, portrait, or other memorial of the men who have done us good service" and "around the walls are the cartouches of our forty-four chapters, each bordered with the chapter's special flower, along with the Order's red rose and magnolia, and containing the chapter's motto and symbol."[12] Despite the enticements of curious relics to be displayed, irreplaceable documents saved from the worms and the dustbins, and a convenient repository for all sorts of ancient vestments, jewels, and outfits of old times, not many outside of Alpha were inspired to dig deep into their wallets to support the effort. Indeed, there was not even substantial support among the Alpha Chapter itself.

Notwithstanding the grand rhetoric and rosy conjecturing of various officers, two years later only $36.00 had been collected.[13] In spite of the various plans to collect monies and offset expenses, and to create a board of trustees to oversee the project, the aggressive solicitation of funds, the pledges of successive conventions, and the efforts of Frank Percy McConnell, Grand Purser, who threw himself into the work of collecting funds for the Hall with "his well-known KA enthusiasm" by sending out "letters and circulars innumerable," the incessant haranguing of Ammen and Hubard, the fact remains that by 1902 the vast sum of $36.00 had somehow shrunk to $27.05. [14]

The hitch in the plan was that after years of effort on the part of Ammen and company, members and alumni of the collective Order were not willing to support an enterprise that would disproportionately benefit the Alpha Chapter. Even to the organizers it was understandable that "there is a natural apathy in many Chapters with regard to a Memorial Hall, seeing that they themselves are without a Chapter House."[15]

Meeting resistance and seeing the flaws in the original campaign, those making the pitch for Memorial Hall changed tact and presented the Memorial Hall not as a Chapter House for the elite Alpha Lodge but as a pantheon for all Kappa Alphas. It was now put forth that although the members of Alpha had worked energetically to accomplish the mission it was not their expectation that the building would be "their hall" or that they would occupy it for free; "on the contrary, they will not be allowed by the trustees to occupy any part of it, unless they pay full rent."[16]

The change in tack did not persuade the hoi polloi and the matter was discussed with varying degrees of candor and reality until the First World War, when "all activities were stopped." After the war, the notion was again resurrected and its most fervent advocate was the Kappa Alpha historian W. B. Crawford, who maintained that the hall would create a logistical and emotional destination to which all members of the Order could gravitate and congregate.

The reluctance of other chapters and alumni may well have been a reaction to the seemingly presumptuous and arrogant demeanor on the matter of Ammen and the cavalier attitude of Alpha. In part, the resistance may also have been a product of self-interest on the part of other lodges; it may have been the result of the efforts of the followers of Verner Jones, who attempted to oust Ammen and William Sprigg Hamilton; it may have been the result of deficient amounts of disposable incomes; or it may have come from the perception that Ammen was using the "Memorial Hall" project as an opportunity to enshrine his own reputation and contributions.

Although the desire to return to Lexington momentarily lay dormant in the hearts and minds of many—it slumbered but did not die. Throughout the first decade of the twentieth century, the plans for a central administrative capital and spiritual "Mecca" faded into the background in the face of other issues. Conversations among senior leaders began anew in the second decade but were waylaid by the exigencies of the Great War. In the 1920s, however, the plan for a national headquarters took a more substantial form.

In 1921, Cyrus Beale introduced the General Headquarters Resolution since the Order had "never established or attempted to establish a General Headquarters, or owned or occupied a building which was used as a General Headquarters building."[17] It was argued that "such buildings or headquarters are common among other well organized college fraternities" and to be lacking such a facility diminished the status and the good name of the Order.[18]

The Convention of 1921 agreed and expressed more pragmatic reasons for the concept other than status: "Whereas, the Kappa Alpha Order has never established or attempted to establish a General Headquarters, or owned or occupied a building which was used as a General Headquarters building, it is our opinion that a building of suitable size and dignity, located in a proper locality within our chosen limits, in which building the Order may or might have or use as a General HQ Offices for the transaction of its business."[19]

Beale's proposal, however, was not a matter of spontaneous inspiration. He related that he and Henry C. Chiles, the Knight Commander, had colluded about such a project for several years. Specifically, we "talked the entire matter over two or three years prior to the 1921 convention" in respect to "getting the alumni members interested enough to put up the money."[20]

The convention, in its wisdom, agreed that the honor of funding such a noble project should fall on the shoulders of the older and more affluent alumni and thus resolved, "Whereas, the Kappa Alpha Order has never heretofore called upon its alumni members as a whole to contribute materially to any fund towards furthering of interest in said Order; and Whereas, the said Order has never established or attempted to establish a General Headquarters ... it is our opinion that a building [be erected] of suitable size and dignity, located in a proper locality be established."[21]

By the following year, 1922, Beale announced that a site had been selected and a title acquired—it was on Monument Avenue in Richmond, Virginia, just opposite of the equestrian statue of Robert E. Lee. An eminent architect, Douglas Ellington, had donated his services to the Order and already drawn up preliminary blueprints for the building.[22] In 1927, however, because of the bureaucratic obstacles, the inaction of certain officials, and the reluctance within certain elements of the Order to produce the necessary funding, the Richmond project was floundering in inertia and apathy. Beale had already advanced $1,300 out of his own pocket to move the plans forward and confessed that he was so disappointed in the intransigence and foot dragging that he "almost felt like quitting."[23]

He, nevertheless, plugged along, hoping that the initial enthusiasm

*Architect Douglas Ellington's proposed National Office, Richmond, Virginia, 1921*

for the General Headquarters would return. But Beale suffered an even greater disappointment at the Thirty-Seventh Biennial Convention when the Alumni Foundation issued a statement recommending that the Kappa Alpha Order should abandon all effort to acquire a building for use as a General Headquarters and in the future to refrain from contacting the Alumni Foundation on this matter.[24]

Beale was understandably bitter about this reversal of circumstances and addressed the situation during the convention, over the objections of the Knight Commander Emmett L. Irwin, "The last Convention, after the Foundation project had been approved by six other Conventions of the Kappa Alpha Fraternity, appointed a committee to determine whether the Convention should have anything more to do with that Foundation. This Convention, upon the report of the committee, abandoned the Foundation, abandoned the idea of a central office, abandoned the work of ten years."[25]

The main reason for the failure of the Richmond venture was likely the opposition of Knight Commander Irwin. While thinking a central headquarters was a good idea, Irwin believed that it ought to be done at the Knight Commander's convenience and thus he established the Order's headquarters in the floor above his medical offices in New Orleans and issued the fiat in the *Kappa Alpha Journal* that "the Central Administrative Office of the Fraternity has been established at Suite 721 Maison Blanche Building, and all chapter reports and correspondence as well as monies should be forwarded to this address. As you know, this office combines the work of the Grand Historian and Grand Purser under the Executive Secretary."[26]

Although the Knight Commander allowed for the *Journal* to be continued in Richmond "until the completion of the present volume," he declared that "ultimately, the work will be taken over by the Administrative Office, thereby concentrating all work of the National Order in this office, which will be of great assistance to both active and alumni chapters and members."[27] With this statement and likely the collusion of the Alumni Association, Irwin short-circuited the extended and frustrating efforts of Cyrus Beale.

*Maison Blanche, New Orleans, 1898*

*Maison Blanche, circa 1900*

The Maison Blanche Building, located at the corner of Dauphin and Canal Streets, opened its doors in 1897 as a department store and was described by the *New Orleans Times-Picayune* as "the finest in the South." In 1908, the original structure was replaced with a more modern version.

The replacement was in the Beaux-Arts style and had a modern but elegant look to it. In the new structure the lower floors were devoted to retail spaces and the upper floors were occupied by medical and professional offices.

While advocating for a Central Administrative Office, Irwin, in essence, continued the tradition of having the administration be subservient to the will and whim of the executive. Although, it was self-evident to most that a complete restructuring of the administration was not only timely but imperative, until a professional and permanent bureaucracy was put in place, such a reality was impractical.

Improved communication and modes of transportation, the exponential growth of the Order, the increased revenues from an expanded base of wealthy alumni, all made this precept plausible. It would not be until the 1940s, however, that the Central Administrative Office would be moved and, even then, in a transitory state, flitting from one location to another—a tenant and not a landlord.

In 1939, John R. Berryman was elected as the new Knight Commander with his term beginning on January 15, 1940.[28] The entire infrastructure of the Order was being replaced and the immediate internal overview was assigned to the Senior Councilor, W. Elliot Dunwody, on January 19, 1940. Shortly thereafter an official bulletin was issued by Knight Commander Berryman, "The Executive Office Administration has been assigned to Senior Councilor Dunwody. By reason of his proximity to Atlanta where the offices will be maintained, he [Dunwody] will be of particular value in assisting the Secretary in … the efficiency … of the Executive Office."[29]

The new Knight Commander, John R. Berryman, resided in Los Angeles and, if matters had followed past customs, the administrative team would have coalesced around him in California. The decision was made, however, that a move would be made to Atlanta, which was both a central point in the eastern territory of the Order and the home of the Senior Councilor and a place convenient to the Executive Secretary. This unusual step signified a shift in the operational procedure of the Order, from a personal and autocratic control to a business and professional paradigm. During this transition the once dispensable office of Traveling Secretary, which had transitioned into the post of Executive Secretary, had become the fulcrum of day-to-day activity.

In an editorial in the *Journal*, Knight Commander Berryman reflected the shift in priorities facing the Order and the nation, "These are times fraught with much uncertainty, in international, national, and individual affairs, and it behooves each of us as individuals and as members of our respective chapters to anticipate the future and get our affairs in the best order possible. A program of preparedness similar to that of the national program is suggested to each chapter and each individual." He extrapolated from the singular to the plural and explained the change in direction in the administration of the Order in utilitarian terminology, "Much the same situation faces your national officers who are engaged in the determination of policies with reference to the operation of the National Order. These situations do not indicate any catastrophe, but merely opportunities for service and a demand for more efficient and more carefully conceived plans for future development."[30]

The business of managing the nuts-and-bolts activities of the Order was left in the hands of the Executive Secretary. In addition to arranging for the moving of the tangibles of the office northward, it was necessary for the Executive Secretary, C. W. "Mike" May, to hire an entirely new staff, to rearrange and coordinate the new policies of the administrative team, and to determine independently for almost two years the business affairs of the office as he "was without an official set of by-laws for reference, the new ones not yet being adopted or distributed."[31]

Therefore, the aggregate accumulations of Kappa Alpha's stay in New Orleans were stowed into "forty-two steel strapped boxes and crates weighing nearly seven tons" and shipped to the new office in Atlanta. There were personal items and documents, sentimental regalia and mementos of past glories, hundreds of books and archived *Journals*, and numerous knickknacks and brick-a-brac among the flotsam and jetsam intermingled with rare treasures that migrated from Canal Street to Five Points.

*National Administrative Offices, Palmer Building, Atlanta, Georgia*

The new location also physically reflected a more-modern and professional persona—linear, clean cut, no nonsense in design and application—the Palmer Building exemplified the modernization of the Order. In creating the *New Directory*, the progressive May resorted to using the new business machine cards that allowed "for a mechanical listing of members by chapters, geographically, by profession, by class, by initiation date, by birth date, or any combination of classifications."[32]

It was announced on March 15, 1941, however, that C .W. May, the Executive Secretary and editor of the *Journal,* had resigned less than eighteen months after the administrative offices had been moved to Atlanta. In May, Ransom Bassett was named the Executive Secretary and was confirmed in that office on August 28 by the Executive Council. In November 1941, Knight Commander Berryman announced that Ransom Bassett, who had been acting as interim Executive Secretary and Editor of the *Journal,* had been unanimously elected to that office and that the administrative offices had been relocated to his hometown. Once again bags were packed and moved to their new hub—303 Martin Brown Building, Louisville, Kentucky.[33]

*National Administrative Offices, Martin Brown Building, Louisville, Kentucky*

In a letter to Walter George, Bassett described the arrangements that he had made concerning the relocation, "Our offices, we think, are going to be very nice to start out with and will be in the Martin Brown Building, Fourth & Broadway, Louisville, Kentucky. The space we had planned on could no longer be held but I believe what is allotted to us now will be better and the total cost will only be one hundred dollars a month instead of the $106.50 as we had planned.... I got a bid for the entire moving of $176 and some odd cents which I think is very reasonable. I also got a concession from the Palmer Building of only having to pay one month's rent of October for $80."[34]

After fourteen years of service as Executive Secretary, Ransom Bassett resigned and the administrative office was returned to Atlanta during the month of July 1954. The first of three office locations in Atlanta from 1954 to 1986 was situated on the second floor of a modern office building at 830 West Peachtree Street, directly across from the Biltmore Hotel. It was a functional but simple office, which reflected the desire to appear professional and at the same time keep the costs to a minimum.

William E. Forester, who had resigned as Central Regional Advisor, agreed temporarily to become the Director of the Administrative Office and assume the responsibility of moving the burgeoning contents of the Order's records and regalia. The formal opening of the new headquarters took place on September 25th with a gathering of Province Commanders.[35] As the transition was more complicated and the need for his services more extended, in April 1954 he was appointed Executive Secretary. In the initial move, Tom Tune was employed as an accountant, and, with Forester's appointment, Tune was elevated to the office of Assistant Executive Secretary.[36]

The return to Atlanta represented a stability and permanence that had been lacking up to this point; from the time of Irwin and New Orleans, the Order had been following the steps of the Knight Commander or Executive Director like the Tabernacle wandering back and forth through the deserts until finally finding Jerusalem. The multiple, temporary, and increasingly transient administrative offices brought along in its wake the incorruptible monuments

*830 West Peachtree Street, Atlanta, Georgia*

of the Order's history, antique regalia, awards, gavels, commendations, portraits, and even the original badges of several of the Founders—in short the collective soul and memory of the fraternity. As time passed and the origins of the Order became more distant, the desire for permanency and the fear of losing what records remained became more acute.

The Kappa Alpha administrative offices remained at 830 West Peachtree Street until 1961, when the Order's growth necessitated a move to a larger venue at 1252 West Peachtree Street, only several blocks away. This building was a modern five-story structure that had been completed only the year before. The offices were on the fourth floor and the suite contained a library, a meeting

*1252 West Peachtree Street, Atlanta, Georgia*

room, and the Executive Secretary's office. The sophistication and elegance of the new office reflected the increasing affluence of the Order. The staff expanded as well as the size of the compound; in addition to the executive offices the headquarters also had working space for the Alumni Secretary and the Traveling Chapter Advisor. [37]

In 1970, the administrative offices again moved westward, this time to 379 Peachtree Road in Lennox Square, the present-day site of a new BB&T bank. But all the shuffling around Atlanta was but a backup plan for the ambitions of the Order. The Centennial Anniversary was right around the corner and many longed for a return to Lexington. In 1956, Knight Commander James L. Duncan announced the launch of the Centennial Campaign, which would provide for scholarships and have sufficient funds on hand "to truly house the Order in the way it should be housed—namely, to have a permanent administrative center in a settled location."[38]

As contributions to the campaign kicked into high gear, the donations became more frequent and more generous. In 1957, the first large gift of $50,000 from an alumnus in Houston was announced and new ways of giving were promoted. And while the Order realized that contributions of that size were the exception, nevertheless all members "through a new plan to be coordinated by the Centennial campaign can participate."[39] Indeed, Roy Parsons, the campaign director, hinted at the prospect of a national headquarters two years before substantial activity took place. He artfully reported that "a few proposals" had been made at the Convention of the preceding year "regarding the site for a National Headquarters Building... and is very definitely in the future plans for the Order."[40]

At the mention of a national headquarters, checks and support flooded in. "I am enclosing my check for the Centennial Campaign," wrote Charles McCrary, "I think it is important for the fraternity to have a permanent home, an imposing edifice in keeping with the traditions of the Order."[41] Alumni organizations in the various lodges across the country did not automatically cede this honor to Lexington, however. McCarthy DeMere, president of the Memphis Alumni

Chapter, was one of the first to pitch his own city as an excellent location for a permanent headquarters.[42]

By 1961, the success of the Centennial Campaign was apparent by the surprising surplus of anticipated funds. Once director of the campaign and now Alumni Secretary, James Young revealed the once and future focus of the fund-raising promotion, "The Centennial Campaign has now assisted the Order in another phase of its operations. Recently the Executive Council adopted a proposal that established a reserve for the purpose of accumulating funds for the building of a National Headquarters Building."[43] Young explained that over the past few years there had been much discussion about such a project because of the "rapidly expanding administrative activities." He hoped, in addition, as Ammen had proposed, "that the building will contain a memorial library which will serve as a repository for the Order's archives and other works of historical interest." The all-important alumni representative admitted that the realization was "long term" but, at least "the studies have begun, and the first positive steps have been taken."[44]

The new plan was augmented by additional contributions of alumni, Young confessed that "the building of a National Headquarters was an objective of the Centennial Campaign from its inception," but that the implementation was delayed until the funds collected reached a point where the Building Fund would not take away from "other vital programs" that the fund-raising campaign supported.[45]

In the fall of 1962, the Executive Council announced its choice for the site of the proposed headquarters—Lexington, Virginia—"as the one pre-eminent location … the founding and spiritual home" of the Order. Despite the jockeying of many different alumni associations for their own hometowns as the spot for the Kappa Alpha "Mecca," there was likely little surprise that their supplications had gone unheeded and less that Lexington was chosen.[46]

The search began in earnest in 1963, several of the first candidates were historic homes recommended by their proximity to the campus of Washington and Lee University, their ties to local luminaries and their imposing physical presence. Chief among them were Col Alto plantation, the Barclay House, Silverwood, and the Mitchell property.

The original tract of land on which Col Alto is situated was purchased in 1819 by James McDowell Sr., father of Virginia governor James McDowell Jr. The main structure was completed in 1827 and given to the former's namesake son. After the younger McDowell's death in 1851, the property changed hands several times. "Among the subsequent owners were a minister, a professor of mathematics at VMI, and a New Orleans judge. In 1898 Col Alto was sold to Henry St. George Tucker."[47] Tucker was a descendant of the second professor of law at the College of William and Mary, St. George Tucker, and the second professor of law at Washington and Lee University, John Randolph Tucker. Henry St. George Tucker followed his father as Dean of the Law School at Washington and Lee in 1899 and served as acting president of the university from 1900 to 1902. Tucker died in 1932 and the house was inherited by his eldest daughter, Rosa Tucker Mason. She lived there until 1960.

Col Alto was of especial interest. In appearance, the main building was an example of the Classical Revival style of graceful proportions. The house, architecturally, is of two stories, Flemish-bond brick structure with a handsome three-part fanlight doorway with Ionic colonettes. In the 1930s, Rosa Tucker Mason commissioned New York architect William Lawrence Bottomley to update the features of the house and he added both modern conveniences, several service additions and a Palladian style veranda.[48] By the time the architect had completed his renovations the house had seventeen rooms, eight bathrooms, twelve fireplaces, a full basement, and four porches.

In the years intervening between the restoration and the death of Mrs. Mason, however, the house and grounds had fallen into disrepair. In 1957, for "the consideration of ten dollars," Mrs. Mason willed the property to Washington and Lee University with the understanding that it would become the residence of the future presidents of Washington and Lee. After Mrs. Mason's death, however, the university decided to remodel Lee's residence on campus and used Col Alto as storage space for books and unused furniture. As late as 1972, the

*Col Alto, Lexington, Virginia*

property was described as being "in need of repair and restoration work on both the exterior and interior."[49]

The second candidate, known as the Barclay House, was located at 109 Lee Avenue. It was designed by Lexington architect, John Jordan, and built between 1824 and 1834 by Benjamin Durst. In 1834, Durst sold the house to David Evans Moore, a former aide to General George Washington. Moore was both a member of the board of trustees for Washington College and in charge of the Arsenal (later Virginia Military Institute). The house fell into the possession of Alexander Tedford Barclay in the 1880s when he married the youngest daughter of David Moore. Mr. Barclay was a businessman and editor of the *Lexington Gazette*. In 1907, Greenlee D. Letcher, commissioner for Mrs. Lucy White, sold the old Barclay House to Mr. W. F. Pierson. Letcher, of course,

*Barclay House (Beaumont), 109 Lee Avenue, Lexington, Virgina*

was a longtime historian to the Kappa Alpha Order and had been a member both of the Alpha Chapter at Washington College and of the Beta Chapter at VMI, his father was wartime governor John Letcher, who is thought to have persuaded General Lee to accept the position of president of Washington College.

The third prospective site was the Gadsden House, also said to have been designed and built by Benjamin Durst Sr. in 1819. The original form of the house was in an "I"—with two rooms flanking a central hall in a structure that was two and a half stories high of a particularly fine Flemish-bond brick. After several occupants, a prominent Episcopal minister, General William Pendleton, who had been Lee's Chief of Artillery for the Army of Northern Virginia, bought the house in 1883, but died before moving in. The property, however, passed to his children who added the "front section in 1885 extending the floor plan to a four room per floor arrangement."[50] General Pendleton's daughters operated an "English and Classical School" in the "Pines," as it was called for many years. The building was also used as a boarding house for many years.[51]

A second and earlier residence of General Pendleton, located at 107 Lee Avenue and locally known as the Episcopal Rectory, was also under consideration. The structure, again the product of a collaboration between Benjamin Durst and John Jordan, was erected for Charles Dorman about 1829. The house was passed along to his son, James Baldwin Dorman, about 1849. The younger Dorman attended both Washington College and Virginia Military Institute, which had been converted from the Arsenal by the elder Dorman's bill. In 1841, while still a student he was appointed Assistant Professor of Modern Languages and joined his father's law practice in 1845. He served in the House of Delegates from 1849 to 1851 and was a strong supporter of abolition and the American Colonization Society. Dorman vehemently opposed secession but joined the Confederate army when Virginia separated from the Union.[52]

General Francis H. Smith, who was the first superintendent of VMI, bought the house in his own name about 1854 but soon sold it to Grace

*The Rectory, 107 Lee Avenue, Lexington, Virginia*

Episcopal Church, where for many years it served as a rectory. General William Pendleton was the first rector to live there, from 1854 to 1883. During the Civil War the roof was raised to make attic space to accommodate students from Washington College. It has been described as "evenly proportioned two story brick structure ... with delicately scaled doorways on both levels ... which has an elliptical fanlight and decorated sidelights ... separated by a one story Doric columned porch."[53]

Also considered was the Reid-White House, which was designed by Samuel McDowell Reid, who later remodeled Mulberry Hill. Reid began detailed specifications for the house as early as 1821, and ordered his carpenter, Edward Sewell, to erect fluted Ionic columns and "fancy doors with sidelights" on both levels. Two elaborate chimneypieces were used to adorn the first floor, while those on the second were to "be finished in middleing style." [54] It is situated on a shady two-and-a-half-acre lot on the same ridge of hills as Washington and Lee University stands at 208 West Nelson Street directly behind the present post office building, which was once the front yard of the house.

It was constructed in the Federal Style and was further modified in the antebellum period with a modification of the roof and additions to the south side.[55] It is interesting to note that Samuel McDowell Reid, who was a clerk of the Rockbridge County Court, was a cousin of James McDowell. He also served as a trustee to Washington College and was the owner of Mulberry Hill.

The house was transferred to his daughter, Mary Louise White, wife of the Greek professor at Washington College and stayed in the family until 1959 when it was sold to Kappa Alpha Fraternity and converted into a chapter house. It was bought in 1975 by Brigadier General Tobias Philbin, who has restored it to its antebellum grandeur.[56]

Other contenders with less illustrious pedigrees were the Mitchell property just east of Lexington, and Silverwood, which was located directly across from Stonewall Jackson Cemetery at 217 South Main Street. Silverwood, is a well-proportioned villa in the Italianate style, built by General Elisha Franklin Paxton in 1857. In 1860, Paxton traded the house to Judge John Brockenbrough in

*Reid-White House. Lexington, Virginia*

exchange for Thorn Hill, which would also later be under consideration for Kappa Alpha's national headquarters. Judge Brockenbrough, was the founder of the Law School and was assigned the task of convincing General Lee to become the president of Washington College. The judge, older and more reluctant to make the longer walk from Thorn Hill, wished to be nearer to the law school. The house was sold to Judge J. K. Edmondson in 1896.[57]

Silverwood's most attractive attributes included its proximity to the town, the cemetery where both Stonewall Jackson and Samuel Ammen were buried, that it was situated on the main line of traffic through town, and that it was already finely landscaped and was supplied with water and sewage services. Its detractions included the price, lack of acreage, and concerns about expansion and parking.

On the other hand, the Mitchell property had the advantages of a sizeable lot, almost 2.5 acres, located not in town but at a convenient crossroads, which would have been suitable for expansion and parking. It was not developed, however, and required improvements that might prove expensive—water, sewage, roadways, and extensive landscaping.

Weighing all the various considerations to be taken into account, the Executive Council considered the Barclay House to be the most desirable choice. On January 6, 1964, the Fraternity Housing Corporation entered into an agreement with Virginia and Edwin Schultz to buy their property at 109 Lee Avenue, known as the Barclay House, for the sum of $30,000.[58]

The document called for a settlement on the first day of May. Even before that early date arrived, however, a roar went up among some of the townspeople. Word had leaked out that the fraternal order was planning to scrap the lovely old building in the middle of town and insert a modern monstrosity. At this early stage of development, with an agreement already having been signed, the determination of the scope and manner of rendering the location into a building suitable to the Order's purposes was still under preliminary considerations.

At an appeals meeting with the Zoning Board of Lexington held on April 21, 1964, Lexington resident and future Knight Commander Henry J. "Hank" Foresman was greeted with anxious and sometime strident requests for information. Almost immediately at the beginning of the session, he was on the defensive, "Quite frankly, at this point, I do not know what particular form the Headquarters will take." He tried to assure the gathering that "the building—whether it be a restoration or whether it will be a new building, will be of colonial design and harmonize with the neighborhood... the architects have recommended that, in any event, certain woodwork, the bricks, and the hand-rolled glass should be very carefully removed even if the building is to be demolished, for the purpose of being reused in a new building."[59] This was not the reassurance that the crowd had sought.

A spokesman for the Association for the Preservation of Virginia Antiquities, Colonel Bates Gilliam, rose to voice the collective opinion of the group, "I feel that this is one of the buildings that we particularly want to see standing for a great many more generations... and I assume that the architectural consultants that he referred to have been made well aware of the feelings of the community."[60]

The local opposition must have caught the Kappa Alpha leadership by surprise for the prospect of the Order's being located in the town had been recently heralded as a boon for the community. The local paper, the *Lexington News-Gazette*, announced the return of Kappa Alpha on its front page, in bold letters, and was greeted by all as an exciting opportunity. Even the most understated opinion implied that universal approval was assured, "No one could find fault with the idea that Kappa Alpha should locate its offices here at the site of its founding.[61]

Hank Foresman, who was spearheading the headquarters effort, in prognosticating potential delays and pitfalls devised a Plan B, just in case. In June, he informed Knight Commander John W. Nowell that he had met with the Director of the R. E. Lee Hotel, which was situated in the middle of town, and that an understanding had been reached with the management of the hotel "to lease the seven rooms on the mezzanine for the sum of $375 per month. The rental would include full janitor service and two permanent parking spaces in the hotel parking lot, as well as all utilities, except telephone."[62] Foresman added that a two-year lease was set to commence the following June and could be extended for an additional year if necessary. A month later, plans for a temporary location had advanced to the stage that the hotel's attorney, William Coleman, agreed in writing that it was willing to enter into such an arrangement with the Kappa Alpha Order.[63]

In January 1964, the sale of the Barclay House was arranged between the Fraternity Housing Corporation and Virginia and Edwin Schultz, the closing date and final signing were set for May 1, 1964.[64] Although the Order both bought the house and had received permission to use the Barclay House as its headquarters in May 1964, nevertheless, Foresman thought that it was prudent to have made the alternative arrangements.[65]

In July 1964, the Executive Council wrote to the editor of the *News-Gazette* to explain that the architects

*Hank Foresman in regalia*

had determined that it would "not be practical for us to restore" the Barclay House "and convert it as a whole."[66] In turn the editor replied, "I cannot honestly conceal my disappointment in learning that Kappa Alpha has apparently decided not to make use of a lovely old house that it has bought here.... I feel that in the destruction of this house we would be losing something quite precious to this town, and I do not stand alone in this belief."[67]

Thus, the battle resumed in earnest. Paul Speake, a longtime leader of the Order, evidently had received a sharp rebuke from the editor in return and suggested, tongue in cheek, to Foresman that the real reason for the ongoing debate had more to do with the weather than the principle, "Unfortunately, the rose beetles were late in arriving this summer and the drought has not been as bad as last year, and the local citizenry found it necessary to manufacture an item of conversation to relieve the boredom of a long hot summer."[68]

Despite the seeming finality of the deal, and that most of the opposition had seen reason after the plans and process had been explained to them, nevertheless, a very small, but quite vocal, group, known locally as the "Rockbridge Hysterical Society," acoustically opposed the razing of the house. Foresman's initial impulse was to turn one part of the townspeople against the other and start up "the damndest fight between the Chamber of Commerce and the Hysterical Society." It turned out that the High Sheriff had become so frustrated with several members of the organization that he had them as a "guests in his establishment on a hot summer afternoon" and "turned a bitch in heat loose in the same cell."[69]

Although the Chamber of Commerce and others were hostile to the efforts of the "Hysterical Society," the determined band continued in its efforts. Several weeks later, in September 1964, a very polite note came from the mayor of Lexington to Foresman relating the events of the last town council meeting where, he said, a majority of the townspeople were happy to welcome the headquarters in their city "whether it is the result of restoration, rebuilding or a complete new structure."[70] There still remained for a few, however, the hope "that the Barclay House can be restored."

Considering the tenacity of the vocal few and already having a temporary backup plan for the delays, Foresman also began to think about other options. One of the more interesting was, as Ammen had proposed at the end of the nineteenth century, actually to have a center on the campus of Washington and Lee. This time, however, Foresman, was proposing the spot where the toast to the two Williams took place between old Central Hall and the Lee Chapel. He wistfully wrote. "As always, I rather expect that some good will come out of this present tempest and who knows, we may end up with a site on the campus of Washington and Lee University next to the Lee Chapel." [71] He believed that the proposal would receive consideration but facetiously said that he did not expect that "the University will throw in the Lee Chapel to sweeten the deal."[72]

Foresman suggested that members of the Hysterical Society call Tom Paulson in San Francisco, at their expense, "regarding the destruction of the hallowed Barkley [Barclay] house, as few, if any, of the 'objectors' are willing to replace mouth with money."[73]

The day following Foresman's letter to Paul Speake an article appeared in the *News-Gazette* under the title "Barclay House" with a history of the building, its historical and architectural significance, and the fact that General Lee was a frequent overnight guest. The article was also liberally sprinkled with the editor's quotes to Mr. Speake (which actually were not in the letter) concerning the civic duties of the Order. "In a letter to Mr. Speake, M.W. Paxton, director of the APVA, stated 'We can think of no better way for the fraternity to promote an appreciation of its heritage than by preserving this handsome house.… We feel, he continued, that KA has a wonderful opportunity here to set an example."[74] In reality, Mr. Paxton had issued a not-so-veiled threat, "I am afraid that Kappa Alpha has placed itself in a position of having quite a public relations job to do in Lexington."[75]

Delays, setbacks, accelerating construction costs, and the predicted public relations problems increased as the editor of the *News-Gazette* had so accurately predicted. There had been talk of leaving the central offices in Atlanta and even abandoning the idea of a permanent headquarters, the most lucrative enticement for contributions to the Centennial Campaign had been predicated on the establishment of a headquarters in Lexington and to abandon that prospect at this late stage in the game was not an option. The continuing fluctuations of fortune struck a nerve in the most ardent supporters of the return to Lexington and some reckoned that the prize in the guise of the Barclay House was not worth the chase.

Thus, shortly afterward, the trustees of Washington and Lee were presented with the proposal to establish the Kappa Alpha Headquarters on campus. After all, they had approved the donation of a tract of land when Ammen had asked at the end of the last century and, although that offer had yielded no results, it was worth another try. Formerly the site proposed by Ammen was bordering the divide between Washington and Lee and VMI; this time it was an area called the Fishwick tract, which was located between the Lee Chapel and the R. E. Lee Memorial Episcopal Church. Foresman's proposition was not received with the same enthusiasm as it had been formerly, and in January 1966, he reluctantly reported that "I have learned this morning that the Trustees of the University had rejected the request."[76]

In March it was announced that Order had sold the Barclay House to Ann Jones Tutwiler of Brushwood near Lexington for an undisclosed sum. It was emphasized, however, that the sale had enabled the Order to recover its entire investment in the property. Although there was still a mandate and obligation to establish a national headquarters and have it located in Lexington, the members of the Executive Council made it perfectly clear that they were not willing to become involved in any project with potential ties to the "Hysterical Society."

The two most viable alternatives now became the Mitchell property and the Ann Smith School. Henry Foresman heard rumors about the old Ann Smith Academy, which had fallen into embarrassing disrepair, was about to be terminated as a public school and abandoned by its owners, the City of Lexington. Foresman recommended a feasibility report for the site and worried about the contentious members of the Lexington School Board. The institution had special significance for the Order, as William and Stanhope Scott had called the Ann Smith Academy home, Samuel Ammen had his first teaching job there, and some of the earliest meetings of the Alpha Chapter were held in a room on the second floor of that building.

The original Ann Smith Academy had been founded by the subscription of many of the town fathers in 1807. It was operated as a school for female students and was the first in the state and likely in the South to educate the fairer sex exclusively. After 1821, the school had a regular succession of principals and teachers, a standardized curriculum and enjoyed a good reputation. Boys were admitted about 1877 and it afterwards was regarded as a good day school with classical features. In 1903, the building was rented to the Lexington School Board on condition that the town would erect a new building on the site by October 1, 1909. "For this purpose there was a bond issue of $20,000 and the ancient building was torn down to make room on the same spot for the High School of Lexington."[77] Therefore, although the building colloquially bore the same name and stood in the same place, it was an entirely different edifice from the one known to the founding fathers of the Kappa Alpha Order.

The Mitchell property, which earlier had been dismissed as being too expensive to upgrade, too far off the beaten track, and lacking the pedigree and venerable appearance that the Executive Council was hoping to secure, now looked far more attractive than before. Weighing the pros of the Ann Smith School, with its fine location and its tangential connections to Kappa Alpha's past, against the costs of repairing, modernizing, adapting the renovations to the liking of local preservation societies—the committee decided against bidding on the building. By contrast, the Mitchell estate seemed a practical alternative.

On July 6, 1967, the Fraternity Housing Corporation purchased the parcel of land "situated in the western part of the City of Lexington, bounded by U.S. 60 on Nelson Street Extended on the northeast bounded by Bord[e]n Road on the south" from the heirs of Dr. Howard Mitchell.[78] Noted architect and Kappa Alpha, Alvin Aubinoe, drew up plans for a simple, unvarnished, but functional base of operations. Local contractors were contacted and negotiations were proceeding.

The former and primary objection to the Mitchell property had been the cost of developing both the building itself from scratch and the improvements necessary for the infrastructure and landscaping of the surroundings. Two years later, even though construction costs in the area had increased dramatically, the Mitchell property now seemed to be the best option.

Once again, however, fate intervened. On August 17, 1969, Hurricane Camille made landfall in Mississippi packing 170-miles-per-hour winds and creating a surge that was twenty-five feet high; it was one of only three category five hurricanes to date to hit the United States. By August 19th, Camille had made its way to Virginia and "so much rain fell in such a short time that, according to the National Weather Service, it was the probable maximum rainfall which meteorologists compute to be theoretically possible."[79] The result was flooding, landslides, destroyed communications, and vast destruction.

The cost of construction estimates and the time frames in which a job could be completed doubled overnight. Far more willing to pay the inflated prices than Kappa Alpha were those who had lost their homes or businesses. Moreover, as a

*Aftermath of Hurricane Camille, August 1969*

result of severe property damage from Hurricane Camille, contractors doubled their original estimates. The Executive Council chose to sell the property. An exasperated Hank Foresman proclaimed, "For all intents and purposes, the idea of a headquarters in Lexington was dead at that time." [80]

The concept of relocating in Lexington, while not dead, lay half-aware in that twilight between deep sleep and waking for many years. It was shaken from its lethargy more than a decade later when Knight Commander Idris Traylor in 1985 declared that a move back to Lexington was obligatory. The Executive Council concurred with Knight Commander Traylor and "voted to move the headquarters from Atlanta ... and be relocated in Lexington, Va., beginning in 1986."[81]

With a firm commitment's having been made, the national staff began to scurry about Rockbridge looking for suitable locations. Citing the rising costs of doing business in Atlanta and noting the obvious excitement of staff, alumni, and active members, no delays in the move were expected or made. "The Order made arrangements to renovate some commercial property on Walker Street overlooking Lexington.... Renovation will be completed in time for the move from Atlanta on December 28."[82]

In January, the resigned but cheerful group, took up quarters on Walker Street in Lexington. Later, former tenants would affectionately recall the "KA & P," their building having once housed a grocery store. It was however beautifully appointed to the fitting of the headquarters. The stay was not as brief as had been reckoned—the administrative staff remained in this spot until 1992—six years; longer than New Orleans, longer than the two previous locations in Atlanta.

Henry Foresman noted that "we looked at every piece of property in Lexington and close to Lexington. It didn't make any difference whether it had a building on it or not—we looked at it."[83] The search for a new site continued but Foresman and associates were, like the sheriff's dog on a hot summer day, both worked up and determined, and, as will be seen in the next chapters, were able to accomplish their plan in a more-consummated fashion than the sheriff's long-denied canine companion.

## *Notes* Chapter 12:

1 Greenlee Letcher, "Letcher on Memorial Hall," *Kappa Alpha Journal* 23, No. 3 (February 1906): 350.

2 "Editorial," *Kappa Alpha Journal* 14, No. 2 (January 1897): 240.

3 "Memorial Hall," *Kappa Alpha Journal* 17, No. 5 (May 1900): 470.

4 Ibid., 469.

5 Samuel Ammen, "A Memorial Hall," *Kappa Alpha Journal* 17, No. 5 (May 1900): 496.

6 "Memorial Hall," 470.

7 Ibid., 472.

8 Ibid., 470.

9 Ibid., 471.

10 Ibid.

11 "Editorial," *Kappa Alpha Journal* 14, No. 3 (January 1897): 240.

12 "Looking Backwards," *Kappa Alpha Journal* 14, No. 4 (March 1897): 273.

13 F. P. McConnell, "More about the Proposed Memorial Hall," *Kappa Alpha Journal* 16, No. 4 (March 1899): 378.

14 Samuel Z. Ammen, "The Memorial Hall," *Kappa Alpha Journal* 20, No. 2 (November 1902): 108

15 Ibid.

16 Samuel Z. Ammen, "The Memorial Hall" *Kappa Alpha Journal* 24, No. 4 (April 1907): 45.

17 *Minutes of the Thirty-First Biennial Convention of the Kappa Alpha Order* (Orlando: W. Crawford, 1921), 31.

18 Ibid., 32.

19 William S. Hamilton, Synopses of the Kappa Alpha Conventions, 1870–1937, Kappa Alpha Archives, Lexington, Va., 1939, p. 43.

20 *Minutes of the Thirty-Fourth Biennial Convention of the Kappa Alpha Order* (Orlando: W. Crawford, 1927), 36.

21 Hamilton, Synopses of the Kappa Alpha Conventions, 1870–1937, p. 44.

22 *Minutes of the Thirty-Second Biennial Convention of the Kappa Alpha Order* (Orlando: W. Crawford, 1923), 60.

23 *Minutes of the Thirty-Fourth Biennial Convention of the Kappa Alpha Order,* 36.

24 *Minutes of the Thirty-Seventh Biennial Convention of the Kappa Alpha Order* (New Orleans: Administrative Office, 1934), 115.

25 Ibid., 27.

26 Emmett Irwin, "The Knight Commander's Message," *Kappa Alpha Journal* 50, No. 3 (March 1934): 342.

27 Ibid.

28 "Proceedings of the Fortieth Biennial Convention" (New Orleans: Administrative Office, 1939), p. 37.

29 "Proceedings of the Forty-First Biennial Convention" (Louisville: Administrative Office, 1941), 7.

30 "The Knight Commander," *Kappa Alpha Journal* 57, No. 1 (November 1940): 3.

31 "Administrative Office," *Kappa Alpha Journal* 58, No. 3 (March 1941): 100.

32 "The Directory," *Kappa Alpha Journal* 58, No. 3 (March 1941): 101.

33 "Administrative Office," *Kappa Alpha Journal* 58, No. 1 (November 1941): 1.

34 Ransom Bassett to Walter George, September 19, 1941, Kappa Alpha Archives, Lexington, Va., 1941.

35 "KA on the Move," *Kappa Alpha Journal* 71, No. 1 (November 1954): 7.

36 "Forester, Tune, Step Up Work," *Kappa Alpha Journal* 72, No. 2 (January 1956): 14.

37 "Central Headquarters Moved," *Kappa Alpha Journal* 78, No. 1 (November 1961): 2.

38 "Knight Commander's Message," *Kappa Alpha Journal* 72, No. 4 (May 1956): 1.

39 "Centennial Program Makes Strides," *Kappa Alpha Journal* 74, No. 1 (November 1957): 18.

40 Ibid., 19.

41 "Wider Participation," *Kappa Alpha Journal* 75, No. 2 (January 1958): 5.

42 "Memphis Alumni," *Kappa Alpha Journal* 75, No. 1 (November 1958): 18.

43 James C. Young, "Fraternally Yours," *Kappa Alpha Journal* 77, No. 4 (May 1961): 11.

44 Ibid.

45 "Positive Action Taken for Headquarters Building," *Kappa Alpha Journal* 77, No. 1 (November 1961): 15.

46 Virginia Department of Historic Resources. National Register of Historic Places Nomination. Col Alto. 1988. Survey File 117-3. Richmond, Va.

48 Ibid.

49 Ibid.

50 Royster Lyle and Pamela Simpson, *The Architecture of Historical Lexington* (Charlottesville: University Press of Virginia, 1977), 79.

51 Ibid.

52 Stephen A. McGuire, "James Baldwin Dorman (1823–1893)," Virginia Memories, Library of Virginia, Richmond, 2010, http://www.virginiamemory.com/online_classroom/union_or_secession/people/james_dorman (viewed May 1, 2015).

53 Lyle and Simpson, *The Architecture of Historical Lexington,* 84.

54 Ibid., 86.

55 Ibid.

56 Virginia Department of Historic Resources. National Register of Historic Places Nomination. Reid-White-Philbin House. 2000. Survey File 117-0014. Richmond, Va.; Lyle and Simpson, *The Architecture of Historical Lexington*, 86.

57 Lyle and Simpson, *The Architecture of Historical Lexington,* 109.

58 Contract for 109 Lee Avenue, Lexington, Virginia, January 6, 1964, Kappa Alpha Archives, Lexington, Va., 1964.

59 "Transcript of the proceedings and evidence introduced at a meeting of the Board of Zoning Appeals of the town of Lexington," April 21, 1964, Recorded by Carole Shorter, Kappa Alpha Archives, Lexington, Va., 1964, 2.

60 Ibid., 4.

61 "Kappa Alpha to Move National Office Here," *Lexington News-Gazette*, August 29, 1962, p. 1.

62 Henry Foresman to John Nowell, June 25, 1963, Kappa Alpha Archives, Lexington, Va., 1963.

63 William Coleman to Hank Foresman, July 9, 1963, Kappa Alpha Archives, Lexington, Va., 1963.

64 "Contract and Agreement of Sale between FHC and Virginia and Edwin Schultz," Kappa Alpha Archives, Lexington, Va., 1964.

65 William Coleman and William Romans to Henry Foresman, May 20, 1964 , Kappa Alpha Archives, Lexington, Va., 1964.

66 Paul Speake to M. W. Paxton, July 23, 1964, Kappa Alpha Archives, Lexington, Va., 1964.

67 M. W. Paxton to Paul Speake, July 11, 1964, Kappa Alpha Archives, Lexington, Va., 1964.

68 Henry Foresman to Paul Speake, August 28, 1964, Kappa Alpha Archives, Lexington, Va., 1964, 1.

69 Ibid.

70 Mayor D. E. Brady to Henry Foresman, September 7, 1964, Kappa Alpha Archives, Lexington, Va., 1964.

71 Foresman to Speake, August 28, 1964, p. 2.

72 Ibid.

73 Ibid.

74 [M. W. Paxton], "Efforts to Save House Fail," *Lexington News-Gazette*, August 29, 1962, p. 1.

75 Paxton to Speake, July 11, 1964.

76 Henry Foresman to Shields Johnson, January 20, 1966, Kappa Alpha Archives, Lexington, Va., 1966.

77 Oren F. Morton, *A History of Rockbridge County, Virginia* (Staunton, Va.: McClure Co., 1920), 210.

78 Rockbridge County Deed Book 299, July 6, 1967, p. 11, Rockbridge County Clerk's Office, Kappa Alpha Archives, Lexington, Va.

79 Lisa Romano, "Hurricane Camille," Encyclopedia Virginia, http://encyclopediavirginia.org/Hurricane_Camille_August_1969#start_entry (viewed April 27, 2015).

80 "Alumni Challenge Order to Finish Dream," *Kappa Alpha Journal* 105, No. 3 (Spring 1994): 4.

81 Steven Russell, "A Place to Call Home," *Kappa Alpha Journal* 108, No. 1 (Winter 1991): 8.

82 "KA Makes Tracks to Lexington," *Kappa Alpha Journal* 102, No. 1 (Winter 1986): 5.

83 Russell, "A Place to Call Home," 9.

*Robert E. Lee Hotel, Lexington, Virginia*

*Rockbridge County Jail, Lexington, Virginia*

# 13

## Home Again

The setbacks in the purchasing of the Mitchell property, following the unexpected opposition in respect to the Barclay deal and all the false starts and dashed hopes, had dampened the enthusiasm for the Lexington relocation in the minds of many, especially a number of the formerly openhanded donors. Even Henry Foresman and friends were temporarily put off the scent. The idea was dead in the water until 1985, when the historically oriented Knight Commander Dr. Idris R. Traylor, Jr. decided enough was enough and ordered a return to the *omphalos* of the Order—Lexington, Virginia.[1] In January 1986, the national administrative office was moved by executive fiat from Atlanta to Lexington.[2] Traylor had the support of many of the alumni—the "Campaign for Kappa Alpha"—a five million dollar drive to establish a permanent headquarters in Lexington was commenced and with a short period of time thereafter H. Lynn Greer reported "that a handful of alumni had already committed more than one third of the five million dollar goal."[3]

For the purpose of strategizing, Richard Barnes, the Executive Director, frequently conferred with Sigma Nu, which had already established its headquarters in town and, having been recently through the process, had access to realistic and tangible figures about the expenses of setting up shop and maintaining offices in the town. Therefore, Barnes was able to report to the Executive Council, with a high degree of confidence that "all current operations on the national administrative offices are feasible and can be more cost effective than in Atlanta."[4]

After early and frantic searches, local KA leaders joined with a group of doctors to renovate a property on Walker Street overlooking Lexington and, it came to pass that having found an abandoned grocery store of suitable size and functionality in that locale, an old A&P store became the first administrative center for Kappa Alpha in Lexington. Executive Director Richard Barnes moved the staff to Lexington along with the Executive Vice President William E. Forester. During the long transition while the Order settled into Lexington, "Hank (Foresman, former KC) was there all the time, helping with the settling in and the introductions to the town."[5] Snuggled into their new digs, with the hustle-bustle and distractions of Atlanta far away, the staff renewed its quest to bring all things up to date; within short order a new computer system was installed and modernization commenced.[6]

The ultimate aim of the move to Lexington was to find a headquarters with an impressive physical and architectural presence, with a historical pedigree, and, if possible, with a personal connection to Kappa Alpha's origins. In 1988, Dr. Idris Traylor made a presentation to the KAOEF Executive Board "regarding 'Spring Meadows' a property which might serve as a National Headquarters, [which was] located approximately one mile outside the Lexington City limits and consisted of 80 acres and a large three story brick residence. It was noted that the entire property was available at the cost of $1,350,000 or the house and five acres at $90,000."[7] The prospect was rejected. The property known as Col Alto, which had been previously rejected, was reexamined and Bill Garner, Executive Director of the KAOEF reported that the "most recent offer to purchase Col Alto... was countered and subsequently rejected by the prospective seller."[8]

In spite of the prolonged search for a permanent home in Lexington, in spite of the tantalizing prospects offered so promisingly and then snatched away by unexpected events and acts of nature, in spite of the protests of cautious town fathers, the answer to the prayer of many came about in an instant and from a most-surprising source.

During the fifth annual Kappa Alpha Alumni Weekend Tour, which had been initiated by the historically minded Knight Commander Idris Traylor in April 1990, a fortuitous turn of events occurred. Kappa Alpha historian Gary Scott "'treated' the alumni and their wives to a tour of the requisite landmarks of Lexington—the Lee Chapel, the campuses of Washington and Lee University and V.M.I., and the Stonewall Jackson House." As part of the expedition, the alumni attended a lecture given by the Professor of Art History at Washington and Lee, Pam Simpson. Dr. Simpson was the first female tenure-track professor at the university and had been at W&L since 1973, she was co-author of *The Architecture of Historic Lexington*, was a prolific lecturer to local community groups, and a member of both the Historic Lexington Foundation (HLF) and the Rockbridge Historical Society. Dr. Simpson's slide projector presentation included a picture of the historic Rockbridge Jail, which had sat abandoned for several years.

She not only gave an interesting history of the structure but also enticed the audience by indicating that "she was looking for someone to take care of this orphaned building."[9] A word to the wise is sufficient—Idris Traylor, Gary Scott, and Senior Councilor Guy Revelle quickly but cautiously swung into action. At the meeting of the Board of Trustees of the KAOEF that August, Knight Commander Julian Pardini announced that he had been "advised that Dr. Traylor, speaking on his behalf, had just received information that the 'Old Rockbridge County Jail Building'... was for sale. The property owned by the county since 1839 consists of the original structure and a 1923 addition. There are other additional buildings, adjacent to this property which will be offered for sale at a later date. Traylor understood that [there] was little interest in the old County Jail as a real estate investment and had been told that it could probably be acquired by a sealed bid, due August 27th, of $51,000. He referred to county documents declaring the building to be structurally sound and passed around photographs of the site. He did stress that the building would need major renovation, but felt that it could be purchased and renovated for $300,000."[10]

William Garner noted, "The timing was right.... The governing boards of the Order and Foundation directed that the building be considered for acquisition if careful review found that it met KA's needs. The board decision coincided within days of Rockbridge County's commencement to aggressively market the property."[11] It was totally unexpected that after decades of enduring the trials and tribulations of finding a suitable location for a headquarters for the Order that the acquisition of the historic jail was effected in a matter of weeks. Foresman, also a local lawyer, had spent so much time and energy in this endeavor was quoted as saying, "I think we were very fortunate that none of the other places worked out."[12] Foresman was particularly amused at the location as he said that he had probably introduced more inmates to that place than anyone else.[13]

On December 14, 1990, the Trustees of the KAOEF wrote a statement of confirmation that they had met in August, and had "approved the naming of a General Headquarters Committee and authorized the Committee to negotiate for the purchase of the building, known as the 'Old Rockbridge County Jail'... the Committee acquired the building at public auction for $120,000 from the County of Rockbridge, Virginia, on September 10, 1990, and signed the settlement papers and paid all costs associated with the purchase and closing on November 27, 1990."[14]

The Trustees also authorized the Committee "to conduct... all legal, financial, contractual, ceremonial, and fundraising activities necessary for the renovation and restoration of the building... and to negotiate arrangements with lending institutions... to hire an architect and contractor or firm qualified in design/construction and to select a recognized professional in interior design."[15] A low-interest loan was obtained "from the Lexington Downtown Development Association, a larger loan from a local bank, and a member fund-raising campaign launched that year... that would bring the cost of the project to $850,000."[16]

In his Biennial Report, then Knight Commander Julian Pardini reported to the Convention, "After five years of laborious search, a National Headquarters building site has been acquired. In the center of historic downtown Lexington, the place of our birth, lies a magnificent structure taking the shape of home for the Kappa Alpha Order.... The building is owned by the Foundation with the Order as its principal tenant. Ownership by the Foundation protects the tax deduction of gifts which are made for the renovation, restoration and refurbishing of the building.... The affordability of the project has been enhanced by substantial contributions toward the completion of the project which have already been obtained. It is hoped that within the next year or so, the entire project will be funded through gifts to the Foundation."[17]

The original Rockbridge County Jail had been planned in 1838, to follow local traditions of architectural style, which were often cast with larger windows, a lower-pitched roof and elaborate woodwork "but were based on traditional plans and presented [with] simple Federal-like facades."[18] The jail was designed by the celebrated Philadelphia architect, Thomas U. Walter, who was most famous for planning the cast-iron dome of the United States Capitol in the 1850s. Lyle and Simpson described Walter as "a thoroughly versatile and pragmatic architect" freely designing in "many styles and when economy called for it, produced subdued" and Federal looking plans.[19] In a testament to his adaptability "the plainness of the red brick design [of the jail] may be attributed to the limited funds available...; the perfection of its balanced, evenly proportioned façade" is prima facie evidence of his talent.[20] Additional architectural flourishes included a focal and attractive pediment that bursts out of the low-hipped roof and accents a "round arched doorway" adorned from above by a delicate fanlight. Thomas Walter "devised the biform plans for the structure in 1838, and the building was completed in 1841," and until its sale in 1990 "claimed to be the nation's oldest continually functioning jail."[21]

The complex consisted of several parts, the once-elegant Classical Revival residence of the magistrate, which connected to the jail proper; stylistically the two components were diametrically opposed. The superintendent's residence was orderly and elegant, classically proportioned with an abundance of light and fresh air; through a gloomy portal, one would enter an architecturally different world—discontinuous and disproportional rooms thrown together in a chaotic fashion—low lighting, dank walls and cold concrete floors.

In a memorandum to his staff, Dick Barnes described the condition of the building at the time of purchase and the grim report indicated that extensive and expensive work had to be done:

> By the time that Kappa Alpha Order purchased the Old Rockbridge County Jail, the residential portion of the building, Walter's prison, and a second cellblock added in the 20th century had all fallen into desperate disrepair. Long neglect had destroyed the interior plaster, the tern[e] roof and its sheathing, much of the exterior cornice, and the railing from the side porch. The exterior brickwork was water damaged. All of the systems of the building were obsolete. The interior paint was peeling off in ribbons. In the jailor's residence, paneling had been nailed to the lower walls in some areas; several interior walls were unsound; the floors were worn out; the original stairwell had been relocated inappropriately; window glass was broken; the window sash was badly deteriorated; some of the interior trim was missing; the upper hall of the residence had been partitioned off into a ramshackle room. In the prison portion of the building, floors were of varying heights. The building was filthy and pigeons were living in the second floor. The building had to be completely rehabilitated.[22]

A large part of the process would be to conjoin the two parts of the structure and incorporate and meld the two disparate styles into a formal and functional setting while being faithful to the historical integrity of the building.

The committee hired a local firm, Sils Construction, which specialized in restoring historic homes, to renovate and update the complex. Their first two objectives were to flush out the pigeons who had been nesting in the attic and to stabilize the basic structure of the building. To arrive at a place to begin reconstruction, the firm first had to remove the "debris that had been left, the old plumbing, and ruined plaster also needed to be hauled away. [Next the] doors, moldings and windows were carefully removed and stored, so that they could be repaired."[23]

The contractors "mended the house's foundation; rebuilt chimneys, replaced the terne roof, repaired original shutters, restored the front door casing, window sills, and damaged cornice molding; and repointed and recoated the brick exterior."[24] They next reinforced floor joists and repaired crumbling walls "making every effort to approximate the original appearance of damaged or lost materials and to salvage and restore original elements."[25]

Following these steps, the next phase involved reconditioning the jail section. This work included "penetrating the stone walls with a water cooled saw" without damaging the adjoining chestnut ceiling timbers; removing the torch-resistant steel bars of the newer cells and jackhammering their concrete floors and deepening the floor to make room for the fraternity printing shop.

In the process of reconditioning the jail, Sils Construction added restrooms, installed new systems for heating, air-conditioning, and sewage; reconstructed a stairwell; put in a dumbwaiter; and created an access to the newly created basement/print shop.

With form following function, a deliberate plan was made to enhance the spaciousness of the interior, with the general rule being that a room approached from two directions seems twice as large. To accomplish this effect, walls were taken down and the space reconfigured. Another objective was to integrate in style and coordinate in the space the superintendent's residence in the front of the building with the Walter cellblock in the back, this was accomplished in part by removing "enormous stones [from the interlocking passageways] and the resulting arch encased to echo the front door."[26] Thus the intent was to make the "environmental elements of an attractive and functional workplace that were consciously omitted from Walter's jail—light, openness, flow—a central light well was carved out of that section which connects the house with the jail."[27]

Karlin Warkentin, a woodworking specialist, copied the original doors and

*National Administrative Offices at Courthouse Square*

casings for the new offices to integrate the old with the new. He also used a photograph from the Washington and Lee archives to replace the lost staircase, which had connected the front of the house from the rear, in such dedication to the original design that "its handrail made [was] from a single Rockbridge County walnut tree, without joints or lamination."[28] The stairwell over which Walter had designed a skylight had long ago been taken out; now it was restored and enlarged "creating an atrium effect that bathes the stairwell [and] the portrait of General Lee in sunlight and reaches clear to the first floor reception area." On the second floor, Sils designed a new plaster arch that replicated the Walter arch on the first floor, with the result of creating a sunny central hallway from which new offices radiated.[29]

Once the essentials of the structure were taken care of, attention was turned to making the building as historically accurate as possible. Memories of the complications of the Barclay House were not forgotten and to be in good standing with the community leaders, the committee thought it prudent to seek the opinions of local authorities. To make sure on both heads, KA and the construction crew sought the advice of the Historic Lexington Foundation, the Lexington Architectural Review Board, and local garden clubs.[30]

Experts in nineteenth-century architecture, interior design, and renovations were consulted and their advice followed. Dick Barnes, the Executive Director of Kappa Alpha, had restored his own 1785 home in nearby Brownsburg, and had a working knowledge of the appropriate actions to be taken. Specialists hired by the contractors made "every effort to approximate the original appearance of damaged or lost materials and to restore original elements of the building."[31]

The *Journal* reported, "No detail has been too small in the restoration process. Masons analyzed existing mortar and identified sand from the same local river to mix new mortar for exterior brick repointing. Rock for the face of the building was cut from the original source."[32] Original doors, shutters, mantles, and guardrails were restored and the 1841 trim was "stripped, mended and repainted and missing pieces were recut with custom knives … a woodwork specialist was employed "to copy original doors and casings for the new offices, further reducing the demarcation between the house and the offices."[33]

In regard to interior design, while the newly invented office areas had a more contemporary color scheme and reconditioned early-twentieth-century lighting fixtures; areas of the Walter building were assigned 1840 color schemes, rooms in the residence section were distinguished by a more complex wall treatment: an Empire paper of green and three colors of gold in the conference room, carpets reproduced by the English firm of Woodward and Grosvenor especially for the project, and a superintendent's room in red damask.[34]

*National Administrative Offices at Courthouse Square*

The final stage of the project was to supply the headquarters with "fine antiques of the mid-19th century… [and] towards that goal, alumni and friends of the Order are being given the opportunity to donate tax-deductible gifts… some of the specific items include: a walnut, cherry or mahogany board room table with seating for ten, sic walnut or cherry executive desks—they should be 1880 or earlier, a walnut or cherry reception desk approximately 36 by 60 inches, matching pair of bookcases (7 feet tall by 55 inches wide), Sheraton or Empire sofas, Walnut or Cherry English sideboard (5 or 6 feet long), fifty-inch mirror with walnut or cherry frame, dark wood American grandfather clock (at least 7 feet tall), Walnut or Cherry Empire chest with four or five drawers, and a list of other desirables."[35]

The end result was one that pleased everyone, both the fraternity and local community leaders. Even architectural historian and preservation activist Dr. Pam Simpson who first instigated the discussion concerning the site in slide show presentation and whose organization, the Historic Lexington Foundation, remarked, "It's one of those happy stories…. We found a private buyer with the means and the sensitivity to carry out a really good restoration."[36] The restored building was recognized by the Association for the Preservation of Virginia Antiquities.[37] The renovation was featured in *Preservation Magazine.*

Although the staff moved in on April 1, 1992, the official dedication of the headquarters took place on Saturday, October 3, 1992, when Idris Traylor, one of the prime movers in the endeavor, announced, "The dedication marks a significant high point in the history of Kappa Alpha Order, when after more than 125 years, KA finally has a home of its own. We can be exceptionally proud of this splendid building and of the renovation that has been accomplished." He was especially gratified to note that "although the building is more than 140 years old, and many of its rooms retain that dignified and elegant character, it is also a very modern, functioning office to handle the contemporary business of servicing undergraduate and alumni chapters across the country."[38]

Even though the move was complete, the fund-raising continued. In 1995, alumni and members were encouraged to help close the financial gap left by the completion of the headquarters, "The total cost of purchasing, renovating and providing a small maintenance endowment for the Order's home in Lexington will be approximately $950,000. As of December 1, 1995 the balance of funds to be raised to complete the project stood at only $41,000. We are looking forward to a celebratory mortgage burning very soon."[39] On August 5, 1996, at the final banquet of the National Leadership Institute in Scottsdale, Arizona, the ceremonial mortgage went up in a blaze to the applause of the gathered crowd.[40]

The relocation and establishment of the National Headquarters had been, counterintuitively, a financial boon to the organization. On the front inside cover of the *Journal* in 1996, KAOEF Executive Director, David Carico, noted that "our assets, largely the headquarters building in Lexington and scholarship endowment funds, have grown from nothing to just over $2,600,000. Contributions have grown from just over $100,000 in 1982 to $462,000 last year."[41]

The incoming pledges, outright donations, and returns on investments encouraged the KAOEF to increase and enlarge its property on Main Street and continue to renovate in a fashion befitting the status of an organization flush with resources. In 1993, the Order began to cast its eyes on a cottage that it had been leasing from the First American Bank of Virginia since moving into the jail the previous year. The structure had been built as a carriage house in the 1880s and converted over to residential use later; for KA it had recently served as a summer residence "for educational and leadership consultants while they are training and working in Lexington."[42]

Later that year the building was purchased for $49,000.[43] In 2001, "The KAOEF Executive Committee voted to purchase from Tom Paulson the property he owns adjacent to our current headquarters ... and the purchase price will be between $500,000 and $550,000 depending on the appraised value."[44] The Paulson property consisted of the First National Bank Building, a much-needed parking lot, and a contiguous set of buildings known as "Lawyers Row."[45] The assessment was for $600,000 and Paulson sold the property for $550,000.

Renovation work started on the properties and in August 2002, Vice President Frank Maresh told the Executive Committee that the "demolition of the annex was complete and the stabilization of Lawyers Row and the exterior of the Bank was currently underway." He added that the original estimates for the work of $75,000 and $100,000 respectively had already been spent and that an additional $50,000 should be budgeted to complete the work.[46] The following year, Executive Director Larry Wiese, who was promoted to that post following Dick Barnes's retirement, advised the Executive Council "that replacement windows and doors were still being installed in the Lawyers Row building and that the painters were scraping the exterior of the Bank Building."[47]

Everything was progressing apace in those halcyon years and with a growing endowment and prudent investment, the expansion of the Order both in terms of acquisition of property and augmentation of staff seemed to be assured. The Order was aggressively buying up neighboring properties and refurbishing them without stint. Nearly all the adjacent buildings were being coopted into a virtual complex, which was not only a mark of prestige for the Order, but also increased the value and appearance of downtown Lexington. Paradoxically, the Historic

Lexington Foundation, the very organization that had been founded to protect the architectural integrity of the old town against the violations of the fraternity in the matter of the Barclay House, turned out to be the greatest beneficiary of the Order's meticulous efforts of historic preservation in the matter of the Old Rockbridge Jail. The Order was on the precipice of being the owner of a block of real estate in the center of its hometown—Courthouse Square.

The world is always changing, however, and as the Scottish poet Robert Burns reminded the harried mouse who so swiftly lost her house to progress, "The best laid schemes o' mice an' men, gang aft agley."[48]

The legend is that the move from Courthouse Square actually began when a cornice of the Old Courthouse fell off the roof of the building and struck an elderly lady passing by, resulting in a substantial suit against the county. The original Rockbridge County Courthouse had been constructed in 1786 on a plan endorsed by Andrew Reid, the architect and owner of Mulberry Hill.[49] But by the 1890s "the Courthouse had fallen into such disrepair that criticism by the local paper was fervent and frequent."[50] In 1896, a local architect, William

*Rockbridge County Courthouse*

G. McDowell, was chosen to design the new edifice, which was completed the following year and was admired for its "massive but beautiful proportions... in the Grecian style" and for its handsome red brick exterior trimmed in Kentucky bluestone.[51]

But a century later, the judicial rampart was showing her age in the most unflattering ways. Not only was she trying to dispense with venerable dowagers by raining chunks of Kentucky bluestone on their heads but also as the local media reported, "Almost everybody agrees that Rockbridge County's aging courthouse is inadequate. Water damage marks the walls on two floors, and the exterior is cracking. Security is another issue. Defendants are dropped off by deputies on a public street, and are held on a courtroom bench while they await their case. Also, officials say the building simply doesn't have enough storage space. Historical documents dating back to the 1700s are stored in the basement along with outdated equipment."[52]

The shortcomings of the courthouse being brought into sharp perspective had an unintended and initially stunning repercussion for Kappa Alpha, which had bought the dilapidated and adjacent county jail in 1990 and after spending almost one million dollars in renovations moved into its new home in 1992.[53] In addition to the Old Jail Building, the Order purchased adjacent property, including the old First National Bank Building, the Old Lawyer's Row complex, the Tom Tune Consultant House, and a parking lot, to secure space for growth, parking and leader education facilities.[54]

The judicial fiat of Judge George Honts III declared that, for the good of the public and the state, the courthouse either needed to be updated and expanded or a new facility had to be built. The judge maintained that the courthouse not only did not meet the needs of the expanding community but also presented certain risks to people and property. The judge decided that either the courthouse needed to be improved or expanded or a new one built. The decision on the new courthouse was rejected at a referendum, and another referendum could not be held for ten years on the same matter (state law). The judge further dictated that the courthouse, jail, and connected municipal offices must be physically adjacent—thus by eminent domain the jail that KA had purchased and renovated at great expense was to be expropriated by Rockbridge County. The referendum was held in 2002 with respect to the construction of a new courthouse, but because of concerns about the design for the new courthouse and the 13.5 million dollar price tag, the proposal failed.[55]

Following Judge Honts' pronouncement, Executive Director Larry Wiese notified the Executive Council and the KAOEF Board of Trustees that the property at Courthouse Square could be subject to seizure by eminent domain. All agreed that counsel needed to be retained. To assist in locating the right attorney, Wiese recommended and the boards agreed to consult member and former/current trustee Gordon H. "Stumpy" Harris, an Orlando attorney recognized nationally as an expert in eminent domain. After an initial call with Stumpy, he and Wiese agreed to schedule a phone call with Staunton, Virginia attorney Colin J.S. "Cal" Thomas who was known to Wiese as one of the "lions of the Virginia Bar" in the Valley. Additionally, Harris and Wiese thought an attorney from outside of Rockbridge would be above local politics. After their call, Stumpy told Wiese, he is the man for the job, and Wiese on behalf of KAOEF retained Cal that day. Cal was instrumental in working with Wiese with the able support and review of Harris in negotiations.[56]

Concerning the legal ramifications of the judge's ruling, the following statement was made at a meeting of the board of trustees of KAOEF on April 26, 2003, concerning the possible condemnation of the downtown offices.

> Executive Director Wiese reviewed the possible condemnation of the headquarters property indicating that the Rockbridge County Circuit Court Judge had sued the County Board of Supervisors for its failure to comply with state guidelines in its maintenance and space available in the County Circuit Courthouse. He reported that due to a failed referendum in November, the courthouse would not be able to be moved from its current location and that Virginia law allowed for courthouse expansion to only occur on

> contiguous property. He indicated that this made the Foundation owned property in Lexington the most likely target. He further reported that the county had hired consultants to develop a plan for expanding the courthouse that would utilize at least part of, if not all, of the Foundation owned property in Lexington.[57]

Director Wiese recommended that the Order begin to examine alternative locations and presented the three most promising sites—Mulberry Hill, Castle Hill, and Thorn Hill—all stately homes with historic pedigrees located in or around Lexington. He also indicated several other locations, including a parcel of land owned by the Sigma Nu National Fraternity.[58]

The president of the Kappa Alpha Order Educational Foundation, Frank Maresh and others, raised the legitimate question of whether or not the headquarters of a national organization should remain in Lexington. Nevertheless, Knight Commander David M. "Dink" Warren answered that, at least for now, the Executive Council supported the concept of an administrative headquarters remaining in Lexington, and Executive Director Wiese pragmatically reminded everyone "that the emotional attachment to Lexington, being the home of Washington and Lee University, and the burial place of General Robert E. Lee, was a strong one that makes for easier fundraising in a capital campaign." President Maresh announced that "he would be appointing an Ad-Hoc Committee to explore new headquarter sites and that the committee would report on its findings at the annual meeting in August."[59] On May 1, 2003,

*Thorn Hill, Lexington, Virginia*

*Mulberry Hill, Lexington, Virginia*

a meeting took place to establish an Exploratory Committee that consisted of Jim Estes, Bill Dreyer, and Frank Maresh. Executive Director Wiese was present at the discussion as well as Ben Satcher and Dink Warren.[60] Frequent consultations took place over the following weeks concerning not only the acquisition of new property but also the many questions about the equitable disposition of the old properties. Attorney Cal Thomas was called in.

Meetings were held the following week with representatives from city hall. KAOEF Trustees Frank Maresh, Jim Estes, and Bill Dreyer inquired into alternative sites for relocation, Maple Hall and Grace Presbyterian Church, and advocated for an immediate inspection of the three most prominent candidates for the next National Administrative Office—Thorn Hill, Castle Hill, and Mulberry Hill. The original itinerary of visitations called for a visit to Thorn Hill first at 3:30 P.M., next to Mulberry Hill at 4:30, and a final stop at Castle Hill at 5:30. Executive Director Wiese rearranged the sequence of the inspection of the properties in order to leave the favorite candidate—Mulberry Hill—as the last to be seen.

Knight Commander Bill Dreyer recently recalled, "I remember that we had visited the two other estates and while impressed thought that they would require much in the way of renovations and updating. When we came up Liberty Hall Road our last stop, and the house on Mulberry Hill came into view, we knew this was home. We were all very excited. I remember calling my wife that night and telling her, if the Order did not decide on this house that we would buy it. She told me to enjoy myself that she was staying in San Antonio."[61] The others members of the committee were equally taken with the site. Future Knight Commander Ben W. Satcher, Jr. and Trustee Rock N. Houstoun later visited all three locations.

The Lexington City Council approved the zoning for the Sigma Nu property and ongoing negotiations were taking place with county authorities over the Old Bank Building and the Lawyer's Row property and the Jail.[62] Dink Warren vowed that the Order would fight the takeover of the Courthouse Square Headquarters "unless adequately compensated."[63] On July 14, Bill Dreyer once again visited Mulberry Hill and reported that he was pleased with the general upkeep of the property.[64]

In late summer, the Exploratory Committee and Executive Director Wiese became laser-focused on the Mulberry Hill property. On August 18, Jim Estes and Larry Wiese had a conference call with real estate agent Steve McLean concerning a lease/option plan on the property. McLean asked for a thirty-day notice to occupy and Jim Estes requested that the option on the lease not begin until the day of possession; discussions also took place concerning what furniture and other items would be appropriate to convey with the house.[65]

Also on this day Executive Director Wiese and Thomas held a call with Dr. Calder Loth of the Virginia Department of Historic Resources concerning historic easements on Mulberry Hill and how that might affect the conversion of a private residence into a place of business, the construction of a consultants' house on the edge of the property, the reconfiguration of the old garage/stables into a printing office and mail room, the erection of a chapel, and the needed additional parking. Arrangements were also made for all the usual inspections.[66] With an outcome in negotiations with Rockbridge County seeming to conclude with the "adequate compensation" promised by former Knight Commander Warren at hand, an alternative location for the offices had been found.

In the fall, Lewis Tyree was anxious to tie the matter up, as he had recently been injured while cutting his lawn, when the tractor had flipped over injuring him.[67] He already had plans to move to a retirement community near Charlottesville and the stability of the Order, along with the watchful eye of the Department of Historic Resources, would keep his beloved home solvent, intact and free from radical change.

In early November, Mr. Tyree received a letter from Virginia McConnell, easements coordinator at the Department of Historic Resources, in which she complied with the vast majority of requests that Mr. Tyree had made on behalf of Kappa Alpha Order. She confirmed the request for locating "a guest house in the southeast corner of the property," additional parking, and the construction of a "small chapel near the northeast corner."[68] The most crucial and uncertain aspect of the department's ruling pertained to the conversion of the historic residential property into, essentially, a business concern. Mrs. McConnell wrote, "The easement does not currently permit the construction of office buildings at Mulberry Hill. When you and your wife donated the easement in 1982, it was the expectation of all parties that the property would remain a single-family residence. However, the DHR easement properties have, because of change of circumstances or financial necessity, been converted to commercial or institutional uses without the loss of their essential historic integrity. Your status as the original donor of the easement, together with your support for this proposal, are particularly persuasive in determining that such use of the property would be consistent with your wishes for its preservation. Accordingly, we are willing to recommend to the Board of Historic Resources that the easement be amended to allow the construction of office buildings at Mulberry Hill."[69]

Inasmuch as the financing was not a problem, the recommendation to amend the historic easement was the last major obstacle to be overcome. Lewis Tyree and Cal Thomas were essential elements in cutting the bureaucratic red tape. Tyree was a tireless public relations specialist in projects that he supported. Described by all as a gracious gentleman of the old school, he charmed everyone who came in contact with him; if he could not accomplish that feat, his wife certainly would. Ten days after the letter arrived from the Department of Historic Resources, the Tyrees hosted a reception and a viewing of drawings and artwork at the house during a Board of Trustees meeting.[70]

Preliminary discussions and consultations concerning the specifics of the contract took place between the time of the reception and the signing of the contract less than a fortnight later on November 25, 2003.[71] Among the provisions of the deed, the Tyrees gave "portraits and furniture that he believes would be appropriate for the home … including the grand piano."[72] Also stipulated was a two-year lease/option arrangement to allow for the sale of the courthouse property and financial arrangements to be made with the purchaser's being responsible for "all maintenance and repairs, general upkeep, utilities, taxes, insurance and all other costs associated with the ownership of the property."[73] Rental payments were $3,000 per month "payable in advance... and will not be counted toward the purchase price."[74]

Mr. Tyree, in addition to providing the nonrefundable element of the monthly rent payments, also provided the incentive carrot of the bottom-line sale price of the house, to wit; if the purchaser closed within the first nine months of the lease—the purchase price would be $1,400,000; if within the next six months—$1,450,000; and if the Order did not conclude the transaction until the last nine months of the contract, the price would escalate to $1,500,000.[75] The Tyrees also made certain that they would have a comfortable grace period to tie up affairs at Mulberry Hill as the deed included as well a proviso to that effect, "regardless of the date of satisfaction of contingencies and vacation of property, the lease shall not start before March 1, 2004 unless otherwise agreed to in writing."[76]

The Order and the KAOEF had the courthouse situation well in hand and turned a disadvantage into a financial coup. A strategically released article in a local paper appeared on November 26, 2003, "Supervisors Draft KA Land Deal." The report announced that the Rockbridge County Board of Supervisors had met on November 24th to discuss the implications both of the failure of the referendum to build a courthouse complex in a new location and the decree by Judge Everett A. Martin Jr. that the courthouse plans proceed as negotiated "during the litigation"; namely, at the location on Main Street.[77]

The two major factors involved in the outcome of negotiations included the failure of the referendum to build a new courthouse complex (and by fact that under Virginia law another referendum could not be held for ten years) and the pronouncement by Judge Honts "that all court facilities should be housed together and not scattered across town. This leaves the county with few options but to expand the current courthouse."[78]

The combination of these judicial orders necessitated that Rockbridge County must purchase the Kappa Alpha Headquarters. Thereupon, the supervisors' chair, Nancy Stagner, was quoted saying in the article that the

"the agreement has gone so smoothly [that] the county has not had to resort to condemning the property."[79]

Caught between the proverbial rock and a hard place of its own making, the county became uncharacteristically pliant and flexible in regard to financial arrangements with the Order. As the Knight Commanders Warren and Satcher had proclaimed and the Executive Director privately assured interested parties, the Order would receive equitable compensation for its time, effort, and property. The Rockbridge supervisors scrambled for options including a bridge loan to make payments or even of the prospect of renting the property from the Order until financing could be arranged.

The article reported that a contract of purchase had been made on "the 17th day of November 2003 … between Kappa Alpha and Rockbridge County."[80] The purchase included the former First National Bank, the Kappa Alpha Headquarters (designated as the Old Jail), and the Old Public Clinic for a "total purchase price of $2,050,000."[81] The county also permitted the fraternity to take away from the Headquarters all of its plaques and memorabilia, rugs and carpets, and strip away all the lighting that was nonrecessed. From the bank, the Order was allowed to remove chandeliers, antique doors and windows, metal railings from outside, and even the bank vaults—if they were deemed "worthwhile."[82]

The difference between the purchase price of the downtown property, $2,050,000 and Mulberry Hill at $1,400,000, was $650,000. This satisfied the remaining debt service of $550,000. There was, of course, enormous expenses in refitting and expanding the estate and its property, but there was an outpouring of enthusiastic support by a committed group of loyal alumni. The assertions of Dink Warren, Ben Satcher, and Larry Wiese were vindicated; the legal and logistical maneuverings of Cal Thomas were fruitful; the generosity and personal involvement of Bill Dreyer, Jim Estes, Idris Traylor, and countless others were rewarded. As Mr. Micawber would have said—"in short, success!"

The four primary options for finance were the lease purchase option, which had the drawbacks of a delay in renovations; a monthly lease expense and pledge of securities in the amount of $500,000; a purchase financed by Mr. Tyree, with the drawbacks of using up the collateral that was slated for renovation expenditures thus having to pledge monies for both the purchase and expenses for refitting the mansion; a construction loan with Suntrust Bank that was capped at $1,200,000 that would have forced the Order to renegotiate for a higher amount at additional interest (the interest rate for the first year was 1.75 percent and floating after that time); or, a loan with BBT Bank that was already approved for $2,000,000 and with access to $500,000 in additional funds for renovation expenses, and a commitment on the part of the bank to lend extra money on the full project and for a new building as well, which was at prime plus .75 percent for three years, and then floating. Community leader and BBT banker David Grist negotiated the best terms. KAOEF chose BBT.[83]

In the Spring 2004 issue of the *Journal* when the editor was on the verge of making the public announcement, it was reported: "The KAOEF Board of Trustees in consultation with the Executive Council and the Executive Director have selected an extraordinary site that could serve Kappa Alpha very well. However, at press time, the closing on the purchase is pending. An announcement should follow soon on the national website and more details will be presented in the next *Journal*."[84] And, indeed, Knight Commander, Ben Satcher did announce in the Fall 2004 issue that "the National Administrative Office has now relocated to Mulberry Hill."[85]

*Notes* Chapter 13:

1 The *omphalos* was a sacred rock in the Temple of Apollo at Delphi and was believed to be the center of the world. The term has been used through the centuries as a metaphorical reference to a place that is most powerful in terms of the religious, political, or military importance or capabilities. *The Oxford Universal Dictionary, Third Edition* (Oxford: Clarendon Press, 1955), 1369; "Omphalos," *The Oxford Classical Dictionary, Second Edition* (Oxford: Clarendon Press, 1992), 752.

2 "Alumni Challenge Order to Finish Dream," *Kappa Alpha Journal* 110, No. 3 (Spring 1994): 4.

3 "KA Makes Tracks to Lexington, Va.," *Kappa Alpha Journal* 103, No. 1 (Winter 1986): 5.

4 Ibid.

5 Buddy Cote, "Letters to the Editor," *Kappa Alpha Journal* 113, No. 1 (Winter 2001): 5.

6 "KA Makes Tracks to Lexington, Va.," 24.

7 "KAOEF 1988 Annual Meeting," August 13, 1988, Kappa Alpha Archives, Lexington, Va., 2001.

8 "KAOEF 1990 Annual Meeting," August 11, 1990, Kappa Alpha Archives, Lexington, Va., 2001.

9 Mary Westheimer, *History of the Kappa Alpha Order* (Phoenix: Heritage Publishers, 1994), 63.

10 "KAOEF 1990 Annual Meeting," August 11, 1990.

11 Westheimer, *History of the Kappa Alpha Order*, 64.

12 Steven Russell, "A Place to Call Home," *Kappa Alpha Journal* 108, No. 1 (Winter 1991): 9.

13 Cote, "Letters to the Editor," 5.

14 "Consent of Trustee: Kappa Alpha Order Educational Foundation," December 14, 1990, Kappa Alpha Archives, Lexington, Va., 1.

15 Ibid.

16 Elizabeth Humphrey, "From Jail to Fraternity," *Historic Preservation* 45, No. 6 (November–December, 1993): 20.

17 Julian Pardini, "A Permanent National Headquarters, Knight Commander's Biennial Report, Convention Minutes, 1991, Kappa Alpha Archives, Lexington, Va., 56.

18 Royster Lyle and Pamela Simpson, *The Architecture of Historical Lexington* (Charlottesville: University Press of Virginia, 1977), 24.

19 Ibid.

20 Ibid.

21 Humphrey, "From Jail to Fraternity," 20.

22 Richard Barnes to Staff, "Memorandum: National Headquarters Restoration," September 10, 1992, Kappa Alpha Archives, Lexington, Va., 1.

23 Ibid.

24 Humphrey, "From Jail to Fraternity," 21.

25 Ibid.

26 Ibid.

27 Ibid

28 Ibid., 22.

29 Ibid.

30 Russell, "A Place to Call Home," 8.

31 Humphrey, "From Jail to Fraternity," 22.

32 "Staff Moves into New Headquarters," *Kappa Alpha Journal* 109, No. 1 (Spring 1992): 12.

33 Humphrey, "From Jail to Fraternity," 22.

34 Ibid.

35 Dick Barnes, "Headquarters Nears Completion," *Kappa Alpha Journal* 108, No. 3 (Fall 1991): 13.

36 Humphrey, "From Jail to Fraternity," 23.

37 "Staff Moves into New Headquarters," 12.

38 "New Headquarters Dedicated in Historic Fashion," *Kappa Alpha Journal* 109, No. 3 (Fall 1992): 11.

39 "National Headquarters Campaign Rapidly Draws to a Close," *Kappa Alpha Journal* 115, No. 3 (Fall 1995): 11.

40 "NLI 1996," *Kappa Alpha Journal* 114, No. 4 (Winter 1996/97): 10.

41 David Carico, "A Message from the Foundation," *Kappa Alpha Journal* 115, No. 3 (Winter 1995): front.

42 "Tom Tune Consulting House," *Kappa Alpha Journal* 110, No. 2 (Fall 1993): 19.

43 "KAOEF Annual Meeting," August 3, 1996, Scottsdale, Arizona, Kappa Alpha Archives, Lexington, Va., 2002, p. 2.

44 "KAOEF Memorandum," May 15, 2001, Kappa Alpha Archives, Lexington, Va., 2001, p. 1.

45 "Joint Meeting of the KAO Executive Council and the KAOEF," April 7, 2001, Kappa Alpha Archives, Lexington, Va. 2001, p. 1.

46 "KAOEF 2002 Annual Meeting," August 11, 2002, Kappa Alpha Archives, Lexington, Va., 2002, p. 5.

47 "KAOEF Conference Call," October 15, 2002, Kappa Alpha Archives, Lexington, Va., 2002, p. 1.

48 Robert Burns, "To a Mouse," in *The Poetical Works of Robert Burns* (Boston: James B. Dow, 1834), 1:136.

49 Lyle and Simpson, *The Architecture of Historical Lexington*, 11.

50 Ibid., 76.

51 Ibid.

52 Transcript of Broadcast for WDBJ News at Six, August 2, 2002. http://scholar.lib.vt.edu/VA-news/WDBJ-7/script_archives/02/1102/110402/110402.m.htm (viewed April 21, 2015).

53 Todd Shelton, "Home Sweet Home," *Kappa Alpha Journal* 120, No. 2 (Summer 2003): 16.

54 "Providing a Home for Kappa Alpha," Kappa Alpha Order Annual Report. 2002–2003, Supplement to the *Kappa Alpha Journal* 120, No. 4 (Winter 2003): 100

55 Jay Conley, "Contractor Submits Courthouse Designs," May 8, 2006, *The Roanoke Times*, http://www.roanoke.com/webmin/news/contractor-submits-courthouse-designs/article_251273de-7bd9-5590-97d7-cc8a08292cea.html (viewed May 1, 2015)

56 Larry Wiese, Personal Journal, January 1, 2003.

57 "KAOEF: Meeting of the Board of Trustees," April 26, 2003, Austin, Texas, Kappa Alpha Archives, Lexington, Va., 2002.

58 Ibid.

59 Ibid.

60 Larry Wiese, Personal Journal, May 1, 2003.

61 Personal Interview with Bill Dreyer. January 19, 2015.

62 Larry Wiese, Personal Journal, June 17, 2003, and July 14, 2003.

63 David Warren, "Knight Commander's Message," *Kappa Alpha Journal* 120, No. 2 (Summer 2003): 2.

64 Larry Wiese, Personal Journal, July 14, 2003.

65 Larry Wiese, Personal Journal, August 18, 2003.

66 Ibid.

67 Personal Communication, Dr. Taylor Sanders to Dr. Martin Clagett, February 20, 2015.

68 Virginia McConnell to Lewis Tyree, November 4, 2003, Kappa Alpha Archives, Lexington, Va., 2003, p. 1.

69 Ibid.

70 Larry Wiese, Personal Journal, November 14, 2003.

71 Virginia Association of Realtors, "Contract of Purchase," November 25, 2003, Kappa Alpha Archives, Lexington, Va., 2003, p. 1.

72 Ibid.

73 Ibid., Addendum, 2.

74 Ibid.

75 Ibid.

76 Virginia Association of Realtors, "Contract of Purchase," November 25, 2003, Addendum, 1.

77 "Supervisors Draft KA Land Deal," *Rockbridge Weekly*, November 26, 2003. p. 1; Douglas Sweeney, " Courthouse Deadline Extended," The Rockbridge Report, Washington & Lee University, March 9, 2006, http://journalism.wlu.edu/rrarchive/03-09-2006/courthouse.htm (viewed May 12, 2015).

78 Todd Shelton, "Home Sweet Home," 16.

79 "Supervisors Draft KA Land Deal," *Rockbridge Weekly*, 1.

80 Ibid., 5A.

81 Ibid.

82 Ibid.

83 "KAOEF Proposed Financing Options for Mulberry Hill," Kappa Alpha Archives, Lexington, Va., 2003, p. 1.

84 "Headquarters to Relocate in Lexington," *Kappa Alpha Journal* 121, No. 1 (Spring 2004): 12.

85 Ben Satcher, "Knight Commander's Message," *Kappa Alpha Journal* 121, No. 3 (Fall 2004): 2.

*View of House Mountain from old front porch of Mulberry Hill*

# 14

## Mulberry Hill

Some might regard the acquisition of Mulberry Hill by Kappa Alpha as predestined. If Washington College can be considered the nurturing mother of the Kappa Alpha Order, then Mulberry Hill, this plot of land on which Liberty Hall Academy was founded, might rightly be called the grandmother. The almost miraculous turn of events that made Mulberry Hill a candidate, at the very moment when the Order was in such immediate and unexpected need, should be considered not serendipity but fate. For the eerie good fortune lay not only in the reality of the confluence of events and timing and location and availability but also in the multiple and intimate connections that lay between the history of the house and the procession of former inhabitants and the fraternity itself—kismet, not coincidence.

The story of Mulberry Hill begins with the Rector of Liberty Hall Academy and progenitor of Washington and Lee University, the Reverend William Graham. The son of a Scot, Michael Graham, who emigrated from Ireland, William was born on December 19, 1746, in the town of Paxton in Pennsylvania. He had little in the way of formal education as a child, but as a young adult decided on a career as a clergyman and attended a school run by the local minister, Mr. Roan.[1]

He advanced rapidly through his studies and within a short time he decided to attend the College of New Jersey (now Princeton), which was under the leadership of John Witherspoon. Witherspoon had graduated from the University of Edinburgh and been a minister at Beith and Paisley in Scotland. He was well versed not only in theology but also in the scientific ramifications of Isaac Newton and the tenets of the Scottish Enlightenment, particularly the School of Common Sense Philosophy. Witherspoon brought his books, scientific equipment, and concepts of political freedom to the New World.

Graham was in good company at Princeton, for some of his contemporaries included James Madison, Aaron Burr, and Henry "Light-Horse Harry" Lee. Steeped in the traditions of the Presbyterian Church and enthusiastic in his devotion to science and utilitarian principles, Graham was an attractive candidate for a schoolmaster in the Presbyterian Scots-Irish valleys of Virginia. Having been recommended to the Hanover Presbytery, he was invited to become a master at its school, Augusta Academy. The small log cabin structure was located at Timber Ridge about 20 miles north of Lexington.

The school grew in reputation and size and in May 1776 Graham became the rector.[2] When the Revolution came to the Valley, however, the Reverend Graham took up the patriotic cause and raised a militia among his students. The enrollment fell swiftly at the school, however, because of the conscription of students and the depreciation of the American currency that was caused by the exigencies of the Revolution and the diminished pool of patrons.

In 1777, Graham found that the lack of revenue at Timber Ridge was so severe that he could not support his growing family on his salary and, thereby, moved his family "to the farm he had purchased at Mulberry Hill near Lexington."[3] Nevertheless, in spite of the distance to Graham's home, several of Graham's students followed him to his new residence and implored him to continue their education. Thus, at Mulberry Hill, Graham continued to instruct his former charges.

The appearance of the original structure at Mulberry Hill was "a 36′ x 63′ one-story-brick rectangle. It rested on a stone foundation that is laterally bank sited. The exposed east and south foundation walls are random ashlar and the rest is coursed rubble." It is likely that Graham built on the site of an earlier

*Interior stone wall, Graham House*

*Unskinned beams in the basement*

residence for "the interior of the basement level offers evidence of the existence of an earlier house on the site. The south section has a corner fireplace on the inside stone partition. It is bricked over and has no stack or relation to the plan above. The south exterior wall is also unusually thick. Part of this can be accounted for by the need to [support] the two fireplaces rising above it, but its thickness [goes]...well beyond where fireplace support is needed. It seems likely that this was a wall of an earlier structure that later needed reinforcement and expansion."[4] The only reasonable explanation for this anomaly is the preexistence of another structure on the property.

The evidence indicates that Mulberry Hill was in Graham's day a one-storied building and "is supplied not only by insurance policies and the change in bond between the floors but also in a change in window moldings." In addition, "there are also two fireplaces in the wall that have been closed… [and] there are fragments still of a beaded chair rail."[5] The relatively unsophisticated appearance of the initial stage of the house is supported by the "unskinned log joists exposed in the basement hall" and "windows [that] are double-hung sash and laid on their side."[6]

One of Graham's earliest students was his neighbor Archibald Alexander, who would become a noted cleric and educator. Alexander gratefully acknowledged

Graham's influence in the course of his life. He recounted that Graham had settled on the "extreme part of my father's property" and recollected that his father was so pleased have a school so near that he made a donation of land for its expansion. Although it has been handed down that classes were conducted in the lower full floor, Archibald Alexander, recalled that "studies were pursued in an upper room of Mr. Graham's."[7] Thus, the simple home at Mulberry Hill, even in Graham's day had attic rooms for sleep or study.

Graham's replacement at Timber Ridge, William Willson, became ill and, in 1780, he closed the school there altogether, making Mulberry Hill the most-conveniently located and most-indispensable center of learning in the valley. Graham may have boarded some students there and others are recorded to have stayed with his neighbors Samuel McDowell, Alexander Stuart, David Gray, Samuel Lyle, and John Lyle.[8] With a growing family and the addition of his two younger brothers, Graham's modest house soon became too claustrophobic for the purpose of teaching, let alone taking in boarders.

In 1782, Graham formally reopened the school in a building on the grounds of Mulberry Hill. It was also in that year that his institution, which he patriotically renamed Liberty Hall Academy, was granted incorporation, thus freeing its masters from military service and also taking it "out of the hands of the Presbytery," and it was thenceforward undenominational.[9]

Graham concluded that the only logical way to continue the school was to conduct classes in a larger building constructed for that purpose. Thus, the first schoolhouse was erected in 1783. It was a frame building rather than the rough-hewn log cabins that were typical for field schools; "other early buildings on Mulberry Hill included a horse stable, a spring house and various smaller buildings."[10] The newly granted status of incorporation not only added to the reputation of an institution that had a well-stocked library, scientific apparatus, and excellent teachers, but also the school, by having the ability to confer degrees, received the status of a college.[11]

Sometime that same year, 1783, the schoolhouse burned down and the "minutes of the Board of Trustees indicate that arson was suspected… a new schoolhouse was erected and again went up in flames in 1790. However, this time it was deemed an accident."[12] In 1791, the Synod of Virginia negotiated with Liberty Hall for the establishment of a seminary. The arrangement ultimately fell through, but the importance of those discussions was that it generated "generous donations to the building fund."[13]

Nevertheless, the Hanover Presbytery once again showed an interest in the academy and encouraged new subscribers to join the growing ranks of supporters. The expanding roster of patrons increased the coffers to the point where all agreed that it would be expedient to raise up a stone edifice rather than a wooden structure.[14] In June 1793, William Cravens, a local stonemason, was contracted to erect the main building and a steward's house. The main building was "to be 30 by 38 feet, three stories in height, with a square roof, a belfry and corner chimneys."[15] In many ways the building resembled the central portion of Nassau Hall at Princeton and "a cupola of identical outline was placed on the 1816 Lexington Arsenal (VMI)."[16]

According to Royster Lyle and Pamela Simpson, "The large stone school building served both as classroom and dormitory for the school, housing some forty to fifty students in the upper floors, and classes, scientific apparatus, and the library on the first floor."[17] Not as much was known about the steward's house but it apparently consisted of a kitchen, dining room, bedroom, and cellar with a smokehouse nearby.

In 1796, William Graham resigned his post as rector to seek a better life for his family in the Ohio Valley land speculation business—but what had been a boon for Benjamin Franklin was not a benefit for all. Graham's former student and assistant George Baxter took over the management of the academy. In 1799, the board of trustees hired a local mason, Richard Bernard, to build the new rector a brick house with the dimensions of 25-by-20 feet and two stories high on a stone foundation with a "handsome dentile cornice and to be done in a substantial and workmanlike manner."[18]

In November 1802, the trustees insured the school and a well-timed expenditure it was for the roof caught fire two months later leaving little more than a romantic shell of its former self. This conflagration provided the inhabitants of Lexington with the opportunity to move the school closer within their grasp. Andrew Alexander agreed to exchange his property on the western edge of town for the Liberty Hall site and, with the help of local philanthropist John "Jockey" Robinson, the arrangement was made and Washington Academy moved to its present location.[19]

On May 11, 1797, a year after he resigned, Graham sold his farm to Andrew Reid for £1,700.[20] Reid was the son of a Scots-Irish emigrant who had first settled in Lancaster, Pennsylvania, and then moved to Augusta County from that place. At the age of twenty-seven, Andrew Reid, already a successful businessman and community leader, was instrumental in the process of carving Rockbridge County out of Augusta County and became the first clerk of the newly formed county. He served in that post for fifty-three years from 1778 until 1831.

Reid's meticulous plans for his house accentuated and complemented his name and reputation. Every detail was executed to add to his stature in the community and serve his sense of pride. The first story is constructed of brick in the Flemish-bond style and originally had a gable roof making it similar in appearance to Hawthorne Hall in Botetourt County.[21]

*Hawthorne Hall, Botetourt County*

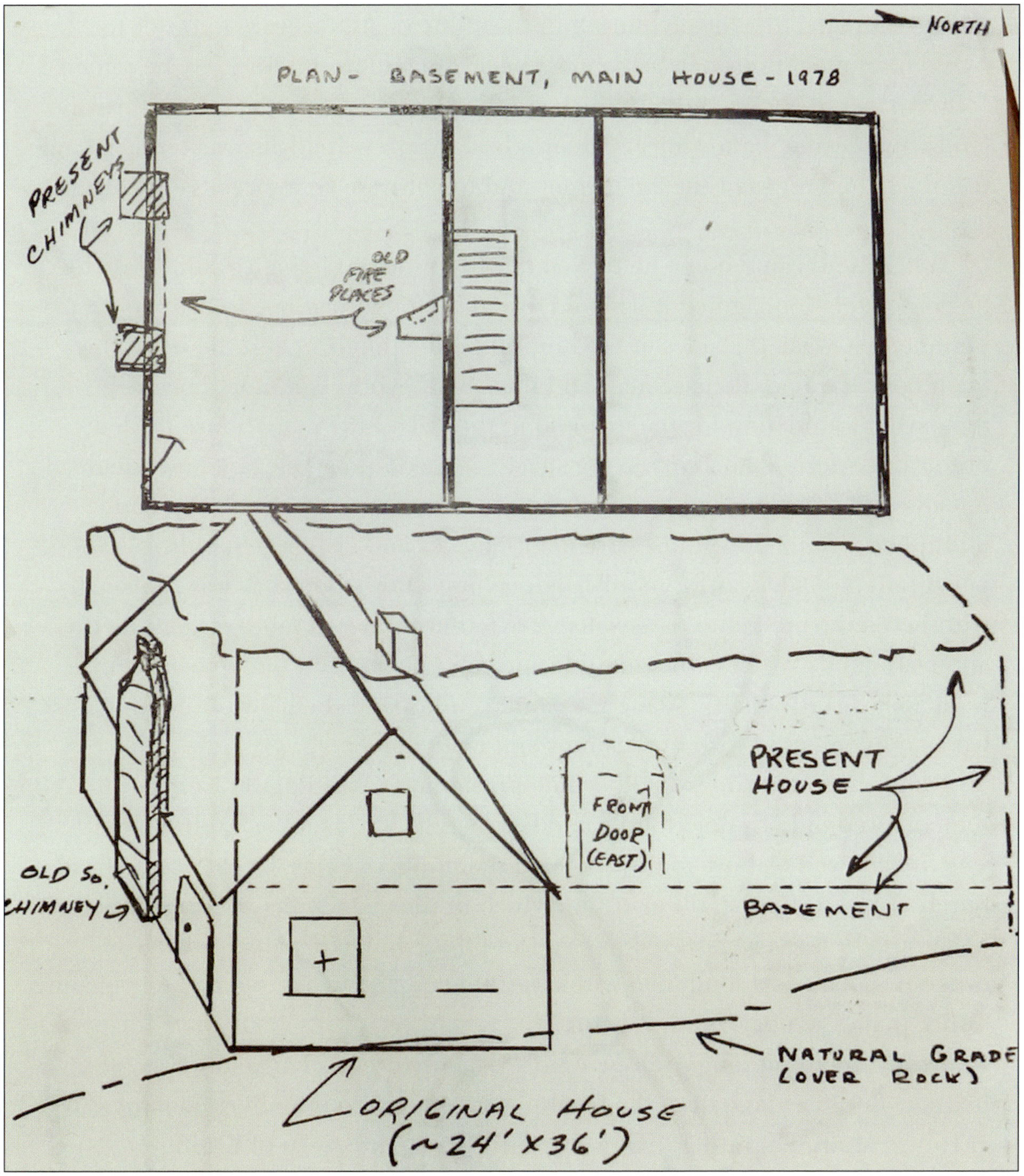


*Andrew Reid's Mulberry Hill superimposed on Graham's Homestead by Lewis Tyree*

Thomas Jefferson, after the Revolution and in his role as minister to France, took great pains to educate himself in the study of architecture in order to frame his conceptions of what is most beautiful and useful. In 1786, he joined John Adams in a tour of the English countryside to view both architecture and landscape design. Following Jefferson's lead, Andrew Reid also visited England to survey the homes of the aristocracy and to cultivate an awareness of correct style.

When Reid came home he turned his attention to Graham's simple abode—he completely reimagined it. The old orientation that had been north-south became east-west; the sides of the house became the front and the back; the main floor became the basement and the small second half-story became the partial foundation for the main floor; the size of the main house tripled; utilitarian exteriors and cozy living spaces segued into an elegant and balanced outside and a polished and refined interior; chimneys changed places and multiplied—framed by impressive mantlepieces and elaborate molding; hand-hewn rafters made way for motif-laden ceilings; raw stonework was replaced with beveled panels, and bare walls were either rendered more elegant by the application of plaster slathered on bison-hair backing and often covered in wallpaper or fashionable shades of paint; candles and the glow of the fireplaces were supplemented with brass lamps and chandeliers.

Henry Ruffner, who would become president of Washington College, remembered old Mr. Reid fondly and later wrote "I remember Andrew Reid well, he allowed us boys to thrash down the mulberries [as] he sat on the front porch of his Mulberry Hill mansion, which in those days was a beautiful picture of shining brasses, well waxed passage and floor and [emanated] that air of order and neatness, combined with ease and comfort which seemed to welcome, rather than to embarrass the visitor."[22]

But even envisioning Andrew Reid's vista involves a change of perception, because in those days, from the front porch one would have been looking out at House Mountain rather than in the direction of the town of Lexington—the front of the house was the back and the back the front.

The original road led around to what now is the back of the house and visitors and vendors would have arrived at the back gardens of today. The old formal gardens were on one side of the front porch and from the other side of the porch delightful aromas would have wafted out of the old bakery and kitchen; slave quarters lay beyond the kitchen toward the ruins of Liberty Hall Academy. It was customary to have a hotbed situated just beyond the circle of the road, so today's formal garden may be filled not only with remnants of left-over dinners or old vegetables but also broken crockery and the other flotsam and jetsam of plantation life.[23]

This theory of orientation is supported by data from the interior of the house. The first floor, which was the main floor, with Graham's house forming the undergirding, consisted of a center hall with two rooms off each side. The flooring of the center hall is composed of narrow boards laid diagonally with a board that is parallel to the walls; it is about five inches higher than the surrounding floors and is not original to the house. The surrounding floors are a uniform four inches wide, of pine, and appear to be original. "The [present] front door … is a modern addition … The rear door, on the other hand, is a double door with each side having three panels with glass above …. [and] appears original … and is probably the original front door."[24]

Ruffner also recalled that "Mr. Reid's favorite seat in summer was on the vine-covered front porch of the family mansion. Here he sat in his arm chair, or rested prone on a wide bench at one end of which was a pillow of folio volumes, a leather bound illuminated edition of Hume's England. The old gentleman was a great favorite of the boys and allowed us to climb cherry trees and thrash down the mulberries without restrain."[25]

It was recorded that the prolific Lexington mason and amateur architect John Jordan moved from his native Goochland County to the Lexington area about the beginning of the nineteenth century and worked locally as a plasterer and apprentice brick mason. It is said that Andrew Reid's reconfiguration of the house that he had purchased from William Graham, Mulberry Hill, was his first major project.

Jordan, about this same time, also worked for Thomas Jefferson as a mason at Monticello. In a letter dated November 14, 1805, Jefferson wrote to John Jordan, "I will ask the favor of you to settle the amount of work done at Monticello with Mr. Dinsmore according to the principles of our agreement. Such a settlement certified by him will be accepted." Dinsmore informed Jefferson that "the Subscriber hath measured the Brick work done by John Jordan for Thomas Jefferson at Monticello and finds it to contain twenty eight thousand eight hundred and eighty Bricks."[26] Jefferson "reluctantly" sold one of his slaves, Brown Colbert, to Jordan; Colbert's wife belonged to Jordan. Eventually Colbert was manumitted along with his family and immigrated to Liberia.

Jordan, however, may have also co-opted some of the Hessians that worked as plasterers at Monticello to execute the fine moldings and firebacks at Mulberry Hill for Andrew Reid. The Hessians, having been captured at the Battle of Saratoga, had fought for the British during the Revolution and decided to settle in America after the war. Many had been trained as plasterers and carpenters, and working in teams, as if in a guild, they devoted themselves to one house per season. The team that Jefferson employed, and almost certainly Reid as well, was led by one Martin Wanscher.

The Hessian plasterers specialized in moldings and fire plates with characteristic but individual detail.[27] At Mulberry Hill there are echoes of Monticello both in the detailed plasterwork and also in the Palladian design of the windows and firebacks. At Mulberry Hill, "The first floor mantles have paneling and pilasters above that reach to the ceiling while the ones upstairs do not."[28] Reflecting that the first floor was done by the Hessians in the first lustrum of the new century, while the second floor mantles were constructed in the 1850s to replicate those of the earlier era.

It was said that Andrew Reid and his wife lived in great luxury at Mulberry Hill. "Silk curtains hung down to the floor… and one [slave] did nothing but care for the roses."[29] In 1831, Andrew Reid stepped down from his position as Clerk of the Superior Court to spend his last days in restful repose at his country estate. Samuel McDowell Reid, Andrew Reid's son, replaced him as clerk of court and six years later, in 1837 when Andrew passed away, as proprietor of Mulberry Hill.

Samuel McDowell Reid was the seventh and youngest child of Andrew and Magdalene McDowell Reid, born on October 21, 1790, and was raised at Mulberry Hill plantation near Lexington.[30] In the first decade of the nineteenth century Reid was a student at Washington College where his father was a trustee. After receiving his collegiate education at Washington College, Samuel Reid "studied law in Stanton under Judge Archibald Stuart, and, while there, was made adjutant of Col. James McDowell's regiment, and served as such in the War of 1812."[31] After the war, he became Deputy Clerk of Rockbridge County "when his father, who held the office for fifty-three years, retired from active life, and Colonel Reid was made his successor."[32]

Samuel Reid married Miss Sarah Hare of Nelson County on February 22, 1820, Washington's birthday. The couple had seven children—two died in infancy, "three grown sons died early in manhood, leaving his home desolate, his name extinct."[33] Two daughters survived him, Mary Louise, who married James J. White, Professor of Greek at Washington College, and Agnes, who married Colonel John De Hart Ross.[34]

After becoming clerk of court, Samuel Reid involved himself in the political, judicial, economic, and intellectual development of the county of Rockbridge and the town of Lexington. In the economic sphere, after the death of his father, Reid expanded his real estate holdings in the area. "By the mid-1840s he had acquired nearly 1,500 acres in Rockbridge County, and several years later he owned buildings worth $5,000 in downtown Lexington."[35] He was a director of the James River and Kanawha Canal and was instrumental in extending the navigation works up the Maury River to Lexington. Colonel Reid was also a founder of the Bank of Rockbridge and built a profitable legal practice over the course of his career.[36]

In addition to being a successful real estate entrepreneur, Reid was also a sought-after lawyer and a social and political force in the small and nepotistic community. By the age of forty-one, when he succeeded to his father's post as clerk of the county court, a more-impressive office than it sounds today,

Samuel had already graduated from Washington College, studied law, served as his father's assistant at court, and had a successful career as a lawyer and businessman. He served as clerk of the court from 1831 until 1856 when he began a two-year stint as clerk of the circuit court.[37] The "Squire of Rockbridge County," as Lexington historian Ollinger Crenshaw called Reid, was elected to the Virginia House of Delegates in 1859 and "served through the war years as a member of the banking committee."[38]

Literary societies were a staple of eighteenth-century cultural life in England and Scotland and they became the fashion in the colonies in the 1750s. Benjamin Franklin formed the "Junto" in Philadelphia in 1724, Thomas Jefferson's only professor, William Small, initiated the Society for the Advancement of Arts and Manufacturing in Williamsburg about 1760, and in Lexington, the Lexington Library Company came into being in 1801. These literary societies, or philosophical clubs, were established both to amuse and to instruct. The Library Company was short lived and a successor, the Franklin Society, was formed in 1816.

One of the founders of the society was Samuel McDowell Reid. Like Franklin's Philadelphia consortium, one of the group's greatest benefits "was that it drew together reflective and articulate men from various social strata."[39] The original members included men classified as "mechanics"—such as Valentine Mason, the printer; John Ruff, the hatmaker, Henry Ruffner, the lawyer; and Samuel McDowell Reid, the clerk of court.[40] Shortly after being organized, the society subscribed to five different newspapers, which was followed by a sustained level of book purchases. The society built its library and reading room in front of the Reid house at the corner of Nelson and Jefferson Streets and rented out rooms for various private schools.[41] Reid was elected the society's first president under its charter and at the time of his death was recognized as its oldest-living member. In his eulogy, the speaker noted that Reid "had always recognized the value of the Franklin Society as an instrument for advancing the interest of the community."[42]

The raison d'etre for the Franklin Society was civic improvement through the democratic and pragmatic participation of all classes. Franklin himself was the most "clubbable" of people and had joined multiple societies both in America and in Britain. These intellectual clubs had the force and intent of creating a more-homogenous society, and, at the same time, having the pragmatic byproduct of utilizing the talents and abilities of all classes. A second tine of this republican fork was the equalization and improvement of education for society in general—women included. Colonel Reid was a powerful proponent for these concepts as well. He was one of the founders of Washington College's Graham Debating Society, of which many of the founders of Kappa Alpha were members.[43]

He interned at law with Judge Archibald Stuart in Stanton and the experiences had a profound influence on Reid's political and philosophical outlook. Stuart, a local boy born in Augusta County in 1757, was first educated at Liberty Hall Academy under the stewardship of William Graham, and from there he attended the College of William and Mary, where it is said he studied law concurrently with Thomas Jefferson. It is likely that Stuart's internship would have been with either George Wythe or St. George Tucker. Interestingly enough, St. George Tucker's descendant, John Randolph Tucker, founded the Law School at Washington College.

Nevertheless, whether actually working with Jefferson, or simply drinking from the same fountain of knowledge, Stuart would have imbibed the elixir of democracy and likely thought of education as the straightest path to arrive there. Colonel Reid seems to have picked up this bug and brought it back to Lexington, for many consider his greatest contributions to the town to have been in the field of education. Reid was a lifelong trustee of the Ann Smith Academy, a prominent school for girls, and instrumental in the development and expansion of his alma mater, Washington College.

In 1810, he was a student at Washington College and less than a decade later, he followed in his father's footsteps as a member of the board of trustees. He held this post for fifty years and for nine of those years he was the secretary. As Reid gained seniority on the board he took charge of the school's finances and he particularly interested himself in its architectural development. "In the early 1840s he initiated a building campaign that transformed the central campus buildings into a harmonious Greek Revival ensemble, an appearance that is preserve[d] down to the present day."[44] Particularly significant, in terms of the physical appearance of the college, were the Ruffner years (1836–1848), "for they included a plan to add a new dormitory, three new faculty houses, and a President's house to flank the main academic group; and an idea to alter the center building itself."[45]

The plan for construction was brought to an abrupt halt in 1841, when the board of trustees worried that the ambitious concept would all but deplete the Robinson Trust. At the crux of the impasse, Samuel Reid proposed a resolution calling for a closer evaluation of the college's finances and a survey of faculty opinions on the question of faculty housing. The findings, announced at the following meeting in March, 1841, surprised many of the trustees: "If the debts due to the college were promptly collected and the remaining lands sold and the proceeds invested in one percent stocks, the contemplated improvements might be commenced and finished without encroaching on the permanent funds of the college."[46] The result was the construction of four new houses "three for the professors and one for the president [that] were placed forward of the main group of buildings and flanked them with two on each side." In addition, the front of the center building was remodeled and annexes were added to each side that conjoined it to the Lyceum and Robinson Hall.[47]

As a part of Reid's agenda for civic improvement was a desire to elevate the architectural sophistication of the town. The most well known representative of the Virginia tradition of the gentleman-amateur architect was Thomas Jefferson, although he was not the first of this group. In Lexington there were many competitors for the title but Samuel Reid must be included among the most prominent. His father had an interesting connection with Jefferson in the use of Lexington builder John Jordan, and likely, the Hessian artisans who lathed plaster of Paris on the walls of both Monticello and Mulberry Hill. But the architectural interactions do not end there.

In the first two decades of the nineteenth century, the Classical style became predominant in local architecture, inspired by Jefferson's successes at Monticello and the University of Virginia. "The quality of these designs as well as Jefferson's own prestige encouraged the popularity of this revival in Virginia to such a degree that it is generally called Jeffersonian Classicism."[48]

As a prominent member of the community with a deep interest in architectural design, Reid "held membership in the building committees for several of Lexington's most prominent structures."[49] It is significant that Samuel Reid was on the board of the committees that chose the architect for both the Rockbridge County Jail and the First Presbyterian Church. In 1838, Reid's committee awarded the contract to build the new county jail to Thomas U. Walter. Five years later, Reid, again a member of the appointing committee, again selected Walter to build the Lexington Presbyterian Church. Walter's style may be described as eclectic; in designing and constructing a building he might use the symmetrical, balanced, and simple elegance of the Federalist style; the domes and classically proportioned "elegance of the Roman orders" (which Jefferson preferred); the heavier, stockier forms of the Greek Revival; or, combine elements of all three. The connection between Reid and Walter and the modifications and additions that Reid orchestrated at Mulberry Hill in the 1850s make it plausible to see Walter's directions in Reid's adaptations.

Turning from the public to the private, Samuel Reid was a significant player in the design and construction of his own personal property as well. In 1821, Samuel Reid purchased a home nearer to the center of town. The Reid-White house has many parallels to Mulberry Hill both in its history and architectural design.

Like Mulberry Hill, the Reid house was built on a previous homestead that had several different owners. Benjamin Borden deeded the property to Samuel McClure in 1752; from 1762 to 1782 it was owned by the Campbell family; in 1788 the house was bought by John Hopkins, who lived there with his son and daughter-in-law, David and Ann Hopkins, who sold the house to Samuel McDowell Reid in April 1821 for $750.[50]

Reid soon began his ambitious plans for the house. Fortunately, his records concerning the planning and execution of this house, including his watercolor elevation and section drawings have remained as a testament to the abilities of the gentleman-architect.[51] By the end of October 1821, he had already drafted specifications for a two-story brick house and contracted English-born carpenter Edward Sewell to build the house. The same brick mason who had his first professional job at Mulberry Hill, John Jordan, and later worked at Monticello, is believed by some to have performed the same duties for the younger Reid. The fact is that Reid had, in essence, designed his own house just as his father had done at Mulberry Hill, an architectural proclivity that must have been in the family genes.

The similarities between the mid-eighteenth-century renovations done to both properties carry strong implications that the moving hand in both was Colonel Reid himself and the additions and changes also reflect his aggregate experience in public architecture and private development. There are notable similarities and parallels between the two properties, both in design, execution, and historical connections. Reid made significant renovations to his residence on Lee Avenue in 1847, and completely revised Mulberry Hill in the 1850s. His changes at Mulberry Hill included the addition of a second floor and a slight departure from the plain-but-elegant treatment of the windows in the Federal style of the main floor to the more ornate Italianate ornamentation of the windows on the second.

The mantlepieces at the Lee Avenue house also resonate with the balance of common sense and good taste that first appeared at Mulberry Hill; the plaster embellishments of the mantels on the first floor are meant to impress—Samuel Reid specified that he wanted "molding planted on 2 fancy chimney pieces," which included "fluted half-round pilasters, a tall bed framing, fluted tablets at the ends of the frieze and fan motif corner." He ordered mantels to be done "in middling style" for the fireplaces of the second floor, however.[52] At Mulberry Hill, likewise, "The interior is most notable for its elaborate late Georgian detailing.... A special feature of the northeast room fireplace is an iron fireback that bears a bas relief of 'fame' blowing on a trumpet—tumbling out from trumpet are [the] sixteen stars and the legend 'Be Liberty Thine.' It is signed 'Halbert and Moses McClurer.' The fireback is one of the finest pieces of folk art yet to be discovered in Rockbridge County."[53] The same economic pragmatism of making the mantels in the "middling style" was shown in the addition of the second floor at Mulberry Hill in the 1850s.

Both the additions made to Mulberry Hill in the 1850s and those to the Reid-White house in 1847, have plaster laid on circular-sawn lath slats; both included the use of newel posts at the end of banisters. In a report for the National Register of Historic Places for Mulberry Hill, it is noted that "the central hallway is unusually wide . . . with an elegant curving Italianate-type stairway. Lath under the stairs is circular sawn and the octagonal newel is mid-19th century in character, suggesting that the stair was added to accommodate the new second floor... in the mid-19th century."[54]

At Mulberry Hill, the brick for the second floor is a variation on the Flemish bond of the main floor. The first floor was for public entertaining and contained a library, a parlor, a dining room, and an office or bedroom. The door of the office, which now leads to the bathroom, at that time opened to the exterior and the rear door let out onto the then front porch. The second floor was for residential purposes and consisted of the staircase leading out onto a central hall with two comfortably sized bedrooms on each side. The kitchen/bakery was outside of the main building and the door leading to what is now the kitchen once let out to the yard and the dependencies. Throughout Reid's life the mansion maintained its original orientation toward House Mountain; the new additions were made to blend in with the original texture of Andrew Reid's design; it retained its air of a relaxed and inviting country house. It is maintained by Washington and Lee University that Lee spent his first night in Lexington at Mulberry Hill.[55]

Samuel McDowell Reid died on September 15, 1869, and Robert E. Lee was one of his pallbearers. Governor John Letcher, with whom Reid is said to have collaborated to entice Lee to come to Lexington, performed Reid's eulogy.[56] In

1910, a sketch of Reid's life appeared in the *Lexington Gazette* enumerating his many accomplishments, which included his service of more than fifty years as a trustee of Washington and Lee University, as a founder of the Graham Debating Society, as a founder and stockholder in the Franklin Society, and as a trustee of more than fifty years of Ann Smith Academy for Girls. The author of the article, Reid's son-in-law, Colonel J. D. H. Ross also recalled his devotion to public service as a member of the Board of Public Works, as "one of the chief organizers and supporters of the Rockbridge County Fair, and of the Virginia State Agricultural and Mechanical Society ... and for many years he was a ruling elder in the Presbyterian Church, and his home was the abode of a generous and an elegant hospitality."[57] Ironically, having been a lawyer almost his entire life, Samuel Reid died intestate and of his seven children, only two of whom survived him—Mary Reid White who married a Washington and Lee professor, James J. White, and Agnes Reid Ross, who married a local businessman, John De Hart Ross.

It was agreed between the two sisters to divide their father's properties among themselves and, in 1871, they signed a partition of the lands. Mary and James White were to have the "Homestead" "or dwelling in the town in Lexington together with the pasture lands attached as their part; Agnes and John De Hart Ross were to obtain the mill, miller's house, and Mulberry Hill farm as their portion of their father's real estate.[58]

*Colonel John De Hart Ross*

Agnes Jane Reid was born on February 20, 1838, in Lexington; her husband, John De Hart Ross, was born at Bel Pre plantation in Culpeper County on May 1, 1840. The couple were married in Lexington on April 7, 1862. Ross had graduated from Virginia Military Institute in 1859 and was an instructor there until enlisting in the Confederate army in 1862. He achieved the rank of first lieutenant of engineers on General Longstreet's staff "and afterwards was lieutenant colonel of 52nd Virginia Infantry. He was twice wounded at Cross Keys."[59]

Having returned to Lexington from the war, Colonel Ross became prominent in the affairs of the area and involved himself in the business matters of the town. He was soon elected a member of the board of directors for the town, became a justice of the peace, and the president of the Rockbridge Agricultural Fair.[60]

In the closing months of the 1880s, the anticipation of easy wealth in land development seized the inhabitants of western Virginia like an untamable itch. The "boom" was on, the local newspaper proclaimed, "To put it mildly, things are getting wild. It is not unusual for eligible building lots to jump $100 in twenty-four hours" and in Glasgow, Virginia, a newspaper correspondent reported that the community's population had doubled overnight.[61] Speculation and the Buena Vista Company had transformed that rustic village overnight and a vast scheme of residential, villa, and industrial sites had been laid off in what, until that time, had been pastureland known as Hart's Bottom.

Buena Vista soon had an elegant hotel, which was in need of expansion as soon as it had been finished; in May 1890, the company moved into a new three-story Victorian building in the middle of town, and soon to be constructed was the Buena Vista Opera House.

New development companies were formed by some of the area's most prominent citizens— the Rockbridge Company by General Lee's nephew, Fitzhugh Lee; the West End Glasgow Land Company by Greenlee D. Letcher; and the Glasgow Improvement Company by John De Hart Ross.[62] It was even rumored that an English syndicate led by the Duke and Duchess of Marlborough was investing up to five million dollars in the projects.

The prospect of easy access to the area by expanding railroad lines along with the stunning vistas, quiet environment, and the genteel and hospitable nature of the local inhabitants, made the Valley and Lexington, in particular, prime real estate for a dormant tourist industry. Thus, one of the earliest and most ambitious projects was the rush to build ornate and elaborate hotels to attract a suddenly wealthy American clientele and the prosperous and adventuresome European traveler.

In the Gilded Age, plans were made to build hotels of the most outlandish architectural styles, satisfy the most decadent of tastes, and impress even the most-jaded travelers. In Goshen, the Palace City Hotel was constructed: "The massive pile of turrets, towers, and columned verandas blended Victorian forms—Queen Anne, stick, shingle and others—into an impressive chateau overlooking the Goshen Valley."[63] A promotional brochure boasted that the hotel had "the best White Sulpher water in America on draught and that the rotunda, drawing rooms, and dining rooms were 'beautifully furnished natural wood.'"[64] At the Palace City Hotel life was to be "gay and easy with swimming pools and tennis courts to provide recreation, orchestras would be constantly present, and after supper the guests could either sit on the porch enjoying the coolness of the evening or go for strolls around the grounds."[65]

The fever that had started in Buena Vista quickly spread to Glasgow and then to remote Goshen, leaving the denizens of Lexington, usually swift to glom onto a good money-making scheme, with their hands in their pockets. An editorial in the *Rockbridge County News* addressed the strange set of circumstances, "There is a growing sentiment in this community that if the same energy displayed and money invested in the development of other towns were made use of in our own, a handsome promise would be returned to the investors and a permanent benefit to Lexington ... shall our county town take advantage of the opportunity now afforded her, or shall she remain content?"[66]

Without further provocation, several local businessmen picked up the banner and formed the Lexington Development Company, chief among them was Colonel John De Hart Ross, its first president, and Robert Catlett, its last. Stock in the company went on sale October 23, 1890, and hungry investors gobbled up the available shares.[67] In little more than a month's time the *Staunton Spectator* reported, "When we called at their office yesterday the paid-in subscriptions amounted to over $590,000 and the amount subscribed was in excess of $600,000. To-day the books will be practically closed."[68] According to the article the immediate and initial plans were to put engineers in the field straightaway to lay off the property and "steps will be taken at once to go to work on two new hotels so as to have them finished in the spring."[69]

A Boston newspaper expanded, "The Lexington Development company has acquired about 1150 acres of land lying immediately adjoining the town upon its western border, and along the railroad and river front, at a cost of about $300,000. Much of it is already improved with costly buildings, mill dams, canals, etc., and the rest finely adapted to the other purposes of the company."[70]

The company's mission, it proclaimed, was "to prepare the lands for settlement by laying off and grading streets, dividing the land into suitable lots, providing a source of pure spring water … and building two hotels."[71] The company's property included not only Ross's estates of Sunnyside and Mulberry Hill, but also, Honeysuckle Hill, Castle Hill, and the old golf course, Fairwinds, and extended north to the Maury River and east, beyond the old covered bridge, to the railroad line.

One of the two hotels was projected to be built on the Mulberry Hill property of Ross' wife. Andrew Reid's mansion was to be demolished and a grand ornate hotel was to take its place, complete with an iron bridge connecting the pleasure palace to the railroad station in town. Before ominous

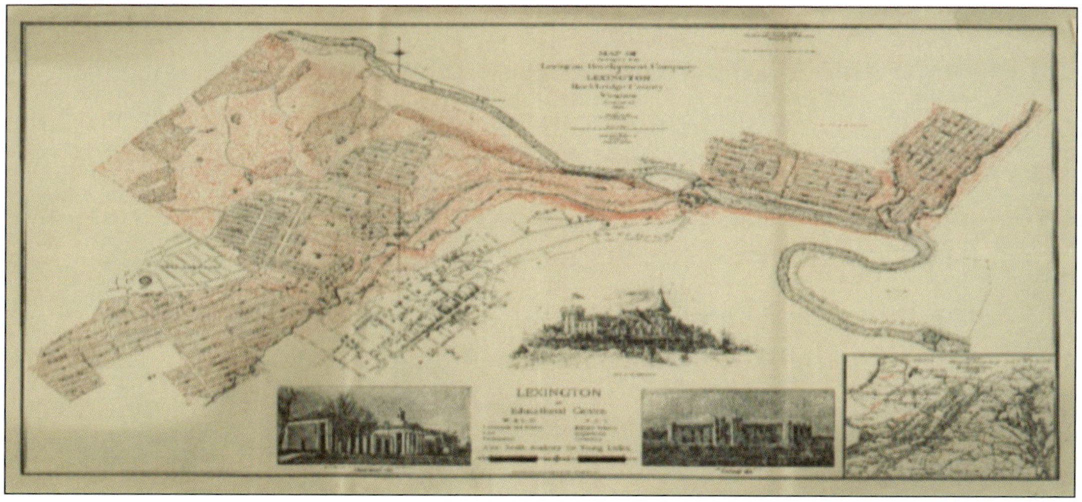


*Map of Lexington Development Company, 1891*

signs on the economic horizon began to appear, the company "planned to further this idea by extending the whole town westward and building new streets and houses on both sides of Mulberry Hill and Liberty Hall and north of the Maury River. The proposal would have doubled the size of Lexington."[72]

Before the end of the year the company had decided to erect a $60,000 hotel on Mulberry Hill, "which would have meant demolishing the house there."[73] For whatever reason, that particular plan was abandoned and the following spring construction commenced on the De Hart Hotel a short distance away, across Covington Turnpike, at Castle Hill. The hotel was described as a "sprawling ornate structure which embodied almost every conceivable type of architecture, from Moorish domes, to Norman tower and battlements'" with the modern conveniences including an elevator and "several bathrooms on each of the upper floors."[74]

Among the town's commercial enticements and conveniences touted were that it possessed one of the best-equipped wood-working mills in the state, a foundry with two cupolas, a machine shop with the latest ironworking machinery complete, a chair factory doing a large and profitable business, a vegetable and a fruit canning factory whose products stood at the very head of the market, two large flour mills, two corn mills, two plaster mills, and one ice factory that supplied the neighboring town.

The expansion of the Gilded Age soon came to an abrupt end. In 1890, one of the most influential banking houses in England that specialized in foreign investments, Baring Brothers, made a questionable arrangement for the government of Argentina. When the details became known, disillusionment took root and, by 1892, the appetite for investment in foreign countries dissipated. The ripple effect struck the United States, already on shaky financial ground by the abandonment of the gold standard, and all of a sudden there was a rush on banks. Investments dried up, overextended railroads went into default, companies failed, unemployment skyrocketed. The boom was over.

In 1892, both the Buena Vista Development Company and the Lexington Development Company "declared bankruptcy and investors were left with

*De Hart Hotel, Castle Hill, Lexington*

worthless paper, abandoned buildings, empty hotels, and a dream that evaporated more quickly than it came into being."[75] In June, there was a hearing concerning the debts and liabilities of the company and the *Roanoke Times* reported, "This was also court day and quite a large crowd were in attendance. Tomorrow the officers of the Lexington Development Company propose to sell all the delinquent stock at public auction."[76]

Although lots were actively marketed in 1891 and 1892, there were few buyers for "within less than a year from its inception, Lexington's great boom was in a state of collapse, with nothing to show for it but a vast, empty hotel, a ready-made site for tennis courts, a wide expanse of unsold lots, and a financial tangle of the first order."[77]

In January 1893, Robert Catlett replaced Ross as president of the company, and the officers "have been diligently at work endeavoring to straighten out the company's affairs, and as a result of their efforts very substantial concessions to the company have been allowed by a number of its creditors. The debts of the company have been reduced by over $20,000 and now amount in round numbers to $40,000."[78] One of the negotiations allowed Colonel Ross to buy back Sunnyside, his home, with sixty acres for the price that he had sold it to the corporation. Colonel Ross and Agnes Reid Ross lived in quiet retirement at Sunnyside for the rest of their lives. On April 10, 1912, the *Lexington Gazette*, reported the celebration of their fiftieth anniversary and later that year Colonel Ross passed away.

With the bankruptcy of the Lexington Development Corporation in 1893, Mulberry Hill was taken over by special court commissioners of the City of Lexington. The property was rented to the family of Colonel Edward Dillon in 1891, when they moved to Lexington, and they remained in the house until his death on August 11, 1897.[79]

On February 17, 1898, Robert Catlett, who succeeded Ross as President of the Lexington Development Company and was at this time the Commissioner for the Lexington Courts, sold Mulberry Hill to the Virginia Fire and Marine Company, which, in turn, sold the mansion to Mrs. Frances Barnum. By 1901, Mrs. Barnum's finances had taken a turn for the worst; it was published that "Frances Courtenay Barnum" was being sued for a debt but that she "had not been served with a copy of the attachment issued… as she is not a resident of the State of Virginia."[80] The job of disposing of Mrs. Barnum's property and satisfying her creditors fell to the court commissioners David E. Moore and W. T. Shields, who sold her property to Mrs. Elinor Jackson Junkin Cox in 1903, for $3,400.[81]

Elinor (sometimes recorded Eleanor) Jackson Junkin was born at Falling Spring in 1866, to the Reverend William Finney Junkin and Anna Aylette Anderson. Elinor's grandfather was George Junkin, president of Washington College from 1848 to 1861. A prounion man with an irascible temper and inflexible attitudes, he left Lexington and after crossing into Pennsylvania, he is said to have wiped the hooves of the horses drawing his carriage "to leave the dust of the South behind him." During his term in office, however, his daughter, married Thomas "Stonewall" Jackson, but died in childbirth. Elinor was named in honor of her erstwhile aunt.[82]

Elinor's father, William Finney Junkin, was born in Philadelphia on May 1, 1831, and was educated at Washington College from which he graduated in

1851. He continued his education in the study of theology at Princeton and graduated from that institution in 1854, at which time he was licensed by the Presbytery of New York and translated to Falling Spring, near Lexington, from 1855 to 1857. He was then sent to the Globe Church in Charleston, South Carolina, where he remained until 1887. In 1888, he "received a call to the pastorate of the church in Montclair, New Jersey, where he served until his death in 1901."[83] He left behind his widow, Anna Anderson Junkin, and four children. Elinor's first husband was Lewis Berkeley Cox.

Cox was born in Georgetown, District of Columbia, on January 7, 1856. His father, Richard Smith Cox, had been employed by the United States War Department. When Virginia seceded from the Union, the family moved to Richmond where the elder Cox offered his services to the Confederate government. He was awarded the rank of major and worked in the Confederate States War Department and was an inmate of the same house as General Lee and was a close friend of George Washington Custis Lee. After the war he settled as a farmer in Loudon County.[84]

His son and Elinor's first husband, Lewis, went to schools in Baltimore and took his first degree in law at Washington and Lee University. In 1879, Lewis continued his education at Columbian University (now George Washington University) and was awarded a Masters of Law and Literature. After graduation, he began a law practice in Oregon. On a trip home and during what must have been a whirlwind romance, he met Elinor Jackson Junkin. On June 27, 1890, at the then ripe age of twenty-four, Elinor married Lewis Berkeley Cox in Montclair, New Jersey, and, in such style that the nuptials were reported the following day in San Francisco under the byline of a society event: "Lewis Berkeley Cox of Portland Oregon, was married this morning to Miss Elinor J. Junkin. It was quite a society event. There were ten bridesmaids. Mr. and Mrs. Cox sail for Europe July 2d, to remain abroad during the summer."[85]

With a society bride at his side and a growing family, Lewis became active not only in the legal community in Portland but in the political arena as well. He served in the state legislature for two years and was elected the chairman

*Elinor Jackson Junkin Cox Latané*

of the Democratic State Convention and president of the State Bar Association in 1892. He died on April 11, 1901, in Portland, Oregon.[86]

When Cox died, he left behind not only his widow but also three young sons. The eldest son of the union was Lewis Berkeley Cox Jr. Berkeley, as he liked to be called, was the valedictorian of his Lexington High School class in 1910.[87] He took his undergraduate degree at Washington and Lee in 1914, and two years later entered its law school. Before he could complete the first year he volunteered for the war effort and was shipped out to France. He received the Distinguished Service Medal for bravery and "extraordinary heroism during the St. Mihiel offensive in September 1915."[88] A second son, Richard Threlkeld Cox, matriculated at Johns Hopkins (where his stepfather was a Professor of History) in 1915, and he was drafted into the army in the first year, but returned after the war to earn a doctorate in physics in 1924. His main area of expertise was the scattering of electrons and probability theory.

In an engaging photograph of the time, the three boys played in the then front yard of Mulberry Hill. According to the commentary on the reverse of the picture, the eldest son, Lewis Berkeley Cox, is seen leaning against the gnarled trunk of an ancient Mulberry tree; Richard Threlkeld Cox is precociously hugging the tree to his brother's left, and the middle son, William Junkin Cox, is up in the branches of the tree; "on the burro is Winthrop Williams, their first cousin who went west to Kansas City." Notes on the back by Isabelle Cox English, daughter of Berkeley Cox, described the inhabitants of the frame of life frozen in time, "up the tree is William Junkin Cox, who was the scamp of the family. It is said that my grandmother, Anna Anderson Junkin, would say 'Berkeley, go see what Billy is doing—and—tell him to stop.' He was charming

*The Cox boys at Mulberry Hill, circa 1904*

and witty all his life."[89] Despite his grandmother's misgivings Billy was the valedictorian of his graduating class at Washington and Lee in 1917, and participated in a number of clubs with his older brother Berkeley.[90] Richard "grew up to be a teacher at Johns Hopkins. He was a philosopher of physics. We have one of his books and we can read all of the words but none of the sentences."[91] Berkeley Cox was described as "an utterly endearing man who grew up to be the General Counsel of Aetna Life and Associated Companies."[92]

Elinor Cox consulted and hired local architect William G. McDowell, who had been born in Lexington in 1850 and graduated from Washington and Lee University in 1872. According to Lyle and Simpson, "He was probably the most active [local] architect of his time."[93] In those same years that McDowell was reimagining Mulberry Hill, he was also busy designing and executing a myriad of public and other private buildings. He was commissioned to renovate the Rockbridge County Courthouse in 1896, to construct a new Law School at Washington and Lee, Tucker Hall; and to erect both a classroom building and the Surgeon's Quarters at the Virginia Military Institute. He was at the same time the inspiration for and a factor in many private homes in the expanding town—including his own at 108 Preston Street.

While the law building on the campus of Washington and Lee was both a departure from McDowell's usual style and inconsistent with the harmony of architectural flow of the colonnade, it was lauded by some as inspirational. In a Washington and Lee publication of its own history, it was described as a "limestone Richardsonian Romanesque style building replacing the old north dormitory, which was destroyed to make way for Tucker Hall, [it was] completed in 1900 and housed the

*Tucker Hall, Washington and Lee University, 1903*

law school. This massive picturesque Victorian structure contrasted sharply with the harmonized Classical red brick buildings on the front lawn."[94] The President of the University, William Wilson "admired the building for its beauty, solidarity of construction, and ability to adapt."[95] To the eyes and sensibilities of most, however, Tucker Hall provided a shocking visual dissonance "to the elegant brick buildings lined neatly along the crest of the hill."[96]

In contrast, the Surgeon's Quarters, reflected the more traditional style of architecture common to many of McDowell's buildings. The structure included a sprawling and ornate front porch framed by a short balustrade and was mirrored by an inverse construction at the top. The residence has a rectangular format with dormer windows in a modified Federalist style. McDowell's own house at 108 Preston Street also had the same large porch supported by Ionic columns with Victorian embellishments, dormer windows, and a hip roof. There are striking resemblances between the exteriors of the Surgeon's residence at VMI and the changes made at Mulberry Hill.

McDowell was responsible for the last extensive renovation to Mulberry Hill. The house, as designed by Andrew Reid, faced scenic House Mountain and a porch was appended to western flank of the house to take advantage of the view. The original gatepost for Mulberry Hill was situated on the southwestern corner

*Post Surgeon's Quarters, VMI, circa 1915*

*Mulberry Hill, after renovations, 1903*

of the property and the road to the front of the house swung around western flank looking out onto House Mountain. The original main entrance gate to the mansion (1) was toward House Mountain (see plan at left); this is clear not only in the placement of the original front door leading out to the porch facing House Mountain, but also from the layout of outbuildings and gardens. There was an old formal garden (3) just to the left of the present rear of the house; as Colonel Reid and his wife were fastidious with regard to this garden, it would have naturally adorned the front of the house rather than the rear. In addition, there are archaeological remains on that side of the house of the former kitchen and bakery—at the edge of the new formal gardens (4), and slave quarters to the right in the direction of Liberty Hall Academy (5).

When McDowell changed the orientation in 1903, he switched the entrance of the property to approximately the same place where Liberty Hall Road now begins. It proceeded from that point directly up the steep incline (where the guest house is now located) and joined the present drive at its upper curve. Inasmuch as the primary approach was still either by horse or carriage, the projection of the path was the logical one.

This redirection made for the most dramatic change to the house, however; instead of facing the west and House Mountain, it now faced east toward the town of Lexington. The emphasis had shifted from seeing to being seen, from a working farm to a social setting, from a place of quiet ease and repose to a center of entertaining and socializing.

At first the new front of the house sat on a grassy knoll, but, in 1911, Thomas Meehan was engaged to construct a new entrance and driveway (6) that led off of Liberty Hall Road instead of its original set of gate posts on the Old Lexington Highway (1). Even the 1911 driveway has been somewhat redirected since that time, as, if it stood as it was, it would run through the present-day guest house and Veterans Memorial. The present corridor runs up path that is not so steep and cumbersome.

In 1911, Elinor was considering changes and her uncle, Francis T. A. Junkin, handled much of the business concerning the property. He consulted the firm

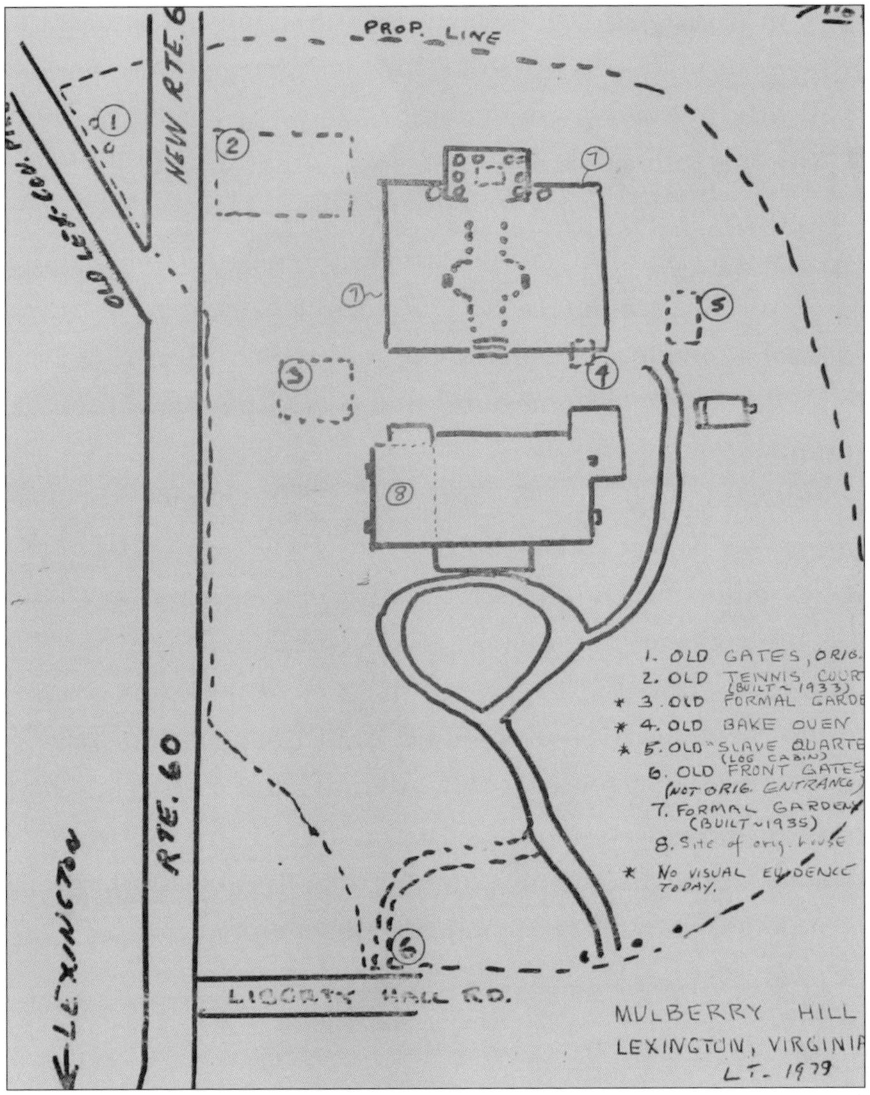


*Sketch of Mulberry Hill's present and past manifestations*

of Thomas Meehan & Sons of Philadelphia and Mr. Meehan, the proprietor, recommended, "The present entrance … necessitates a steep grade and an abrupt turn, both of which are objectionable and dangerous to the present mode of conveyance, the automobile."[97] Mr. Meehan advocated that the road be diverted to a pathway of more moderate grade and the lower portion be filled in until a 15 percent grade was achieved. He also recommended the removal of "buildings C"—the old kitchen (4), and "D"—the old slave quarters (5), and that the garage or carriage house be changed into a more utilitarian fashion. He noted that "the ground floor is intended for the carriage house and stable and is on the level with the road or slightly above it."[98] The structure then included three levels, which is indicated by his suggestion that the "floor above be used for the domestics or a farmer and that the basement for the cows and the farm utensils. This arrangement brings the cattle to the pasture fields and at the same time centralizes all the farm interests."[99] Meehan advocated that the entrance to the lower level be made by means of the "old road," referring to the original approach to the house—curving around that part of the mansion that faced House Mountain.

Another indication that Mrs. Cox intended for the home to be a center of visitation and guests is that McDowell reinvented the second story that had been added by Samuel McDowell in the mid-nineteenth century. The National Register of Historic Places nomination recorded that not only was the central porch added in 1903, but also the plan of the second floor was greatly altered: "The two southern rooms were untouched, but a great central space was created at the expense of the other rooms.... The second story east façade had a central-transom doorway and closets were inserted and lit by two oval windows."[100] It was at this time that the great Ionic columns, like those on McDowell's own house, were added to support the stairs and the ceiling.

*Mulberry Hill, after renovations, front view, circa 1903*

*Mulberry Hill, after renovations, rear view, circa 1903*

In addition, at that time, both the north and south sides of the house had two windows flanking the two fireplaces on each side, but the north side was altered by the addition of the two-story kitchen wing. The first floor of the wing is constructed of brick and the second of mansard-type siding. Both for convenience and to balance the kitchen wing, a second two-story wing was built on the south end of the house. A Victorian porch, later replaced, was set "in antis" between the two new wings.[101]

To support all this new construction and give height to the second floor parlor, the roof was adjusted as well. McDowell reused the mid-nineteenth century rafters, which were joined and pegged rather than nailed, and simply lifted them above the "original plate," removed the former dormer windows, and created a fashionable hip roof to enhance both the appearance and the functionality of the building.[102]

The house in many ways manifested the extroverted nature of its owner and became a beehive of activity. The still young and affluent Mrs. Cox must have attracted many admirers for it was reported in the Lexington papers that on October 17, 1905, "Mrs. Elinor Jackson Junkin Cox was wedded to Dr. John Holladay Latané yesterday afternoon at the R. E. Lee Memorial Episcopal Church.... Immediately following the marriage a reception was held at Mulberry Hill, the hospitable home of the bride's mother, Mrs. William F. Junkin."[103]

Inasmuch as Dr. Latané became a KA while attending Washington and Lee and was the faculty advisor to the Alpha Chapter, it is not unlikely that there were several members attending both the wedding and the reception at Mulberry Hill. Among those under his supervision was the longtime Kappa Alpha historian, Greenlee David Letcher.[104]

The family unit of assorted Andersons, Latanés, Rusts, and Williamses made Mulberry Hill their full- or part-time home, depending on their separate social and professional agenda. Anna Anderson Junkin, however, was in her element at Mulberry Hill "where she often gathered around her, her children grandchildren, and great grandchildren."[105] The house was known for its gracious hospitality, and many old friends, distant relatives and distinguished

*John H. Latané, Faculty Advisor to Alpha Chapter, Kappa Alpha Fraternity, 1904*

guests would be treated to dinners, recitals, and social gatherings at the house.

Dr. Latané, as many of the other inhabitants of Mulberry Hill were in the past and would be in the future, had academic connections to Washington and Lee. He was born in Staunton on April 1, 1869, the son of Bishop James Allen Latané; he attended school in Baltimore and graduated from Baltimore City College in 1889. He next entered Johns Hopkins as a graduate student, where he was a student of Professor Woodrow Wilson and specialized in American diplomatic history and received his doctorate in 1895.

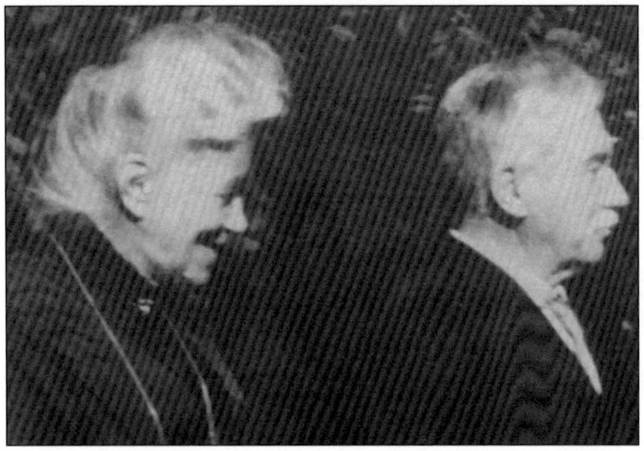

*Anna Aylett Anderson Junkin and brother William A. Anderson*

In 1898, he lectured at Johns Hopkins and became a professor of history at Randolph-Macon College where he taught from 1899 to 1902. In 1902, he was elected as the Chair of History at Washington and Lee University and was named a Special Lecturer at the Naval

War College. In 1913, he left Washington and Lee to take a position at Johns Hopkins. Known as an outspoken idealist, he supported many of the policies of his old professor including the League of Nations. In 1924, his name was placed in nomination for the Woodrow Wilson Medal of 1924.

The matriarch of the family, Anna A. Junkin, passed away on May 1, 1911.[106] It was chiefly because of her mother's wish to be close to the family that Mrs. Latané returned to Lexington and made her home, Mulberry Hill, a gathering spot for her extended Junkin-Anderson family. In 1913, Dr. Latané left Washington and Lee and returned to Baltimore to teach at Johns Hopkins. Mrs. Latané and her four children remained in Lexington at Mulberry Hill. Although her husband returned home as often as possible, Mrs. Latané wanted to join him in Maryland.

Mrs. Latané's uncle, Francis T. A. Junkin, wanting to help his niece, concerned himself in the Mulberry Hill property. He intended to either develop the estate or turn it to another use. In 1914, he consulted Robert Cridland, a noted landscape architect from Philadelphia, about changing the nature of

*Anna Aylett Anderson Junkin and relatives on the new porch, Mulberry Hill, 1905*

the estate. Junkin wrote, "A proposition which developed soon after you last wrote Mrs. Latané, to establish a military school as a sort of preparatory school for the Virginia Military Institute is now being worked up. The location is ideal... and there will be a great deal of work in and around Mulberry Hill if it and the building on the adjoining hill, known as Castle Hill [on which the De Hart Hotel had been built during the boom of 1892], are turned into a military school."[107]

Dr. Latané continued to teach in Baltimore and the scheme to transform Mulberry Hill into a preparatory school for VMI did not materialize. The Latanés rented out the house per interim to Forest Fletcher, the Associate Professor of Physical Education at Washington and Lee.[108]

Fletcher was born in Lincoln, Nebraska, and grew up in Chicago where he participated in the Chicago Athletic and Pleasure Club with the legendary Knute Rockne. Both Rockne and Fletcher went on to attend Notre Dame, where Fletcher became the captain of the track team and was a champion hurdler and sprinter setting five indoor world records. In 1912, he competed in the Olympic Games in Stockholm with teammate Jim Thorpe. Fletcher came to Washington and Lee in 1914 to teach physical education and coach track. In 1917, he organized a band of Washington and Lee students into an ambulance brigade that served in France during World War I. As a result of his heroic actions he received the Croix de Guerre. After the war, Fletcher returned to Lexington and served as instructor and coach of the track and basketball teams for twenty-six years. He died in 1945 following a long illness.[109]

Thus, in 1923, Mulberry Hill was sold to yet another academic with connections to Washington and Lee University, William Jett Lauck. He was born in 1879 in Keyser, West Virginia, into the family of William Blackford Lauck. He graduated from Washington and Lee University in 1903. As a student, Lauck was a winner of the Graham-Lee Debating Medal and Editor-in-Chief of the student publication *Ring-tum Phi* from 1899 through 1901.[110] Having completed his studies at Washington and Lee, he briefly attended the University of Chicago as a graduate student, and then returned to Lexington to marry his college sweetheart, Eleanor Moore Dunlap, and teach at his alma mater. His graduate thesis, "The Causes of the Panic of 1893," won an award and was published in 1905.[111]

His intense interest in public affairs turned his attention from academia to the real world, and he held a series of government jobs in conjunction with his research and teaching obligations. Among his early forays into government service was his stint as the Director for Industrial Investigations for the U.S. Immigration Board (1907–1910), land chief examiner for the Tariff Board (1910–1911). Soon after, Lauck became interested in issues involving labor and unions; he was a union representative to the railway labor boards (1912–1919) and became a consulting economist for John L. Lewis and the United Mine Workers (1919–1939).[112] Lauck also worked for the Roosevelt administration and assisted on the legislative drafting committee for the National Recovery Act in 1933, and assisted the Senate on its revision in 1935. In 1937, he also became a consultant for the United Auto Workers.

Whether Lauck actually lived at Mulberry Hill is in question and although it was reported that he added electricity to the house, there are indications that the Latanés updated the plumbing, wiring, and landscaping in 1914. During the 1920s, Lauck lived on a large estate in Chevy Chase, Maryland, with a staff of three servants and belonged to both the Chevy Chase Country Club and the Cosmos Club in Washington. He was a greater expert at national labor relations and global economics than he was in personal finance and by 1930, he was forced to "sell his beloved Chevy Chase home and relocate to Fredericksburg to an older house overlooking the Rappahannock River."[113]

In 1931 while in continuing financial straits, Jett Lauck sold Mulberry Hill to yet another Washington and Lee professor, Lewis Tyree Sr. This time, however, Lauck was able to turn a profit—he more than doubled his money. He purchased the estate from Elinor Latané for $13,000 and sold it to Professor Tyree for $32,000. Lauck continued his associations with both the federal government and the labor unions with fluctuating success until his death in 1949.

In an interesting connection, Elinor Latané's son, Lewis Berkeley Cox, and Lewis Tyree were both faculty members at Washington and Lee in 1921, as well as members of the same honor society—Delta Sigma Rho.[114] They assuredly knew one another and it is not unlikely that Dr. Tyree had been a visitor to Mulberry Hill during the early 1920s. It is also a possibility, that Berkeley Cox and his younger brother, William Junkin Cox, remained at Mulberry Hill until, and perhaps even after, the property was sold to Dr. Lauck, to complete their education at Washington and Lee. In the ΔΣP portrait (*opposite page*) in the bottom horizontal pairing, Lewis Tyree is on the left and Berkeley Cox on the right.

Lewis Tyree followed in the mold of many of the stewards of Mulberry Hill—he came from an old Rockbridge family and was a professor at Washington and Lee University. His father, Dr. Cornelius Tyree, was born in Amherst County, Virginia, on September 14, 1814, to Jacob and Martha Tyree. He attended both the College of William and Mary, where he studied algebra, history logic, chemistry, and Greek, and Columbian University (now George Washington University) in Washington, D.C.[115] In 1839, he was ordained with the Greenbrier Association "in Fayette County [Virginia, now West Virginia] and was soon after transferred to do missionary work in Rockbridge County."[116] On May 9, 1841, he was one of three ministers who organized the First Baptist Church of Lexington and served as its first pastor. The church had a mixed congregation until 1867, "when its colored members organized a church of their own, the Lexington African Baptist Church."[117]

*William Jett Lauck, 1903*

The elder Lewis Tyree was born in Salem, Virginia, in 1892, and graduated from Fork Union Military Academy in 1908.[118] He earned both a BA and a MA from the University of Virginia in 1912, he taught Summer School at the university that

*Lewis Tyree Sr. and Berkeley Cox, ΔΣΡ, 1921*

summer and was dean at Fork Union for the 1912–1913 session. In 1913, Tyree taught English at Washington and Lee University, while pursuing his law degree and was awarded the LLB in 1915.[119]

After graduation, he moved to Richmond where he taught at John Marshall High School for a year while waiting to qualify for the bar on June 14, 1917.[120] He then "opened an office for the practice of law at 1125 Mutual Bldg., Richmond, in association with the firm of Gunn & Matthews."[121] But World War I intervened and he left for the naval training school in Newport in the fall.[122] He became an ensign and was assigned to the Overseas Transportation Service from 1917 to 1919.[123]

When Tyree returned from active service in 1919, he became a Professor of Law at Washington and Lee, teaching Contracts, Bills and Notes, and Chancery Practice, as well as Evidence and Legislation. He took a sabbatical in 1925 to do graduate work at Columbia University and while there taught part-time at the New Jersey School of Law (Rutgers). He was offered a permanent position at that institution and for a while taught both at the New Jersey School of Law and at Washington and Lee University "commuting by train weekly between Lexington and Newark."[124]

On Halloween 1931, Lewis Tyree bought Mulberry Hill from his fellow professor, William Jett Lauck.[125] The advantages and opportunities for research and advancement at Rutgers, however, drew him back to New Jersey, where he taught law until 1957. Tyree continued to travel between New Jersey and Virginia, living near Newark "in a house constructed during the Revolutionary War at Paulinskill Lake."[126]

In 1921, Lewis Tyree married Winfred Scott West, born in 1902, who was ten years his junior. She was the daughter of Colonel and Mrs. Barrington West and related to the Grigsby and Sellars families of Lexington. The couple's first child, Lewis Tyree Jr., came in 1922, followed by Mary West Tyree in 1928, and Scott West Tyree in 1930. Scott Tyree's obituary stated that he grew up in Lexington, but attended Blair Academy in Blairstown, New Jersey. After high school, he studied American literature at Yale University and graduated with honors in 1953.[127]

It is likely that the family moved with Dr. Tyree to New Jersey sometime before 1930, for Mrs. Tyree listed her residence as Milburn, Essex County, New Jersey, in the U.S. Census of 1930. The census, however, finds her back in Lexington in 1940. Several visitors to Mulberry Hill after Kappa Alpha purchased the house informed the Assistant Executive Director for Advancement, Jesse Lyons, that they had rented rooms from the Tyrees when they were students at Washington and Lee and VMI.

Lewis Tyree Sr. seems to have made only a few significant changes to the estate after he purchased it in 1931. The first was to lay out a formal boxwood garden in the western, or now rear, portion of the house to "frame a magnificent view of House Mountain."[128] The second was to take down all of the remaining outbuildings except the old stable, which was turned into a caretaker's cottage. The old freestanding kitchen was still standing when Elinor Cox bought the house and Professor Lauck may have had it torn down after he bought the house in 1921. He seems to have bought it only for rental and investment purposes, however, and likely gave little thought to improvements or expansion.

The third area of renovation was the rear porch. In 1903, William G. McDowell, the architect, converted the old one-story front porch into an exterior connector between the additions that he added at the time. The replacement porch had two levels that extended out past the old western walls—the extension on the northern side of the house contained the new kitchen and a wing with bathrooms added to both the first and second floors on the southern side. The first story of the kitchen wing was made of brick, while the second floor was covered in mansard-type siding.

In 1903, the connecting porch between the two new additions was of an ornate Victorian affectation; in 1957, Mr. Tyree replaced the overwrought former design with one that was cleaner, simpler, and more classically proportioned.[129] Updates were made in regard to the kitchen and bathrooms, wiring, heating, and plumbing.[130]

After Lewis Tyree Sr.'s death in 1957, Mulberry Hill was left to his wife, Winifred, for life and then to devolve on his three children—Lewis Tyree Jr., Mary T. Schambach, and Scott West Tyree.[131] The property was sold, however, within several months to Mrs. Tyree's cousin, Susan Shelby Grigsby, for $75,000, in April 1957.[132] It is assumed that Mrs. Grigsby lived on the estate with Mrs. Tyree, for when Mrs. Grigsby passed away less than four years later in 1961 she left the property to Winifred Tyree in consideration of her love and affection.[133]

Winifred Tyree made an agreement with her eldest son, Lewis Tyree Jr., that after her death he had a three-month option to purchase the estate for the

The Battle of Lexington *by Lewis Tyree Jr.*

same price that Susan Grigsby had bought it in 1957—$75,000. It is assumed that the purchase money would have been divided between the two remaining heirs, Mary Tyree Schambach and Scott West Tyree.

Scott Tyree had attended Blair Academy in New Jersey as a child, graduated from Yale, and worked as a business executive in Evanston, Illinois. After retiring, he moved to Aladdin, Wyoming, where he wrote Western novels until the time of his death in 2003.[134]

Mary West Tyree Schambach married James Schambach, who was later the president of the American Label Company in New York City. Mrs. Schambach, like her brother Scott, likely grew up in central New Jersey and met her husband there. She lived near Orange, New Jersey, for much of her life. Thus, while the connections to Lexington were tenuous for Scott Tyree and Mary Schambach, they were deeper for their elder brother, Lewis Tyree. Winfred Tyree died on October 8, 1973, and Lewis Tyree purchased the farm in the summer of 1974.[135]

Lewis Tyree the younger was born in 1922 and graduated from the Massachusetts Institute of Technology with a degree in mechanical and cryogenic engineering in 1944.[136] At MIT he joined Alpha Tau Omega fraternity. After graduation, he enter the Army Corps of Engineering and attained the rank of lieutenant. While stationed on Iwo Jimo, with an invasion of Japanese forces impending, Lieutenant Tyree was charged with destroying 600 tons of explosives that had been brought to the island to aid in the construction of an airfield. He later reported that in order to detonate one pallet of explosives would certainly create a chain reaction among the others and that all would explode at the same time. Tyree wrote, "It was with great trepidation that we exploded the 600 tons of dynamite. We were not at all certain that Iwo would not sink... on the day of the blow everyone else retreated to Mt. Suribachi except my sergeant and I who used a plunger type detonator from the top of a nearby cliff."[137] Both Iwo and Tyree survived.

After the war, Lewis Tyree briefly worked as an engineer for the Joy Manufacturing Company in Pittsburgh, Pennsylvania.[138] It may have been here that he filed his first patent, along with co-workers Samuel Collins and Win Paget. The design was for an Oxygen Purity Improvement Method and Apparatus.[139] Mr. Tyree moved from Pittsburgh to Oak Brook, Illinois, where he lived for many years and served as a consultant to a number of major corporations. He held more than forty patents in the field of cryogenics, the use of extremely low temperatures, and was listed in *Who's Who in America*.[140] He was for many years the Chief Technical Officer and Executive Vice President of Liquid Carbonic Industries, and listed his last patent in conjunction with that company in 1983.[141]

After a long and successful career, Lewis Tyree Jr. and his wife Dorothy H. Tyree returned to Lexington and Mulberry Hill. Mr. Tyree was particularly interested in the history of the house and his family's personal connections with it. He took great pains to contact and collaborate with various historians, preservationists, archeologists, and local authorities to establish a more-accurate account of the estate's background. He drew many diagrams of the different stages of Mulberry Hill's development and even executed an oil painting of the Battle of Lexington in 1864. The couple's devotion to the property was so pronounced that they donated a historic easement to the Virginia Department of Historic Resources in 1982, which would later prohibit the construction of office buildings on Mulberry Hill.

Old age and infirmities, however, caused the couple to desire the amenities and conveniences of a retirement community. Judicial orders were made in 2002, which made the evacuation of the Order's Headquarters on Courthouse Square almost a certainty. Then Mayor of Lexington, former VMI Superintendent and alumnus LTG John Knapp, suggested Executive Director Wiese call Tyree regarding Mulberry Hill. That day, Tyree called Wiese himself. As recorded in the previous chapter, a deal was struck, and a deed signed in the fall of 2003. All the permits were obtained, all the financial arrangements were concluded, and now was the time for the conversion of the property from a private residence into a commercial property. But with all the changes to come, Mulberry Hill was to remain a home. On May 11, 2004, the sale was officially closed, on June

10th the first official staff meeting was held at Mulberry Hill, and on July 14th a Wednesday night fund-raising reception was held. The unofficial move in happened in October 2004, and the official dedication on August 6, 2005.

The first steps of the transformation from a private home to a public institution included updating the plumbing, the heating, and the electrical and communication systems and then transforming the garage into a print shop, mail room and temporary archives. It would also be imperative to expand parking for employees and visitors.

The priorities were set out in a progress report formulated by Executive Director Larry Wiese to the KAOEF Board of Trustees and Executive Council in April 2004. The first matter on the agenda was the manor house itself, specifically, "retrofitting the existing structure to accommodate the business operations of the Order and Foundation until an additional administrative building is complete." The subcategories of this phase included preparing the manor house for the upgrading and installation of telephone, electrical, security and computer systems, and removing extraneous materials from the attic and basement areas so that they could be used as controlled environments for storage of equipment and related materials.[142]

The phone system needed new wiring and the installation of a phone box for multiple extensions; extensive wiring and the addition of wireless modems were needed for the advanced computer systems to be installed; more-sophisticated security systems needed to be added; and, upgrading electrical service to 600 amps (including the basement and attic) were required.

The second priority was to create an annex by turning the old garage space into a "1000 square foot area to be used as printing facility, mail-room, and additional office space which may include a temporary archivers."[143] This renovation was to include a HVAC system, and rewiring and revamping the interior into office space.

The third area on the report addressed the need for reconfiguring the roadway leading to the house and developing a parking area that would serve the needs of the staff and at the same time not detract for the aesthetics of the house. The anticipated date of completion was projected to be in the fall of 2004, in time for the unofficial occupation of the house, now headquarters.

The first floor needed little modification: the room that had been the parlor was still the parlor; the dining room at the western portion of the house now became a conference room; the downstairs bedroom now served as the office of the Executive Director; and the former study became an office for the assistants to the Executive Director. A reception desk was stationed in the central hall, French doors led to the rear patio and porch and a magnificent view of the formal gardens and House Mountain. The kitchen was modernized and adapted for communal usage.

The staircase from the first floor ascends onto a landing overseen by a grand portrait of Robert E. Lee on his horse and continues up another short flight of stairs to the second floor, which had previously consisted of a central hall and four spacious bedrooms. In 1903, the central hall had been widened to form a ballroom or upstairs parlor with two of the former bedrooms somewhat diminished by the transition. The McDowell configuration remained constant to the 1903 version in shape but not in function. The bedrooms had become office space, the consultants were crowded into a single office (but now the old central ballroom has become their workplace) and the area over the kitchen was transformed into the financial offices.

The Tyrees left behind several valuable works of art, furniture, and most impressive an early Steinway piano, made in Germany in 1883, which may well have been the first of its kind in America. David Warren donated a number of beautiful and utile pieces of furniture including the conference table and Neoclassical sideboard. The beautiful Federal-style chairs, a gift of Thomas Paulson, surrounding the conference table were transferred from the former offices in Courthouse Square. The large equestrian portrait of General Lee that hangs above the central stairway was painted by American artist Natalie Eynon Grauer for the Greenbrier Hotel in 1932.[144]

The greatest changes were to take place in the garage, however. The original carriage house became a garage about 1915, and was used in that capacity for

*Veterans Memorial and Entryway to Kappa Alpha National Administrative Offices, April 2015*

a number of years. By 1985, it had become so dilapidated that Lewis Tyree tore it down and rebuilt a three-bay garage in its stead. It was an open plan with a section in the rear that served as a workshop and storage area. The cabinets that had served as storage serve the same purpose today. The inside of the first floor was gutted, however, heavily insulated two-by-eight walls were installed for climate control and noise reduction, and the whole was rearranged into three distinct areas—the first, in the rear was a combination print shop and supply depot; the second area is in the front left-hand side of the building and it serves as the mailroom; and the third is now the office of the archivist, Kent McMichael. Before the renovation, the only entrance to the garage had been the door on the right of the building but, in order to facilitate supplies coming into the print shop, a new sidewalk was laid and a second door installed on the left side of the building.

The last structural addition to the Mulberry Hill grounds was a guesthouse begun in 2009 for the traveling field staff. Construction started in the fall of 2009 with the basement meant to house the archives of the Order. As such, it had to be securely built and climate controlled. Therefore, the first step was to construct a concrete shell reinforced with steel rods; next was to cut doors and windows out of the solid shell and install climate control and security systems for the archives. The second stage was to build the living quarters for the staff. The house contains five bedrooms, four bathrooms, a common area, a kitchen, and two porches.

The final addition has been the construction of a Veterans Memorial and Entryway. It is situated behind the guest house on the former Miller property which was acquired in 2011. The entryway was proposed to the Buildings and Grounds Committee in the spring of 2013 and evolved into a project that included a marquee, a memorial garden, and plaques to honor fallen heroes, and a walking path to the formal gardens. It is to be dedicated at the 76th Convention. The set of plaques honor members of Kappa Alpha who were awarded the Medal of Honor; members who were the first to die in wars since the founding of the Order; the distinguished veterans of Kappa Alpha; and donors to the Sesquiscentennial Celebration.

The symbolic importance of Mulberry Hill to the Kappa Alpha Order is significant. The foundation was built by the Reverend William Graham and once housed the Liberty Hall Academy. The academy transitioned into Washington College when the first president of the United States ensured its reputation and existence through his good opinion and the shares of Canal Stock that he bestowed on the fledgling institution. When the Civil War broke out, students from Washington College drew on their history for their name—the Liberty Hall Volunteers. After the war, General Robert E. Lee, the hero of the South and a close friend of the proprietor of Mulberry Hill, Samuel McDowell Reid, reportedly spent his first night as president of Washington

College as a guest of Colonel Reid. Not only his spirit but the ghosts of others who had ties both to the college and to the Order roam her halls. Kappa Alpha Order is the common thread that binds together the university and the house with the shared values of ethos, attitude and duty.

The founders of the nascent fraternity no doubt often strode past her gates and mulberry bushes on their way from their country haunts to campus and it is not unlikely that they spent many evenings enjoying the hospitality of the house. Lee's affiliation to the house and sentimental ties to his young telegraph operator, Jo Lane Stern, impressed on the first members of the Order the concepts of honesty, utility, and duty. In many ways the character of the house, the ethos of the college, and the expectations of the fraternity have formed an unbreakable alliance—and one is synonymous with the other.

In terms of location, history, and connections between the Order and the estate, there could not have been a better home for the National Headquarters than Mulberry Hill. The century-long endeavor to return to its home has finally been realized and all the trials and tribulations of the past seem to have been only part of the price that comes along with obtaining one's end. Thus, as the Order had its origins in Washington College and Washington College its genesis at Mulberry Hill, the question "Will the Circle Be Unbroken" seems to have its answer—by and by, Lord, by and by.

*Notes* Chapter 14:

1 Hugh Grigsby, "The Founders of Washington College," in *Historical Papers, No. 1* (Baltimore: John Murphy, 1890), 16.

2 Ibid., 18.

3 Oren F. Morton, *A History of Rockbridge County, Virginia* (Staunton, Va.: McClure Co. 1920), 130.

4 Virginia Department of Historic Resources. National Register of Historic Places Nomination. Mulberry Hill. 1982. Survey File 117-10. Richmond, Va.

5 Ibid.

6 Ibid.

7 James Waddel Alexander, *The Life of Archibald Alexander* (New York: Charles Scribner, 1854), 16.

8 Morton, *A History of Rockbridge County*, 190.

9 Ibid.

10 Royster Lyle and Pamela Simpson, *The Architecture of Historical Lexington* (Charlottesville: University Press of Virginia, 1976), 149.

11 Morton, *A History of Rockbridge County*, 190.

12 Washington and Lee University Archaeology Program, http://archaeology.wlu.edu/mboard4.html (viewed April 23, 2015).

13 Lyle and Simpson, *The Architecture of Historical Lexington,* 147.

14 Ibid.

15 Ibid.

16 Ibid.

17 Ibid., 149.

18 Ibid.

19 Ibid.

20 Rockbridge County Deed Book C, p. 193, in Julian Nexsen, "Mulberry Hill," May 23, 1975, Unpublished Research Paper, W&L Special Collections, Washington and Lee University, Lexington, Va., 9.

21 Virginia Department of Historic Resources. National Register of Historic Places Nomination. Mulberry Hill. 1982. Survey File 117-10. Richmond, Va.

22 Henry Ruffner, *Historical Papers, No. 4, 1893* (Baltimore: John Murphy Co., 1893), 37.

23 A hotbed is an area where organic debris was buried; the decaying matter would generate heat and become an environment that would be favorable to the early and accelerated growth of vegetation, much like a modern composting pile.

24 Julian Nexsen, "Mulberry Hill," May 23, 1975, Unpublished Research Paper, W&L Special Collections, Washington and Lee University, Lexington, Va., 7.

25 Ruffner, *Historical Papers, No. 4, 1893*, 37.

26 Thomas Jefferson to James Dinsmore, January 3, 1806, Archives, Massachusetts Historical Society, Boston.

27 Nexsen, "Mulberry Hill," 9.

28 Ibid.

29 The Rev. William McClung, *The McClung Genealogy* (Pittsburgh: McClung Printing Co., 1904), 47.

30 Col. J. D. H. Ross, "Sketch of Colonel Samuel McDowell Reid," *Lexington Gazette*, August 24, 1910, p. 1. Colonel Ross was Samuel Reid's son-in-law.

31 Col. J. D. H. Ross, "Sketch of Colonel Samuel McDowell Reid," 1; Judge Archibald Stuart was born in 1757 and educated at Liberty Hall Academy and at the College of William and Mary. After the Revolutionary War he studied law under Thomas Jefferson and returned to Rockbridge. He was elected to the Senate of the Virginia and was subsequently chosen its president. In 1799, he was elected Judge of the General Court of Virginia, assigned to the Augusta District, and served until 1831. J. Lewis Peyton, *History of Augusta County* (Staunton, Va.: Samuel Yost & Son, 1882), 309.

32 Ross, "Sketch of Colonel Samuel McDowell Reid," 1.

33 Ibid.

34 Ibid.

35 Virginia Department of Historic Resources. National Register of Historic Places Nomination. Reid-White-Philbin House. 2000. Survey File 117-0014. Richmond, Va.

36 Ibid.

37 Ibid.

38 Ibid.

39 Richard Owan, "John W. Fuller and the Franklin Society Library of Lexington," *Virginia Magazine of History and Biography* 93, No. 3, (July 1985): 324.

40 Ibid.

41 Virginia Department of Historic Resources. National Register of Historic Places Nomination. Reid-White-Philbin House. 2000. Survey File 117-0014. Richmond, Va.

42 Ibid.

43 Ibid.

44 Ibid.

45 Lyle and Simpson, *The Architecture of Historical Lexington*, 154.

46 Ibid.

47 Ibid., 155.

48 Ibid., 23.

49 Ibid., 21.

50 Virginia Department of Historic Resources. National Register of Historic Places Nomination. Reid-White-Philbin House. 2000. Survey File 117-0014. Richmond, Va.

51 Ibid.

52 Ibid.

53 Virginia Department of Historic Resources. National Register of Historic Places Nomination. Mulberry Hill. 1982. Survey File 117-10. Richmond. Va.

54 Ibid., Section 7/ page 1.

55 Abigail Gage, "Geotechnical and Geophysical Survey of Mulberry Hill," Department of Anthropology, Unpublished Paper, 2003, Leyburn Library, Special Collections, Washington and Lee University, 3. It is reported by others that it was actually Professor White's residence in town.

56 Virginia Department of Historic Resources. National Register of Historic Places Nomination. Reid-White-Philbin House. 2000. Survey File 117-0014. Richmond, Va.

57 Ross, "Sketch of Colonel Samuel M'Dowell Reid," 1.

58 "Deed of Partition. James White and Wife and D. H. Ross and Wife," Kappa Alpha Archives, Lexington, Va.

59 "Colonel John De Hart Ross," *Lexington Gazette*, April 10, 1912, p. 5.

60 Ibid.

61 Royster Lyle, "Rockbridge County's Boom Hotels," *Virginia Cavalcade* 20, No. 3 (Winter 1971): 5.

62 Ibid., 9.

63 Ibid., 11

64 Ibid.

65 Ibid.
66 Ibid., 12.
67 Ibid.
68 "The Lexington Development Company," *Staunton Spectator*, November 26, 1890, p. 3.
69 Ibid.
70 "Lexington Development Company," *Cambridge Tribune*, April 4, 1891, p. 4.
71 Lyle, "Rockbridge County's Boom Hotels," 12.
72 Lyle and Simpson, *The Architecture of Historical Lexington,* 42.
73 Lyle, "Rockbridge County's Boom Hotels," 12.
74 Ibid., 13.
75 *Lexington Gazette*, December 18, 1912, p. 5.
76 "Lexington Development Company," *Roanoke Times*, June 7, 1892, p. 3.
77 *Proceedings of the Rockbridge Historical Society*, Vol. 5. (Lexington, Va.: The Society, 1941–2002).
78 *Highlander Recorder* (Virginia), March 10, 1893, p. 2.
79 "Death of Mrs. Frances P. Dillon," *Lexington Gazette*, March 27, 1912, p. 5.
80 *Lexington Gazette*, August 14, 1901, p. 1.
81 "The Sale of Mulberry Hill," *Lexington Gazette*, April 29, 1903, p. 3.
82 Lawrence B. Thomas, *The Thomas Book* (New York: Henry Thomas Co., 1896), 556.
83 *Minutes of the Seventy-eighth Annual Session of the Synod of New Jersey* (Trenton: MacCrellish & Quigley, 1900), 40.
84 Julian Hawthorne, *The Story of Oregon* (New York: American Historical Publishing Co., 1892), 2:391.
85 "A Society Event," *Morning Call* (Allentown, Pa.), June 28, 1890, p. 1.
86 "Multnomah Bar's Tribute to Lewis B. Cox," *Morning Oregonian* (Portland), April 23, 1901, p. 8.
87 "Closing of High School," *Lexington Gazette*, June 15, 1910, p. 1.
88 "Two D.C. Lieutenants at Walter Reed Hospital Decorated for Bravery," *Washington Times*, April 11, 1919, p. 13.
89 Photograph, Album at Mulberry Hill Parlor.
90 *The Calyx 1917* (Lexington: The Students of Washington & Lee University, 1917), 74.
91 Photograph, Album at Mulberry Hill Parlor.
92 Ibid.
93 Lyle and Simpson, *The Architecture of Historical Lexington,* 92.
94 "Chapter Two: A Brief History of Washington and Lee: Preservation Master Plan 2005," Washington and Lee University, Lexington, Va. , 14.
95 Ibid.
96 Ibid.
97 J. Franklin Meehan to Francis Junkin, February 11, 1911, in *Francis T. A. Junkin Collection* (Leesburg: Thomas Balch Library, 1911), 1.
98 Ibid., 2.
99 Ibid.

100 Virginia Department of Historic Resources. National Register of Historic Places Nomination. Mulberry Hill. 1982. Survey File 117-10. Richmond, Va.

101 Ibid. "In antis" is defined: "Columns in antis are placed between two projection sections of wall, in an imaginary plane connecting the ends of the two wall elements." Richard Guy Wilson, ed., *Buildings of Virginia: Tidewater and Piedmont* (Oxford, Eng.: Oxford University Press, 2002), 517.

102 Ibid.

103 "Dr. Latané and Mrs. Cox married yesterday afternoon," *Lexington Gazette,* October 18, 1905, p. 3; "Dr. Latané Weds," October 21, 1905, *Ring-tum Phi* 9, No.4 (Washington and Lee University), 1; Lyon G. Tyler, *Men of Mark in Virginia* (Washington, D.C.: Men of Mark Publishing Co., 1908), 4:241.

104 Latané was a fellow of the Royal Historical Society (London) and was a Chevalier, Legion of Honor (France). W. B. Crawford, *Directory of the Kappa Alpha Order, 1865–1929* (St. Augustine: The Record Company, 1929), 58.

105 "Death of Mrs. William F. Junkin at Mulbery Hill," *Lexington Gazette*, May 3, 1911, p. 5.

106 Ibid.

107 Francis T. A. Junkin to Robert B. Cridland, August 7, 1914, Francis T. A. Junkin Collection, Thomas Balch Library, Leesburg, Va., 1914, p. 1.

108 *1917 Washington and Lee University Bulletin* 16, No. 1 (1917): 11.

109 "Forest Fletcher," http://www.generalssports.com/information/hall_of_fame/fletcher_forest (viewed April 22, 2015).

110 *Calyx 1903* (Lexington, Va.: The Students of Washington & Lee University, 1903), 76, 127.

111 Leon Fink, *Progressive Intellectuals and the Dilemmas of Democratic Commitment* (Cambridge, Mass.: Harvard University Press, 1999), 216.

112 Ibid.

113 Ibid., 225.

114 *The Calyx 1917*, 262.

115 George B. Taylor, *Virginia Baptist Ministers: Fourth Series* (Lynchburg: J. P. Bell Co., 1913), 118.

116 Ibid., 119.

117 Morton, *A History of Rockbridge County*, 178.

118 *The Legacy*, New Jersey School of Law (Newark: The Student Council, 1928), 26.

119 *The Legacy*, 26. See also *The Calyx 1915* (Lexington: W. Bell Co., 1915), 28.

120 "Lawyers Qualify, *Richmond Times-Dispatch,* June 14, 1917, p. 7; "Leaves for Newport," *Richmond Times-Dispatch,* September 4, 1917, p. 7.

121 *University of Virginia Alumni News* 5, No. 7 (Charlottesville: General Alumni Publications, 1916): 83.

122 "Leaves for Newport," *7.*

123 *The Legacy*, 26.

124 "Lewis Tyree," http://law2.wlu.edu/faculty/profiledetail.asp?id=371 (viewed April 22, 2015).

125 Rockbridge County Deed Book, 156, Rockbridge County Courthouse, Lexington, Va., 381.

126 "Lewis Tyree," http://law2.wlu.edu/faculty/profiledetail.asp?id=371 (viewed April 22, 2015).

127 *Black Hills Pioneer* (Spearfish, South Dakota), May 13, 2003; *Rapid City Journal* (South Dakota), May 12, 2003.

128 Virginia Department of Historic Resources. National Register of Historic Places Nomination. Mulberry Hill. 1982. Survey File 117-10. Richmond.

129 Ibid.

130 Ibid.

131 Rockbridge County Deed Book, 238, p. 446.

132 Ibid., 440.

133 Ibid., 551.

134 "Scott W. Tyree," *Gillette News Record,* Gillette, Wyoming, May 13, 2003, p. 27.

135 Rockbridge County Deed Book, 342, p. 310; "Miss Schambach Weds in Virginia," *New York Times,* November 26, 1984.

136 "Record Attendance for Soph Prom Now Expected," *The Tech* 51 No. 4 {November 7, 1941): 1.

137 Lewis Tyree, "Letters to the Editor," *Journal of Military History* 59, No. 3 (July 1995): 577.

138 *Technological Review* 51, No. 7 (May 1949): 369.

139 "U.S. Patent Office, Patent 2,671,318," March 9, 1954.

140 Obituary, "Lewis Tyree Jr.," *Chicago Tribune*, August 8, 2004.

141 "Ice-making and Water-heating," U.S. Patent Office, Patent 4373345A, February 15, 1983.

142 Larry Wiese, "Mulberry Hill Project Progress Report," April 2004, p. 1.

143 Ibid.

144 Mark C. Grove, "Replacement Value: Insurance scheduling" (Mark C. Grove, Fairfax and Charlottesville, Va. 2007).

*Beta Kappa Chapter, University of Maryland, 2014*

*Mulberry Hill, 2015*

# Epilogue

The telling of the tale of the Kappa Alpha Order is one that is encompassed by connections, interconnections, and reconnections—in short, an unbroken circle. The fact that the National Headquarters lands on the same plot of ground from which it emanated seems to have been predestined. Wherever the trail breaks off, it picks up anew; whenever a goal seems unattainable, by some sort of contortion of fate, it is attained; whatever the immediate and almost insurmountable obstacle, it is—by work and determination—overcome. But the strength of the Order lies not in a building, nor by its storied history, but in the aggregate and universal character of its members.

The axiom that the shortest distance between two points is a straight line is not the path of our narrative—rather it is one of twists and turns, it breaks off and reappears, and then it pops up again in the most unexpected places. Consider that piece of land, that plot of earth, that realm of knights, has changed hands more often than a subway token; nevertheless, the very spot where the Order's nurturing mother, Washington College, was founded, became the Order's permanent home. Mulberry Hill passed from one owner to another, but, strangely enough, all had a connection to the Order and its history; sometimes intimate, sometimes tenuous.

The personalities that possessed and inhabited the old estate all left their stamp, in one way or another, on the birth, growth, and expansion of the fraternity. The founder of Mulberry Hill was the rector of Liberty Academy, which transformed itself into Washington College, the birthplace of the Order. After the Civil War, the spiritual inspiration for the Order was a guest of Mulberry Hill's owner, Samuel McDowell Reid, who in turn played an important role in the development of the college and the town. The son-in-law of Colonel Reid, J. D. Ross, a former professor at VMI turned developer, had plans to knock down the house to make way for a decadent hotel, but, at the last moment, it was aborted, the best-laid plans went awry, and the home was saved. Elinor Junkin Cox, the granddaughter of the former president of Washington College, George Junkin, and the niece of Stonewall Jackson, bought the house at the turn of the century. Her father-in-law, Richard Smith Cox, had been a housemate of General Lee during the war; his eldest son, Lewis Berkeley Cox, was educated at Washington and Lee and was a member of the same club at Washington and Lee as Lewis Tyree, a later owner of Mulberry Hill.

After Mr. Cox died in 1901, Mrs. Cox married John Holladay Latané in 1905. Dr. Latané was not only another Washington and Lee professor but also a member of Kappa Alpha and its faculty advisor at the university. Mulberry Hill was sold to yet another Washington and Lee professor, whose son attended the college and was the last proprietor of the estate before Kappa Alpha Order purchased it—just at the very time that the Order was in urgent need of getting a home and Lewis Tyree the younger in desperate need of finding a caretaker for his.

But the importance of Kappa Alpha's story is more than an encapsulation of the history of its National Headquarters and the supernatural twists and turns in the Order's installation there. It reflects a microcosm of the history of the state, of the South, and of the nation. After the Civil War, it was touch and go for the young lodge; its nascent founders, veterans inured by the hardships of battle, yet still naïve boys, making the decisions to forge forward despite the difficulties of Reconstruction—like Virginia and the South and the nation. Their tenacity and persistence was rewarded by an expansion that was, at the time, unimaginable—like the nation.

The growing empire soon extended to the western coast and the Order adapted to the times as did the nation. As the nation grew so did the fraternity, projected lodges were being vetted in the territories. Although the concept of territories seems remote and distant, history is never far behind. Consider that in the 1960s when Barry Goldwater ran for president, his antagonists protested that he was not eligible to run because he was born in the Arizona territories. But like the nation, as the Order extended, it adapted. The exponential growth of lodges and members, both active and alumni, necessitated a greater sophistication in management, communication, and a linear structure. Just like the country, the Order underwent a process of streamlining until the Great War arrived and then, for its duration, there was a time for thinking about the greater good and those members who had marched forward into the horrors of the trenches.

Both the country and the Order were flush with victory and enthusiasm after the war and the twenties was a decade of growth, stability, and the establishment of a cohesive national organization. A watershed moment was the Convention of 1923, when the Old Alpha and the New Order met. From this point onward all matters were handled in a more-clinical and organized fashion and the process of vertical integration began. And then the Crash of 1929.

The nation and the Order held its collective breathe, hoping against hope that the new U.S. president could pull the nation out of the devastating economic situation. The number of students attending college dropped precipitously, donations from alumni stagnated or stopped, lodges closed their doors. Yet the Order and the nation endured. Slowly through measures that in the 1920s would have been impossible, the policies of the government breathed reluctant life into the economy and as the nation began to exhale again, so did Kappa Alpha Order.

And then Germany invaded Poland and a purpose larger than normal life became more important, both to the Order and to all Americans. For the duration of World War II, the young men were dispersed to foreign strands—defeating he enemy and coming back alive were the only things that really mattered. For the Order, normal life also disappeared; lodges closed down, meetings were left unattended, conventions postponed. But like the ordinary citizens, the Order did its part to the best of its ability. The *Kappa Alpha Journal* looked more like *Stars and Stripes* than a college publication; articles entitled Stars-Bars-Chevons, KaKa Talk, War Service Issue, Camp Chatter, Eternals, To Brothers in Service, Go Getter Patton, Alford's Leadership, Desert Journey, Military Notes, and Legion of Honor demonstrated a unified purpose and desire to connect every member past and present of the fraternity and give them both comfort and recognition.

As the outcome of the war became more apparent, the leadership of the Order began to prepare for the return of the soldiers and the revitalization of the fraternity. The surge of new and former undergraduates, accelerated by both the return of the nation's sons and the impetus of the GI Bill, caused an explosion in the ranks of the Order. Lured by the comradeship to which they had become accustomed during the campaigns of the past four years and with the prospect of hard-to-find housing, recruits joined fraternities in droves. The cascade of enthusiasm, patriotism, and rising economic stature boosted the popularity of fraternities, in general, and Kappa Alpha, in particular, for more than a decade and a half.

In the sixties, the growing mistrust of the military-industrial complex, the rebellion against traditional values and mores, the hatred for anything establishment reflected in the attitudes and protests of the baby boomers also had an impact on the desirability of being fraternal. As the Vietnam War dragged on, self-deprecation and apathy seemed endemic. The numbers of fraternities and lodges diminished and on some campuses even disappeared. Kappa Alpha was one of the first fraternal organizations to address the question of inclusiveness and embraced recruits from every segment of society.

The increasing importance of academic achievement and the more mature outlook of many college students today has attracted high-quality candidates to an organization that supports and recognizes those efforts. The result is a body of active and alumni members who have not only a social side but a pragmatic one as well. This universal character helps the institution, as a whole, and all of its discrete and component parts, to achieve collective and individual goals.

From the 1980s to today the nation and the Order have been through many highs and lows. But being a member of the Kappa Alpha Order gives each and every member the confidence that not only does somebody care but also that someone will act on the desire to be helpful.

The parallels between the history of the Order and the nation are self-evident. Kappa Alpha's past is the nation's past in a more localized distillation and I can only believe that the trend will continue into the future.

To the readers, paraphrasing the confession, forgive me for what I have done and left undone. I know that many will wonder why certain points of Kappa Alpha's history have not been addressed, why important events have been overlooked, why people so significant to the Order's survival and growth have gone unmentioned. This work was intended to be a mega-narrative, however, the big story, a work that tries to tell a story of the major phases and changes within the history of the Order. I hope this work has, in some measure, accomplished that purpose. Excelsior.

# *Acknowledgments*

In the process of the making of any work, not a single hand but many hands are responsible for the end result. In some cases, this is a self-evident truth; that a new car needed various skills and levels of expertise is obvious to everyone; a beautifully designed piece of furniture, perhaps less apparent—but on consideration—yes, of course; a lumberjack had to cut the tree, a miller needed to turn the timber into smooth planks of wood, there was also a variety of vendors who provided tools, varnishes, and polishing clothes. But for a picture or a book, the artist or the author is usually assigned the full credit. This assumption is the consequence of instinct rather than deliberation. No man is an island, wrote the poet Dunne, nor is any work.

The significance of an acknowledgment section relates, in discrete segments, to the people and institutions that make any composition possible. The traditional components often include a special recognition to those who provided financial and logistical support and encouragement; the scholars and academics who have inspired by their enthusiasm and informed with their expertise and experience and made the telling of the tale more accurate and true by their revelations; the third segment is devoted to the cohorts, colleagues, and collaborators that worked diligently to ensure that the author and the work did not stray too far from the true path; and, last but not least, to the people most affected by the doing of the deed—friends and family. Frequently, many people who should receive thanks and gratitude do not find their names because of sheer numbers or a last-minute oversight or the faulty memory of the author.

I, therefore, would like first to express my appreciation for all the support, both financially and emotionally, to various members of the Kappa Alpha Order; especially to Larry Stanton Wiese, Executive Director of the Order, Jesse

Lyons, and Kent McMichael—all of whom worked diligently to guarantee that all documents needed were open and available, any equipment necessary to the investigation of the history of the Order was attained, and that I always felt comfortable and confident of their support. I am also grateful for the kind and gracious reception that I was afforded by the generous and amicable staff of Mulberry Hill.

Special thanks go to Knight Commander William E. Dreyer for his leadership and generous support for the Sesquicentennial Celebration; to all former Knight Commanders and particularly to Dr. Idris R. Traylor, Jr., the distinguished scholar, for his guiding hand; and to Sesquicentennial Committee Chairman and Kappa Alpha historian Councilor C. Douglas Simmons III. Also playing significant roles were members of the KAOEF Board of Trustees, including former and current Presidents Barry B. Donnell and Todd D. Reaves. I thank them for their generous support for this book. A special mention of gratitude is extended to Bensley H. L. Field, who made possible by his unstinting support the gifting of a copy of this book to every registered undergraduate attendee at the Sesquicentennial Celebration and 76th Convention in Roanoke, and Lexington, Virginia; and to all the donors listed in the front of this work who selflessly contributed to the cause.

And with pride, I would like to thank William A. "Bill" Wood and his wife Edna for opening up their home, family records, and collections to the Order. They have granted use and delivery of hundreds of documents never before seen relating to the Wood family; many of these found their way into this story and the narrative of the Order. Bill is the grandson of James Ward Wood and a true Kappa Alpha brother, his wife Edna is a KA rose if there ever was one. Their homestead in Lost River, West Virginia, is the place from which Wood set out in 1865 to travel to Lexington, Virginia, and Washington College.

The validity of a work of a historical nature rests on the accuracy, the depth, and the perspectives presented in the study itself. Often this phase of the process is the most gratifying for it involves collaboration, brainstorming, vetting of concepts, and interpretation. In the instance of this inquiry, the author has been extremely fortunate to be in the company of such a distinguished and eclectic group of historians, archivists, and scholars.

The gentleman who both set me on this path and picked me up all along the way is Brent Tarter, a well-known scholar of Virginia history, historian at the Library of Virginia, senior editor and co-founder of the *Dictionary of Virginia Biography*, and most recently the author of the acclaimed *Grandees of Government*. Brent has been a kind and consistently supportive friend for many years.

Taylor Sanders, who was a beloved professor of History at Washington and Lee University for forty-two years and an expert in early Virginia studies, graciously served as second reader for this work. His knowledge of local history and especially the workings of the Presbyterian community of Rockbridge County clarified confounding and competing information from the early history of the area and the university.

James E. Scanlon, Professor Emeritus of history at Randolph-Macon College and author of *Randolph-Macon College: A Southern History*, supplied arcane tidbits from the college's past and context to its foundation and formation.

The guardians of the gates and the knowers of all things past and present are the archivists and their assistants. Most of the hidden gems of research, the facts that allow both a more complete story and a greater comprehension of these matters are uncovered, exposed, and explained by the staff of libraries, archives, and special collections. The major repositories consulted in the course of this investigation were located at the Leyburn Library at Washington and Lee University; the Sandor Teszler Library at Wofford College in Spartanburg, South Carolina; the Virginia Baptist Historical Society, located at the University of Richmond; the archives at the McGraw-Page Library at Randolph-Macon College in Ashland; and the Kappa Alpha Archives in Lexington, Virginia.

Tom Camden and Lisa McCown of the Leyburn Library Special Collections were especially helpful in pointing out Ollinger Crenshaw's typewritten notes for his opus, *General Lee's College*. They also were careful to steer me toward the correspondence of Thomas Thom, Hugh Moran and Jo Lane Stern—all of whom were contemporaries and participants in the founding days of Kappa Alpha and the events that brought General R. E. Lee to Washington College. I would also like to thank Mr. Camden for his support and encouragement in the use of digital photography as one of the safest and noninvasive methods of recording often fragile and delicate manuscripts.

Philip Stone, archivist of the Sandor Teszler Library of Wofford College in Spartanburg, South Carolina, contributed original papers from the Delta Lodge of Kappa Alpha and information concerning the founding and early days of the institution. We are also grateful for the handsome 1854 photograph of the main building of the institution.

I am very grateful to Mary Virginia Currie and Laurie Preston of Special Collections at the McGraw-Page Library for their diligent inquiry into the missing and mysterious letter from Robert E. Lee to the administration of Randolph-Macon College in the matter of the establishment of a lodge of the Kappa Alpha fraternity in Ashland. Although the letter was not found, it was remembered. A companion letter to Jabez Lamar Monroe Curry and the administration of Richmond College also went missing.

I wish to thank Mrs. Darlene Herod of the Virginia Baptist Historical Society, which maintains the archival holdings at the University of Richmond, for her assistance in exhuming the early minutes of the Eta Chapter at Richmond College and directing me to the Eta Chapter's original minutes and the *History of the University of Richmond* by Reuben Alley. The combination of the two and the account of Richmond College in 1865, which Mrs. Herod also made available, brought to the surface many unknown facts concerning the establishment of the lodge.

I am indebted to the always-informed and instructive Francis Pollard of the Virginia Historical Society for pointing out the path to the original Zeta Chapter Minute Book and to important information about John Jordan, who played such an influential role in the architecture of historic Lexington.

Travis F. Shaw of Special Collections at the Thomas Balch Library in Leesburg located and provided critical information from the Francis T. A.

Junkin Collection concerning the reorientation and transformation of Mulberry Hill from the plantation of the past into the elegant mansion of the present.

The images and illustrations that enhance and enrich this volume could not have been possible without the kindness and dedication of many individuals. I would like to thank several of these often unsung heroes for their contributions: Chris Kemp, Head of Digital Initiatives at the University of Richmond; Chuck Barber of the Hargrett Library, University of Georgia; Courtney Chartier of MARBL, Emory University; Kathryn Stallard, Director of Special Collections at Southwestern University; President David Sallee, his Executive Assistant, Danya Beinke, and Director of Communications, Cara Dahlor, all of William Jewell College; Quatro Hubbard, Archivist at the Virginia Department of Historic Resources; Pamela Yeager of the University of Louisville Photographic Archives; and, Ryan Ledwith, Alumnus Advisor to the Alpha Xi Chapter, University of California–Berkeley.

I am also beholding to my old friend and great-nephew of John Holladay Latané, David Latané, Chair of English at Virginia Commonwealth University, for his insights into family history, and to Leon Fink, author of *Progressive Intellectuals and the Dilemmas of Democratic Commitment*, for his commentary of Jett Lauck and his connections with Mulberry Hill and Washington and Lee University.

I am most especially beholden to Kent McMichael, archivist of the Kappa Alpha Order, for edifying and enlightening commentaries in understanding some of the contextual issues relating to the Order's history and, with great patience and accessibility, doing a good part of the actual digging, exhuming, and explicating the documents critical to a more-reliable and documented narrative of the Order's existence and import.

Last but not least I would like to thank the team of professionals who made this book possible. Jesse S. Lyons, Assistant Executive Director for Advancement and Editor of the *Kappa Alpha Journal*, is to be commended for his unflagging devotion and energy as editor of the project. His contributions have been crucial. Kandy Harvey, designer and production coordinator from the University of Virginia Printing Office, has used her talented eye and substantive experience to make this volume inviting and engaging. Thanks to Julie Campbell, editor of the *Washington and Lee University Alumni Magazine* and Associate Director of Communication and Public Affairs for the University, for her careful reading and comments.

Special thanks and gratitude to Emily Jones Salmon, senior copy editor emerita in the former Publications Division of the Library of Virginia and co-editor of *The Hornbook of Virginia History* and co-author of *Historic Photos of Richmond* for stepping in at the last minute to proof-read, copyedit, and index the work. She is a miracle. Emily's husband, John Salmon, ably assisted Emily in this work. John was State Historian for the Virginia Department of Historic Resources and is the author of *The Official Virginia Civil War Battlefield Guide*.

I am obliged to my technical and research assistants in this process; without their contributions and technical assistance I would have been overwhelmed. Among those individuals were both my own son, Richard Graham Clagett II (who also assisted me in the research of *Scientific Jefferson: Revealed*), my daughter, Alexandra Helena Bowen Clagett, Nicholas Bell, Brent Buswell, Preston Pritchett, and Taylor C. McMichael.

And finally I want express my deep appreciation to the other members of my family—my mother, Dorothy Potter Clagett, who passed away during the process of the writing of this volume—and, most especially, to my much-enduring wife, Elizabeth Ann Pristernik Clagett, for her patience and grace.

# *Bibliography*


**Primary Sources: Manuscripts**

Alderman Library, Archives University of Virginia
———. Calohill Mennis Papers

Boatwright Library, University of Richmond, Richmond, Virginia
———. Eta Lodge Minutes

Kappa Alpha Archives, Lexington, Virginia
———. Alpha Catalogue of 1884
———. Ammen Papers
———. Letcher Papers
———. Miscellaneous Papers
———. Tazewell Hubard Correspondence Books
———. Wood Papers

Leyburn Library, Washington and Lee University, Lexington, Virginia
———. Hugh Moran Papers
———. Jo Lane Stern Papers
———. William Taylor Thom Papers

Library of Congress, Washington D.C.
———. Papers of Thomas Jefferson
———. George Washington Papers

Massachusetts Historical Society, Boston, Massachusetts
———. Papers of Thomas Jefferson

Thomas Balch Library, Leesburg, Virginia
———. Francis T.A. Junkin Collection

United States Patent Office, Washington D.C.

Virginia Historical Society, Richmond, Virginia
———. Zeta Lodge Register

Wofford College Archives, Spartanburg, S.C
———. Delta Chapter Minutes

**Primary Sources: Printed**

Ammen, Samuel. My History. Typescript Copy. Kappa Alpha Archives, Lexington, Virginia.

Crenshaw, Ollinger. Typescript Notes for General Lee's College. Archives, Leyburn Library, Washington and Lee University, Lexington, Virginia.

Hamilton, William Sprigg. Biographies: General Officers, Kappa Alpha Order, 1868–1936. Kappa Alpha Archives, Lexington, Virginia.

———. Chronological History of the Kappa Alpha Order, N.D. Kappa Alpha Archives, Lexington, Virginia.

———. History of Kappa Alpha, Gamma Chapter, N.D. Kappa Alpha Archives, Lexington, Virginia.

———. Memoranda Book of Kappa Alpha Order, N.D. Kappa Alpha Order, Archives, Lexington, Virginia.

———. Synopses of the Conventions, 1870–1937. Kappa Alpha Order, Archives, Lexington, Virginia.

Virginia Department of Historic Resources. National Register of Historic Places Nomination. Col Alto. 1988. Survey File 117-3. Richmond, Va.

Virginia Department of Historic Resources. National Register of Historic Places Nomination. Mulberry Hill. 1982. Survey File 117-10. Richmond, Va.

Virginia Department of Historic Resources. National Register of Historic Places Nomination. Reid-White-Philbin House. 2000. Survey File 117-0014. Richmond, Va.

### Secondary Sources: Books

Adams, Herbert Baxter. *Thomas Jefferson and the University of Virginia*. Washington, D.C.: Government Printing Office, 1888.

Alderman, Edwin Anderson. et al., eds. *Library of Southern Literature*. Vol. 7. Atlanta: Martin & Hoyt Co., 1907.

Alexander, James Waddel. *The Life of Archibald Alexander* New York: Charles Scribner, 1854.

Alley, Reuben. *History of the University of Richmond: 1830–1971*. Charlottesville: University Press of Virginia, 1971.

Apperson, John. *Repairing the March of Mars*. Macon: Mercer University Press, 2001.

Austin, J. W. *Related Families of Botetourt County Virginia*. Baltimore: Clearfield Press, 2000.

Baird, William Raimond, and Jack L. Anson, *Baird's Manual of American College Fraternities*. New York: The Alcolm Co., 1905.

Bassett, Ransom, ed. *Kappa Alpha Laws*. Louisville: Kappa Alpha Order, 1947.

Burns, Robert. "To a Mouse" in *The Poetical Works of Robert Burns*. Vol. 1. Boston: James B. Dow, 1834.

*The Calyx 1917*. Lexington, Va.: The Students of Washington & Lee University, 1921.

Chick, Joseph S. *History and Catalogue of the Kappa Alpha Fraternity*. Nashville: Kappa Alpha Order, 1891.

Clagett, Martin. *Scientific Jefferson: Revealed*. Charlottesville: University Press of Virginia, 2009.

Crawford, W. B. *Directory of the Kappa Alpha Order, 1865–1929*. St. Augustine: The Record Co., 1929.

———. *Directory of the Kappa Alpha Order, 1865–1922*. Atlanta: Index Printing Co., 1922.

Crenshaw, Ollinger. *General Lee's College*. New York: Random House, 1969.

Crocker, H. W., III. *Robert E. Lee on Leadership*. New York: Three Rivers Press, 1999.

Doherty, William O. *Snowballs and Skirmish Lines: A History of the Fincastle Rifles*. West Haverstraw, N.Y., N.D.

Doty, William Kavenaugh. *Samuel Zenas Ammen and the Kappa Alpha Order*. Charlottesville: Surber-Arundale Co., 1922.

Epstein, Steven. *Wage and Labor Guilds in Medieval Europe*. Chapel Hill: University of North Carolina Press, 1991.

Fink, Leon. *Progressive Intellectuals and the Dilemmas of Democratic Commitment*. Cambridge, Mass.: Harvard University Press, 1999.

Freeman, Douglas S. *R. E. Lee: A Biography*. Vol.4. New York: Charles Scribner's Sons, 1934.

Garrett, Franklin M. *Atlanta and Environs*. Vol. 2. Athens: University of Georgia Press, 1969.

Hawthorne, Julian. *The Story of Oregon*. Vol. 2. New York: American Historical Publishing Co., 1892.

Lee, Captain Robert E. *Recollections and Letters of Robert E. Lee*. New York: Doubleday, Page & Co., 1904.

*The Legacy*, New Jersey School of Law. Newark: The Student Council, 1928.

Levin, Jack, ed. *Sociological Snapshots 5*. Thousand Oaks: Pine Forge Press, 2008.

Luscombe, David, and Jonathan Riley-Smith, eds. *The New Cambridge Medieval History, Volume 4: c.1024–c.1198*. Cambridge, Eng.: Cambridge University Press, 2004

Lyle, Royster, and Pamela Simpson. *The Architecture of Historical Lexington*. Charlottesville: University Press of Virginia, 1977.

McGehee, Larry T. *Southern Seen: Meditations on Past and Present*. Knoxville: University of Tennessee Press, 2005.

Meriweather, Colyer. *History of Higher Education in South Carolina: Circular of Information, No. 3, 1888*. Washington, D.C.: Government Printing Office, 1889.

*Minutes of the Twenty-eighth Biennial Convention*. Kissimmee, Fla.: Kissimmee Valley Gazette Press, 1915.

*Minutes of the 59th Convention of the Kappa Alpha Order*. Nashville: Kappa Alpha Order, 1981.

*Minutes of the Seventy-eighth Annual Session of the Synod of New Jersey* Trenton: MacCrellish & Quigley, 1900.

*Minutes of the Thirty-First Biennial Convention of the Kappa Alpha Order*. Orlando: W. Crawford, 1921.

*Minutes of the Thirty-Second Biennial Convention of the Kappa Alpha Order*. Orlando: W. Crawford, 1923.

*Minutes of the Thirty-Seventh Biennial Convention of the Kappa Alpha Order*. New Orleans: Administrative Office, 1934.

Morton, Oren F. *A History of Rockbridge County, Virginia.* Staunton, Va.: The McClure Co., Inc., 1920.

*1917 Washington and Lee: University Bulletin Catalogue*. Lexington, Va.: Washington and Lee, 1917.

Peyton, J. Lewis *History of Augusta County*. Staunton, Va.: Samuel Yost & Son, 1882.

*Proceedings of the Fortieth Biennial Convention*. New Orleans: Administrative Office, 1939.

*A Record of the Members of Kappa Alpha Fraternity*. New York: Kellogg Press, 1892.

Ruffner, Henry, and Samuel Campbell. *Historical Papers: 1890*, No. 1. Baltimore: John Murphy & Co., 1890.

Scanlon, James Edward. *Randolph-Macon College: A Southern History*. Charlottesville: University Press of Virginia, 1983.

Semple, Robert. *A History of the Rise and Progress of the Baptists in Virginia*. Richmond: John Lynch Printer, 1810.

Shackelford, George Green. *Jefferson's Adoptive Son: The Life of William Short, 1759–1848*. Lexington: University Press of Kentucky, 1939.

Taylor, George B. *Virginia Baptist Ministers: Fourth Series*. Lynchburg: J. P. Bell Co., 1913.

Thomas, Emory. *Robert E. Lee: A Biography*. New York: W.W. Norton & Co., 1995.

Thomas, Lawrence B. *The Thomas Book*. New York: Henry Thomas Co., 1896.

Tyler, Lyon G. *Men of Mark in Virginia*. Vol. 4. Washington, D.C.: Men of Mark Publishing Co., 1908.

*University of Virginia Alumni News*, Vol. 5, No.7 Charlottesville: General Alumni Publications, 1916.

Van Cleve, Charles Liggett. *The History of Phi Kappa Psi From Its Foundation in 1852 to Its Fiftieth Anniversary*. Philadelphia: Franklin Printing Co., 1902.

Westheimer, Mary. *The History of the Kappa Alpha Order* Phoenix: Heritage Publishers, 1994.

Wise, Jennings C. *The Military History of the Virginia Military Institute*. Lynchburg, J. F. Bell Co., 1915.

Young, Charles C. "The Origin of Kappa Alpha," in *A Record of the Members of Kappa Alpha Fraternity*. New York: Kellogg Press, 1892.

Young, Virginia E. *Randolph-Macon College*. Charleston: Arcadia Publishing, 2011.

### Secondary Sources: Articles

"Administrative Office." *Kappa Alpha Journal* 58, No. 3 (March 1941): 100.

"Administrative Office." *Kappa Alpha Journal* 58, No. 1 (November 1941): 1.

"Alpha Pi's New Chapter House." *Kappa Alpha Journal* 23, No. 3 (February 1906): 326–330.

Altbach, Philip. "From Revolution to Apathy: American Student Activism in the 1970s." *Higher Education* 8, No. 6 (November 1979): 622.

"Alumni Challenge Order to Finish Dream." *Kappa Alpha Journal* 110, No. 3 (Spring 1994): 4.

"At the University of California – Berkeley." *Kappa Alpha Journal* 12, No. 4 (June 1895): 336–342.
Ammen, S. Z. August 28, 1904, "Northern Extension." *Kappa Alpha Journal* 22, No. 1 (October 1904): 6–12.
Ammen, Samuel Z. "The Convention of Ninety-Three." *Kappa Alpha Journal* 11, No.1 (October 1893): 4–14.
———. "The Early History of Alpha." *Kappa Alpha Journal* 1, No.3 (April 1884): 1–7.
———. "Founders of Kappa Alpha: General Jo Lane Stern." *Kappa Alpha Journal* 38, No. 1 (November 1921): 19–23.
———. "The Founders of Kappa Alpha: James Ward Wood." *Kappa Alpha Journal* 37, No. 3 (May 1921): 218–221.
———. "The General Catalogue of 1900." *Kappa Alpha Journal* 18, No. 3 (January 1901): 256–260.
———. "The Memorial Hall." *Kappa Alpha Journal* 20, No. 2 (November 1902): 108–109.
———. "The Memorial Hall." *Kappa Alpha Journal* 24, No. 4 (April 1907): 449–452.
———. "A Memorial Hall." *Kappa Alpha Journal* 17, No. 5 (May 1900): 469–472.
———. "The Founders of Kappa Alpha." *Kappa Alpha Journal* 38, No. 1 (November 1921): 19–22.
Barnes, Dick. "Headquarters Nears Completion." *Kappa Alpha Journal* 108, No. 3 (Fall 1991): 13.
Barnes, Richard. "Lights, Camera, Action." *Kappa Alpha Journal* 99, No. 1 (Winter 1981): 6–7.
Berryman, J. R. "From Me to You." *Kappa Alpha Journal* 61, No. 4 (May 1945): 1.
Berryman, John. "From Me to You." *Kappa Alpha Journal* 66, No. 2 (January 1950): 1.
Boney, B. F. "The Rising Hope of Our Land: University of Georgia Students Over Two Centuries." *Georgia Historical Quarterly* 74, No. 1 (Spring 1990): 117.
Brassieux, J. M. "One of Our Noble Founders." *Kappa Alpha Journal* 18, No. 1 (September 1900): 15–16.
Brewer, John. "Chapter Letters." *Kappa Alpha Journal* 82, No. 1 (January 1966): 23.
Brown, Herbert. "Do Fraternities Have Social Rights." *Kappa Alpha Journal* 77, No. 4 (May 1961): 12–13.
Brown, Walter. "Against Union with Northern Kappa Alpha." *Kappa Alpha Journal* 1, No.4 (June 1884): 1–4.
Burnley, H. T. "The Convention of 1905." *Kappa Alpha Journal* 23, No. 1 (October 1905): 5–14.
Carico, David. "A Message from the Foundation." *Kappa Alpha Journal* 115, No. 3 (Fall 1996): front.
"Centennial Program Makes Strides." *Kappa Alpha Journal* 74, No. 1 (November 1957): 18.
"Central Headquarters Moved." *Kappa Alpha Journal* 78, No. 1 (November 1961): 2.
Clark, Daniel A. "The Two Joes Meet—Joe College, Joe Veteran: The GI Bill, College Education, and Postwar American Culture." *History of Education Quarterly* 38, No.2 (Summer 1998): 173.
"Constitutional Committee Makes Report." *Kappa Alpha Journal* 52, No. 1 (November 1935): 9.
"Convention." *Kappa Alpha Journal* 62, No. 1 (November 1945): 4–5.
Cote, Buddy. "Letters to the Editor." *Kappa Alpha Journal* 118, No. 1 (Winter 2001): 5.
Creyke, Geoffrey. "Fraternity Housing Corporation Story." *Kappa Alpha Journal* 69, No. 3 (March 1953): 17–21.
"The Directory." *Kappa Alpha Journal* 58, No. 3 (March 1941): 101.
"Does Your Chapter Need a House." *Kappa Alpha Journal* 68, No. 3 (March 1952): 12.
"Editorial." *Kappa Alpha Journal* 14, No. 3 (January 1897): 240.
"Editorial." *Kappa Alpha Journal* 30, No. 2 (January 1913): 301–302.
Feller, R. T. "Fraternity Housing: A Look at the Fraternity Housing Committee after Ten Years." Kappa *Alpha Journal* 74, No. 3 (March 1958): 11–13.
"FHC to take new approach." *Kappa Alpha Journal* 99, No. 3 (Summer 1982): 18.
"5th Chapter Officers School." *Kappa Alpha Journal* 66, No. 4 (May 1950): 5.
"The Flat Hat Club." *William and Mary Quarterly* 23, No.1 (January, 1917): 161.
"Forester, Tune, Step Up Work." *Kappa Alpha Journal* 72, No. 2 (January 1956): 14.
"A Fossil from the Tertiary." *Atlantic Monthly* 44 (1879): 101.
"4th Chapter Officers School." *Kappa Alpha Journal* 66, No. 1 (November 1949): 8–10.

Fullilove, Sanford. "From the Knight Commander." *Kappa Alpha Journal* 30, No. 2 (January 1913): 202–206.
———. "Knight Commander's Opening Address." *Kappa Alpha Journal* 23, No. 3 (February 1912): 36–38.
———. "The New Directory." *Kappa Alpha Journal* 39, No. 1 (November 1922): 46–48.
Garner, William. "Merger Benefits Order." *Kappa Alpha Journal* 109, No.1 (Spring 1992): 8.
"The Greek Press." *Kappa Alpha Journal* 9, No.1 (October 1891): 84–92.
Guepper, Dani. "Gamma Rho Stresses Service." *Kappa Alpha Journal* 82, No. 1 (January 1966): 40.
Hamer, P. B. "Kappa Alpha Development." *Kappa Alpha Journal* 30, No. 2 (January 1913): 169–176.
Hamilton, William S. "Kappa Alpha Chronology." *Kappa Alpha Journal* 62, No. 2 (January 1946): 9–12.
"Headquarters to Relocate in Lexington." *Kappa Alpha Journal* 121, No. 1 (Spring 2004): 12.
"History of Alpha Chapter." *Kappa Alpha Journal* 69, No. 1 (November 1952): 44–45.
Hodge, Dean. "Changes in College Students' Value Patterns in the 1950's, 1960's, and 1970's." *Sociology of Education* 49 (April 1976): 155.
"Howard P. Locke." *Kappa Alpha Journal* 68, No. 1 (November 1951): 3.
Hubard, Tazewell T. "The K.C.-ship and the K.C.s." *Kappa Alpha Journal* 11, No. 3 (April 1894): 321–342.
Humphrey, Elizabeth. "From Jail to Fraternity." *Historic Preservation* 45, No.6 (November-December, 1993): 20.
Irwin, Emmett. "The Knight Commander's Message." *Kappa Alpha Journal* 50, No. 3 (March 1934): 342.
James, W. A. "Alpha-Lambda and Johns Hopkins University." *Kappa Alpha Journal* 19 No. 4 (March 1902): 356–358.
"John Rorher." *Kappa Alpha Journal* 64, No. 1 (November 1947): 5.
"KA Celebrates 125 Years of Excellence." *Kappa Alpha Journal* 107, No. 2 (Summer 1990): 8–11.
"Kaka Talk." *Kappa Alpha Journal* 62, No. 3 (March 1946): 8–9.
"KA Makes Tracks to Lexington." *Kappa Alpha Journal* 102, No. 1 (Winter 1986): 5.
"K.A. on the Move." *Kappa Alpha Journal* 71, No. 1 (November 1954): 7–10.
"KAOEF." *Kappa Alpha Journal* 99, No.3 (Summer 1982): 1–3.
"KAO Endorses Muscular Dystrophy as Its National Philanthropy." *Kappa Alpha Journal* 93, No. 3 (Spring 1976): 1.
"K.A.O. Selects Headquarter's Location." *Kappa Alpha Journal* 79, No. 1 (November 1962): 24.
"Kappa Alpha Chapter House Company." *Kappa Alpha Journal* 23, No. 1 (October 1905): 48–52.
"Kappa Alpha Directory." *Palm of Alpha Tau Omega* 49, No. 2, (May 1929): 202.
"The Kappa Alpha Journal." *Kappa Alpha Journal* 18, No. 2 (November 1900): 73–88.
*Kappa Alpha Journal* 63, No. 1 (November 1946): 48.
"KASF Awards Irwin Scholarships." *Kappa Alpha Journal* 84, No. 3 (Summer 1968): 8.
"The Knight Commander." *Kappa Alpha Journal* 57, No. 1 (November 1940): 3.
"Knight Commander's Message." *Kappa Alpha Journal* 72, No. 2 (January 1956): 1.
"Knight Commander's Message." *Kappa Alpha Journal* 72, No. 4 (May 1956): 1.
"The Knight Commander's Message." *Kappa Alpha Journal* 79, No. 1 (November 1962): 1–21.
Letcher, Greenlee. "Letcher on Memorial Hall." *Kappa Alpha Journal* 23, No.3 (February 1906): 347–353.
"A Letter from Judge Hardeman," Jo Lane Stern to John Hardeman, April 27, 1870. In *Kappa Alpha Journal* 19, No. 2 (November 1901) 172–175.
Locke, Howard P. "The Tax Division of the Department of Justice: Its Function and Operation." *American Bar Association Journal* 30, No. 6 (June 1944): 319–325, 363–366.
"Looking Backwards." *Kappa Alpha Journal* 14, No. 4 (March 1897): 273–276.
Lyle, Royster. "Rockbridge County's Boom Hotels." *Virginia Cavalcade* 20, No. 3 (Winter 1971): 5.
"McCall Donation." *Kappa Alpha Journal* 74, No. 4 (May 1958): 12.
McConnell, F. P. "More about the Proposed Memorial Hall." *Kappa Alpha Journal* 16, No. 4 (March 1899): 377–378.

McGilvary, E. B. "A few voluntary remarks." *Kappa Alpha Journal* 1, No.3 (April 1884): 7–9.
"Memorial Contributions to Scholarship Fund." *Kappa Alpha Journal* 74, No. 1 (November 1957): 18–19.
"A Memorial Hall." *Kappa Alpha Journal* 14, No. 3 (January 1897): 240.
"Memphis Alumni." *Kappa Alpha Journal* 75, No. 1 (November 1958): 17.
Miller, W. Karl. "Alpha Pi Reports." *Kappa Alpha Journal* 23, No. 5 (June 1906): 607–612.
Morris, James W. "Union with Northern Kappa Alpha." *Kappa Alpha Journal* 1, No. 2 (January 1884): 1–4.
Murrill, Paul. "From the Catalogue Editor." *Kappa Alpha Journal* 18, No. 3 (January 1901): 149.
Myers, Frank. "Fraternity to College." *Kappa Alpha Journal* 63, No. 4 (May 1947): 8–11.
"National Headquarters Campaign Rapidly Draws to a Close." *Kappa Alpha Journal* 113, No. 3 (Fall 1995): 11.
"New Headquarters Dedicated in Historic Fashion." *Kappa Alpha Journal* 109, No. 3 (Fall 1992): 11.
"The New Plan." *Kappa Alpha Journal* 11, No. 1 (October 1893): 31–33.
"The New President of the Old-Time Telegraphers." In *Telegraph and Telephone Age* (April 16, 1921): 186.
"NLI 1996." *Kappa Alpha Journal* 113, No. 4 (Fall 1996): 10–11.
"NLI stresses Big Five." *Kappa Alpha Journal* 89, No.3 (Fall 1972): 1.
Nowell, John. "An Open Letter." *Kappa Alpha Journal* 78, No. 3 (March 1962): 20.
"Officers Schools Held in 3 Cities across U.S." *Kappa Alpha Journal* 75, No. 1 (November 1958): 14–15.
"Officers Training School Will Be Held in Memphis." *Kappa Alpha Journal* 77, No. 4 (May 1961): 9.
Olson, Keith W. "The G. I. Bill and Higher Education: Success and Surprise." *American Quarterly* 25, No. 5 (Dec., 1973): 601.
"Our Fraternity at Wofford." *Kappa Alpha Journal*, (May 1891) 3, No.8, 432–443.
"A Plan and a Plea for the K.A. Review." *Kappa Alpha Journal* 1, No. 3 (December 1879): 101–103.
"Plans Completed for 1960 Training School for Officers." *Kappa Alpha Journal* 76, No. 4 (May 1960): 10–11.
Parks, R. L. "Union with Northern Kappa Alpha." *Kappa Alpha Journal* 1, No. 3 (April 1884): 9–11.
"Positive Action Taken for Headquarters Building." *Kappa Alpha Journal* 78, No. 1 (November 1961): 15.
"Providing a Home for Kappa Alpha." Kappa Alpha Order Annual Report: 2002–2003: Supplement to the *Kappa Alpha Journal* 120, No. 4 (Winter 2003): 10–11.
Rees, Carl. "Scholarship." *Kappa Alpha Journal* 65, No. 1 (November 1948): 11–14.
Rose, Richard. "The Emergence of Secret Societies in Antebellum Georgia Colleges." *Georgia Historical Quarterly* 70, No. 1 (Spring 1986): 55.
Russell, Steven. "A Place to Call Home." *Kappa Alpha Journal* 108, No. 1 (Winter 1991): 8–9.
Satcher, Ben. "Knight Commander's Message." *Kappa Alpha Journal* 121, No. 3 (Fall 2004): 2.
"Scholarship Fund." *Kappa Alpha Journal* 65, No. 4 (May 1949): 2.
"Scholarship Report." *Kappa Alpha Journal* 74, No. 1 (November 1957): 2–3.
"Second Chapter Officers School." *Kappa Alpha Journal* 64, No. 1 (November 1947): 8.
Shaffer, Robert. "Status of the Greek System." *Kappa Alpha Journal* 100, No. 3 (Summer 1983): 6–9.
Shelton, Todd. "Home Sweet Home." *Kappa Alpha Journal* 120, No. 2 (Summer 2003): 16–17.
Shrager, Rick. "The Impact of Living Group Social Climate on Student Academic Performance." *Research in Higher Education* 25, No. 3 (1986): 274.
Slifer, H. Seger. "Postwar Education." *Kappa Alpha Journal* 60, No. 5 (August 1944): 2.
Smith, Leon. "Epsilon Chapter." *Kappa Alpha Journal* 7, No. 5 (February 1890): 201–203.
"Staff Moves into New Headquarters." *Kappa Alpha Journal* 109, No. 1 (Spring 1992): 12.
"Stanford." *Kappa Alpha Journal* 13, No.1 (October 1895): 80–87.
"The Star Chapters." *Kappa Alpha Journal* 72, No. 1 (November 1955): 36.
"Statement of Contributions." *Kappa Alpha Journal* 74, No. 1 (November 1957): 18–19.
Stephenson, John W. "A Decade of Development." *Kappa Alpha Journal* 109, No. 1 (Spring 1992): 8.
"Syndicated Story Outlines a Major Fraternity Problem." *Kappa Alpha Journal* 77, No. 3 (March 1961): 39.

*Technological Review* 51, No. 7 (May 1949): 369.
"Third Chapter Officers School." *Kappa Alpha Journal* LXV, No. 1 (November 1948): 2.
"The 38th Biennial Convention." *Kappa Alpha Journal* 52, No. 1 (November 1935): 92–93.
"Tom Tune Consulting House." *Kappa Alpha Journal* 110, No. 2 (Fall 1993): 19.
Traylor, Idris. "The Kappa Alpha Journal: A 100 Year History." *Kappa Alpha Journal* 96, No. 1 (Winter 1978): 2–7.
Turner, Charles W. "The Franklin Society, 1800–1891." *Virginia Magazine of History and Biography* 66, No. 4 (Oct., 1958): 432–437.
"12th National Training School," *Kappa Alpha Journal* 75, No. 1 (November 1958): 14.
Tyree, Lewis. "Letters to the Editor." *Journal of Military History* 59, No. 3 (July 1995): 577.
"University of California History." *Kappa Alpha Journal* 19, No. 2 (November 1901): 150–152.
*University of Virginia Alumni News* 5, No.7 (Charlottesville: General Alumni Publications, 1916): 83.
"Want to Help the Scholarship Fund and Be Insured Too." *Kappa Alpha Journal* 71, No. 1 (November 1954): 3–10.
Warren, David. "Knight Commander's Message." *Kappa Alpha Journal* 120, No. 2 (Summer 2003): 2.
"White Province." *Kappa Alpha Journal* 62, No. 2 (January 1946): 15.
"Wider Participation." *Kappa Alpha Journal* 75, No. 2 (January 1958): 5–21.
Williams, James. "Official Communication." *Kappa Alpha Journal* 3, No.4 (January 1886): 13–14.
"Year End Statistics 1981–1982." *Kappa Alpha Journal* 99, No. 3 (Summer 1982): 23–25.
Young, James C. "Fraternally Yours." *Kappa Alpha Journal* 77, No. 4 (May 1961): 11.

**Newspapers:**

*Baltimore Sun*
*Cambridge* (Massachusetts) *Tribune*
*Chicago Tribune*
*Gillette News Record* (Wyoming)
*Highlander* (Virginia) *Recorder*
*Lexington* (Virginia) *Gazette*
*Lexington* (Virginia) *News-Gazette*
*Morning Call* (Allentown, Pennsylvania)
*Morning Oregonian* (Portland)
*New York Times*
*Religious Herald* (Richmond, Virginia)
*Richmond Times-Dispatch*
*Ring-tum Phi* (Washington and Lee University)
*Roanoke Times*
*Rockbridge Weekly*
*Washington Times*
*The Washington Star*

**Unpublished Papers:**

Nexsen, Julian. "Mulberry Hill," May 23, 1975, Unpublished research paper, Archives, Leyburn Library, Archives Washington and Lee, Washington and Lee University, Lexington, Virginia.
Gage, Abigail, "Geotechnical and Geophysical Survey of Mulberry Hill," 2003, Unpublished Paper, Archives, Leyburn Library, Washington and Lee University, Lexington, Virginia.

**Internet Sources:**

Romano, Lisa. "Hurricane Camille" http://encyclopediavirginia.org/Hurricane_Camille_August_1969#start_entry (viewed April 27, 2015).

Scott, Gary. "History of the Xi Chapter Kappa Alpha Order Southwestern University, Georgetown, Texas." http://www.williamson-county-historical-commission.org/GEORGETOWN_TEXAS/Xi_Chapter_Kappa_Alpha_Order_Southwestern_University_Georgetown_williamson_county_Texas.html (viewed April 27, 2015).

Transcript of Broadcast for WDBJ News at Six, 2 August 2002. http://scholar.lib.vt.edu/VA- news/WDBJ-7/script_archives/02/1102/110402/110402.m.htm (viewed April 27, 2015).

Lewis Tyree." http://law2.wlu.edu/faculty/profiledetail. (viewed April 22, 2015).

# *Illustration Credits*

4 Governor's Palace, Williamsburg, Va. Courtesy of Library of Congress.

5 Thomas Jefferson to Thomas McAuley, June 14, 1819. Courtesy of William and Mary College.

8 The Rev. William Graham, Mulberry Hill. Courtesy of Kappa Alpha Order.

12 Liberty Hall Academy. Courtesy of Special Collections and Archives, James G. Leyburn Library, Washington and Lee University.

15 Historic Map of Rockbridge County. Courtesy of the History Museum of Western Virginia.

16 Colonnade, Washington College, Lexington, Va., circa 1870. Courtesy of Special Collections and Archives, Washington and Lee University.

20 Washington to Trustees of the Washington Academy, June 17, 1798. Courtesy of Special Collections and Archives, Washington and Lee University.

22 Ruins of Liberty Hall. Courtesy of Special Collections and Archives, Washington and Lee University.

23 Graham Hall. Courtesy of Special Collections and Archives, Washington and Lee University.

27 Henry Ruffner. Courtesy of Special Collections and Archives, Washington and Lee University.

27 George Junkin. Courtesy of Special Collections and Archives, Washington and Lee University.

31 Fort Sumter, April 15, 1861. Courtesy of Library of Congress.

34 Jo Lane Stern. Courtesy of Kappa Alpha Order.

40 Battle of Williamsburg, May 5, 1862. Courtesy of Library of Congress.

44 Jericho Mills, Virginia. Courtesy of Library of Congress.

45 Major General Thomas Lafayette Rosser. Courtesy of Library of Congress.

48 Chesterfield Bridge, North Anna River, May 23, 1864. Courtesy of Library of Congress.

51 View of the Confederate Gunboat *Drury* (*Drewry*). Courtesy of Library of Congress.

52 Civil War Map of Rockbridge County. Courtesy of Kappa Alpha Order.

54 Union Troops in a victory parade, May 1865. Courtesy of the Library of Congress.

55 John Letcher, Governor of Virginia (1860–1864). Courtesy of the Virginia Military Institute Archives.

59 Main Street, Lexington, Virginia, circa 1865. Courtesy of the Virginia Military Institute Archives.

60 Stationery, Washington College, Hugh Moran Papers, 1867. Courtesy of Special Collections and Archives, Washington and Lee University.

# *Index*